MW00850089

A History of
Horoscopic Astrology

by

James Herschel Holden, M.A.

Fellow of the American Federation

of Astrologers

Second Edition

Copyright 1996, 2006 by James Herschel Holden

No part of this book may be reproduced or transcribed in any form or by any means, electronic or mechanical, including photocopying or recording, or by any information storage and retrieval system without written permission from the author and publisher, except in the case of brief quotations embodied in critical reviews and articles. Requests and inquiries may be mailed to: American Federation of Astrologers, Inc., P.O. Box 22040, Tempe, AZ 85285-2040.

First Printing: 1996
Second Edition: 2006

ISBN 10: 0-86690-463-8
ISBN 13: 978-0-86690-463-6

Cover Design: Jack Cipolla

Published by:
American Federation of Astrologers, Inc.
6535 S. Rural Road
P.O. Box 22040
Tempe, AZ 85285-2040.

Printed in the United States of America

Contents

Preface

During the last twenty years I have frequently been asked to recommend "a good history of astrology." I have been unable to do so because in my opinion there was no such book. The closest thing to it is the Geschichte der Astrologie by Wilhelm Knappich (Frankfurt am Main: Vittorio Klostermann, 1988. 2nd ed.), but this book only exists in the German language (and a French translation). I know of no comparable book in English.

The astrological histories I have seen are mostly "cultural" histories, i.e. they mention specific astrologers and discuss the times in which they lived, their patrons if any, and the opposition they encountered from ecclesiastical and other sources. But, while often quite interesting to read, they seldom give any details as to the techniques employed by those astrologers.

So far as I am aware there is no good "technical" history of Western astrology that covers the last two and one half millennia. There are a few excellent studies on specific periods, but these are by academicians who are not astrologers, and many of whom write about astrology as a repugnant but mildly interesting subject that gives them an opportunity to exercise their scholarly talents in a field that is not overcrowed by other academics.

On the other hand, the histories written by astrologers, with a few exceptions,[1] are based on insufficient knowledge both of the older astrologers and their works and of the historical periods in which they lived. Therefore the farther back in time such histories go, the more inaccurate they become.

The most informative academic historian is Lynn Thorndike, whose monumental *History of Magic and Experimental Science* is a treasure trove of information on astrology from the 1st through the 17th centuries, although it is noticeably weaker in the 17th century. Thorndike spent

---

[1]The principal exception is the well-written and well-documented technical history by Geoffrey Dean, *Recent Advances in Natal Astrology* (Subiaco, Western Australia: Analogic, 1977). It is very detailed, but it covers only the first 75 years of the 20th century.

more than thirty years reading old books and MSS and taking notes. Best of all, he reported these sources without prejudice. He sometimes notes that a particular astrologer was illogical or inconsistent, but he also notes that some academic and ecclesiastical critics of astrology were equally illogical and inconsistent.

Some other academics, while doing the history of astrology a great service by presenting detailed information from original sources, maintain an attitude towards the subject similar to what we might expect from Yasser Arafat if he undertook to write a history of Zionism. Those who read their books and papers must make allowance for their narrow and to some extent warped view of astrology.

An example is the frequently found statement that the adoption of the Copernican or heliocentric theory of our solar system "sounded the death knell of astrology," or some similar dramatic declaration. Actually, since astrologers mainly work with geocentric planetary positions, it is immaterial whether they are calculated from a geocentric or a heliocentric theory, so long as the positions are accurate. And astrology was never based on the theory that the earth was the center of the universe. It is a practical science like engineering. The reasons why it works might be interesting, but they are not essential to its use.

A related topic that interests academic historians much more than it does astrologers is the philosophical background of astrology. It is possible that a few astrologers may have been led to astrology from their knowledge of Stoic philosophy or some other philosophical system, but the majority of them, like virtually all of their clients, are drawn to astrology because it is a system of divination. The desire to know something about the future is innate in human beings. That alone is the thing that first sparked an interest in astrology and that has kept it alive since.

Those readers who are particularly interested in philosophy will have to look elsewhere for discussion of that subject in relation to astrology. But they should keep in mind that such discussions generally leave the false impression that astrologers and their clients based their decisions to practice astrology and to consult astrologers on philosophy. They didn't!

In compiling the present history I have tried to present the facts as I understand them in an objective manner. I have been interested in the history of astrology for most of my adult life, and I have the good fortune to have some language skills that have enabled me to investigate the older literature of astrology. At the same time, I am familiar with the major academic studies of astrology that have appeared in English and with some of those in other modern languages. However, I have used my own judgment in combining information from original sources, astrological histories, and academic studies.

Thus, the present history is both technical and cultural. In it I have traced the principal features and techniques of modern astrology back to what I believe to be their origins. I have named those astrologers whom I felt to be most important in the history of astrology. And I have given some information about how they worked and the social conditions under which they lived. This is necessary because the world has changed in many ways since the early days of astrology.

In each of the time periods discussed there were many astrologers whose names and books are not mentioned in this history. This is a short history, not a detailed one; hence, the names and books that are mentioned are those that I felt were the most important. In order to give some mention to everyone who is known to have been active in astrology, a book at least three times the size of the present volume would be required.

In particular, I wish to emphasize that this book is not intended to serve as a comprehensive guide to contemporary astrologers. Hence, many names of currently popular authors and lecturers are not mentioned. The reason for this was stated in the preceding paragraph.

In a number of cases I have given extracts from the astrologers' books. Some of these extracts are important in themselves, but others are merely intended to give the reader some idea of what those books contain. In a few cases I thought the extracts were sufficiently entertaining to interest the reader. Where the extracts are from writings in another language, the translations that are not attributed to anyone else are my own.

I usually cite the titles of books or papers in their original language, and in most cases I also give English translations of the original titles, but in some instances I cite the translated titles in the text and relegate the original titles to a footnote. The names of some early authors may exist in three forms: the vernacular, the Latin, and the English. Ordinarily I use the form that is most familiar to 20th century astrologers, but in a few cases I have preferred the vernacular. I have occasionally shortened Arabic names, keeping only the most familiar part, since some of them go on and on.

In transcribing words and names from the Arabic language, I have used the transliteration that is now customary. The reader who does not know Arabic may wonder why some of the small superscripted commas in Arabic words or names are turned one way and some are turned the other. These represent two different consonants in Arabic—one (as in Māshā'allāh) is a glottal stop and the other (as in 'Alî) is a laryngeal, which represents a constriction of the throat. Also, the Arabic definite article *al* is always written as *al*, but before certain initial consonants it is assimilated in speech to the initial consonant. For example, the name of the 11th century astronomer al-Zarqālî is written thus, but it would be pronounced as if it were written az-Zarqālî. I have preferred the written form. But either is correct.

I would like to emphasize that the present work is primarily a history of *Horoscopic Astrology* as it developed in the West. Therefore I have not devoted much space to the early omen astrology of the Babylonians. Those who wish to sift through the reports of the astrologers and the 10,000 or more omens and compare one series of Babylonian omen compendia with the others can consult the books I mention in that section of the history. In particular the new book *Mesopotamian Astrology* offers a comprehensive bibliography.

Nor have I pursued the development of horoscopic astrology in the Far East. Indian horoscopic astrology is an offshoot of Greek astrology, but it has been modified to suit the different social conditions in India and elaborated by Indian astrologers. I have indicated the relations between Western astrology and Indian astrology in the appropriate places. The bibliographic references will serve as a guide to reliable sources for the further study of Indian astrology.

Some other divinatory methods that are not discussed here are Numerology, Palmistry, and the Hebrew Cabala. These have some relation to astrology, but astrology has no relation to them. It is true that some astrologers have also been interested in one or more of these subjects, but astrology is the art or science of the relations between astronomical phenomena and terrestrial life, especially human life. These other divinatory arts do not use astronomy as their basis. The fact that they use some astrological terminology does not qualify them to be considered as branches of astrology.

My aim in this book has been to provide a brief historical account of how horoscopic astrology developed from its beginnings into what is practiced today by Europeans and their dispersed relations around the globe (and by non-Europeans who have adopted Western astrology).

At the end of the historical account I have discussed some questions that frequently arise in connection with astrology. I hope that these discussions will clarify some of the questions or at least give the reader the advantage of seeing them from a different perspective. In some cases the discussions are responses to questions that have most often been answered from only one point of view, in which case it seems appropriate to review the quality of the answers that have been given and the reasoning behind them.

Those readers who do not wish to wade through the entire book but would like information about certain persons or about specific subjects are advised to consult the indices of persons and of subjects. In compiling the Index of Persons, I have also included the names of publishers and publishing houses, since occasionally the publisher's name may be known but not the author or the exact title of a book. In the main text I have tried to mention the first date of publication of each book, but this has not always been possible. And my citation of subsequent editions is not intended to be complete. The reader who requires more detailed information should consult the usual bibliographic resources.

The Index of Subjects also contains the titles of all the books mentioned in this history. Most of the titles are listed in their original language, but the first referenced page will usually give an English translation of titles in another language. A few titles appear in the Index in both their original language and in English translation. The reader should be aware that verbatim and even facsimile reprints are sometimes issued under revised or totally altered titles.

Many popular English-language books have been translated into other European languages. I have only mentioned a few such translations, since they can all be found listed under their authors' names in the appropriate library catalogues and other bibliographic references.

Finally, I would like to express my thanks to my friends Gail Stephens, who encouraged me to write this book, Kris Brandt Riske, who edited the first and second drafts of the book and offered numerous suggestions for its improvement, and Phil Riske, who drew the astrological figures and put them in computer format. I especially want to thank Kris Riske for converting my word processor files—a difficult task—into publishing files and for supervising the publication of the book. Without their encouragement and help, it would not have been published. Some other individuals who very kindly answered questions that I put to them are mentioned on the page following this. To them also I would like to express my sincere appreciation for their contributions.

J.H.H.
April 1996

Consultants

The following individuals have, in response to my queries, very kindly furnished information for certain entries in this history. I wish to thank them for contributing their special knowledge.

SÁNDOR BELCSÁK

JERRY BRIGNONE

JANY BESSIÈRE

THOMAS GAZIS

SUSAN GOLIK

PATRICE GUINARD

GERHARD HOUWING

H.M. ISHIKAWA

THEODORE KRITZA

GRAZIA MIRTI

HENRY OWEN, JR.

MARTHA RAMSEY

MARILYN SEBECK

Preface to the
Second Edition

The first edition of this book is now sold out, and public demand for it continues. Therefore, I have taken the opportunity to review the work and make some useful revisions before it is reprinted. The main text of the History remains largely unchanged; however, the errors that were noted in the first edition are corrected, and a number of items of information are added. I have also included notices of some persons who were inadvertently omitted from the first edition. Sadly, some prominent astrologers have passed away in the last decade; their years of demise are shown. Finally, the Bibliography has been enlarged to include some important books that have come to my attention since 1996.

I want to thank Kris Brandt Riske for taking on the tedious task of revising the Indices. Readers who wish to cite locations in the book should be careful to mention the second edition, since most of the page numbers have changed slightly from the first edition.

James Herschel Holden
February 2006

The First Period

Babylonian Astrology

The Babylonians invented astrology. In the second millennium B.C. they adopted the constellations that had already been recognized by the Sumerians in the third millennium,[1] and they began to observe and record celestial phenomena. By the 16th century B.C. they had begun to compile a list of phenomena with (what they believed to be) corresponding mundane events. This is known to us from many individual documents and from the standard compilation *Enuma Anu Enlil*, which was found in several copies in the library of the Assyrian king Ashurbanipal (reigned 669-c.627 B.C.). It consists of seventy tablets, containing some 7,000 *omina*. Tablets 50 and 51 contain an astronomical compendium called *Mul.Apin.*[2]

The material contained in these Babylonian treatises became known to the Jews during their captivity in Babylon (587-539 B.C.) and passed to the Persians when they conquered Babylonia in 539 B.C. Through the Persians it passed to Egypt during the period of Persian domination (525-404 B.C.) and to northwest India (now Pakistan) by 509 B.C. Some of this material was translated into Egyptian and Greek in the West and into Sanskrit in the East. Instances of this are found in a demotic papyrus[3] on eclipse *omina* of the late second century A.D. (but ultimately derived from Babylonian material of c. 500 B.C.), in Ptolemy's *Tetrabiblos*, Book

---

[1] Ulla Koch-Westenholz, *Mesopotamian Astrology* (Copenhagen: Museum Tusculanum Press, 1995), states that while the Sumerians had named the constellations and some individual stars, there is no evidence that they had developed astrology.

[2] For a discussion of these texts and bibliographic information, see Reiner, Erica & Pingree, David, *Babylonian Planetary Omens* (Bibliotheca Mesopotamica, vol. 2) (Malibu, Calif.: Undena Publications, Pt. 1 1975, Pt. 2 1981). MUL.APIN is in Pt. 2

[3] See R.A. Parker, *A Vienna Demotic Papyrus on Eclipse- and Lunar-Omina* (Providence: Brown University Press, 1959).

1

2, in the Indian *Gargasamhitā* (first century A.D.), and elsewhere.[4]

It is important to understand that Babylonian astrology was a primitive form of *mundane* astrology,[5] not *natal* astrology.[6] Obviously, however, it provided a foundation for *elections*,[7] since, if an omen indicated good or bad fortune for a particular activity, the idea would naturally occur that an activity undertaken at that time would have a correspondingly good or bad outcome. The idea must also have occurred to some astrologers that an omen might be directed into a preferred channel instead of just letting it run its own course. Koch-Westenholz relates an interesting example.[8] Reporting on a lunar eclipse that was to occur in January 673 B.C., the astrologer Nergal-etir wrote to King Esarhaddon:

> If you make (the observation) for the well-being of the king, the city and its people, they will be well. In the beginning of the year a flood will come and break the dikes. When the Moon has made the eclipse, the king, my lord, should write to me. As a substitute for the king, I will cut through a dike, here in Babylonia, in the middle of the night. No one will hear about it.

Babylonian omen astrology was practised by astrologers who were scribes, priests, or exorcists, or a combination of these. In the period before the seventh century B.C. astrologers interpreted celestial phenomena after it happened or not too far in advance, since they did not have a good understanding of eclipse theory or planetary motions and were thus unable to do much in the way of forecasting the phenomena very far in advance. Their typical occupation was to write reports[9] and explanations of

---

[4] See David Pingree's early paper "Astronomy and Astrology in India and Iran" in *Isis* 54 (1963): 229-246, and his detailed review of Indian astronomical and astrological literature, *Jyotihsastra. Astral and Mathematical Literature* (Wiesbaden: O. Harrassowitz, 1981). Also, see his survey article "Astrology" in the *Dictionary of the History of Ideas* (New York: Charles Scribner's Sons, 1973-1974. 5 vols), vol. 1.

[5] The branch of astrology dealing with large groups of people—for example, those living in a particular city or nation.

[6] The branch of astrology dealing with the characteristics and life of a particular individual. This is the most popular branch of astrology.

[7] The branch of astrology dealing with the selection of a propitious time for beginning some endeavor—departing on a trip, laying the foundation stone of a building, opening the doors of a store for the first time, meeting a person for a definite purpose, or placing a bet, etc.

[8] Ulla Koch-Westenholz, *op.cit.*, p. 12. This book contains an extensive bibliography of books and papers on Babylonian astronomy and astrology.

[9] See the examples given by Ulla Koch Westenholz, *op. cit.*, and also those given by R.C. Thompson, *The Reports of the Magicians and Astrologers of Nineveh and Babylon in the British Museum* (London: Luzac, 1900. 2 vols.; New York: AMS Press, 1977. 2 vols. repr.)

phenomena for the king and to answer queries that the king sent to them. Some queries were fairly simple: on one occasion the king wrote "Mars was seen, why didn't you write?"[10] Here we have an early example of a client who knows something about astrology and wonders what a certain planetary position signifies for him.

Some of the astrologers conducted ritual propitiations of the Sun, Moon, or planets. And, since there was a common belief in demons, some of the astrologers functioned as exorcists. The Babylonians also practised other forms of divination, such as inspecting and interpreting the entrails of sacrificial animals, or assessing the significance of any sort of unusual occurence. The astrologers and the other diviners belonged to the small group of literate Babylonians, and as such they were considered to be "wise men" who might be called upon to supply any sort of knowledge that might be required by the king.

Babylonian constellations included the twelve zodiacal constellations (first mentioned as such in a late 5th century text, although some individual constellations were mentioned much earlier). They were of uneven length with gaps between some of them. Later, in the 4th century, when the Babylonians began to invent mathematical theories for calculating solar, lunar, and planetary positions, they were obliged to invent the 360 degree circle and the "signs" of the zodiac. This was done for convenience in studying the past records of planetary positions and phenomena, not for astrological reasons. The "signs" had the same names as the corresponding constellations but were defined as having exactly 30 degrees each. Once the Babylonians had devised mathematical theories to generate ephemerides, the calculated positions were necessarily referred to these new signs.[11] These methods of generating lunar, solar, and planetary positions passed to the Indians and to the Alexandrians and may also have passed to the Persians, although nothing much is known of Persian astronomy before the 3rd century A.D.[12]

Babylonian planetary theories were developed to fit previous records of positions referred to the 31 so-called "normal"[13] stars. And these stars had fixed positions in the newly invented signs. Consequently, the calculated positions produced by the theories were referred to what we would call a fixed or "sidereal" zodiac. The theories themselves were purely nu-

---

[10]Ulla Koch-Westenholz, *op. cit.*, p. 71.

[11]O. Neugebauer, *The Exact Sciences in Antiquity* (New York: Harper & Brothers, 1962. paper), points out that the Babylonians invented solar and lunar ephemerides so that they could determine in advance the number of days (either 29 or 30) in each lunar month in a particular year and thus be able to construct a calendar for that year. As a byproduct the ephemerides also enabled them to predict eclipses.

[12] See Pingree's article, "Astronomy and Astrology in India and Iran," *loc. cit.*

[13]A modern scholarly term that refers to those fixed stars in or near the zodiac that were often mentioned in the Babylonian astral literature.

3

meric and had no relation to "orbits," which was a concept unknown to the Babylonians.[14] Calculated positions were within a few degrees of their true values.[15]

The acquisition of the ability to predict solar, lunar, and planetary positions, to determine in advance the appearances of the Moon and the occurences of eclipses caused a change in the way Babylonian astrologers thought about their art. In the old days a celestial phenomenon was considered to be of divine origin, hence subject to the whim of the gods, but now it was seen that such phenomena followed mathematical rules. There was order in the universe. It may have been established by the gods, but once they had set the celestial machine in motion, they evidently let it run unattended.

This obviously reduced the need for propitiation of the gods when an unfavorable celestial omen appeared. Nor was there any use in praying that an eclipse would not happen, when calculation showed that it would. Consequently, the link between astrology and religion gradually dissolved. More and more the astrologer became the practicioner of a technical art.

We may now examine the features of Babylonian astrology that were later adopted by the Alexandrian inventors of horoscopic astrology—the so-called "Greek" astrology.

Babylonian astrologers said that when a planet was in a certain sign it was in its "secret house," viz. the Sun in Aries, the Moon in the Pleiades (in Taurus), Mercury in Virgo, Venus in Pisces (and also in Leo!), Mars in Capricorn, Jupiter in Cancer, and Saturn in Libra. These "secret houses" became the *exaltations* of the planets in the later Greek astrology.[16] Another feature of Babylonian astrology was the subdivision of the signs into twelfths, called in Greek *dodecatemoria* 'dodecatemories'.[17] The rulership of these was assigned to the signs in sequence beginning with the

---

[14] All available texts relating to Babylonian solar, lunar, and planetary theories were edited, translated, and discussed by O. Neugebauer, *Astronomical Cuneiform Texts* (London: Lund Humphries, 1955. 3 vols.) Babylonian astronomy is discussed thoroughly by Neugebauer in his *A History of Ancient Mathematical Astronomy* (New York Heidelberg Berlin: Springer Verlag, 1975. 3 vols.)

[15] By "true values" I mean true values referred to the fixed zodiac. In 400 B.C. the Babylonian fixed zodiac as defined by their solar ephemerides had its zero point at about 352° of the tropical zodiac. Hence the Babylonian longitude of the Sun at the vernal equinox was about 8 Aries. See my paper "The Classical Zodiac" in the A.F.A. *Journal of Research* 7, No. 2 (1995): 9-16.

[16] See Ulla Koch-Westenholz, *op. cit.*, pp. 134-136, and Julius Firmicus Maternus, *Mathesis* (Leipzig: B.G. Teubner, 1907-1913. 2 vols.; 1968. 2 vols. repr. with corrections and addenda in vol. 2), II. iii. 4 ". . . the Babylonians have wished those signs in which the stars are exalted to be their domi

[17] The few contemporary English-speaking astrologers who use these subdivisions usually call them *dwads* (from the Sanskrit word dvādaśāmśa 'twelfth'), having picked up this term from Hindu astrology manuals.

whole sign itself. Thus, the first dodecatemory of Gemini was assigned to Gemini, the second to Cancer, etc. This technique also passed to the Greek astrologers.[18] Still another was the grouping of the signs into *trigons* or triplicities: four sets of three signs each at 120-degree intervals, e.g. Aries-Leo-Sagittarius.

At some time between the 7th and 5th (or perhaps as late as the 4th) century the Babylonians developed the concept of natal astrology. It consisted of determining the positions of the Sun, Moon, and planets in the zodiac on the date of birth, perhaps noting the conjunction of one of the moving bodies with one of the normal stars. There is no trace of rising sign, midheaven, or celestial houses.

It is reasonable to suppose that natal astrology was first made available to the king and his family, then to other courtiers, and later to rich or important persons of the city—in other words, to the elite. Naturally, most of those who were in a position to demand this service from the astrologers would have done so. And those of lesser status would have offered payment. However, it seems doubtful that more than a small percentage of the population would have been able to avail themselves of astrological services—one restriction would have been the limited number of trained astrologers. But with increasing demand more astrologers would have been trained, and at some point they would have divided themselves into two classes—court astrologers, whose principal function was to advise the king and his ministers, and professional astrologers to serve the public.

Most of the cuneiform "horoscopes" that have been published belong to the 3rd century (one is dated doubtfully to the end of the 5th century); and one of them appears to be a conception "horoscope." These "horoscopes" only occasionally give the native's name, but they all give the planetary positions and sometimes a few other celestial phenomena, followed by a few short "readings"—"he will become rich," "he will grow old," or something of the sort.[19] (We hope the clients for whom these "horoscopes" were prepared didn't have to pay very much for them.)

As an example of this Babylonian natal astrology, we may cite the following:

Year 77 (S.E.), (month) Siman, the 4th in the last part of
the night the 5th. Aristokrates was born. That day Moon in

---

[18]See Ulla Koch-Westenholz, *op. cit.*, pp. 168-169.

[19]See A. Sachs, "Babylonian Horoscopes," *Journal of the Cuneiform Society* 6 (1952):49-75. Also, Frederick Cramer, *Astrology in Roman Law and Politics* (Philadelphia: The American Philosophical Society, 1954), pp. 6-7, for photographs of some of the horoscopes of Sachs's paper. The horoscopes are given in regular text—no diagrams of any sort. I have modified Sachs's translation slightly. That pioneer paper is now replaced by Francesca Rochberg,, *Babylonian Horoscopes* (Philadelphia: American Philosophical Society, 1998), a fine work with pictures of the Babylonian texts.

Leo; Sun $12°30'$ in Gemini. The Moon set its face from the middle toward the top. (The relevant omen reads:) "If, from the middle toward the top, it sets its face, (there will ensue) destruction." Jupiter in $18°$ Sagittarius, the place of Jupiter (means his life will be) regular, well; he will become rich, he will grow old; (his) days will be numerous. Venus in $4°$ Taurus. The place of Venus (means): Wherever he may go, it will be favorable (for him); he will have sons and daughters. Mercury in Gemini, with the Sun. The place of Mercury (means): The brave one will be first in rank, he will be more important than his brothers. . . . Saturn: $6°$ Cancer. Mars: $24°$ Cancer. . . . The 22nd and 23rd of each month. . . .

The Babylonian date of this "horoscope" is equivalent to 3 (and 4) June 235 B.C. Note that the astrologer's client was a Greek, which probably means that his birthdate was given to the astrologer in one of the Greek calendars, so that the astrologer had to convert it to the Babylonian calendar. The Babylonian fixed zodiac began about 5 degrees before the equinox in 235 B.C.[20] Adding $5°$ to the tropical longitudes calculated for 3 June, we find the Sun in 12 1/2 Gemini as stated, the Moon in 9 1/2 Leo, Mercury at 21 Taurus, Venus at 27 Aries, Mars at 24 1/2 Cancer, Jupiter at 18 1/2 Sagittarius, and Saturn at 29 Gemini. The Babylonian calculations were reasonably good except for Venus and Saturn. But (at least by later standards) Saturn in Gemini is better astrologically than Saturn in Cancer, while Venus in Aries is worse than Venus in Taurus.

Technical Procedures

How did a Babylonian astrologer make a "horoscope" for a client? Fairly easily if his client was a fellow Babylonian. He merely asked for the client's birthdate and then consulted his ephemerides to find the solar, lunar, and planetary positions for that date. The ephemerides were recorded on clay "tablets,"[21] and, if the astrologer did not have a personal set, he

---

[20]See my paper "The Classical Zodiac" in the A.F.A. *Journal of Research, loc. cit.*, where it is shown that in 235 B.C. the zero points of the so-called Systems A and B of Babylonian ephemerides were at 355.1 and 354.8 respectively of the tropical zodiac.

[21]The word "tablets" gives a false impression. Most of us think of the pictures of Moses holding fairly large flat board-like "tablets." Babylonian "tablets" might better be termed "slabs" or even "lumps." Those who needed to write kept a supply of damp clay in a box. When they wanted to write, they took out a handful of appropriate size, slammed it down on a flat surface to smooth and flatten it on one side (both sides, if more space was needed), took up their stylus and began to press it into the soft clay. When they finished, they laid it aside to dry. An office or library probably had a worker whose task it was to prepare more or less uniform clay "tablets" in advance, so that the scribe had only to pick one up and begin to write.

could go to the library (in one of the principal cities) and consult the library's set. The time of day was unimportant, so the astrologer simply copied the positions out of the ephemeris onto a fresh clay "tablet" and added whatever text he thought necessary—the date, perhaps the client's name, and a very brief interpretation. There were no diagrams because there was nothing to diagram. Presumably the astrologer handed the "tablet" to the client if the client was literate, but in most cases he probably kept it for his own archives if he expected any further visits from the client (it is presumably these tablets that have been found by archaeologists).

If the client were a foreigner, then the astrologer had a preliminary problem to solve: how to equate a birthdate in a foreign calendar with the corresponding date in the Babylonian calendar. Probably from the fourth (or at the latest, from the third) century on a Babylonian astrologer would have understood the principal calendars used by the Greeks as well as the very simple calendar used by the Egyptians, and later he might have had some idea about how the Roman calendar worked. With care he could probably have equated an Athenian or Macedonian date to an equivalent Babylonian date within a day or two. An Egyptian date could have been equated exactly if the Babylonians had gone to the trouble to do so, but there is no indication that they did. A Roman date would have had a possible error of more than a month prior to its regularization in 45 B.C. by order of Julius Caesar! Hence, it is doubtful that anyone except Babylonians and Greeks (and natives of other Middle Eastern countries that used lunar calendars) got a "horoscope" for even the right day.

Suppose that someone wanted a mundane forecast—will it rain this month, how will the next barley harvest turn out, will there be war? To answer such questions the astrologer would consult his ephemerides to see where the transiting planets would be during the specified time period. He would also check to see if there would be an eclipse within the preceding six months or a year. He had set rules for judging the effects of an eclipse, and for those as well as for the indications from the planetary positions he could consult the standard astral omen book *Enuma Anu Enlil*. A similar procedure could have been used to select a favorable time for an undertaking.

This then was Babylonian astrology (and astronomy) as it existed at the time of the founding of what was to become the home of western horoscopic astrology—Alexandria, Egypt.

Some of the ancient historians mention that the Babylonian priest and scholar **Berosus**[22] established a school at Kos around 290 B.C. where he

---

[22]He was also the author of a historical and cultural account of the Babylonians, which is unfortunately lost. The fragments of his works that had been identified up to the early nineteenth century were translated by I.P. Cory in *The Ancient Fragments....* (London, W. Pickering, 1832. 2nd ed.; Minneapolis: Wizard's Bookshelf, 1975. repr.). Pliny, *Natural History,* Loeb Classical Library (Cambridge, Mass.: Harvard University Press & London: William Heinemann Ltd.), vii. 123, says the Athenians erected a statue with a gilt tongue to Berosus "because of his marvellous predictions."

taught astronomy and astrology. His astrology must have been like what was just described. Consequently it would have been discarded a century later when horoscopic astrology was invented by the Alexandrians. However, it may have given rise to the later custom of calling astrologers "Chaldeans."

The Roman architect **Vitruvius**, *Architecture*, ix. 6, tells us that Berosus was succeeded by his pupil Antipater and (perhaps another pupil) Athenodorus, "who left a method of casting nativities, not from the time of birth, but from that of conception."[23]

Some Important Points

- Babylonian omen astrology began to be compiled around the 16th century B.C. It consisted of aphorisms for mundane astrology. Crude as it was, it established the fundamental principle that celestial phenomena were related to mundane occurrences.

- Babylonian omen astrology eventually spawned a rudimentary form of electional astrology. The astrologer simply selected a future time when the omens would be favorable for whatever action was to be undertaken.

- In its latest form Babylonian omen astrology passed to the Persians and through them to the Egyptians; it also passed in some manner to the Indians. Neither the Persians (so far as is known) nor the Egyptians made much use of it, but it found a better reception in India, where there are considerable reflections of it in the earliest Sanskrit astrological material.

- The early Egyptians had no astrology of their own and little astronomy,[24] but they had mapped the sky into constellations, most notable of which were the 36 decans that were originally used to tell time at night. The decans seem to have had individual characters that were considered to be lucky or unlucky (as were some of the days in the Egyptian calendar). By the Ptolemaic age it was apparently believed that the decan rising at the time of birth gave an indication of a lucky or an unlucky nativity. This led to the concept of the ASC as the prime astrological factor and ultimately to the celestial houses.

- The early Hindus had some rudimentary astrology based on Moon positions in the *nakshatras*[25]) but little astronomy. They had no zodiac. They later acquired the Babylonian omen astrology as men-

---

[23]Vitruvius, *De architectura*, ed. & trans. by Frank Granger (Loeb Classical Library, 1934. This may put the origin of the astrological method of determining the conception date back to the early third century B.C.

[24]See the article "Egyptian Astronomy, Astrology, and Calendarical Reckoning" by Richard A. Parker in the *Dictionary of Scientific Biography* (New York: Charles Scribner's Sons, 1970-1980), Supplement.

[25]Individual asterisms, usually 27 in number. After the introduction of the zodiac in the second century A.D., they were regularized into 13°20' subdivisions.

tioned above, but even then they had only what we would call omen and electional astrology. (The so-called "Vedic" astrology [a late 20th century term] that is advertised today did not exist in Vedic times; it is in fact what was called "Hindu" astrology until recently.) The fact that the Hindus have traditional horoscopes for Buddha and Rama and other ancient real or fictitious persons does not mean that the horoscopes were made by contemporary Hindu astrologers (or that they are anything more than speculative horoscopes)—the Greeks had horoscopes for figures of the Trojan War (12th century B.C.),[26] who may very well antedate the Vedas, but their horoscopes were made a thousand years or more later.

- In its latest period Babylonian astrology developed a rudimentary natal astrology based on planetary positions in the signs and conjunctions of the planets with the normal stars.
- The Babylonians had no orbital theory and no trigonometry, but they developed (in the 4th century) ingenious numerical methods of calculating solar, lunar, and planetary positions, by means of which they were able to calculate extensive ephemerides by a step-by-step process.
- They invented the 360 degree circle and the mathematical zodiac consisting of twelve 30-degree "signs." This was a fixed zodiac.[27]
- Babylonian "horoscopes" were based solely on the day, month, and year of birth. No account was taken of the time of day, although it was occasionally reported.
- The Babylonian priest Berosus is said to have established a school of astrology on the island of Cos around 290 B.C., but it was not the source of horoscopic astrology, which was invented in Alexandria, Egypt, a century later.

---

[26]Several of these horoscopes are cited in Book 6 of the *Mathesis* of Julius Firmicus Maternus (4th century). They give the appearance of having been postulated rather than calculated, and Firmicus himself was evidently sceptical, since he says that so-and-so "is said" to have had such a chart.

[27]That is, it was fixed with relation to the fixed stars. In other words, a star in Leo would always be in Leo. In the second century B.C. Hipparchus invented a "tropical" zodiac, which was measured from the vernal equinox. Since the position of the vernal equinox slowly moves backwards through the constellations ($1°$ in 72 years), the tropical longitudes of the fixed stars advanced at the same rate. Hence a star at the beginning of Leo would in about 2,160 years move all the way through Leo and into the beginning of the next sign, Virgo. The Hindus, having learned astrology from the Babylonians and from the earliest Alexandrian astrologers, still use a fixed zodiac. The Western world uses the tropical zodiac.

The Second Period

Classical Greek Astrology

The city of Alexandria, Egypt, was founded after 332 B.C. by order of Alexander the Great (356-323). One of his field marshals was Ptolemy (367-283), who claimed Egypt as his portion of the Macedonian Empire after Alexander's death. The new city rapidly became an important cultural and commercial center. Its population consisted of three main groups: Greeks, Egyptians, and Jews. Thus, the cultural, religious, and (what passed for) scientific traditions of the Greeks, Egyptians, and Babylonians were intermingled in one place.

Ptolemy, who became King Ptolemy I Soter (reigned 305-283), ordered the construction of a great library. It soon attracted scholars from throughout the Greek-speaking world. A library requires a book trade to furnish its shelves. Stationers and copyists set up shop. Commercial enterprises of all sorts sprang up. Alexandria had trade connections with India and Ceylon (now Sri Lanka), as well as with all the Mediterranean and Near Eastern lands. This facilitated the diffusion of knowledge between Alexandria and outlying regions.

The society of 3rd and 2nd century Alexandria is faithfully reflected in the Greek astrological texts. The royal court, government officials, religious functionaries, rich individuals, merchants, scholars, artists, musicians, artisans, workers, criminals, and slaves are all mentioned. Combined with sociological information gleaned from papyrus documents and inscriptions, the astrological texts give a comprehensive picture of Egyptian society in the Ptolemaic era. Fortunately for the history of astrology, the Belgian scholar Franz Cumont (1868-1947) assembled these sources into a fascinating book, *The Egypt of the Astrologers.*[1]

---

[1]Franz Cumont, *L'Égypte des astrologues* (Brussels: Fondation Égyptologique Reine Elisabeth, 1937). In French with indices of Greek and Latin words.

1 1

Some modifications were introduced by astrologers who lived later when Egypt had become part of the Roman Empire, but even the latest writers preserve words and phrases that go back to the early Ptolemaic era. Cumont's book is a necessary tool for anyone who wishes to edit, translate, or study Greek astrology.

The scholars and "scientists" of Alexandria were particularly active in the 3rd and 2nd centuries. Among them were the inventors[2] of Western horoscopic astrology. Their real names are unknown, since they chose to issue their books under the names of gods, kings, heroes, or wise men of the past. Their books are lost except for scattered fragments preserved by later authors. However, the essential features of their astrological theories have been transmitted to us through the writings of the later Greek astrologers.

In keeping with the three major elements of the Alexandrian population, the system of astrology they invented combined the following elements:

- The Babylonian zodiac with sign positions of the planets and fixed stars, the triplicities of signs, the exaltation signs of the planets, the dodecatemories (the 2°30' subdivisions of the signs),[3] and the emphasis on the importance of eclipses in mundane astrology.

- The Egyptian concept of the 36 decans, with the rising decan (and consequently, the rising sign[4] that contained it) as a prime indicator

---

[2]One of my valued colleagues objects to the word "inventors." He points out that Greek horoscopic astrology, even in its early 2nd century form, was a new and very complicated system, and he thinks it doubtful that it could have been "invented" by one or more individuals all at once. He would prefer me to say that horoscopic astrology "appeared" at that time. My rejoinder is that Euclid, who lived perhaps a century before the Alexandrian astrologers, wrote the elements of geometry in a comprehensive and near perfect form, and if he could do that all at once, there seems to be no reason why some later Alexandrians or perhaps two generations of them could not have created horoscopic astrology.

[3]It is interesting to note that the classical Greek astrologers had two quick methods to find the dodecatemory position of a planet: (1) multiply the degrees (and minutes, if given) of the planet by 12 and cast the resulting product from the beginning of the sign in which the planet is posited, or (2) do the same thing but multiply by 13. Weak arguments are advanced for the second procedure in the Greek astrological literature. But both of these procedures have been found in cuneiform documents (without any explanation), so it appears that the Alexandrian astrologers inherited both methods (with no explanation) and some of their successors adopted 12 as a multiplier, while others adopted 13. See Ulla Koch-Westenholz, *op.cit.*, pp. 168-169.

[4]In Greek astrology the rising sign, which consituted the first (celestial) house, was called *horoskópos* "horoscope." In modern astrology the term "horoscope" refers to the entire chart, and the first house is called "ascendant." Also, in modern astrology the term 'horoscope' is usually restricted to a *natal* horoscope. The diagram drawn for a question, an election, or something else is usually called simply a "chart."

of destiny. The decans were regularized to 10° each and assigned by threes to the signs of the zodiac. Their names are given in corrupt Latin and Greek transliterations by Firmicus (4th century A.D.) and Hephaestio of Thebes (early 5th century).[5] They were also subdivided into thirds—the 3°20' subdivisions, called in Greek *leitourgoí* 'ministers' and in Latin *munifices* 'duty-officers'[6]—which are quite possibly the origin of the Hindu *navamsas* or "ninths," which play such an important role in modern Hindu astrology.[7]

- The Greek characteristics of the planetary gods and Greek philosophical concepts such as the four elements,[8] the alternation of male and female, etc., and most importantly the system of sign rulership based on the distance of the planets from the sun (a concept unknown to the Babylonians and Egyptians) and the speed of their motion in the zodiac. The same sequence of planets[9] was used to assign rulers to the decans and to the hours of the day and the night—the so-called planetary hours[10]—and from the latter the planetary rulers of the days of the week.[11]

---

[5] See Firmicus's list of names in *Mathesis*, iv. 22, and the Greek and Egyptian names in the article by Richard A. Parker cited above.

[6] Mentioned by Firmicus, *Mathesis*, ii. 4, and in the "Discourses of Hermes to Tat" in *Hermetica* ed. and trans. by Walter Scott (Oxford: Clarendon Press, 1924. 4 vols.), vol. 1, pp. 414 ff.

[7] Hindu astrologers today use two horoscopes—a regular one (called "rasee") and a subsidiary one (called "navamsa") constructed by multiplying all the longitudes of the regular chart by 9.

[8] Fire, earth, air, and water.

[9] Called *heptázonos* 'heptazone' in Greek: Saturn, Jupiter, Mars, Sun, Venus, Mercury, Moon. All of these are sometimes called "planets" by astrologers, using the original definition of the word—"moving bodies." Modern astronomers restrict the word "planet" to a sizable body moving around the sun. And modern astrologers usually use the term "planets" as the astronomers do.

[10] A system of hour-rulership that was established as follows. The first hour (sunrise to 1 hour later) of the day is ruled by the planet which rules the day, the next hour is ruled by the next planet in sequence, and so on. Since there are 12 hours of the day and 12 hours of the night, making a total of 24 hours, the sequence of 7 planets will be gone through 3 times completely and the count will advance 3 steps into the planetary sequence at the beginning of the next day. Hence, if we begin with "Sun-day," the first hour is ruled by the Sun; then the first hour of the next day will be ruled by the Moon, hence it will be "Moon-day"; and the first hour of the next day after that will be ruled by Mars, hence it will be "Mars-day" ("Tiuw's-day" or Tuesday to English speakers, but Mardi to the French), etc.

[11] The planetary rulers of the weekdays are somewhat obscured in English, since the names of some of the Teutonic gods have been substituted for the names of the Roman gods—Saturday, Sunday, and Monday are recognizably Saturn-day, Sun-day, and Moon-day, but Tuesday (Tiuw's-day) is Mars-day, Wednesday (Woden's-day) is Mercury-day, Thursday (Thor's-day) is Jupiter day, and Friday (Freya's-day) is Venus day.

13

To these elements the inventors added the fundamental horoscopic concept of the celestial houses—originally conceived as a simple sequence of signs beginning with the rising sign[12]; the idea of *sect* (diurnal and nocturnal), significations of planets in signs, planets in houses, planets in aspect; the lots,[13] the terms,[14] and the other familiar features of horoscopic astrology.

Whether the inventors were accustomed to draw a chart is unknown. The earliest diagrams that have been found are simply circles, sometimes with a cross drawn within to indicate the cardinal houses of the horoscope.[15] These early charts, like those we use today, are drawn with East at the left and South at the top because that is the way Egyptians drew their geographical maps. (It was Ptolemy who reversed the traditional directions and drew geographical maps with West at the left and North at the top.) Here is an English translation of one from a papyrus document of the early 1st century A.D.:

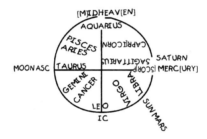

Fig. 1 (after Neugebauer & Van Hoesen).

[12]This system has no name in the ancient literature. I have termed it "Sign-House," since each sign constitutes one of the celestial houses. See the further note below.

[13]A *lot* (nowadays called a "part") is a point in the zodiac that is calculated by measuring the distance from one point to another point (usually from one planet to another planet) and adding the distance to a third point (usually the ascending degree of a horoscope). The resulting lot is supposed to represent the combined influences of the two points. For example, the most frequently used lot is the Lot of Fortune, calculated by measuring from the Sun to the Moon and then adding the distance to the ascending degree. It is supposed to be a special indicator of financial circumstances (the idea being that if you are rich, you are fortunate; if you are poor, you are unfortunate).

[14]Subdivisions of the signs of the zodiac. There were several different systems, but the only one in common use was that "according to the Egyptians," which had five subdivisions of irregular length within each sign. These subdivisions were assigned to the five visible planets Mercury, Venus, Mars, Jupiter, and Saturn.

[15]See the reproduction of a diagram found on a papyrus document of about 15 A.D. in O. Neugebauer & H.B. Van Hoesen, *Greek Horoscopes* (Philadelphia: The American Philosophical Society, 1959), p. 18, Fig. 9, and the discussion on p. 163.

14

In other original sources the Sun is occasionally represented by a small circle with a ray attached and the Moon by a crescent, but no symbols are used for the planets or the signs of the zodiac.[16] In most cases the names of the signs and planets were simply written on the chart in the appropriate places. It is evident that the earliest astrologers were content to list the sign positions of the planets and the ascending sign. With this information it was easy to visualize the house placements of the planets, so a chart was actually unnecessary. Most likely the use of a chart only became customary when astrologers had abandoned the simple Sign-House[17] system of house division and adopted one of the later systems that divided the houses irregularly.

Having devised the horoscope for natal astrology, it was obvious that it could also be used for the birth of an event or an action. This concept spawned the branch of astrology the Greeks called *katarchic* 'related to beginnings,' which included what modern astrologers call *horary*[18] and *electional*[19] astrology. A horoscope could also be used to forecast mundane events by considering the positions at the time of an eclipse or at the beginning of the year,[20] but this was only done in a rudimentary way at first. This branch of the art is now called *mundane* astrology.

---

[16]Neugebauer & Van Hoesen, *op. cit.*, pp. 19 & 163, point out that the symbols by which the planets and signs are represented today first appear in medieval MSS. And it might be added that the manuscript symbols differed somewhat from their modern forms, which were regularized by the 15th century printers. The manuscript symbols of the signs were pictorial, while the symbols for the planets were simply modifications of the Greek letters of the planets' names, e.g. K for Saturn (Kronos), Z for Jupiter (Zeus), Φ for Venus (Aphrodite), etc. They were adopted merely for convenience and had none of the "esoteric" meaning that some modern astrologers have attributed to them.

[17]This is my own name for the original system of horoscopic houses. See my paper "Ancient House Division" in the *AFA Journal of Research* 1, no. 1 (1982): 19-28.

[18]Horary astrology deals with questions put to an astrologer by a client (called "querent" in the literature). The astrologer erects a chart for the moment when the querent asks the question. There are special rules for answering the different types of questions that might be asked. A chart can also be erected for the time of an event that has already occurred. It is properly called "a horary chart set for a time certain," but is usually called simply "a horary chart."

[19]Electional astrology is concerned with selecting a favorable time for taking some action, particularly an action which is the beginning of something that is expected to continue into the future, e.g. the time of a marriage, the time of the launching of a ship, the time of signing a contract. Hence, it is a horary chart set for a time certain *in the future*. There are special rules for various types of undertakings. The first astronomer royal, John Flamsteed (1646-1719), drew up such a chart for the founding of Greenwich Observatory in 1675. (See a facsimile of the chart in A.J. Pearce, *A Textbook of Astrology*, 2nd ed., p. 18.) This action of his has proved to be an embarrassment to modern astronomers.

[20]This appears in a rudimentary form in Ptolemy, *Tetrabiblos*, Book 2. But

This system of horoscopic astrology was set forth in books issued under the names of **Hermes**[21] (the Greek god equivalent to the Egyptian god Thoth), **Hanubius** (Chnubis, Anubio?), **Aesculapius,**[22] **Nechepso & Petosiris,**[23] and **Abram**[24] in the 2nd century B.C. None of their books have come down to us intact. What we know of them is from citations and remarks made by later astrologers. To accompany these fundamental treatises of horoscopic astrology, solar, lunar, and planetary tables were constructed. These, or another similar set of tables are referred to by later astrological writers as the *Eternal Tables*. Their exact structure is uncertain, but they were probably calculated from epicyclic models.[25] However, they may have included a set of abbreviated ephemerides, one for each planet, that covered a period of years that constituted a recurrence cycle for the planet, such as eight years for Venus. If so, by determining the number of years elapsed since the years of the table and casting out multiples of the cycle, the astrologer could determine which year in the table corresponded approximately to the year for which he desired to cast a horoscope. Then it would be an easy task to find the desired planetary position. But whatever their structure was, the tables gave zodiacal positions referred to a fixed zodiac,[26] which we may call "Alexandrian." This might

---

Ptolemy was mainly interested in sign positions and appearances at the time of eclipses and at the time of the syzygy that occurred before an equinox or solstice. The idea of erecting a complete chart for an eclipse or an Aries Ingress and interpreting it as if it were a horary chart set for a time certain did not develop until the early Middle Ages.

[21]See the section on Hermetic literature below on p. 85.

[22]Hanubius (the Egyptian Anubis?) and Aesculapius (the Greek Asklepios) were evidently early writers. In the preface to Book 4 of the *Mathesis*, Firmicus lists them ahead of Nechepso and Petosiris. However, Pingree would assign the poet-astrologer Hanubis (Anubio) to the 2nd or 3rd century A.D.

[23]Nechepso was the name of an Egyptian king who ruled around 600 B.C., and Petosiris was the name of an Egyptian priest of the 4th century B.C. who seems to have still had a reputation in the 2nd century. Obviously these men had nothing to do with astrology, but the real writers of the book or books issued under their names evidently desired to give the impression that their work was based on older Egyptian knowledge. See the informative entry for Petosiris by Pingree in the *Dictionary of Scientific Biography*.

[24]Nothing is known of Abram (or Abraham). He might have been a Jew.

[25]See the reference to the perihelion of Mercury in the section on Ptolemy and Vettius Valens. If the *Eternal Tables* were calculated from a strictly numerical theory such as the Babylonians used, then there would be no "perihelion" of Mercury. A contrary opinion is expressed in the earlier papers listed in Pingree's article, "Astronomy and Astrology in India and Iran," *loc. sit.*, p. 236 n.53. The authorities mentioned there assume that the tables were similar in construction to the Babylonian tables.

[26]The zero point of the Greek tables was some 3° or 4° from the zero point of the Babylonian zodiac. For details, see my paper "The Classical Zodiac," *loc. cit.* The reason for the discrepancy is unknown.

be an indication that they were prepared before Hipparchus constructed solar and lunar tables that yielded positions referred to the tropical zodiac (last half of the 2nd century B.C.).

These tables were used by astronomers, astrologers, and ephemeris makers until the 4th century A.D., when they began to be displaced by the newer tables of Claudius Ptolemy, which ostensibly referred positions to the tropical zodiac.[27]

Hipparchus (fl. 160-126) discovered the phenomenon of precession in the 2nd century B.C. He prepared the first comprehensive catalogue of stars and evidently prepared tables of the Sun and the Moon as well as specialized tables for computing eclipses.[28] These tables produced positions in the tropical zodiac. However, for reasons unknown, they did not come into common use.

Technical Procedures

How did a Greek astrologer make a horoscope for his client? Fairly easily if the client knew his birthdate in the Alexandrian calendar. Otherwise, the calendar conversion problem arose. The astrologer would need to have some knowledge of the lunar calendars in use by the Greeks and the natives of Middle Eastern countries. And he would also need to know something about the Roman calendar. If he were a very careful astrologer, he would also need to know the longitude and latitude of the birthplace. The longitude would be "so many hours east or west of Alexandria," and the latitude would be the "clime" in which the place lay. Climes were bands of latitude in which the longest day was so many equinoctial hours. These bands were several degrees wide, and tables of rising times for the signs were available for each clime, or the astrologer could calculate them himself if he lacked a table.[29] An indifferent astrologer would simply ignore all this and calculate the horoscope as if the client had been born in Alexandria, thus falsifying the Moon position by as much as one degree and perhaps getting the ASC wrong by a whole sign for clients born at a considerable distance from Egypt.

If his client were an Egyptian, matters were simple. The astrologer merely asked for the client's birthdate and birth time and then consulted

---

[27]Ptolemy used a value of the precession that was too small (36" per Egyptian year instead of 50") and the true epoch of his tropical zodiac was in the 2nd century B.C. rather than the year 137 A.D., so his longitudes were already 1° too small in his own time, and the error increased steadily at about 0°24' per century thereafter. But this was not noticed until much later.

[28]His tables are mentioned by Pliny, *Natural History* (Loeb Classical Library), Book 2, Section 53.

[29]The procedure is given by Vettius Valens, *Anthology*, i. 6, "The Rising-time of the Signs." The rules are simple enough to commit to memory, but an astrologer who was accustomed to receive clients from a variety of climes probably either acquired a listing of the rising times for the climes or used the rules to write out a list that he could keep at hand.

17

his ephemerides or made the necessary calculations from tables to find the solar, lunar, and planetary positions for that date. The Egyptians measured time in *seasonal* hours from sunrise ("hours of the day") and from sunset ("hours of the night"). The astrologer noted the degree and sign of the Sun. It would be on the ASC at sunrise and on the DSC at sunset. If the client reported that he was born at the 5th hour of the day, the astrologer had two procedures available to find the ASC at the 5th hour: (1) the "rough and ready" procedure—multiply the given hour by 15° and add that many degrees to the Sun position; or better (2) consult a table of "horary times," which gave the length of a seasonal hour of the day for the Sun in each of the signs, multiply the horary times from the table by the given hour; thus converting the time since sunrise in seasonal hours into the time since sunrise in "equinoctial hours"; then consult a table of rising times of the signs in equinoctial hours, and, starting from the sign and degree position of the Sun, deduct the rising times of the succeeding signs until only an hour or so was left; then the remainder of the time divided by the rising time of the sign times 30° would give the rising sign and degree. Procedure (1) might well have an error as great as 20° or more even in moderate latitudes. Procedure (2) would probably yield the ASC degree with an average error of less than 10°. The astrologers were aware of the inherent errors in both these procedures, so they sometimes rectified the ASC degree by one of several available methods.

If the client were a Roman or a native of some other country, calendar conversion was required before anything further could be done. Probably a professional astrologer kept a notebook with instructions on how to make the calendar conversions that were most likely to be needed in his practice. There was a good chance for error in making such conversions, but this was unavaoidable. Fortunately, after the Romans conquered most of the Mediterranean region and regularized their own calendar (45 B.C.), the calendar problem gradually became easier because people throughout the empire began to keep double dates—Roman and local—and the client might already know what his birthdate was in the Roman calendar. From 8 A.D. on, Roman dates were very easy to convert to the Alexandrian or "Egyptian" dates employed in the ephemerides and astronomical tables. (There was a possible error of a few days in converting Roman dates between 42 B.C. and 8 A.D. due to an error the Romans had made in reckoning Leap Year in that interval.)

Another problem the astrologer had to cope with was when the day began. Those countries using lunar calendars usually began the day at sunset of the preceding day. The Romans began the civil day at midnight (although they reckoned the hours from sunrise and sunset). The Egyptians began the day at sunrise. Inattention to these differences might cause the astrologer to calculate the chart for the wrong day.

Having determined the rising sign, the celestial houses were instantly known, since the Sign-House system merely counted the houses in whole signs from the rising sign. The horoscope was then complete. The astrologer could write on a piece of papyrus the client's name, his birthdate and time, the planetary positions, and the rising sign. It was not necessary to draw a diagram because the house positions of the planets could easily be visualized.

The early astrologers paid no attention to the astronomical midheaven. The tenth sign from the rising sign was the midheaven sign. A century or so later, a few astrologers began to calculate the astronomical MC degree and to note its house position—the 9th or the 10th house in moderate latitudes. It was not considered to be the "cusp" of the 10th house but rather what modern astrologers would call a "sensitive point"—something like the so-called Vertex.[30] Even those astrologers who mentioned it attached little importance to it. Ptolemy only uses it in connection with his method of rectifying the birthtime, and even there it is mentioned as a second choice.

Ephemerides might or might not be available (they could probably be found in Alexandria or Rome where there was more demand for them), but astronomical tables, such as the *Eternal Tables*, were available by which positions could be calculated for any date. Probably most astrologers had a set. These were used until Ptolemy's *Handy Tables* became generally available in the 4th century. By then the accuracy of the older tables would have been seriously reduced. As mentioned above, they referred positions to a fixed zodiac, while positions from the *Handy Tables* were referred to a nominally tropical zodiac.

Something should also be said about how the ordinary citizen knew what time it was. There were of course no clocks or watches. The sundial was the daytime timepiece and the water clock was used at night by those who felt a need to know the time after sundown. Some large cities had sundials in public places (there was one in the Forum at Rome). The only city known to have had a public mechanical clock was Athens (fragments of its mechanism have been identified in recent years). Christian churches do not seem to have had bells prior to the 5th century. Hence, the citizen who wished to know the time was pretty much on his own. Sundials came in all sizes including small ones that could be carried about almost like a pocket watch. The problem with a portable sundial is that it must be oriented correctly in order to get a correct reading of the time. This might be difficult to do in some cases.

Water clocks were invented for night use, but they could also be used in the daytime. The simplest ones consisted merely of a jar with a small hole in the bottom and lines painted on it to indicate the hours. If a cloudy spell set in for several days, the sundial would be useless, the water clock

---

[30] A 20th century invention of the astrologer L. Edward Johndro (see below). It is the point where the prime vertical circle intersects the ecliptical circle in the west.

could not be set accurately, and people would simply have to guess what time it was.

A few technically-minded astrologers may have employed an astrolabe or some simpler astronomical device to determine the time more accurately, but it is doubtful that this was done very often.

Hours were reckoned a bit differently from our modern usage. Sunrise was the 12th hour of the night and sunset was the 12th hour of the day. Hence, if someone said he was born "at the first hour" of the day, he meant 1 hour after sunrise. The "middle of the second hour" would mean 1 1/2 hours after sunrise. Noon then was at the 6th hour of the day, and midnight was at the 6th hour of the night. We can convert this ancient method of time reckoning to our own by using the old schoolboy saying, "the English hour you can fix if to the Roman you add six." According to this rule, the 3rd hour is nine o'clock, either day or night. If the sum exceeds 12, then subtract 12. For example, the 9th hour of the day is the 15th hour or 3 PM. Obviously this method of conversion gives only a rough approximation, since it takes no account of the variable length of the day and the actual time of sunrise, but the error decreases towards noon and midnight.

Astrology in the Roman Republic and under the Empire

Astrology caught the fancy of the Roman elite in the 1st century B.C.[31] The Roman politician Lucius Cornelius Sulla (138-78 B.C.) had such faith in his horoscope that he concluded his *Memoirs* when his chart indicated that his life was about to end.[32] The Roman senator and amateur astrologer **Publius Nigidius Figulus** (c.100-45 B.C.) announced (in September of 63 B.C.) to a startled father that his new born son Octavius would become "the ruler of the world." And when he was 18, that son Octavius and his friend Marcus Agrippa (63 B.C.-12 A.D.) visited the astrologer **Theogenes** at Apollonia, Illyria. The astrologer predicted a splendid career for Agrippa.[33] Octavius at first refused to give the astrologer his own birth data for fear his future might not be so bright as his friend's. But finally he relented, and Theogenes was so impressed by Octavius's horoscope that he threw himself at his feet. For the rest of his life Octavius had great faith in his destiny, and many years later, when he

---

[31] See the richly detailed book *Astrology in Roman Law and Politics* by Frederick H. Cramer for a comprehensive, but unsympathetic, account of astrology and astrologers in the Hellenistic and Roman world down to 235 A.D.

[32] Cramer, *op. cit.*, p. 62. Cramer cites Plutarch's life of Sulla, which says Sulla died at the indicated time. Cramer, skeptical as usual, refuses to believe Plutarch and says "The implication that he actually died at the precise time foretold by the Chaldeans must, however, be dismissed . . ."

[33] He had one! And to this day his name is the most prominent one in Rome, M. AGRIPPA being inscribed on the front of the Pantheon in the center of Rome.

was the reigning emperor Augustus, he issued a silver coin with his Moon sign Capricorn on it.[34]

Romulus and the Founding of Rome

Marcus Tullius Cicero (106-43 B.C.) reports that the Roman scholar Marcus Terentius Varro (c.116-c.27 B.C.) had a friend **Lucius Tarutius Firmanus** who was an amateur astrologer. In Cicero's book *De divinatione* [On Divination], which he wrote around 45 B.C., he says[35] that Tarutius had investigated the birthdate of Romulus, the eponymous founder of Rome, and the foundation date of Rome itself. He had in effect worked out a speculative birthdate for Romulus and a speculative foundation date for Rome.

Plutarch (c.46-120 A.D.) gives some details in his *Life of Romulus*. He says that Romulus was conceived in his mother's womb in the first year of the second Olympiad on 23 Choiac of the Egyptian calendar, in the third hour, when the Sun was totally eclipsed, and he was subsequently born on 21 Thoth at sunrise. These dates equate to 24 June 772 B.C. a little after 8 AM LAT and 24 March 771 B.C. a few minutes after 6 AM LAT.[36] There was in fact an eclipse of the Sun on the morning of the conception date, but it was partial rather than total.

Plutarch then says that Romulus was 18 when he founded the City on 9 Pharmouthi between the 2nd and the 3rd hour, and he adds that "that day was precisely the 30th of the month, and there was an eclipse." Cicero notes that the traditional foundation date was 21 April in the Roman calendar and that on the foundation date the Moon was in Libra. In the years prior to 45 B.C. and far enough back to be before the Roman calendar missed three intercalations the month of April roughly corresponded to Pharmouthi. However, there is an inconsistency here because in the year 754 B.C. 9 Pharmouthi would have corresponded to 4 October in the Julian proleptic calendar, which is of course not the tradi-

---

[34]Suetonius, *The Lives of the Twelve Caesars*, trans. by Joseph Gavorse (New York: The Modern Library, 1931), p. 111. Augustus was probably born on 23 September of the Roman Republican calendar in the year we call 63 B.C.—see the discussion by Agnes Kirsopp Michels, *The Calendar of the Roman Republic* (Princeton: Princeton University Press, 1967), pp. 180-181. In that year the Roman Republican calendar was fairly close to the proleptic (astronomical) Julian calendar; hence, we can conclude that Augustus was born on either the 21st or the 22nd of September of the proleptic calendar, on both of which days the Moon was in Capricorn in the fixed zodiac of the Alexandrian astrologers. From historical evidence alone it is not possible to determine which day.

[35]Book 2, Sect. 98. Published as Cicero: *De senectute, De amicitia, De divinatione.* (Loeb Classical Library).

[36]See also the horoscope published by Manly Palmer Hall, *The Story of Astrology* (Philadelphia: David McKay Co., 1943), p. 61. Even though this horoscope by Tarutius is speculative (in fact, Romulus himself is a historical speculation), it is the earliest accurately calculated horoscope that has come down to us.

tional 21 April.[37]

Further information comes from two late writers, Caius Julius Solinus[38] (fl. 230 A.D.) and Joannes Laurentius Lydus (490-c.565). Solinus says that on 21 April of the foundation year Jupiter was in Pisces; Saturn, Venus, Mars, and Mercury were in Scorpio, the Sun in Taurus, and the Moon in Libra. Venus and Mercury of course cannot be in Scorpio when the Sun is in Taurus, but this is perhaps a scribal error. Lydus says the Sun was in Taurus, the Moon in Virgo, Saturn in Libra, Jupiter in Leo, Mars in Libra, Venus in Taurus, and Mercury in Aries. These positions do not agree with those of Solinus and could not occur around 754 B.C., so we may ignore them.

We may also ignore the date 21 April because if the Sun is assumed to be in Taurus and the Moon in Libra, it cannot be the 30th day of the (lunar) month, and there cannot be a solar eclipse. Presumably, then, the date actually found by the astrologer was 9 Pharmouthi = 4 October in 754 B.C. If we calculate the positions for about 8:30 A.M. of 4 October 754 B.C. and add about 16° to them to relate them to the fixed zodiac that was in use in the 1st century B.C., we find Sun 20 Libra, Moon 12 Scorpio, Mercury 12 Libra, Venus 18 Scorpio, Mars 6 Scorpio, Jupiter 5 Aries, and Saturn 23 Scorpio. If the date 9 Pharmouthi is correct, then the positions recorded by Solinus are somewhat in error. In particular, a date two days earlier would put the Moon in Libra conjunct the Sun (hence it would be the 30th day of the lunar month) and leave the others in the same signs. There was, however, no eclipse at that time.

Aside from the Sun, which was perhaps deliberately changed from Libra to Taurus because Solinus knew that the Sun should be in Taurus on the 21st of April, the other discrepancies could be due to errors in calculating backwards from ephemerides that were perhaps reasonably accurate in the 2nd century B.C. but which could not be extended cyclically for 600 years without losing accuracy.

At the date just established Romulus would have been seventeen years and six months old; hence, in his eighteenth year, which tallies with tradition.

All these dates are of course speculative and therefore, from a present-day point of view, worthless for astrological purposes. But the fact that there was a Roman astrologer in the 1st century B.C. with sufficient

---

[37]But it seems very unlikely that there were any astronomical tables based on the Roman calendar, so the coincidence of Pharmouthi with April was just that—a coincidence. Tarutius would have had to make his calculations using the Egyptian calendar in order to use the tables that were available.

[38]I see no reason to suppose that Solinus had access to Ptolemy's tables, so if he calculated the positions himself, he must have used something like the *Eternal Tables*, and tables of that sort cannot yield accurate positions when they are extended six centuries from their original epoch (2nd century B.C.?). Of course, it is entirely possible that Solinus merely copied the positions from some earlier writer, but whoever used tables of that kind would have incurred the same source of error.

technical skill to work them out shows that horoscopic astrology was known in Rome at that time and also that fairly accurate solar and lunar tables were available (probably those of Hipparchus that are mentioned by Pliny[39]). The discrepant positions for the foundation date recorded by Solinus may be medieval copying errors, or they may be errors made by Solinus or his source, or they may be errors made by Tarutius. We cannot tell.

We continue with some astrologers who flourished under the emperor Tiberius (42 B.C.-37 A.D.) and his successors.

Manilius

At the beginning of the 1st century, the Roman poet **Marcus Manilius** wrote the *Astronomica*, the earliest classical work on astrology that has survived intact. He completed it a few years after the death of Augustus in 14 A.D. It deals almost entirely with the signs of the zodiac, the fixed stars, and the houses of the horoscope. The planets are hardly mentioned. It is historically valuable because of its early date.[40] Manilius evidently believed in the Stoic philosophy and in the idea that the world was like a giant machine whose future motion was predictable. This was compatible with the idea that since planetary motions were predictable, the course of events in a human life should also be predictable.

Manilius gives rather poetical interpretations of the signs when they are in the ASC and when they are occupied by the Moon.[41] It is easy to see that he has taken note of the fact that the emperor Augustus had the Moon in Capricorn and that the reigning emperor has Libra rising[42]:

> ii. 507 Capricorn on the other hand turns his gaze
> Upon himself (what greater sign can he
> ever marvel at),
> Since it was he that shone propitiously on
> Augustus' birth?)

> iv. 547 When autumn's Claws begin to rise,
> Blessed is he that is born under the equili-
> brium of Libra.

---

[39]*Natural History* (Loeb Classical Library), ii, Sect. 53, (trans. by H. Rackham) "the courses of both stars [Sun and Moon] for 600 years were prophecied by Hipparchus"—plainly a reference to a set of astronomical tables.

[40]See the excellent edition and translation by G.P. Goold, *Manilius Astronomica* (Loeb Classical Library, 1977). Goold's Introduction gives a thorough explanation of those features of Greek astrology covered by Manilius.

[41]The ancients commonly noted an individual's Moon sign rather than his Sun sign.

[42]In the fixed zodiac that was in use at the time. But it seems likely that Tiberius also had Libra rising. See my paper, "The Horoscope of Tiberius." The translations that follow are by Goold, *op. cit.* However, I have taken the liberty of casting his prose translation into lines.

As judge he will set up scales weighted
with life and death;
He will impose the weight of his authority
upon the world and make laws.
Cities and kingdoms will tremble before
him and be ruled by his command
Alone, whilst after his sojourn on earth
jurisdiction in the sky will await him.

We are fortunate in having most of Augustus's birthdata. We know the place of birth (the Palatine Quarter of Rome), the year, the month, the time of day,[43] and that he was born on one of the two days in the latter half of the month when the Moon was in Capricorn in the Alexandrian zodiac. This narrows the date down to either 21 or 22 September[44] 63 B.C. at about 5:40 AM LAT. By calculating the tropical longitudes of the planets for that time on 21 September, which, for astrological reasons, I consider to be the most likely date, we can draw Augustus's horoscope, first in the Alexandrian zodiac and second in the tropical zodiac.

Further along in the book, Augustus's successor Tiberius is lauded:

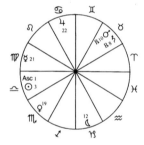 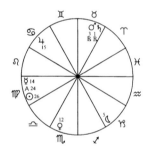

Fig. 2. Alexandrian Zodiac   **Fig. 3. Tropical Zodiac**

iv. 773   Italy belongs to Libra, her rightful sign:
            Beneath it Rome and her sovereignty of the

---

[43]Suetonius, *Lives of the Twelve Caesars*, Augustus, Sect. 5, says he was born *paulo ante solis exortum* 'just before sunrise', which probably means that the ASC degree was 1 or 2 degrees less than the Sun's longitude.

[44]As mentioned previously, Augustus was probably born on VIII.Kal.Oct. in the Republican calendar of 63 B.C., which by numeration was the 23rd of September. See the discussion by Agnes Kirsopp Michels, *loc. cit.,* pp. 180-181. But the number of days in the months was different in the Republican calendar (September, for example, had only 29 days), and dates in the Republican calendar do not agree with those in the Julian proleptic (astronomical) calendar. The dates given above are in the Julian proleptic calendar and are determined by the location of the Moon.

world were founded,[45]
Rome, which controls the issue of events,
Exalting and depressing nations placed in
the scales:
Beneath this sign was born the emperor,
who has now effected a better
Foundation of the city and governs a world
which hangs on his command alone.

He evidently had the Moon in Libra, and he was born on 16 November 42 B.C.,[46] probably in the early morning. See my paper, "The Horoscope of Tiberius," in the AFA *Journal of Research*, vol. 13.

In Book 3 Manilius discusses at some length a subsidiary system of houses counted from the Lot of Fortune.[47] To these he gives the name *athla* a Greek word meaning 'labors' or 'tasks' and here probably merely signifying the facet of life over which each of these houses rules. The rulerships he assigns are these: home, warfare, business; law, marriage, means; dangers, social class, children; character, health, success. Presumably Manilius found this doctrine in some Greek astrological treatise, but if so it made no impact on anyone else, for this scheme is not mentioned by any other writer. In Book 4. 408-501 he also gives a list of the injurious degrees in each sign, of which he says some are too cold, some too hot, and some sterile from either excessive or insufficient moisture. There are 102 of them.[48]

Finally, it should be recalled that Manilius subscribed to the Stoic philosophy, which held that fate directed the affairs of men. Some memorable lines occur in the 4th book:

fata regunt orbem, certa stant omnia lege

---

[45]Cicero states in his book *On Divination*, ii. 98, that his friend Lucius Tarutius Firmanus had determined that Rome was founded when the Moon was in Libra (see above).

[46]This was probably equivalent to 17 November in the Julian proleptic calendar, but the Moon would have been in Libra in the Alexandrian zodiac on both the 16th and the 17th days of that calendar.

[47]To construct a subsidiary chart with the Lot of Fortune in the first house was a standard practice, but all other astrologers who mention it assign the same meanings to the houses of this chart as they do to those counted from the ASC. Manilius assigns a completely different set of meanings which is found nowhere else.

[48]See the list on p. xi of vol. 4 of A.E. Housman's edition of Manilius (Cambridge: Cambridge University Press, 1937) and on p. lxxxviii of Goold's edition and translation. Goold's list has one more (12 Aries) than Housman's (who has a question mark at that point). Housman points out that the list given by A. Bouché-LeClercq, *Astrologie Grecque* (Paris: Leroux, 1899; Brussels: Culture et Civilisation, 1963. repr. in facs.) , p. 236, being based on J.J. Scaliger's last edition (Strasbourg, 1655), contains more than a dozen errors and that the total is not 70 as Bouché-Leclercq says, but 98! No other astrologer offers this list of unfortunate degrees, and if there is some plan behind it, it has remained undiscovered.

15 longaque per certos signantur tempora casus.
    nascentes morimur, finisque ab origine pendet.
    hinc et opes et regna fluunt et, saepius orta,
    paupertas, artesque datae moresque creatis
    et vitia et laudes, damna et compendia rerum.
20 nemo carere dato poterit nec habere negatum
    fortunamve suis invitam prendere votis
    aut fugere instantem: sors est sua cuique ferenda.

Goold translates them as follows:

    Fate rules the world, all things stand fixed by its
      immutable laws,
15 And the long ages are assigned a predestined
      course of events.
    At birth our death is sealed, and our end is
      consequent upon our beginning.
    Fate is the source of riches and kingdoms
    and the more frequent
    Poverty; by fate are men at birth given their
      skill and characters,
    Their merits and defects, their losses and gains.
20 None can renounce what is bestowed or possess
      what is denied;
    No man by prayer may seize fortune if it demur,
    Or escape if it draw nigh: each one must bear
      his appointed lot.

Manilius's book does not seem to have been very popular. And the only ancient astrologer who seems to have read any part of it is Firmicus Maternus (4th century); but while he paraphrases some of Manilius's remarks about the fixed stars in Book 8 of the *Mathesis*, he does not mention Manilius as his source.

Thrasyllus

The emperor Tiberius (42 B.C.-37 A.D.) had a personal friend named **Tiberius Claudius Thrasyllus** (d. 36 A.D.), who served him as court astrologer. Thrasyllus was a native of Alexandria and a grammarian (i.e., a literary scholar) by profession, but he was also very skilled in astrology. He wrote a treatise called *Pinax* 'Table' that was known to later astrological writers, such as Porphyry (c.233-c.304) and Hephaestio of Thebes (5th century), but has unfortunately perished. However, a chapter summary is preserved which gives us some idea of the contents.[49]

---

[49]The text is edited by Franz Cumont in *Catalogus Codicum Astrologorum Romanorum* (Brussels, 1898-1953. 12 vols.), VIII.3, pp. 99-101. This catalogue is hereinafter referred to as CCAG.

This begins first with the nature of the signs . . . some being human in form and others animal, some masculine and some feminine, some equinoctial and some tropical; but [he says] that the tropics do not occur at the first degrees of the sign as some reckon, but rather at the 8th degree, and that the width of the Moon and the Sun is a single degree.[50] And he states that of the 12 signs some are commanding, some servile, some are quadrupedal and some are not, some are fixed, some double-formed, some double-bodied, some terrestrial, some amphibian, and those that are fecundative and those that are prolific and those that are sterile, and those that are absorptive and other odd [classifications], and the crooked ones, and the two-colored ones; and to which winds each of the signs is allotted, and the domiciles and exaltations and chariots and royal positions, and the falls of the seven stars. . . .[51]

And he says something about the heptazone according to the tradition handed down, as he says, by Petosiris and Nechepso; and he says something about the natures of the 7 planets, and that some are particularly at home in some signs; then that Saturn and Jupiter go with the Sun, but Mars and Venus with the Moon because the former are said to be of the sect of the Sun and the latter of the sect of the Moon, and he says Mercury is common . . . and he talks about the Nativity of the World . . . and he says of the angles that the ASC [degree] and [the part of the sign] rising after it and [the part] rising before it is said to be an effective sign and the DSC opposing it, and the MC, which is the right square that rises before it, and the remaining [angle] the IC, which is also called the Under-earth Angle and is the left square of the ASC; and that there are 4 cadents and 4 succedents associated with the angles; and that the cadent of the ASC is called the Bad Daemon and that the one farthest off from that cadent [is its] opposite, the Bad Fortune. Then he relates that the rising sign is called Life; and its succedent, Livelihood; and the 3rd [house] has the topic of brothers; and the [angle] under the earth, parents; and the succedent to it, children; and the one that follows, injuries;

[50]Twice too big! The mean diameters of the Moon and Sun are 0°31' and 0°32' respectively.

[51]An exhaustive concordance of the epithets of the signs of the zodiac is contained in Wolfang Hübner's excellent work *Die Eigenschaften der Tierkreiszeichen in der Antike* [The Qualities of the Zodiacal Signs in Antiquity] (Wiesbaden: Franz Steiner Verlag, 1982). To use the book fully, you need to know German, Latin, and Greek.

and the DSC, the wife; and the one that is succedent to the
setting angle, which is found to be the eighth in order from
the ASC, is called fortune[52] and death. Having said all this .
. . he gives as an example the inspection of a horoscope; and
these things he also talks about, the times of life, which
[planets rule which] and how they distribute them, and
about how [the native] will obtain his livelihood, and about
the remaining [topics] from the chapters—brothers, I
mean, and parents, and children, and injuries, and his fortune in life; in which also [he discusses] the condition of
predominance, and what things the stars decree when they
predominate over each other.

And he also relates by what rationale the so-called
Trismegistos Hermes calls and uses each twelfth of the natal chart, how he declares the ASC to be the tiller,[53] and indicative of [the native's] fortune in life and his soul; and yet
the same [house] is also indicative of brothers,[54] and its
succedent signifies hopes[55]; and the 3rd action, but it is also
indicative of brothers; and he calls the 4th the foundation of
happiness and prosperity and indicative of the paternal estate and of the possession of slaves; and he calls the 5th
Good Fortune; but the 6th is indicative of the Bad Daemon
and punishment and injury; and the 7th, the descending
house, is indicative of death and the wife; and he calls the
8th life and livelihood[56]; the 9th of foreign things as well as
being indicative of spending one's life abroad; and the
10th, which is also the MC, he said is [the native's] fortune
in life, and his livelihood and life, showing about children,[57] and conception, and actions, and praises, and posi-

---

[52]This word should probably be deleted, as the word 'fortune' is not usually associated with the eighth house.

[53]A common epithet of the *horoskopós* or ASC, and an appropriate one since it
is the principal house of the horoscope and the one from which the others are
counted.

[54]The text appears to be corrupt here. A portion of the significations of the 3rd
house (brothers) has accidentally been copied after the significations of the ASC.

[55]The 2nd house is usually called the Gate of Hades and is primarily the house
of livelihood. But evidently it was originally also a house of hope, for Paul of Alexandria, *Introduction*, ed. by Emilie Boer as *Pauli Alexandrini elementa
apotelesmatica* (Leipzig: B.G. Teubner, 1958), Chapt. 24, says of it "For the
house was also established as the giver of good hopes." He uses almost the same
phrase of the 11th house, ". . . but it is also indicative of good hopes."

[56]The terms 'life' and 'livelihood' are usually assigned to the ASC and the second house respectively.

[57]Valens, *Anthology*, iv. 12, also mentions the 10th and 11th houses as presid-

tions of authority and leadership; and he calls the 11th sign in the chart the Good Daemon; and the 12th the *proanaphora*[58] and the Bad Daemon, and it is indicative of livelihood and the subordination of slaves.[59]—And these things [are contained in] Thrasyllus's *Pinax* [which is dedicated] to Hierocles.

In addition to this book, a popular divination tract is also attributed to Thrasyllus. It is mentioned here and there in the literature and also c. 115 by the Roman poet Juvenal in Lines 575-576 of the 6th of his *Satires*:

....Who, if her husband is going forth to camp or return-
    ing home from abroad,
Will not go with him when the numbers of Thrasyllus
    have called her back.

Thus we see that the "Thrasyllan numbers"—apparently some sort of easy-to-use numerological system—were still popular a century later. Whether Thrasyllus was actually their author is uncertain.[60]

Balbillus

Thrasyllus's son (by a daughter of King Antiochus III of Commagene) **Tiberius Claudius Balbillus** (d.c. 81) was also court astrologer to later emperors, including Claudius, Nero, and Vespasian. Balbillus accompanied Claudius to Britain as chief military engineer, and on his return received an important post in the province of Egypt. Later he served (54-59 A.D.) as Prefect of Egypt.[61] Balbillus wrote an astrological treatise *Astrologumena* addressed to Hermogenes; it is lost, but there is a synopsis of it.[62]

---

ing over children, as does Ptolemy, *Tetrabiblos* (Loeb Classical Library), iv. 6, who directs the astrologer ". . . to observe the planets that are in the midheaven or in aspect with it or with its succedant, that is, the house of the Good Daemon, or, in default of such planets, those connected with the diametrically opposite places. ." [Robbins's translation]

[58]Literally, "rising before (the ASC)."

[59]These rulerships too are unusual.

[60]See the discussion in Wilhelm Gundel & Hans Georg Gundel, *Astrologumena* (Wiesbaden: Franz Steiner Verlag, 1966), p. 150. The best text of Juvenal's *Satires* is that by A.E. Housman (Cambridge: Cambridge University Press, 1931. corrected reprint of the 1905 ed.). The translation of the *Satires* by G.G. Ramsay in the Loeb Classical Library is convenient but sometimes more of a paraphrase than a translation. Cramer, *op. cit.*, pp. 160-161, renders the astrological references in the *Satires* sometimes more skillfully and sometimes less so.

[61]See Cramer, *op. cit.*, for an account of his life.

[62]The synopsis is preserved in the so-called Parisian Epitome of astrological works in CCAG 8.3, pp. 103-104.

Summary of Balbillus's Astrologumena

First, he goes through [a section] about the periods of life, beginning the investigation from the *aphetic* places[63]; and he says that there are 4 aphetic places: Saturn, Mars, the Sun, [and] the Moon; and he takes the principal aphetic place to be [the planet] in the MC; but if there is none in it, he takes the aphetic place from the ASC or from the DSC or from the IC. And if [several] stars possess these [places], then that one which is in the MC is reckoned to be the sole aphetic place. And the *anaeretic* place[64] for the aphetic places is judged to be the one of them that happens to be 1st after [the aphetic place?],[65] since he says that if indeed the anaeretic place comes to the aphetic place and it is aspected by the ray of a benefic, the anaeretic place does not destroy [the native's life]; but only if an anaeretic sign is not found; and this is when it is rising before the aphetic place and its square.

2. And he relates that Jupiter and Venus [are] of the benefics, but Mercury is common, and some other things relating to the aphetic place and the anaeretic place are discussed in detail. By which method he directs the topic of the time periods of life to be investigated, in which also the Moon aspecting the aphetic place must be carefully observed, for he says it then becomes more powerful. And [he says] that if there are two anaeretic places, and one of them is aspected by the Moon, this [configuration] will be more powerful for causing death; and he lays down a similar observation about Mercury; and he gives rules about the casting of rays, giving examples of the foregoing.

3. Then he also talks about determining the dodecatemoria.

4. And he deals with the method of intervals, saying this: "Doubling the rising-times of each sign and taking a fifth, and if it leaves behind 1 day, put opposite the one a 10, and if two a 20; for example, if Gemini rises in 28 [times], double the 28, [it makes] 56; divide by 5; [it makes] 11; [multiply this by] 5; it makes 55; [subtract this from 56], the

---

[63]The *aphetic* place, literally 'the starting place', is that point in the horoscope from which a direction or profection is measured.

[64]The *anaeretic* place, literally 'the destructive place', is the termination of a direction or profection that is assumed to measure the length of life of the native.

[65]The text is defective at this point.

remainder is 1, which is equivalent to 10; but if it had been 2, it would have been 20, and similarly with the rest.

5. Besides, [he talks] about the end of the parents—how it will come about [as indicated] by prediction, and about dissension between them, and about [indications] of many children or few children, and about freedom and slaves and the conception of children, and about banishment and living abroad and [poverty?][66] and things resembling these. And he gives various methods of finding the ASC and the new Moon, and the apprehension of the stars without analysis.[67]

These are the chapters [of the book] of Barbillus that we have seen. Barbillus lived . . . .[68]

From a chapter of Balbillus's book which dealt with the length of life two example horoscopes of the 1st century B.C. are preserved in the 81st chapter of the the late 14th century Byzantine astrological compendium, *The Apotelesmatic Book* by Palchus.[69] The same excerpt contains the following description of a system of profections:[70]

And he says about the transfer of time [periods] that when each star is in its own exaltation it is allotted its complete cyclical years; i.e. the least [years]. For example, the Sun 19, the Moon 25, Saturn 30, Jupiter 12, Mars 15, Venus 8, [and] Mercury 20. But if they are not in the [exact] degree of that same exaltation, for each degree [of separation] it is necessary to take away as many days as are the years of the star, and for each sign [distant] that same number of months.

And he also says to allot to each star assuming the [role of] apheta its years divided by 129 and to give the Sun a 19th part, the Moon a 25th part, Saturn a 30th, Jupiter a

---

[66]The text is corrupt.

[67]This could mean a method of judging a horoscope without detailed analysis or possibly a method of determining the planets' places without extensive calculation.

[68]From the Parisian Epitome (CCAG VIII.3, pp. 103-104). The epitomator misspelled the author's name and wanted to indicate when Balbillus lived, but he didn't know what to put down, so he left a blank space.

[69]Palchus, *Apotelesmatikē biblos*, Chapt. 81, edited in CCAG VIII.4. The two horoscopes are re-edited, dated, and discussed by O. Neugebauer and H.B. Van Hoesen, *Greek Horoscopes*, pp. 76-78.

[70]Profections are movable points in a horoscope that are assumed to begin at some definite point in the chart and move away from it at a specified rate per year of the native's life. In general they do not correspond to actual astronomical motions.

12th, Mars a 15th, Venus an 8th, and Mercury a 20th, and to allot to each one first its own part, and second to the one after it, and third to the one lying next [to it], and [so on] down to the 7th. And, second to receive the times is the one lying after the apheta, and to allot to it and to those lying next to it similarly and the third similarly and [so on] down to the 7th. In the same manner and by the same method he says the times are allotted.

This system of time periods used for predictive purposes is set forth in detail by Vettius Valens and Julius Firmicus Maternus (see below).

Three other important astrological writers apparently flourished later in the 1st century A.D.:

Critodemus

Critodemus is mentioned by Pliny in his *Natural History* and must therefore have written prior to 77 A.D. when Pliny completed that work. Having reviewed the evidence, Pingree concludes[71] that Critodemus must have flourished towards the end of the 1st century B.C. or the beginning of the 1st century A.D. He wrote a book entitled *Horasis* or 'Vision', which is lost, but of which we can gain some idea from the partial summary preserved in the Parisian Epitome[72] and from the extensive excerpts cited by Vettius Valens (2nd cent.), who is our principal source for fragments of his work. Judging from Valens, *Anthology*, Books 8 and 9, Critodemus set forth an elaborate method for determining the length of life. From another book of his, called *Pinax* or 'Table', Hephaestio of Thebes (*Apotelesmatics*, ii. 10) cites several aphorisms indicating short life, such as: "When the lights are in the last degrees of the signs, they make short-lived persons; when the Moon is in the nodes aspected by the Sun and Mars, it makes short-lived persons; etc."

Teucer

He is called **Teucer of Babylon** and was apparently a native of Babylon, Egypt, formerly a military outpost but now a suburb of Cairo. His description of the natures of the planets and the signs of the zodiac are preserved in the MSS and were used by Vettius Valens (2nd cent.) and later by "Rhetorius."[73] Teucer is first mentioned by name by Porphyry

---

[71] David Pingree, *The Yavanajātaka of Sphujidhvaja* (Cambridge, Mass.: Harvard University Press, 1978. 2 vols.), vol. 2, pp. 424-426.

[72] CCAG VIII.3, p. 102. It begins: "1. He talks in detail about the transfer of chronocratorship from the Sun, when it transfers to the other six planets, and what the transfer to each of these signifies. 2. He takes up the subject of assignment — what does the Sun signify when it assigns [chronocratorship] to itself and when it is configured with one of the other [planets]. . . ."

[73] Pingree uses Rhetorius's name in double quotes to indicate astrological texts that may be by Rhetorius but have not yet been proved to be. See the entry for Rhetorius below.

(300). Here are some excerpts from his description of the planet Mars:[74]

Mars by nature is fiery and burning and drying; of [the parts of] the body, it rules the head, the seat, the [genital] parts, the bile, the blood, the excretion of feces, the hinder parts. And it signifies middle brothers and injury and sickness, violence, malice, war, robbery, arson, adultery, banishment, captivity, seduction of women, miscarriage, cutting and dissolution, attack by soldiers or armed robbers, trickery, lies, theft, perjury, burglary, grave-robbing, and those things similar to these. And it is of the nocturnal sect, and red in color, and sharp-smelling; and of the metals, it has iron; and in common with Mercury it has the mouth.

. . . .

This star taking the role of chart-ruler in a nocturnal nativity and when it is oriental in its own domiciles or with [other stars] of its own sect, makes persons who are courageous, warlike, reckless, terrible, unrestrained, fearless in fights and in foreign [military] service, very dangerous, those who are deprived of the paternal, maternal, and personal possessions of their early years, those who experience injuries or cuts, especially if it aspects the Moon, and it is the cause of burning; and if [it aspects] the Sun, [they are] unstable and immoderate around women, being involved with worthless or adulterous ones; whence, for these same [natives], the one who is unstable around children becomes sorrowful. But if it is found in a diurnal nativity, and if it is effective in a domicile of the opposite sect, it will change the foregoing for the worse, making arrogant, godless, blasphemous persons, mistreating many people, completely unrestrained, not pursuing their actions [to completion], easily diverted, sparing no one, ...[75]

Dorotheus

Dorotheus of Sidon,[76] an astrologer and poet, wrote five books (the *Pentateuch*) on astrology in verse. Pingree dates him to c. 75 A.D. His book survives partially in Greek excerpts (cited by Hephaestio of Thebes

---

[74]From the Greek text ed. by David Pingree in App. II to his edition of *Albumasaris de revolutionibus nativitatum* (Leipzig: B.G. Teubner, 1968), pp. 254-259.

[75]Notice the distinct difference in the predictions for diurnal and nocturnal nativities.

[76]The Arabic version calls him "Dorotheus the Egyptian," which is evidently a deliberate alteration of the text, since Firmicus, *Mathesis*, ii. 29, has "Dorotheus of Sidon."

c. 415 A.D.) and in an incomplete and interpolated Arabic version made c. 800 A.D. from a 4th century Pahlavi (Middle Persian) translation, but it was apparently unknown to Vettius Valens, who lived a century later than Dorotheus. The first four books of the *Pentateuch* are devoted to nativities, and the last book to elections and questions.[77]

We may say at the outset that Dorotheus's astrological techniques are entirely different from those of Ptolemy (see below). In *Pentateuch* i. 1, he says "I tell you that everything which is decided or indicated is from the lords of the triplicities. . ." And, to the considerations arising from their positions, he adds constant reference to house positions and lots and their rulers. The reason is simple: Dorotheus was in the mainstream of Greek astrology, and Ptolemy was not.

It is plain that Dorotheus used the Sign-House system of house division —the original system of the Alexandrian founders of horoscopic astrology. (Hence, when he speaks of the midheaven, he simply means the tenth sign from the ASC sign.) Also, he used the original concept of aspects, viz. that it is the signs that are in aspect. Hence, any planet in Aries is square any planet in Cancer, regardless of degree positions within the signs. The concept of "orbs" so familiar to modern astrologers was unknown to him.[78] He pays special attention to *sect*,[79] to appearances,[80] to

---

[77]The Arabic text with the Greek and Latin texts of all known excerpts is edited along with an English translation of the Arabic by David Pingree, *Dorothei Sidonii Carmen Astrologicum* (Leipzig: B.G. Teubner, 1976). The Arabic text is very neatly hand-written. The Preface and notes are of course in Latin. The excerpts that follow are from Pingree's translation, but I have altered his wording slightly.

[78]In modern astrology aspects are measured from one planet to another and a certain margin of deviation is allowed. For example, Mars in 10 Aries makes a perfect square to 10 Cancer (and to 10 Capricorn). But if a planet is within 8 to 10 degrees of 10 Cancer, it is still considered to be in square to Mars. The allowable deviation is called the "orb" of an aspect. Thus, if Mars were in 28 Aries and Saturn in 2 Cancer, Dorotheus would have considered them to be in square, but a modern astrologer, measuring the actual distance between the planets, which would be 64 degrees, would consider them to be in sextile with an orb of 4 degrees—a very considerable difference!

[79]*Sect* refers to the distinction between diurnal and nocturnal nativities and diurnal and nocturnal planets. A diurnal nativity is one in which the Sun is above the horizon. Diurnal planets are the Sun, Saturn, and Jupiter; nocturnal planets are the Moon, Mars, and Venus; Mercury is variable—sometimes diurnal and sometimes nocturnal. The "ruler of the sect" (called the "Light of the Time" in early modern astrology) is the Sun for diurnal births and the Moon for nocturnal births. These distinctions were very important in Greek astrology but are virtually unknown to modern astrologers.

[80]Appearances are positions of the planets with reference to the Sun or to the Moon and include the stations of the planets (static retrograde and static direct), oriental, occidental, etc.

34

house position, to terms, to which end of an aspect is more powerful,[81] and to other features of Greek astrology that are scarcely mentioned by Ptolemy. These will appear in the excerpts from the *Pentateuch* cited below. Also, Dorotheus explains three methods of timing predictions, one of which depends on a simple twelve-year cycle, another upon an elaborate system of symbolic directions that is also mentioned by Vettius Valens (*Anthology*, iv. 1, and vi. 6), Firmicus Maternus (*Mathesis*, ii. 26-27, and vi. 33-39), and Hephaestio of Thebes (*Apotelesmatics*, ii. 29), and a third upon what we would call the zodiacal primary progression of the ASC degree.[82]

Book 1, Chapter 21 "Knowledge of the Number of Brothers and Sisters" contains one example nativity, Chapter 24 "Judgments Concerning the Matter of Fortune and Property in Nativities" contains seven example nativities, and Book 3, Chapter 2 "The Hyleg" contains yet another.[83] These examples range in date from 7 B.C. to 44 A.D. Some of them were apparently of prominent persons but none have been identified with historical personages. Except for two charts that appear in fragments of a book by Balbillus, these are the oldest literary horoscopes known.[84] Here are the first two charts from Chapter 24:[85]

> A native was born when the ASC was Gemini and the positions of its [the nativity's] planets in the sphere were according to this diagram:

---

[81]This is generally determined by noting which end of the aspect is held by the planet that is on the right as viewed from the center.

[82]The ASC degree is progressed according to the rising-times of the signs under the clime of birth to the zodiacal body or aspect of the planets, noting the terms it is in at each aspect. The technique is ancient, since it is mentioned by Thrasyllus, and probably goes back to Nechepso and Petosiris. However, the first example given in the *Pentateuch* (a Persian horoscope of 381 A.D.) is an obvious interpolation, and only the second (using a chart for 44 A.D.) can be from Dorotheus.

[83]Pingree dates this chart to 20 October 281, since he wishes to ascribe it to the Persians, but a better fit to the positions given in the text is 2 October 44, which is also consistent with the dates of Dorotheus's other example charts. The reason why it has degrees while the earlier charts have only sign positions is because degrees are needed for the calculation of directions, while they are not needed simply for the delineation of a chart by his method.

[84]Firmicus's *Mathesis*, Book 6, contains charts of persons real and legendary who lived much earlier, but they are obviously schematically speculative, while the charts given by Balbillus and Dorotheus are valid horoscopes.

[85]From Pingree's translation of the Arabic version of the *Pentateuch*. I have slightly altered his translation. Note that the charts are drawn Arabic style with the ASC at the top, i.e. the chart is rotated 90° in the clockwise direction. Whether the original Greek text had this type of chart (or any charts at all) is unknown. The dates cannot be determined to the exact day because only the sign positions of the planets are given, and the Moon usually stays two days in each sign.

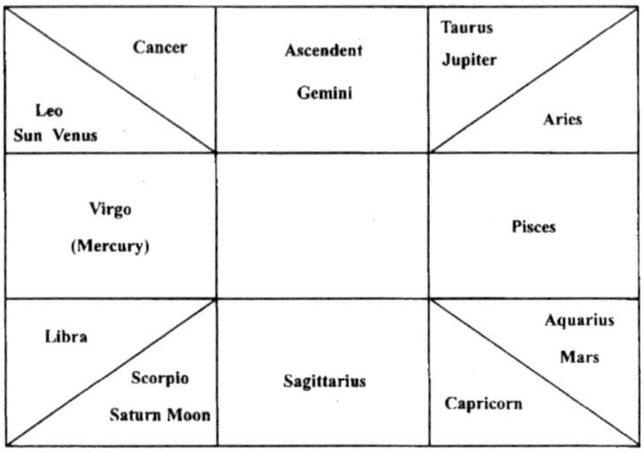

Fig. 4 Horoscope set for 1-3 August 43 (after Pingree).

The nativity was nocturnal, and I found the first planets in the matter of fortune to be Mars and Venus because they are the lords of the triplicity of the sign in which the Moon is; and both of them are in the cadents so that this man should be needy, poor, not finding his daily bread, [and] miserable. And this was more evident in him than what I told you.

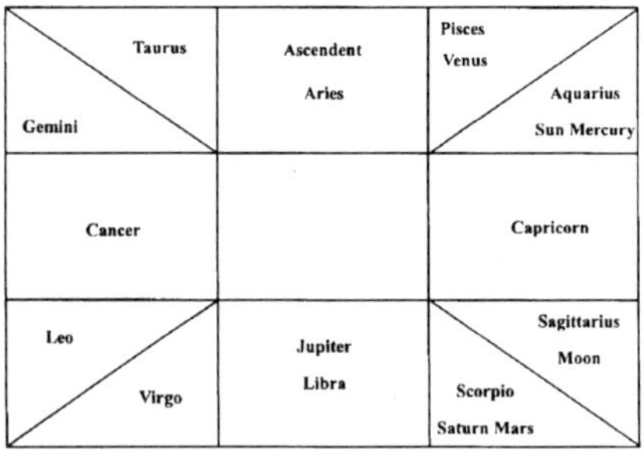

Fig. 5 Horoscope set for 25-26 January 13 (after Pingree).

This nativity was diurnal, and Aries was becoming visible at that hour in the East from out of the depths of the sea, and the lord of the Sun's triplicity was Saturn, then Mercury. Saturn was in what follows the angle of the West and Mercury in what follows the angle of midheaven, which is the house of fortune, so that the native should be wealthy, rich, powerful in business affairs, great in property, seizing eminence and fortune and increasing in them.

As an example of Dorotheus's techniques for judging a particular matter, here are his instructions for judging marriage prospects:

36

Book 2, Chapter 1.

Look at Venus where it is and which are the first, second, and third lords of its triplicity as, if they are with Venus or in an angle or in trine to it [Venus], then there is a good indication because Venus is full [of significance] for the matter of marriage. If you find the lords of the triplicity of Venus with it or in the angles or what follows the angles [the succedents], rejoicing in their light and direct in [their] motion, all of this is a good indication in the matter of marriage so that the father of the child was happy. But if you find the lords of the triplicity of Venus in a bad place[86] or a cadent [house], corrupted, or they are under the rays of the Sun or near the West, then predict differently from that [circumstance] about the badness of the marriage because the natives will be of those who will never marry or whose marriage is with slave girls or whores or old women who are disgraced or those young in years, or he is a leaser of whores; we have seen someone in [a nativity] like this who leased his wife, and he was disgraced in this. If you find the lords of the triplicity of Venus in a bad place, but Venus is with a benefic planet and [they are both] beneficial in one house, then he will marry an agreeable wife. But when the lords of the triplicity of Venus come in between [Venus and the benefic] they indicate disaster and disgrace because of women and anxiety and grief because of them. . . .

If you find the malefics aspecting the sign of the wedding, which is the seventh from the ASC, and you find the lord of this place cadent or corrupted by the aspect of the malefics or by a bad position, then it indicates what I will tell you. If the lord of that place is Saturn, then the injury is because of the fathers and mature men or because of the dead. If the lord of that place is Jupiter, he will attain this because of kings or wealthy men or because of the decree of his city. If it is Mercury, then this calamity and injury is because of argument and talk, and some of them will marry a woman who has been in service as a concubine, but thieves stole her away. If the lord of that place is Mars, it indicates a marriage [that is] shameful [and] disgraceful. . . .

Chapter 2. Knowledge of the Lot of Wedding.

Look at the place (which I shall tell you) of the Lot of Wedding. Count from the degrees of Saturn to Venus and

---

[86]Such as the 6th, 8th, or 12th house.

add to it the degrees of the ASC [by day] or subtract it thirty at a time from the ASC [by night]; wherever it reaches, then there is the Lot of Wedding. If you find any of those planets in this place or in quartile to it [the lot], then this is the indicator of the wedding. Look: perhaps then a malefic or an angle of the lot is in the sixth or the twelfth [of the nativity] so that this happens to be in a sign full of grief [and] scanty in benefit.

Chapter 3. Knowledge of the Lot [in] the Nativity of a Woman.

If you want to see in the nativity of a woman the Lot of Marriage, then count from the degrees of Venus to Saturn and add to it the degrees of the ASC. If you find any of the planets in [the place of] the lot or in quartile of this place, then it is the indicator. If it is Mars, then it indicates women who will marry [several] men in succession and will play the whore with men. If the lord of the Lot of Wedding is in the seventh sign and the lord of the lot is Saturn, then it indicates that that man who will marry her is an old man, and if Saturn is in its own domicile, then it indicates that he will be her grandfather or her paternal uncle or her maternal uncle or one of those possessing realtionships with her. . . .

Always if you find Venus in nativities of men or women in a bad place, then it indicates a disgraceful marriage.

And following this, Dorotheus goes on for four more chapters giving great detail on various possible combinations of the significators and their effects; Chapts. 8-13 are on children. Chapts. 14-19 give the significations of the mutual aspects of the planets; Chapts. 21-27 the significations of the planets in the houses; and Chapts. 28-33 the significations of the planets in the domiciles of the other planets.

Book 3 is on the *haylaj* as the Persians called it, which is what we usually call the *hyleg*, and the *kadhkhudah* or ruler of the chart.[87] The hyleg is what the Greeks called the *aphetic place* or simply the *apheta*. This is the starting point of a direction, either astronomical or symbolic, which is used to determine the length of life. The "ruler of the chart" is the planet or point in the chart that is determined by rules to be the predominant planet in the horoscope. The Arabic version of the *Pentateuch* apparently contains some genuine Dorothean material along with some sizable interpola-

---

[87]The *alcochoden* of the 12th Century Translators and the late medieval astrologers. It is the Greek *oikodespótes*, which, like its Persian translation means 'house-lord', i.e. the ruler of the nativity.

tions by the Persian translator.[88]

Book 4 is on the "transfer of years," i.e. on the successive transfer of rulership over the years of the life of the native from one sign (house) to the next. This is a standard technique of Greek astrology, for it is found in Dorotheus, Ptolemy, Vettius Valens, Firmicus Maternus, Paul of Alexandria, etc. The chapter begins like this:

Chapter 1

When a native is born, the lord of the [first] year is the lord of the house [ASC] in which the native was born. Thus count from the ASC a year for each sign until you reach the year which you desire; the lord of that house is the lord of the year. Look at the lord of this sign, whether it is a benefic or a malefic, and in the radix how its position was and in which foundation it was. From the radix is known what is concerning him [the native] at the beginning of the year, and the beginning of the year is always when the Sun enters the beginning of the minute in which it was on the day of the native's nativity. If the lord of the sign is occidental, misfortune will reach the native. If the planet is also under the Sun beams and is retrograde, then [something] similar to this [will happen]. [But] if the planet is under the Sun beams and is direct, then it will be better for him and it will be good....

Valens also said: Look at the planet which is the lord of that year; if it is seen on the day on which the Sun enters the minute in which it was on the day of the native's birth, then see at that hour in which this degree rises what [is] the ASC, which [is] the sign which rises from the East....

Now I will make clear to you [what happens] if the year reaches where the planets were in the nativity. If the year reaches the sign in which Saturn was and Saturn is in it or aspects it from trine or quartile or the seventh,[89] then the native will have a bad reputation [in that year], and there will reach him folly and injury and hostility from men and [from his] city, and some of them the government will be angry at and treat as an enemy. . . .

Dorotheus continues with more detail and also explains how to determine which house is the house of a particular month or a particular day of

---

[88]It appears that iii. 1.1-26 and iii. 2 are Dorothean. Chapt. 2 contains a chart that Pingree dated unconvincingly to the year 281, but I believe it should be dated to the year 44. See note 83 above.

[89]That is, from opposition.

the year in question.

Book 5 is devoted to Horary and Electional astrology. Here are some excerpts:

Chapter 1.

.... He says in this book[90] that he is following the tracks of the learned men who practised from among the learned of Babylon and Egypt since they were the first who looked concerning the science of the stars and their calculation and the revolution of the sphere and the motion of the seven stars and the rising-times of the twelve signs so that he might extract this from their books, then give this to himself as an example in his following [them]. He says that wherever he looked concerning what they dealt with and arranged of the science of the stars, he followed the best of their science and acquired it and explained it and collected it and extracted it from their books as he made it an example for himself in his following their tracks, and he made it this book like a bee when it follows the most delicious of fruits, and the best of it is made into honey; then he began to write for this book a comprehensive introduction in which he mentions the power of the seven and the twelve, and their soundness and corruption.

Chapters 2-4 instruct the reader to note first the sign that is rising and whether it is crooked or straight or tropical or twin. By this he means whether it is one of the signs that rises rapidly (Capricorn-Gemini) or one that rises slowly (Cancer-Sagittarius) or whether it is a cardinal or a mutable sign. In general, the signs rising rapidly indicate success and the signs rising slowly indicate delay and trouble. Benefic planets in or aspecting the ASC "help bring this action to a successful conclusion," while malefics in or aspecting the ASC in one of the slowly rising signs cause "slowness . . . and trouble and pain." If both malefics and benefics are in the ASC or aspecting it, "the action will be middling with a mixture of good and evil in it." The ASC in a tropical [cardinal] sign indicates "the breaking off of the end of this action before it is finished, and it indicates that he will commence this action a second time." The ASC in a twin [mutable] sign indicates that the "action which he commences at that hour will not be finished until an action other than this occurs in it, and it [the second action] will be finished before the first action is finished; it happens thus in every action in which the ASC is a twin [mutable] sign."

At the end of Chapter 4 Dorotheus defines the fire and air triplicities as diurnal and the earth and water triplicities as nocturnal and says to note

---

[90]Note that what we have is a paraphrase or summary of the original text, not a literal translation.

whether the ASC and the Moon are in diurnal signs by day or in nocturnal signs by night "because this is what is best in calculation."

Chapter 5 "The Corruption of the Moon" lists those conditions which impedite the Moon and prejudice its indications. Among them are its being eclipsed, under the Sun beams (but this is favorable for secret actions), in the Burnt Path [here defined as Libra and Scorpio],[91] in the last degrees of a sign [because it is then in the terms of Saturn or Mars], or in a cadent house. . . .

> Look concerning the totality of every commencement in the manner of Valens the Philosopher. . . .[92]

> Look at which of the stars the Moon is separating [from]. If you find it separating from the benefics, then it is good for every action which he commences....Together with this look at the lord of the navamsa[93]. . . .

> Look concerning the commencement of every matter at the ASC and the Moon. The Moon is the strongest of what is [possible] if it is above the earth, especially if this is at night; the ASC is the strongest of what is [possible] if the Moon is under the earth by day. This is what he says in the introduction of his book . . . .

Of the various horary questions that Dorotheus discusses, theft is the one to which he gives the most attention (nine pages in Pingree's translation). Evidently this was a common problem in antiquity. His treatment of the subject is very detailed. Here are a few excerpts:

> Look: if the Moon is in Aries..., then it indicates that what was stolen is garments, suit[s] of clothes, or trinkets worn on the head and face. If the Moon is in Taurus, then it indicates that what was stolen is gold or silver or trinkets with which they are adorned or something useful for vows and for mosques and deities. If the Moon is in Gemini, then what was stolen is dirhams or denarii[94] or some of what is necessary in taking and giving [in trade], or a ledger in

---

[91]More commonly defined as the last half of Libra and the first half of Scorpio.

[92]An obvious interpolation, since Vettius Valens lived a century after Dorotheus. The quotation that follows does not appear in the received Greek text of Valens, but may have been present in the Persian translation of his *Anthology*.

[93]Here is another interpolation by either the Persian or the Arabic translator. The Arabic text has a word from Hindu astrology, *nubahr* (or *naubahr*). (Cf. al-Bîrunî, *The Book of Instruction* (see below), Sect. 455, where it is spelled *nuhbahr*.) These are the ninths of a sign, which in Greek are called *leitourgoi* 'ministers' [sc. of the decans],but in Sanskrit they are called simply *navāmśas* 'ninths'.

[94]Common Arabian and Roman coins. Here simply = 'money'.

which is a book, or an idol useful for the deities. If the Moon is in Cancer, then it indicates that what was stolen is a costly gem [or something] moist. . .

If the indicator of the characteristic[s] of the thieves is Mars, then this thief will be red in [his] color, reddish in [his] hair, lank-haired, sharp in [his] vision, fat-cheeked in [his] face, [having] gaiety, a master of joking, capricious, turning himself from [one] condition to [another] condition, sharp in [his] glance; he rushes to injure men and to obliterate their thing[s]. . . .

Capricorn indicates that the thief is thin-legged, miserable in [his] two [legs], slim, a male; the figure of his face resembles a goat's in the dark; lank in [his] beard, sharp-eyed; his glance is toward the ground, his opinion does not change from [one] situation to [another] situation; he is trivial in [his] thought and consideration[s]. . . .

If Mercury is the one which aspects the ASC or the Moon, then it indicates that the thief entered the house by a ruse and subterfuge and cleverness and the wish for trouble for the people of the house in which he committed the robbery.

And here are Dorotheus's general instructions for making an election as given in Chapter 30:

Look concerning each matter that you commence at the lord of this action from among the stars. Sometimes one commences a matter when the benefics aspect the Moon and the ASC and the lord of this action is under the Sun beams or impeded or does not aspect the ASC and is in a bad house; then this action will be bad and have no good in it. If you want to buy land or give power of attorney to someone, then look concerning this at the power of Saturn and Jupiter. If [the matter] is a taking away or a gift or a quarrel or a practice or a partnership or an insult or love or trade or seeking culture or [something] like this, then look concerning this at the power of Mercury. If it is a wedding or marriage or something pleasant of the acts of Venus, then look concerning this at the power of Venus. If it is a fight or arms or what is similar to this, then look concerning this at the power of Mars. If it is a matter of the government or a matter of kings or a request before kings, then look concerning this at the power of Jupiter. If it is one of the matter[s] evident and apparent in which secrecy and a ruse and evil are not seen, look at the power of the Sun, also together with Jupiter. Every time Jupiter aspects a star it turns it toward good. Venus does this [also], but not in momentous affairs unless Jupiter is with it or aspects together with it. The power of Venus is in the love which is between two [people] or food or perfume or what is similar to this. In every time and in every situation Jupiter is good because it increases the properness and good or diminishes from the evil and misfortunes and destroys them.

Dorotheus's Book 5 is the oldest treatise on horary and electional astrology that has come down to us. It was well-known to the Arabian astrologers, and much of our received tradition goes back to it ultimately.

Manetho

Another astrological poet writing in the early years of the 2nd century under the name **Manetho**[95] was the author of six books of astrological verse entitled *Apotelesmatics*. The author attempts to give his book an air of antiquity by addressing "King Ptolemy" as if he were a contemporary.[96]

BOOK I (V):

Greetings, O Ptolemy, you who hold the kingly honor
Of our land, world-nourishing Egypt.
I bring to you these gifts, worthy of a royal rule,
Sleepless at night and working hard by day,
So that whatever Petosiris himself cursorily
Said, those same things I shall relate in detail
In heroic rhythms and hexameter verses,
So that you may understand all the things that we
    have learned
Whose lot it is to inhabit the sacred soil of Egypt.

BOOK V (VI):

From the secret holy books, King Ptolemy,
And the arcane columns, which the most wise Hermes
    devised,

---

[95]The elements of his horoscope are given in Book iii, 738-750 of his *Apotelesmatics*, from which his birthdate can be deduced as the 27th or 28th of May 80 A.D. See Neugebauer & Van Hoesen, *Greek Horoscopes*, p. 92.

[96]The last legitimate Ptolemy was Cleopatra's youngest brother Ptolemy XIII, who died in 44 B.C., but the author probably had in mind Ptolemy I Soter (367-283 B.C.). And his own name, Manetho, is that of the famous historian of Egypt, who lived under Ptolemy I. Therefore, the astrological author may have merely adopted Manetho as a pseudonym to make his work appear to be of ancient origin.

Having found Asclepius, the adviser of prudent wisdom,
And he distinguished the proper providences of the
    heavenly stars,
Shaping in modelling wax, he has brought
To the flower-gathering Muse the outpouring gift of the
    bees,
By which, through the black night under the chorus of
    the heavenly stars
I found this doctrine speaking through the fatal threads;
For no one has yet thought out the ornament of this wis-
    dom
Except only Petosiris, a man who was my very close
    friend.
No light labor was this, Ptolemy!

Very flowery! However, unlike Manilius, who was mainly a poet,
Manetho was also a technical writer. And, also, unlike Manilius, he deals
more with the planets than with the signs. His book, which has survived in
a fragmentary state in a single MS, contains valuable excerpts drawn from
earlier writers whose works have not come down to us intact.[97]

Ptolemy and Valens

The two principal astrological writers of the 2nd century were **Claudius Ptolemy** (c.100-c.178) and **Vettius Valens** of Antioch (120-c.175).
Ptolemy is usually considered to be the prime astronomer, geographer,
and astrologer of the Classical World. His *Syntaxis* (*Almagest*) is a compendium of Greek astronomy,[98] his *Handy Tables*[99] eventually became
the standard set for astronomical calculations; his geographical works
constitute an excellent Atlas-Gazeteer[100] and the only one to have come
down to us from classical antiquity; and his book on astrology, the

---

[97]Edited and translated into Latin with a commentary by Arminius Koechly in
Poetae bucolici et didactici (Paris: Firmin Didot, 1931. repr. of the 1862 ed. which
was a repr. from Koechly's 1858 ed.). Koechly has rearranged the order of the
books in his edition, whence the double numbering, e.g. "Book III [II]." See
Gundel-Gundel, *Astrologumena*, pp. 159-164, for a detailed review (in German)
of the contents of the several books.

[98]See the English translations by R.C. Taliaferro, *The Almagest by Ptolemy* in
Great Books of the Western World (Chicago, 1952), vol. 16; and by G.J. Toomer,
Ptolemy's Almagest (London: Duckworth, 1984). The standard edition of the
Greek text is by J.L. Heiberg, *Claudii Ptolemaei opera quae extant omnia* (Leip-
zig: B.G. Teubner, 1898-1903. 2 vols.), vol. 1.

[99]See the French translation of Ptolemy's *Introduction* to the tables and Theon
of Alexandria's *Commentary* and edition of the tables by the Abbé Nicolas Halma
(1755-1828), *Tables manuelles des mouvemens des astres* (Paris, 1822-1825) 3
vols.

[100]Greek text and tables ed. by C.F.A. Nobbe, *Claudii Ptolemaei Geographia*
(Leipzig, 1843-1845. 3 vols. repr. 1898 and 1966); and the edition by Jos. Fischer,

Tetrabiblos, has been wrongly considered by most modern astrologers to be the ultimate sourcebook of astrology.

Actually, Ptolemy seems to have been a well-educated, intelligent man who took on the task of summarizing and systematizing the accumulated knowledge of some of the sciences, perhaps working under the patronage of the otherwise unknown Syrus, to whom all his books are dedicated. This may explain why his books do not seem to have become generally available until the end of the 3rd century. They may have been retained by Syrus's descendants as family property for several generations. Vettius Valens, who lived in Alexandria for about twenty-five years after the completion of Ptolemy's books, had never heard of him! And Firmicus Maternus in the first half of the 4th century had evidently not actually seen his books.[101]

The first astrological writer to mention Ptolemy was the Greek philosopher Porphyry (c.232-c.304), who wrote an *Introduction to Ptolemy's Tetrabiblos*[102] about 295. However, once the *Handy Tables* became available, probably in the 4th century, they were eventually adopted as standard authorities by the astrological community. The oldest known horoscopic positions calculated from Ptolemy's tables are for the date 30 November 380 in Hephaestio of Thebes, *Apotelesmatics* ii. 1 (written about 415). (The second oldest is the Persian horoscope of 26 February 381 mentioned above, which is found as an interpolation in Dorotheus, *Pentateuch* iii. 1.)

It has recently become apparent that Ptolemy was not the great astronomer that he was formerly thought to be. Robert Newton has shown that nearly all of the "observations" mentioned in the *Syntaxis* have been adjusted to fit positions calculated from his tables and that his star catalogue is simply that of Hipparchus with the constant 2°40' added to the longitudes and the resulting longitudes rounded off if they happened to end in 25' or 55'.[103] To Newton's many examples I can add one more that seems particularly significant. The papyrus horoscope of 81 A.D. states that it was calculated with the *Eternal Tables* and that Mercury was in 10 Aries,

---

S.J., *Claudii Ptolemaei Geographiae Codex Urbinas Graecus 82* (Leyden: Brill - Wiesbaden: Harrassowitz, 1932) [Greek text and tables in 4 parts]. The maps are reproduced in A.E. Nordenskiöld's *Facsimile-Atlas,* of which the English version printed at Stockholm in 1889 was reprinted in facsimile by Dover Publications (New York, 1973)

[101]Firmicus mentions Ptolemy three times (*Mathesis*, ii. Preface; ii. 29, and iii. 13), but it is obvious that these are second-hand references, for he attributes the doctrine of antiscions to him, a topic that Ptolemy does not mention.

[102]Edited by Emilie Boer and Stephen Weinstock in CCAG V.4 (Brussels: Belgian Royal Academy, 1940).

[103]The "observations" that form the basis of Ptolemy's work have been proven to be mostly fraudulent, and his theoretical astronomy is not as good as it might have been. See the detailed discussion by Robert R. Newton, *The Crime of Claudius Ptolemy* (Baltimore & London: The Johns Hopkins University Press, 1977).

its perihelion. This is the exact position of the perihelion derived by Ptolemy in *Syntaxis*, ix. 7, after lengthy calculation based upon "observations."[104] This can scarcely be a coincidence. In fact, it shows that Ptolemy simply took the position of Mercury's perihelion from the *Eternal Tables* and then adjusted his "observations" and calculations to produce that same figure.

It is equally plain that Ptolemy's astrological work, the *Tetrabiblos*, was in reality an abriged[105] and deviant version of the standard Greek astrology of his day. Undoubtedly his greatest contribution to astrology was his adoption of Hipparchus's tropical zodiac as the reference circle.[106] This had no immediate impact on Western astrology, but it was adopted by the late classical astrologers and also passed to the Arabian astronomers and astrologers. Thus, it established the tropical zodiac as the Western standard. Ptolemy explains his reasons for abandoning the fixed zodiac of the Alexandrian founders of astrology in *Tetrabiblos*, i. 22:

> . . . it is reasonable to reckon the beginnings of the signs also from the equinoxes and solstices, partly because the writers make this quite clear, and particularly because from our previous demonstration we observe that their natures, powers, and familiarities take their cause from the solstitial and equinoctial starting-places, and from no other source.[107]

Western astrologers have followed this precept for 1,700 years. The

---

[104]This was noted by Neugebauer & Van Hoesen in *Greek Horoscopes*, p. 26, but they failed to grasp its significance. In fact, it confirms and even extends Newton's demonstration of Ptolemy's fraudulent handling of his astronomical data, since the odds against Ptolemy's having derived the exact same value for the perihelion as that used in the older tables are very large.

[105]He says explicitly in *Tetrabiblos*, iii. 1, ". . . we shall decline to present the ancient method of prediction, which brings into combination all or most of the stars, because it is manifold and well-nigh infinite, if one wishes to recount it with accuracy . . . and furthermore we shall omit it on account of the difficulty in using it and following it." (Robbins's translation in the Loeb Classical Library edition). Here are some of the things Ptolemy "declined to present": (1) the influences of the planets in the signs; (2) the influences of the planets in the celestial houses; (3) the influences of the mutual aspects of the planets; (4) the method of using the Lots (other than the Lot of Fortune); and (5) the method of reading a chart by means of derived houes, house rulers, and dispositors! This list could be extended.

[106]It seems to be expecting too much of them, but if astronomers would take the trouble to do a little historical research before they burst into print, they would avoid exposing their ignorance on such matters. But apparently this is too much to hope for. Still, it is amusing to see them trot out the same unfounded argument about the zodiac every ten or fifteen years as if it were something newly discovered.

[107]Robbins's translation.

occasional argument advanced by 20th century astronomers when they run out of anything else to do that "astrologers are using the wrong zodiac" is thus based on ignorance, particularly since the astronomers' own handbooks define the vernal equinox as "the First Point of Aries."[108]

Book 1 of the *Tetrabiblos* defines various technical terms and supplies other information needed by the astrologer. Of particular interest is Chapter 9 "The Power of the Fixed Stars," which specifies the nature of the individual stars and constellations by likening them to the nature of one of the planets or to the combined natures of two of the planets. This seems to be the original source of this sort of information, although Ptolemy may have taken it from some older writer.

Ptolemy disparaged all the subdivisions of the zodiac except the terms,[109] of which he gives three different versions: (1) the original "Terms According to the Egyptians," no doubt those of Nechepso and Petosiris; (2) the Chaldean Terms (from the school of Berosus?); and (3) a set of terms that Ptolemy says he found in an old book. None of the astrologers whose works have survived used the Chaldean Terms, and Ptolemy's Terms were only occasionally mentioned. The Terms According to the Egyptians were used almost exclusively in the Classical Period and in the Middle Ages.[110] See Appendix 1 for a table of the terms according to the Egyptians.

The terms of a planet were considered to be "sub-domiciles" of that planet; hence a planet in its own terms was strengthened in its influence.

Ptolemy made considerable use of appearances and the natures of the signs of the zodiac. He used the syzygy that immediately preceded birth for various purposes, and was rather fond of the Lot of Fortune,[111] for which he simplified the calculation by employing the same rule for both

---

[108]Cf., for example, the *Explanatory Supplement* (London: H.M. Stationery Office, 1961), p. 24, "The ascending node of the ecliptic on the equator is referred to as "the vernal equinox," "the first point of Aries," or simply as "the equinox." Apparently astronomers don't read their own books.

[109]Areas within each 30-degree sign that were assigned to the rulership of a particular planet. Usually there were five such areas, and they were assigned to Saturn, Jupiter, Mars, Venus, and Mercury in an irregular sequence that varied from sign to sign. The most popular system was that "according to the Egyptians," but Vettius Valens cites some other systems, most notably that of Critodemus.

[110]But some modern astrologers used Ptolemy's Terms, e.g. William Lilly, who gives a table of them in his *Christian Astrology*, p. 104, and Vivian Robson, who reproduces Lilly's table in his *Electional Astrology*, p. 210. (Publication data for these books is given under the authors' names below.)

[111]The lots (or "parts," as they are called today) are what modern astrologers call "sensitive points" in the zodiac calculated by subtracting the longitude of one planet from the longitude of another planet and adding the difference to the ascending degree. Usually the order of the two planets was reversed if the chart was a nocturnal one. These lots were an early feature of horoscopic astrology. The so-called Lot of Fortune was the principal one. It was calculated by subtracting the Sun from the Moon (by day, or the Moon from the Sun by night) and adding

diurnal and nocturnal nativities,[112] but he ignored all the other lots. He used general significators rather than accidental significators.[113] Aside from his adoption of the tropical zodiac, his most significant contribution to astrology was his method for determining the length of life by means of what are now called primary directions.[114] Although his explanations were generally misunderstood, they sparked a continuing interest in primary directions and in house division.

The *Tetrabiblos* has an excellent systematic arrangement, and, having been compiled from older Greek astrological works, contains valuable material that might otherwise have been lost. Book 2, for example, is devoted to mundane astrology, which, as Ptolemy rightly points out, takes precedence over natal astrology, since the fate of an individual is necessarily subject to the more universal fate of the place where he resides. Mundane astrology is the oldest kind of astrology, so some of his material goes back ultimately to the Babylonians.

Books 3 and 4 are devoted to natal astrology. Book 3, Chapter 2 explains Ptolemy's method of rectifying the ASC degree. He says to find the time and degree of the syzygy (new or full Moon) preceding the native's birth. Then determine which planet had the most domination over the longitude of the conjunction or over the longitude of whichever luminary was above the earth at the time of the opposition. Then the natal ASC should have the same number of degrees as that planet. But if the estimate ASC degree is considerably different from the degree of the planet, then consider whether the MC degree corresponding to the estimate ASC degree is closer to the degree of the planet, and, if so, then use the planet's degree to establish the degree of the MC and from it the degree of the ASC. This method was used during the Middle Ages and the early Modern Period. It

---

the difference to the ascending degree. Originally, perhaps, the lots were determined by simply counting the whole signs from one planet to the other and then counting the same number from the ascending sign.

[112]This simplification was not adopted by the astrologers of the Classical Period. The medieval astrologers were aware of it, but generally did not use it. But modern astrologers, supposing Ptolemy's simplification to be the original method and the true original (Moon - Sun + ASC by day, and Sun - Moon +ASC by night) to be a deviant method, have almost universally followed Ptolemy.

[113]General significators are planets that are assigned to certain matters or persons in every horoscope. For example, the Sun to the father, the Moon to the Mother, Mars to the husband, and. Venus to the wife. Accidental significators are planets that are assigned to matters or persons because they are sign rulers of the houses ruling those matters or persons in a particular horoscope. For example, the ruler of the fourth house for the father, the ruler of the fifth for a child, the ruler of the seventh for the wife (or husband), the ruler of the tenth for actions, career, prestige, etc. Accidental significators are obviously much more individually specific.

[114]He advocated what we would call Placidian primaries, although this was not understood by astrologers until the 17th century. (See the entry for Placidus.)

was sometimes given the name *animodar* (from the Arabic *al-namūdār* from a Persian word).[115]

In Book 4, Chapter 10, Ptolemy notes again that:

> ". . . among all genethlialogical inquiries whatsoever, a more general destiny takes precedence of all particular considerations, namely, that of country of birth, to which the major details of a geniture are naturally subordinate, such as the topics of the form of the body, the character of the soul and the variations of manners and customs, it is also necessary that he who makes his inquiry naturally should always hold first to the primary and more authoritative cause, lest misled by the similarity of genitures, he should unwittingly call, let us say, the Ethiopian white or straight-haired, and the German or Gaul black-skinned and wooly-haired, or the latter gentle in character, fond of discussion, or fond of contemplation, and the Greeks savage of soul and untutored of mind; or, again, on the subject of marriage, lest he mistake the appropriate customs and manners by assigning, for example, marriage with a sister to one who is Italian by race, instead of to the Egyptian as he should, and a marriage with his mother to the latter, though it suits the Persian. Thus in general it is needful first to apprehend universal conditions of destiny, and then to attach to them the particular conditions which relate to [the] degree [of compliance with that destiny].[116]

Book 3, Chapter 10 "The Length of Life," sets forth a method to determine how long the native will live. In his instructions and examples Ptolemy used the Equal House system of house division and proportional semi-arcs to zodiacal positions for calculating arcs of direction. This one chapter has occasioned more astrological controversy than any other ever written. We cannot examine it in detail here, but it should be plain to anyone that the premier astronomer of antiquity would not have devised a system of house division requiring elaborate trigonometrical calculations without bothering to explain it. The houses after all are used merely to determine which planet or point in the zodiac will be the aphetic place. Ptolemy says nothing about directing planets to intermediate house cusps.

---

[115]This and some other common technical terms transliterated from the Arabic are explained by Paul Kunitzsch, *Mittelalterliche astronomisch-astrologische Glossare mit arabischen Fachausdrücken* 'Medieval Astronomical-astrological Glossary with Arabic Technical Terms' (Munich: Verlag der Bayerischen Akademie der Wissenschaften, 1977).

[116]Robbins's translation. Cf. the remarks of Firmicus in *Mathesis*, i. 10, where he emphasizes the point that the stars produce variations in the characteristic physical and mental type of the different races.

Why should he? His directions are based on the simple principle of bringing one point in the sky to another point in the sky that has a similar relation to both the horizon and the meridian. This is merely matching appearances and has nothing to do with house position. His examples are quite plainly what we would call Placidian zodiacal primaries. Why their principle was not immediately obvious to everyone is puzzling.[117]

In giving instructions as to how to delineate a given horoscope for the topics of bodily form, temperament, mental characteristics, parents, siblings, marriage, children, friends, status, action, sickness, death, etc., Ptolemy mainly relies on the planets, their positions, and mutual configurations. The *Tetrabiblos* contains elaborate lists of planetary epithets (now called "key-words"). The signs the planets are in are also often mentioned and the Lot of Fortune is considered where appropriate, but the houses (aside from indicating angularity) play a very secondary role. This procedure is quite different from that used by Dorotheus and the other Greek astrologers. As an example of his method of delineating the horoscope with reference to a particular topic, let us consider his rules for describing the wife (or husband) from the natal horoscope:

For men, he says to look at the Moon and see whether it is in oriental quadrants or occidental quadrants. (He explains later that in this case the oriental quadrants are those from new Moon to first quarter and from full Moon to last quarter), then to look at the quality of the Moon's sign and the planet or planets to which the Moon applies. A position in an oriental quadrant indicates an early marriage or marriage to a younger woman, while the occidental quadrants indicate a late marriage or marriage to an older woman. Signs of a single form or application to only one planet indicates a single marriage, while signs of double form or application to more than one planet in the same sign indicate more than one marriage. And similar considerations apply to women's marriages, except the Sun is the indicative planet instead of the Moon. Applications to malefics indicate an unhappy marriage, and applications to benefics indicate a happy marriage. He says nothing at all about the seventh house of the horoscope.

All this is completely different from the instructions given by Dorotheus (see above). As a result, we have a mixed tradition that adopts Ptolemy's rules but adds some of those given by Dorotheus. And in general this applies to the other topics—the tradition is a mixture of standard Greek astrology with the deviant rules prescribed by Ptolemy, who largely ignores the houses and pays no attention to any of the lots besides

---

[117]For a discussion of the efforts of Regiomontanus and his successors to maintain that Regiomontanan primary directions (which have a completely different basis from Ptolemaic—i.e. Placidian—primaries) were what Ptolemy "meant" in *Tetrabiblos*, iii. 10, see my translation of J.B. Morin's *Astrologia Gallica*, Book 22 (Tempe, Az.: A.F.A. Inc., 1994), especially Chaps. 8 & 9 and my notes thereto.

his hybrid Lot of Fortune.[118]

Ptolemy cites no astrological authorities by name,[119] he gives no example horoscopes, and he certainly was not a practicing astrologer. Nevertheless, his book has preserved valuable material from earlier writers. And his own, sometimes rather acute, observations on the philosophical and theoretical background of astrological practice are first rate, and in a class by themselves, since most of the other astrological literature that has come down to us does not discuss these matters.[120] But by the astrologers of late antiquity and those of the Middle Ages and early modern period he was considered to be a prime astrological, as well as astronomical authority.

In modern times his reputation among astrologers was greatly enhanced by the fact that his book the *Tetrabiblos* was the only Greek astrological treatise that was available in a modern language translation. This fact plus his reputation as a great astronomer led most astrologers to assume that his book was the original source of horoscopic astrology and that every technique that was not found in the *Tetrabiblos* was an "invention of the Arabs."

Vettius Valens was an entirely different sort of person. Originally from Antioch (probably the modern Antakya, Turkey), he moved to Alexandria, Egypt, where he worked as a professional astrologer and proprietor of an astrological school. There he wrote what was perhaps intended as a textbook for his students—dedicated to his friend (or pupil) Marcus and entitled simply *Anthology*. It consists of nine books, but it begins abruptly without a preface, so the first few pages were lost somewhere along the line of descent from Valens's autograph copy to the archetype of the extant Greek MSS. It was probably passed down from one astrologer to another, for in the year 250 or shortly thereafter someone extended the lunar table in *Anthology*, i. 17, as far as the Emperor Philip I (reigned 244-249). And at some time after 455 a later owner added at the end of his copy the horoscope of some unidentified person (who was born in 431 and was forecast to die in 505) and the horoscope of the last effective Western Roman Emperor Valentinian III (419-455), who, from the data given, was born at sunrise on 2 July 419.[121]

---

[118]*Hybrid* because he uses the same rule for both diurnal and nocturnal charts. Consequently, his nighttime "Lot of Fortune" is actually the "Lot of the Daemon."

[119]Once (in *Tetrabiblos*, iii. 10) he mentions an opinion "according to the ancient," which may well be a reference to Petosiris or to Nechepso.

[120]See some of his comments cited at length below.

[121]The positions of the Sun, Moon, ASC, and the Sun's longitude at the preceding full Moon are given. They were calculated from Ptolemy's *Handy Tables*, which in 419 yielded positions about 2°17' less than true tropical longitudes. Also, the natal positions were calculated for about 6 A.M. in Spain or 7 A.M. in Italy, while sunrise would have been more than an hour earlier in Spain or nearly two hours earlier in Italy. The astrologer rectified the chart and determined the native's length of life by following a procedure given in Book 8 of the *Anthology*.

Book I is devoted to the fundamentals—the natures of the planets, signs, and the terms according to the Egyptians; how to find the ASC and MC, the rising-times of the signs, the longitude of new and full Moons, how to find the weekday from the calendar date, masculine and feminine degrees, various phases of the Moon, a set of instructions for finding the approximate positions of the Sun, Moon, planets, and the lunar nodes, two lists of epithets (key-words) associated with combinations of two and three planets respectively, and finally two chapters on conception and 7-months children.

If the instructions for calculating the planetary positions were reasonably accurate, then most of the information needed to cast a horoscope and even to make an interpretation would be contained in this book. However, the instructions for calculating the planets in the received text are garbled, incomplete, and sometimes worthless. Whether this is due to carelessness on the part of the copyists, or whether the instructions and the numbers given, particularly those for Mars, Venus, and Mercury, were wrong to start with is uncertain.[122]

Book II begins with the triplicities and their rulers, then takes up the lots (parts), planets in the houses, planetary aspects, houses counted from the Lot of Fortune, various other lots, and special topics, such as travel, parents, free and servile nativities, injuries and illnesses, marriage, children, brothers, and violent death. Many example horoscopes are cited to illustrate the rules.

Book III. Chapter 2 "The Authentic Degrees of the Angles" explains the so-called "Porphyry system" of house division and attributes it to an otherwise unknown astrologer, Orion.[123] The following chapters discuss various technical matters related to determining the length of life. Critodemus is cited. Again, there are example horoscopes.

Book IV takes up methods of dividing the native's life into time-periods in order to make predictions. How to find the apheta or starting-point for the prorogations. How to determine favorable or effective times down to the individual day. Examples are given.

Books V-IX continue the discussion of the methods set forth in Book IV with special reference to the length of life, climacteric years, and effective months and days of particular years. Since several different procedures are discussed, these books contain a hodge-podge of different

---

[122]For a discussion of the instructions for finding the solar, lunar, and planetary positions, see O. Neugebauer, *A History of Ancient Mathematical Astronomy*, vol. 2. (Some of Neugebauer's remarks about the lunar table are not correct.) Actually, the solar, lunar, and nodal instructions are not too bad. Those for Saturn and Jupiter yield positions within half a sign or so. But the instructions for Mars and Venus are badly confused, and the instructions for Mercury are worthless.

[123]Orion must have written before Valens (150-175 A.D.), and Valens wrote 150 to 175 years before Porphyry (c. 295 A.D.), so Orion may have been the inventor of the "Porphyry system." See also under **Porphyry** below.

methods. Books VIII and IX contain instructions for using some special tables devised by Critodemus for determining the length of life. Some related matters are also discussed, such as determining the proper birth hour of twins, decumbiture[124] and horary charts, masculine and feminine nativities, charts indicating monsters (badly deformed children or animals), and finally, conception and its relation to the length of life.

True to its title, the *Anthology* contains a variety of astrological techniques drawn from several earlier writers. There is some order to the chapters, but also a certain amount of disorder, as if Valens suddenly remembered something he had forgotten to include earlier and just inserted it wherever he was. In this respect it contrasts sharply with the *Tetrabiblos*. But there is much here that is not in Ptolemy's book. In particular, the symbolic directions,[125] which were in common use by the Classical Greek astrologers, offer a fertile field for astrological research.

According to Pingree, the *Anthology* was translated into Middle Persian in the 3rd century, and the Persian version was later (perhaps in the 8th century) translated into Arabic. A substantial portion of the Arabic text could be assembled from extant MSS. If this becomes available, it might be possible to construct a superior text of the *Anthology* by comparing the Greek and Arabic versions.[126]

Unlike Ptolemy, Valens cites nearly two dozen authors by name, and includes 123 actual horoscopes in his book,[127] including the chart of the Emperor Nero (37-68), which none of Valens's editors have recognized. He gives all the necessary influences and delineations of the signs, planets, aspects, lots, house positions, and special configurations; and he takes up special topics like violent death, illustrating the indicative configurations with actual examples drawn from his own casebook and from the works of his predecessors. His *Anthology* is one of the two most extensive and comprehensive treatises of Greek astrology that have come down to us.[128] Unfortunately, it was first published in 1908 and until recently was

---

[124]A *decumbiture*, as its name implies, is a horary chart set for the time certain when someone took to bed because of illness. From this chart, the astrologer could make a diagnosis and prognosis of the illness.

[125]The 12-year profection and the 10-year and 9-months profection.

[126]Pingree announced his desire to publish the Arabic fragments two decades ago, but so far he has evidently not had an opportunity to do so.

[127]Most of the horoscopes in O. Neugebauer's & H.B. Van Hoesen's excellent book *Greek Horoscopes* (Philadelphia: The American Philosophical Society, 1959) are in fact from Vettius Valen's *Anthology* (latest edition by D. Pingree, *Vettii Valentis Antiocheni Anthologiarum libri novem* [Leipzig: B.G. Teubner, 1986]). The reader who does not know Greek can study them in *Greek Horoscopes.*

[128]The other is the *Mathesis* of Julius Firmicus Maternus, which is discussed below. It is in Latin, but most of the text is translated from earlier Greek sources.

only available in the original Greek.[129] Hence, it is virtually unknown to modern astrologers. This is unfortunate because it contains many techniques that are not mentioned by Ptolemy. For example, Book 1, Chapt. 21 "Conception," gives a very detailed account with examples of how to calculate a conception chart from a given horoscope.[130] This is the technique that is now called the "Prenatal Epoch," or, in older books "The Trutine of Hermes."[131] (For the origin of this technique, see below in the section on Porphyry.)

As examples of Valens's treatment of the fundamentals, we may cite the following extracts from some of the chapters:

Book I, Chapter 1. The Nature of the Stars.

> Mars signifies violence, battles, robbery, screaming, assault, adultery,[132] carrying off of goods, banishment, exile, estrangement from the parents, captivity, abortions, embryotomy, living together, marriage, carrying off of wealth, lies, those unacquainted with hope, violent theft, piracy, plundering, lovers' quarrels, anger, fighting, cursing, hatred, [and] punishment. It also brings about violent murders and wounds and bloodshed, attacks of fever, ulceration, [skin] eruptions, inflammation, imprisonment, tortures, manhood, perjury, deception, seniority in bad things,[133] working with fire or iron, craftsmen, workers in hard materials. It also makes military commanders and commanders-in-chief, soldiers, sovereignty, hunting with dogs, the chase, falls from heights or from quadrupeds, clouded vision, [and] apoplexy. Of the parts of the body, it rules the head, the backside, the genitals; of the inner [parts], the blood, the spermatic passages, the bile, the excretion of feces, the posterior parts, going back, laying one-

---

[129]An English translation was published in Project Hindsight (see the Bibliography below).

[130]The horoscope is evidently that of Vettius Valens himself. It is set for 8 February 120. Pingree believes it is Valens's chart because it is the most frequently used example chart and because its companion conception chart is given. I earlier adduced what seems to me to be an even more cogent reason: in *Anthology* vii. 6.127-160, Valens tells of six men on a ship at sea that was nearly sunk in a storm, and he gives all their horoscopes. It is dificult to imagine how he could have obtained this data unless he was one of the six. And one of their charts, that of 8 Feb 120, is the most frequent example chart in the *Anthology*, so it is probably Valens's own horoscope.

[131]Its basic rules are very briefly stated in Aph. 51 of the *Centiloquy* falsely attributed to Ptolemy, but that is a later work (see below).

[132]The adultery of Ares (Mars) with Aphrodite (Venus), the wife of Hephaestus (Vulcan), was notorious among the Greeks.

[133]The translation is uncertain here.

self backwards.[134] And it has [all] that which is hard and cut off. Of substances, it rules iron and ornament of clothing because of Aries, and wine, and legumes. It is of the nocturnal sect, in color red, and pungent in taste.

Book I, Chapter 3. The Sixty Terms.

The first 8 of Taurus [are] Venus's: fertile, prolific, watery, lecherous, condemned, hating strife. The next 6 of Mercury: intelligent, prudent, evil-doers, having few offspring, poor-sighted, causing death. The next 8 of Jupiter: high-minded, manly, fortunate, ruling and beneficent, magnanimous, temperate, loving modesty. The fourth [terms], the 5 of Saturn: barren, childless, eunuch-like, vagabonds, reprehensible, theatrical, joyless, toilsome. And the final three [are] of Mars: masculine, tyrannical, fiery, harsh, murderous, temple-robbers, utterly bad, not infertile, but destructive and not long-lived.[135]

Book IV, Chapter 12 The Nomenclature of the 12 Houses and the Dodecatropos.

Let the beginning be from the ASC, which is life, tiller, body, breath. The 2nd, livelihood, Gate of Hades, overshadowed, giving, receiving, joint-ownership; the 3rd, brothers, living abroad, Queen,[136] authority, friends, relatives, strong feelings,[137] slaves; the 4th, praise, the father, children, [the native's] own woman, elderly persons, action, the city, the home, property, dwellings, changes, changes of place, dangers, death, restraint, mystical matters; the 5th, the house of children, friendship, association, the act of freeing slaves, something good or a kindness; the 6th, slaves, injuries, enmity, sickness, debility; the 7th, marriage, success, union with a woman, friendship, living abroad; the 8th, death, benefit from things of the dead, an ineffective house, punishment, debility; the 9th, friendship, absence from home, benefit from foreign things, God,

---

[134]Here again the meaning is uncertain.

[135]There is a complete Italian translation of Valens's chapter on the terms in the present author's paper, 'I significati dei Termini Egiziani' in *Linguaggio Astrale* 103 (Summer 1996), the English version was published in the AFA *Journal of Research*.

[136]The word *theá* 'Goddess' seems to have fallen out of the text here, since most of the other Greek astrologers mention it. (Cf. also the 9th house, where both God and King are mentioned.)

[137]*Epikardía*. Or, reading *epikarpía*, 'revenue.'

King, sovereign, astronomy,[138] oracular responses, manifestations of the gods, prophecy, mystical and hidden matters, association; the 10th, action, praise, advancement, children, the wife, change, innovative actions; the 11th, friends, hopes, gifts, children, freedmen; the 12th, a foreign woman, enmity, slaves, injury, dangers, legal judgments, sickness, death, debility.

Each of these houses denotes that which it signifies, but it also works together with the nature of the opposite house.[139]

Some further remarks on the significations of the houses are cited below.

Valens gives much attention to making predictions from natal horoscopes and sets forth several different techniques for doing this. In explaining prediction by means of the twelve-year cycle in Book V, Chapter 7, he gives the following nativity (it is the horoscope of the emperor Nero):

For the sake of an example, let the Sun, Mars, Mercury, [and] the ASC be in Sagittarius; the Moon in Leo, Saturn in Virgo, Jupiter in Scorpio, [and] Venus in Capricorn. The Moon was allotted the second [period], since she was separated from Saturn by 2 [signs][140]; and similarly both the Sun and Mars, Mercury, [and] the ASC [with regard] to Venus. And Saturn and Jupiter and Venus [have] the third [period]; and Saturn the fourth and fifth; and the Moon the sixth; and the seventh empty of all these; and Venus the eighth; and the Sun, Mars, Mercury, [and] the ASC the ninth and tenth; and Jupiter the tenth and the 11th; and Venus the twelfth. And the chart leads to the 31st year. The effective stars and the climacteric ones are found thus: the beginning of the aforesaid climacteric [years] is in the 3rd part of the third [period]; for the preceding two, or the first and second, are ineffective because the first [period] is effective as far as 12 [years], and the second as far as 24, and the third as far as 36, and so on in similar fashion. And it is aspected thus: since the 31st year falls in the 11th [year] of the third [period], and since Saturn and Jupiter and Venus were allotted the third [period] in the nativity, search for

---

[138]Knowledge of the stars, comprising both astronomy and astrology.

[139]A clear statement of an important principle of Greek astrology that has been largely lost from the tradition. Only J.B. Morin insisted upon its observance (see below).

[140]We would say, 'by 1 sign', but the ancients counted both ends of an interval.

the [planets] that are passing over rulership at the time, but never the 11th passing to another or to each other. For example, in the previous nativity at the time there were the stars Sun, Jupiter, [and] Mercury in Gemini, Saturn in Virgo, Mars [and] Venus in Taurus, [and] the Moon in Pisces. And the stars allotted to the 11th were Jupiter and Saturn and Venus; and we find the Moon returning to Venus, Jupiter to no [planet]; [so] I go immediately into the fourth, [and] I find the 32nd in the eighth. None of the rulers of the fourth are climacteric, [so] I go into the fifth, and the Moon and Saturn of the fifth are effective, and these are found returned to each other. I go into the sixth; none through the sixth is separated; I go into the part of the seventh, [which is] empty of all stars; as was said, the seventh is found. Mars and Venus to Saturn. And I go into the table of the eighth [period], and Venus is the ruler of the eighth because of 4, not being returned to any; next, in the climacteric [year] of the ninth [period], the Sun, Mars, Mercury, the ASC, [and] Venus rule the ninth; and in this part is the 36th [year]; in the fourth year were found the Sun, Jupiter, [and] Mercury returned to Saturn. Again, I go into the tenth [period], and the Sun, Mars, Mercury, Jupiter, [and] the ASC will rule the tenth [period].; and in the fourth part of this the Sun, Mercury, [and] Jupiter are found passing rulership to Saturn.

Inevitably then these times become active and effective for the [successive] intervals whenever the [planets] that are ruling them in the nativity were at the time of passing of rulership having that [same interval] which they have in the nativity.

Nero, having lost the loyalty of the Praetorian Guard, felt obliged to commit suicide. On the morning of 9 June 68 he thrust a dagger into his throat and bled to death. He was 30 years and 5 months old; hence in his 31st year.

Valens gives us an early testimonial to the use of derived houses by the Greek astrologers; the first six houses will serve as an example:

IX. 3. 6. Wherefore in fact the houses from the ASC are taken thus:

The 1st, life and the foundation of times and the breath of life (i.e. the ASC itself); but of brothers it is [the house of] the Good Daemon, which is the house of friends; and of parents, [the house] of action; of the wife, the house of marriage; of children, the ninth [house].

The 2nd is livelihood and current income; but of brothers, the Bad Daemon, and the house of slaves and enemies and the cause of evil; and of parents, the Good Daemon and the house of friends; and of children, [the house] of action and repute; and of the wife, the house of death. And when the ruler of the [previous] conjunction or full Moon is found in this sign or its opposition, it shows banishment, and likewise both the conjunction and the full Moon are observed carefully.

The 3rd [house is that] of the life of brothers; and of parents, [the house] of enemies and slaves; and of the wife, the ninth. And it is also the house of the Goddess and the Queen.

And the 4th is the house of the life of the parents, and of secret or hidden things and of foundations and property and things found; of brothers, [the house] of livelihood; and of the wife, of repute and action.

And the 5th [is the house] of the life of the children; and the house of Good Fortune; and of brothers [the house] of brothers, both illegitimate and legitimate; and of the wife, [the house of the] Good Daemon.

The 6th [is the house] of injury and sickness and the cause of suffering; but of parents [it is the house] of brothers; and of brothers, [the house] of parents, legitimate or false; and of the wife, enemies and slaves.

Valens also uses the most important subsidiary house system used by the Greek astrologers—houses counted from the Lot of Fortune. Here is the first part of an interesting chapter:

II. 21. The 11th House of the Lot of Fortune for Prosperity.

And we have found the 11th house of the [Lot of] Fortune to be very potent, the giver of possessions and goods, and especially when the benefics are on it or are aspecting it. For the Sun and Jupiter and Venus grant gold, silver, and adornment, and the greatest wealth, and gifts from greater persons and from kings, and those having a good moral attitude towards the common people; and they are benefactors of many people. But the Moon and Mercury [indicate] increases and decreases and [a general] unevenness of livelihood, sometimes liberal and generous to others, but sometimes turning away from the needy and from loans, because of the Moon's having increases and decreases of its light, and because Mercury is common to both good things and evil things. Mars hinders the things that are given or gained, denoting decreases, robberies, fires, judicial sentences, those spending money on public or royal business, or those becoming free to act and accusing, except if the nativity chances not to be military or renowned; for thus from this cause and from violent or dangerous acts and from theft in acquisition they will be generated if indeed the star chances to be in its own domicile; and in addition, it will accomplish the action in some frightful manner, and it will make a loss. Saturn suitably configured makes lords of building sites and foundations, but unsuitably configured or out of sect it denotes banishments, reductions, shipwreck, poverty, indebtedness. Saturn with Mercury and Mars [denotes] those who are spoken of abusively because of some instance of legal judgments or malpractices or for the sake of secret or violent actions. Saturn [with] Mercury, Mars, [and] Venus [denotes] those who suffer harm from poisons or from feminine persons and become involved in charges. Saturn, Mars, Mercury, Venus, Jupiter, [and] the Moon, those who benefit from inheritances and those who acquire from shipowning and from dwelling abroad or from actions involving water or wetness. Generally, then, Saturn and Mars in the MC or in the succedent[141] to the MC of the Lot [of Fortune], and ruling the wealth-bringing [house],[142] are indicative of banishment.

Therefore, it is necessary to look first at the phases of each star, and in accordance with its own combination [of influences] and its relationship to each other [star] to describe [its action]. And not only do the stars that are in the wealth-bringing house show the preceding things, but also the sign itself acts in accordance with the nature of the star and with its own nature.

Finally, we may say that without Vettius Valens's *Anthology*, we would know much less about Nechepso and Petosiris and Critodemus. Into his book Valens gathered these and many other valuable excerpts from writers whose books have not come down to us. And he has provided us with over a hundred actual nativities from his own personal collection. In short, the *Anthology* affords us our best look at the materials available to and the procedures used by a Greek astrologer of the Classical Period.

---

[141]That is, the 11th house from the Lot of Fortune.

[142]Again, the 11th house from the Lot of Fortune.

Antigonus

Antigonus of Nicea was a physician and astrologer who apparently lived towards the end of the 2nd century. He is remarkable for having compiled a book of "notable nativities"—to use Alan Leo's phrase. So far as is known, this was the first book of its kind, although some earlier astrologers had included example nativities in their works—Dorotheus and Valens, in particular. And still earlier books may also have contained examples because Ptolemy, in discussing the different systems of terms, mentions that ". . . the degrees of these terms [the Egyptian] are consistent with the nativities that have been recorded by them as examples."[143]

Antigonus's collection was evidently sizable, for Palchus mentions the sixth nativity of the third book, and "Rhetorius" Chapter 21 "The Division of Times," cites an opinion of Antigonus's "from the 4th chapter of the 4th book."[144] No such book is known to have been compiled by the Arabs or by the medieval European astrologers, and in fact the next collection of nativities was published by Jerome Cardan *Examples of One Hundred Genitures* (Nürnberg, 1547), followed in 1552 by a considerably larger collection published at Venice by Luca Gaurico in his *Astrological Treatise* (see below under these authors in the Fourth Period).

Fortunately, a copy of the book was available to Hephaestio of Thebes, who cites three horoscopes from it, the most interesting of which is the natal chart of the Emperor Hadrian.[145]

Apotelesmatics, Book II. Chapter 18.22 ff.

...Someone, Antigonus says, was born having the Sun in the 8th degree of Aquarius, and the Moon and Jupiter and the ASC, [all] three, in the 1st degree of the same sign Aquarius, Saturn in the 10th degree of Capricorn, Venus in the 12th degree of Pisces, Mars with it in the 22nd degree, and the MC in the 22nd degree of Scorpio. This person was adopted by an emperor,[146] a relative [of his], [and] he himself became emperor too around his 42nd year; and he was

---

[143]*Tetrabiblos*, i. 21. Robbins's translation.

[144]Noted by Wilhelm Gundel and Hans Georg Gundel, *Astrologumena*, p. 222 and n.3.

[145]See Cramer, *op. cit.*, pp. 162-178, for a discussion and partial translation of the text along with a reproduction of the emperor's horoscope and the Greek text as it appears in one of the MSS. The chart is in the square format, which is not necessarily that used by Hephaestio or Antigonus, if indeed either of them used a chart. Also, see the discussion by Neugebauer and Van Hoesen, *Greek Horoscopes*, pp. 90-9. The two other horoscopes from Antigonus are also discussed in GH; they are nos. L40 and L113IV, tentatively identified as relatives of Hadrian.

[146]The Emperor Trajan (53-117). His paternal aunt Ulpia was the paternal grandmother of Hadrian, who was therefore Trajan's 1st cousin once removed, and at the time of Trajan's death his closest living male relative.

both intelligent and well-educated and he was worshipped like a god in the temples and sacred places, and he was united to only one woman,[147] and from [the time] of her virginity he was childless; and he had one sister; and he came to be in rebellion and dissension against his own people. And when he was about 63 years old, he died, having succumbed to dropsy [and] asthma.

And why these things occurred may be investigated in this way: in fact, he became emperor because the two lights were both in the ASC and especially because the Moon, which was in sect, was joined partilely[148] to it and to Jupiter, which was going to make its morning appearance in 7 days, and with the doryphories[149] themselves being found in their own domicile, Venus for example being in its own exaltation and with Mars in its own triplicity and having a position in its own degrees, and with both of them being in their own places and succedent to the Moon. And besides the cosmocrator Sun is in doryphory to it in the succeeding degrees, and [the Sun] itself has as doryphories Saturn, which is in its own domicile, and Mercury, both of them being in their morning rising. And it should also be noted that the Moon is going to conjoin a certain bright one of the fixed stars in the 20th degree; for not only must one look at the conjunction of the Moon with the planets, but also with the fixed stars. And he was very great and courageous and affable because the two lights were angular, especially in the ASC and in a human and masculine sign. And he was intelligent and well-educated and deep because Mercury chanced to be in its morning phase with Saturn in the 12th sign[150] and in doryphory to the Sun. And from his earliest age this was denoted because of the phase; for the morning risings always act in youth, but the evening [appearances] show their actions with the passage of time.

---

[147]Vibia Sabina (d. 128), who was Trajan's grandniece. She was married to Hadrian in 100, but they were never close. It is possible that their marriage was like that of Frederick the Great (1712-1786) and his wife Elizabeth Christine (1715-1797).

[148]"Partile" is a technical term signifying that the conjunction or aspect is in the same degrees of the signs involved. Thus two planets in 1 Aquarius are partilely conjoined, and a planet in 1 Aquarius would be in partile trine to another planet in 1 Gemini.

[149]Literally 'spear-bearers,' a technical term referring to planets that appeared before the rising of the Sun and after the setting of the Moon.

[150]That is, the 12th house.

And it is always necessary to look at the ruler of the culminating house,[151] whether it is well posited and in aspect with the house, for when it is oriental it makes noted and effective persons and those hard to overcome; and when it is occidental, if it is also well situated, as in the preceding horoscope (Mars, the ruler of Scorpio, is not impedited in Pisces in its own triplicity and its own degrees and aspecting the culminating house); but if the ruler of the culminating house is evilly placed, it makes the opposite. And if when the rulers of the houses that are not effective chance to be in the effective houses, they show a middling sort of livelihood, for the [star] of Jupiter bestows the original and generous and munificent and practical [side] of the present configuration, since it is in the ASC and is a doryphory to the Sun and is in the same angle with the Moon. And the cause of his having many adversaries and conspiracies resulted from the blockading of the two lights containing the power by the two malefics, by Saturn, which is in its morning rising and is a doryphory, and by Mars in its evening [setting]. And his triumphing over his enemies happened especially because of Mercury's being in the domicile of Saturn with Saturn and because both of them chanced to be in the 12th [house].

And the honoring and worshipping of him by all happened because of the angular star of Jupiter's being a doryphory to the Sun; for always being a doryphory thus to the Sun and to the Moon, it makes those who are extolled by those of equal or higher rank and who are accompanied by personal guards and who are bowed down to. And he had the [quality of] beneficence because of Jupiter's chancing to be [configured] thus. And his doing good to many and, as I was saying, his having been bowed down to by many happened because of the position of the Sun and the Moon angularly doryphoried by the 5 planets, [each dignified] by domicile; for always, either the Sun or the Moon, or especially both of them, chancing to be in the effective angles (that is, the ASC or the MC), and particularly when they are doryphoried by all the stars, they make those who are born with such a configuration to be kings ruling over very many nations. But also, Mercury and Saturn chancing to be in the 12th in their morning risings and in doryphory with the Sun make [him] intelligent, well-educated, and not benevolent but rather deceitful.

---

[151]The MC.

And it happened that this person was joined to one wife from maidenhood not because Venus was there, but because the Moon was moving under the Sun beams. And in general you should judge in every horoscope [that] when Venus chances to be angular or succedent and the Moon is making an application to Venus and with the other stars chancing to be together with Venus or else in aspect with it, they certainly make marriages for the one who is born thus; but if only the Moon is making its application to Venus, it will be indicative of a single marriage; and also if the Moon does not apply to Venus, nor to any one of those [stars] that are with it or even in aspect with it, and it is moving into the new Moon phase or the full Moon phase, and Venus is with one star, then it makes monogamous persons just as in the foregoing nativity.

These considerations that seemed pertinent to Antigonus are almost completely different from those that would occur to a modern astrologer reading the same chart. In particular, the Classical Greek astrologers carefully noted appearances, positions in triplicity and in terms.

The emperor was born at Italica (37N26 6W03) near Seville, Spain on 24 January 76 and died on 1 January 138. According to the details given by Antigonus, he was born about 23 minutes before sunrise or at about 6:38 AM LAT with 1 Aquarius rising. The positions given are as follows:

Planet	Antigonus	Antigonus–5°	Tropical
Sun	8 Aquarius	3 Aquarius	2.7 Aquarius
Moon	1 Aquarius	26 Capricorn	27.7 Capricorn
Mercury	12 Capricorn	7 Capricorn	6.9 Capricorn
Venus	12 Pisces	7 Pisces	14.0 Pisces
Mars	21 Pisces	16 Pisces	19.2 Pisces
Jupiter	1 Aquarius	26 Capricorn	26.6 Capricorn
Saturn	16 Capricorn	11 Capricorn	29.9 Sagittarius
ASC	1 Aquarius	26 Capricorn	
MC	22 Scorpio	17 Scorpio	

These positions are of course referred to the fixed zodiac used by the Alexandrian astrologers, which differed from the tropical by about 5°05' in the year 76.[152] Hence, referred to the tropical zodiac, the positions were approximately those shown in the third column above, while the positions from modern calculations are those shown in the fourth column. The agreement is surprisingly good for Mercury and rather poor for Venus and Saturn. Possibly the discrepancies for the latter two planets are due to scribal errors.

---

[152]See my paper "The Classical Zodiac" in the AFA *Journal of Research*, vol. 7, no. 2 (1995).

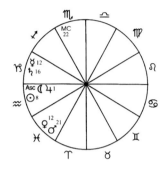
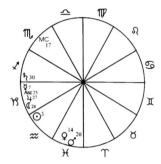

Fig. 6 Original Chart   **Fig. 7 Tropical Chart**

In Antigonus's chart the Moon, Jupiter, and the Sun are all rising in Aquarius. However, in the tropical chart the Moon and Jupiter are in Capricorn, while only the Sun remains in Aquarius. Also, the ASC has now become Capricorn instead of Aquarius, and the modern calculation shows that Saturn had not quite emerged from Sagittarius into its own sign Capricorn. However, we cannot suppose that Hadrian's birthtime was recorded any more accurately than "in the middle of the 12th hour of the night" or "not long before sunrise" or something of the sort, so even in the tropical zodiac he might have had 1 Aquarius rising.

The uncertainty of the rising sign reminds us of the horoscope of the Emperor Augustus, who had early Libra rising in the fixed Alexandrian zodiac, but late Virgo rising in the tropical zodiac.

Antiochus of Athens

Another important astrologer who apparently flourished in the latter half of the 2nd century is **Antiochus of Athens**.[153] He wrote two treatises on astrology, *Introduction* and *Treasury*, both of which are lost, but summaries[154] and extensive excerpts are preserved. Of the twenty-eight chapters of the *Introduction* listed in the Parisian Epitome, twenty are found as chapters of Porphyry's *Introduction* (see below). The other book, the *Treasury*, apparently formed the basis of the first fifty-three chapters of the astrological compendium of Rhetorius the Egyptian (see below), and six of these chapters are also found in Porphyry's *Introduction*. It would appear that two-thirds of the chapters in Porphyry's book are taken from Antiochus, and 55 out of the 117 chapters of Rhetorius are from Antiochus.[155] Pingree says that extensive fragments of Antiochus's works

---

[153]See David Pingree, *The Yavanajātaka of Sphujidhvaja*, vol. 2, pp. 421-422, and David Pingree's paper "Antiochus and Rhetorius" in *Classical Philology* 72 (July 1977): 203-223.

[154]See the Parisian Epitome edited in CCAG, VIII.3, pp. 104-119.

[155]The complicated intertwining of the works of Antiochus, Porphyry, and Rhetorius is set forth by Pingree in "Antiochus and Rhetorius," *loc. cit.*

are preserved in an Arabic version by al-Saymarî, al-Qasrânî, and other Arabian writers under the name Antîqus, but these have not yet been completely edited, and it is possible that they mainly cover the same material as that covered by Porphyry and Rhetorius.

Judging from the available fragments, Antiochus wrote a thorough introduction to astrology, in which he defined all the technical terms and then discussed the houses of the horoscope, the lots, the rising times of the signs, and the conception chart. The Greek fragments of Antiochus mention Nechepso and Petosiris, Hermes, and Timaeus[156] (1st cent. A.D.?). Antiochus himself is mentioned by Porphyry, Firmicus, and Hephaestio of Thebes (it is Hephaestio who says that Antiochus was an Athenian).

Porphyry

Porphyry (233-c.304) was a well-known Greek philosopher to whom is attributed an *Introduction to Ptolemy's Tetrabiblos*[157] which was apparently written c.295. The title is something of a misnomer, since the book is actually a sort of encyclopedic dictionary of astrology. The author says specifically that Ptolemy neglected to give adequate definitions of some of the technical terms of astrology, and he also omitted some that should have been included. Thus the book is actually one to be be read before reading the *Tetrabiblos*. It is best-known for Chapt. 43 "Determination of the Angular, Cadent, and Succedent Houses to the Degree," which explains the earliest quadrant system of house division—the so-called Porphyry system, which trisects the zodiacal arcs of each quadrant. Actually, the earliest mention of this system is by Vettius Valens who wrote more than a century before Porphyry. In *Anthology* iii. 2, "The Authentic Degrees of the Angles," he attributes the "Porphyry" system to an otherwise unknown astrologer, Orion, who must therefore have written before Valens wrote the *Anthology* (c.150-175 A.D.).

Chapters 37 & 38 deal with constructing the conception horoscope. Chapter 38 "The Conception Sign of the Moon" contains this statement from Antiochus of Athens: ". . . But Petosiris says, that 'wherever the Moon was at the [time of] conception, that same [place] or its opposite will rise at birth. And wherever the Moon was posited at [the time of] birth, that same [place] was rising at the [time of] conception.' Furthermore, some also take the ASC of conception in the same way.'" This statement ascribes the origin of the technique detailed by Valens to Petosiris. This same attribution is found in Hephaestio of Thebes, *Apotelesmatics*, ii. 1 and iii. 10, but Hephaestio may have taken it from Porphyry.

In addition to the two dozen or more chapters Porphyry copied from Antiochus's *Introduction* (see above), Porphyry's *Introduction* contains

---

[156]See Gundel-Gundel, *Astrologumena*, p. 111.

[157]*Introductio in Tetrabiblum Ptolemaei* ed. by Emilie Boer and Stephen Weinstock, CCAG V.4 (1940). The last three chapters (Chapts. 53-55) are thought to be spurious and may even be translations from medieval Arabic works.

seven chapters that agree almost verbatim with chapters in the 6th century astrologer Rhetorius's book (see below). Apparently both Porphyry and Rhetorius took these chapters independently from Antiochus's *Treasury*.

Firmicus Maternus

Julius Firmicus Maternus, (c.280-c.360)[158] a native of (Syracuse?) Sicily was a Roman lawyer of the senatorial class and an amateur astrologer, who translated much material from the earlier Greek writers into Latin (about 90% of the text of his *Mathesis* is preserved[159]). The date of composition has been disputed. The German historian Th. Mommsen (1817-1903) concluded that it was written between 334 and 337 A.D. because in the Preface Firmicus speaks of the eclipse of 334 as being one of the more recent ones and later he mentions the Emperor Constantine the Great who died in 337. But Firmicus also mentions the consulship of his friend Quintus Flavius Maesius Egnatius Lollianus Mavortius, a high Roman official, who is known to have been consul in 355. Thorndike therefore argues that it took Firmicus more than a decade to write the *Mathesis* and that it was not completed until 355 or shortly thereafter. Thorndike's conclusion seems more reasonable to me.[160] Be this as it may, the book was written for and is dedicated to Firmicus's friend Lollianus Mavortius, and Firmicus tells us how he came to write it:

Book I.
Introduction.

1. Long ago, Mavortius my lord, I promised I would dedicate this little treatise to you, but for a long time a hesitant modesty restrained me and called me back with doubtful trepidation from the task of writing, for my frail talent could not conceive that it was capable of knowing anything

---

[158]I have assigned these dates for the following reasons. In *Mathesis*, vii. 1, Firmicus mentions "our Porphyry," which probably indicates that he had once studied under him. Porphyry died c. 304, so if we subtract 24 years we come to c. 280 for the year of Firmicus's birth. And since I have agreed with Thorndike (see below) that Firmicus did not complete the *Mathesis* until 355 or shortly thereafter, I put the date of his death c. 360, at which time he would have been 80 years old. At any rate, he flourished in the first half of the 4th century.

[159]Edited by W. Kroll, F. Skutsch, and K. Ziegler, *Iulii Firmici Materni Matheseos libri viii* (Leipzig. B.G. Teubner, 1897-1913), 2 vols. repr, 1968. English translation by Jean Rhys Bram, *Ancient Astrology Theory and Practice* (Park Ridge, N.J.: Noyes Press, 1975). The first edition of the entire work was published at Venice in 1497; it was followed by the Aldine edition (Venice, 1499), which contains spurious material. The Aldine edition was reprinted with a few minor changes at Basel in 1533 and 1551, along with the works of other astrologers.

[160]See Lynn Thorndike, HMES 1, pp. 525-538, for a discussion of the available facts. Thorndike also gives a useful topical survey of the *Mathesis*.

it would judge fit for your ears.

2. For, when you were in charge of the province of Campania,[161] ennobling yourself with the greatest dignity of honor through your meritorius administration of it, I chanced upon you, worn out by the diversity of a long journey and numb from the winter snows. There you strove to relieve the debility of my weak and fatigued body with the most considerate and faithful alleviations of friendship.

3. Later, when my health, restored by your care and medication, had recalled me to my wonted condition, recollecting our past experiences in turn and calling to mind a variety of true stories, we related them.

4. After we talked of our activities and their progress, you questioned me, as you remember. about the situation of the whole of Sicily (where I live, and from whence I am sprung). And with an evincing of true reason you inquired about all those things which the old fables tell of: what Scylla and Charybdis are. . . .

5. . . . . at length you changed the subject of your conversation to the Sphere of Archimedes, showing me the wisdom and learning of your divine genius: what the nine spheres are; what the five zones [of the earth] are which are colored by differing natures; what the twelve signs perform; what the ceaseless wandering of the five planets accomplishes; what the daily motion of the Sun and its yearly revolution accomplish; what the rapid motion of the Moon and the assiduous increases and diminutions of her light accomplish; also in how many revolutions that greater year of which they speak is completed, which restores the five planets, the Moon, and the Sun to their original places, the which is accomplished in 1,461 years; what causes the Milky Way and the eclipses of the Sun and Moon; why the whirling rotation of the sky never causes the Big Bear to rise or set; what part of the earth is subject to the north and what part to the south; what force suspends the earth itself in the middle with poise and balance; how great a space of land the Ocean (which they call the Atlantic Ocean) encloses like an island with its surrounding waves.

6. When the facile instruction of your vivid description had conveyed all these things to me, Mavortius, gem of good men, I too dared to proffer something in the way of an

---

[161]A region of central Italy just south of Rome.

unasked discourse, with the result that I promised I would set forth for you whatever the ancient sages and divine men of Egypt, as well as the learned Babylonians have handed down to us concerning the force of the stars and their powers through the instruction of their divine doctrine.

7. And thus I was rash, as I knew I was, to make that promise; and to tell you the truth, I often wished to be reprehended with severe reproof and to alter that which had been promised if I might have been permitted to do so; but the encouragement given by your conversation diminished my temerity and urged me to begin what I have many times [since] set aside out of desperation. For when the governorship of All the East[162] had been handed over to you by the serene and venerable judgment of our lord and emperor Constantine Augustus,[163] you lost no time in demanding from me that which I had promised you without your having asked for it.

8. And so I sent to you, the Proconsul and Designated Ordinary Consul,[164] the promised work, praying and requesting indulgence for it, lest in this book the weight and pleasing quality of the perfect oration, the best treatments or grave and well-founded opinions might be required by the judgment and eloquence of your learning. I have but slight talent and a plain form of speech,[165] and, what must truly be acknowledged, a very modest learning in astrology; all of which, though it frightened me with various [kinds of] desperation, nevertheless I entered upon the task of writing, so that, notwithstanding my being involved in these arduous and most difficult promises, I might not escape the most learned judgments of your widom, Lollianus.

The *Mathesis* is the lengthiest astrological treatise that has come down

---

[162]The eastern part of the Roman Empire.

[163]Constantine II was joint emperor 337-340, but some think the text is corrupt and should read Constans instead of Constantine. Constans II was joint emperor 337-353 and sole emperor 353-361. Both Constantine II and Constans II were sons of Constantine I the Great (d. 337). Their names are easily confused.

[164]Mavortius was Consul in the year 355. It would seem that Firmicus spent twenty years writing the *Mathesis*, despite Mommsen's contentions to the contrary.

[165]This is partly polite modesty and partly the truth. As flowery as Firmicus's speech seems to us today, other writers of his time with literary pretensions went even further. Also, he must have despaired of turning the mostly pedestrian Greek of the astrological treatises into elegant Latin prose with proper attention to metrics.

to us from the classical period. It consists of eight books, of which the first forms an introductory essay on astrology, and the rest set forth the fundamentals of Greek astrology. Several sections contain material that is found nowhere else, although some of these unique sections (e.g. the significations of the planets in the individual signs of the zodiac) are marred by sizable lacunae.

Interestingly, Firmicus only mentions Ptolemy three times—in each case as having favored the use of antiscions. But the *Tetrabiblos* does not even mention antiscions. Hence, we can infer that Firmicus had never read Ptolemy's book but had only read something in some other book that seemed to attribute this attitude to Ptolemy. This then is another indication that as late as the middle of the 4th century the *Tetrabiblos* had not yet become generally available to astrologers.

Firmicus gives only one example nativity, which of course he does not identify by name, although he says to Mavortius, "you know very well whose it is." The German historian Mommsen identified it as that of Ceionius Rufius Albinus who was consul in 335 and Prefect of the City of Rome the following year. From the horoscope elements given by Firmicus (*Mathesis*, ii. 29) we can determine that Albinus was born on the 14th or 15th of March 303 around 9 PM. He was Prefect of the City of Rome in 336/7 and Consul in the year 345.

At the end of the second book, Firmicus gives professional astrologers a set of injunctions for regulating their life style and professional conduct. It is an entirely unique document. Nothing of the sort is found anywhere else in astrological literature until the 17th century, when William Lilly (without acknowledging his source) rewrote it to adapt it to his own time.[166] It is worth quoting in full.

> II. 30. What Sort of Life and What Sort of Practices Astrologers Ought to Have.
>
> 1. Now you, who venture to read these books, when you have received all the knowledge of divinity and when, steeped and initiated in the secrets of nature, you have come to know the system of this sacred work, shape yourself in the image and likeness of divinity, so that you may always be adorned with the commendation of goodness. For it behooves him who daily speaks of the gods or with the gods to shape and instruct his mind, so that he may always approach the imitation of divinity.
>
> 2. Wherefore, both learn and pursue all the ornaments of virtue, and, when you have instructed yourself therein, be easy of access, so that if anyone wishes to learn about

---

[166]*Christian Astrology* (London: Partridge & Blunden, 1647), p. [9].

something, he may approach you with no terror of trepidation. Be chaste, righteous, prudent, content with a small living and with small means, lest the ignoble greed for money defame the glory of this divine science. Take pains to surpass in your practices and way of life the practices of good men and the way of life of priests; for the high priest of the Sun and the Moon and the other gods, through whom all earthly things are governed, ought always to instruct his mind in such a manner that he may be adjudged by the testimonies of all men to be worthy to be involved in such great ceremonies.

3. You will of course give responses publicly, and advise the questioners of this beforehand—that you are going to say to them in a clear voice everything about which they ask, lest by chance anything be sought from you about which it is not permissible to ask or to reply.

4. Take care that you make no reply to anyone who is asking anything about the state of the nation or about the Roman emperor's life, for it is neither proper nor permissible for us to learn anything about the state of the nation because of nefarious curiosity. But he is a miscreant and deserving of every reproof if, having been asked, he speaks about the fate of the emperor, because he will neither be able to say nor to discover anything. For you should know that even the haruspices, however often they have been asked about the emperor's situation by private citizens and have wished to reply to the questioner, always the entrails which had been destined for this [question] are found to be disarranged with an intricate confusion of the [normal] order of the blood vessels.

5. But neither was any astrologer able to expound anything truly about the emperor's destiny. For the emperor alone is not subject to the courses of the stars, and he is the only one in whose destiny the stars have no power of decreeing. For since he is the ruler of the whole world, his destiny is governed by the judgment of the highest gods; and because the earthly expanse of the whole world is subject to the emperor's powers, likewise he himself is constituted in the number of the gods whom the principal divinity appointed to make and preserve all things.

6. This fact confounds even the haruspices, for whatever divinity they have invoked, because he is of lesser power, he will be unable to explain the substance of the

greater power which is inherent in the emperor. For all free men, all ranks of society, all of the rich, all of the nobles, all honors, and all powers serve him. Having been allotted the power of license of a divine and immortal deity, he is placed in the principal ranks of the gods.

7. Wherefore, whoever inquires anything about the emperor, I do not wish you to embarrass him with a harsh and severe response, but persuade him with gentle speech that no one can discover anything about the life of the chief of state, so that, warned by your persuasions, he may, the error of his mind having been corrected, lay aside that furor of rashness. But I do not wish you to give any reply if anyone asks about anything evil; lest, when he has received a capital sentence for his illicit mental desires, you may seem to have been the cause of his death, which is alien to the priestly way of life.

8. You should have a wife, a home, and an abundance of honorable friends. Be constantly accessible to the public. Remain apart from all contention. You should not undertake any harmful business, nor let augments of money tempt you at any time. Keep separate from all eagerness for cruelty. You shall never rejoice in the disputes of others or in perilous and pernicious enmities; but let a quiet moderation be pleasing to you in all association. Shun seditions; shun always boisterous contentions.

9. Bind the faith of friendship with strong ties. Take pains that your faith remain uncorrupted in all your actions. You should never pollute your conscience with false testimonies. You should never make use of the interest from money, lest a wretched augment of money be conferred upon you from the misfortunes of others. You should never promise or demand the faith of an oath, especially if it is demanded because of money, lest the divine assistance of the deities may seem to be implored because of a wretched gift of money.

10. To erring men, especially those to whom the ties of friendship have joined [you], show the right way of living, so that, shaped by your instruction, they may be freed from their former errors of life, so that you can educate the corrupt desires of men not only by responses but also by counsels. You should never be present at nocturnal sacrifices, either those that are held in public or in private. Nor should you discuss matters secretly with anyone, but openly, just

as you understood it above, under the gaze of all, you should reveal the learning of this divine art.

11. In delineating genitures I do not wish you to explain clearly the faults of men, but, as often as you come to such a place, suspend your response with a certain trepidation of modesty, lest you should seem not to [simply] expound but rather to reproach that evil which the courses of the stars have decreed for the man.

12. Always withdraw yourself from the enticements of spectacles, lest anyone think you are a proponent of any part [of them]. For the high priest of the gods ought to be separated and removed from the depraved enticements of spectacles.

13. When you have adorned your mind with these ornaments and defenses of virtue, undertake this work and with secure courage of mind go through the later books that we have written about the astrological decrees. But if you transfer your mind to any degree from those practices which we have spoken of concerning morals, see that you do not come to the secrets of this discipline with an instinct of preposterous cupidity or with a sacrilegious ardor of rashness.

14. Neither should you intrust the arcana of this religion to the errant desires of mind, for the perverted minds of men ought not to be initiated into divine cerimonies. But neither can the learning of this venerable science be at any time firmly fixed in a mind busied and polluted with corrupt desire, and it always suffers the greatest loss when the immoral will of its professors stains it.

15. Therefore, be pure and chaste, and if you have separated yourself from all nefarious actions which are wont to destroy the mind, and if a right vow of living has freed you from all hatred resulting from evil deeds, and if you keep yourself purged [of evil] and mindful of the divine seed, [then] enter upon this work and commit to memory the following books, so that divinity may bequeath the whole science to you and draw near to your mind with a hidden prophetic majesty, so that, having attained the true knowledge of divinity, in defining the fates of men and in explaining the course of life you may be instructed not so much by those things you have read but rather by your own mental judgments, so that more may be conferred upon you

by your divinity of mind than by your mastery of what you have read.

This lengthy injunction contains several points: keep out of politics, maintain a good reputation, be honest, don't be greedy, don't disparage your clients if you see they have faults, but instead try to direct them into a proper course of action, always act in an ethical manner, and finally, learn astrology thoroughly, so that you understand it and can give valid responses without having to parrot what you have read in your textbooks. This passage is one of the few in Greek astrology that expresses any explicit religious sentiment. Firmicus believed that astrology was a divine science, and he lived in the beginning of a period in which the rulers of the Roman Empire were making an uneasy transition from being gods on earth to being appointed by a particular god to be rulers on earth. His injunction against trying to read the emperor's horoscope would have saved some 16th and 17th century astrologers from incurring the wrath of the popes by predicting their imminent demise.[167] Absolute rulers, whether divine or secular, resent speculation about their destiny. Perhaps the main message of this passage is simply: maintain a good reputation, stay out of trouble, and be careful about what you predict.

The *Mathesis* could perhaps be characterized as a collection of lengthy excerpts from the earlier Greek astrologers. It is systematic in that it takes up one subject at a time and dwells on it at length, but it does not set forth any systematic way to read a chart. In fact, following several sections, Firmicus tells us that if we use the technique (and delineations) just given we can find all the secrets of the horoscope. But since there are several of these, we are left at a loss as to how to synthesize them. Nevertheless, we are given much material that is not found in the earlier writers whose books have come down to us.

Book I is an extended introduction or preface to the remaining books.

Book II explains the fundamentals of astrology—signs, planets, aspects, houses, terms, etc. It contains the only explicit example horoscope in the entire book—the nativity of the consul Rufius Albinus (mentioned above). Unfortunately, there is a large lacuna in the text, comprising the significations of the signs Taurus–Aquarius and several chapters about the individual planets. It is interesting to note that in the chapter about the decans he adds this note: "Some [writers] who want to explain this matter more subtly add to each decan three divinities that they call 'duty-officers,' i.e. *leitourgoi*, so that nine 'duty-officers' are found in each sign, since three 'duty-officers' are assigned to each decan.[168] Furthermore,

---

[167]See below, p. 180.

[168]The Latin word *munifices*, which I have translated as 'duty-officers' is the equivalent of the Greek *leitourgoi*, which signifies those who carry out official duties assigned to them by a superior official. Firmicus alone among the astrologers preserves this bit of early astrological lore. But it is mentioned in the *Corpus*

they distribute among these nine 'duty-officers,' which they say are fixed in each sign, the infinite powers of the divinities; for they say that sudden accidents, pains, sicknesses, colds, and fevers are denoted by them, and whatever else it is that is accustomed to happen to those who neither hope for it nor know about it [in advance]; and they also will have it that monstruous human births are caused by them."[169]

Book III begins with the Thema Mundi or Horoscope of the World, which he says was devised by Hermes, handed down to Aesculapius and Hanubius, and adopted by Petosiris and Nechepso. The chart has Cancer rising with the Moon in it, the Sun in Leo, Mercury in Virgo, Venus in Libra, Mars in Scorpio, Jupiter in Sagittarius, and Saturn in Capricorn—each planet in the 15th degree of its sign. He states that there was of course no actual horoscope of the universe, for there was no one present when it was created by the divine mind, but the divine wise ancients devised this chart as a sort of teaching tool for astrologers. He then explains its significance in detail. Following this, Firmicus explains in detail the significations of the planets in the twelve houses.[170] There are separate sets of significations for the Sun and a planet in the same house. Unfortunately, the significations of the Moon in houses five through eight are missing, as is its signification in the 11th house, since he says it has the same signification there as it has in the 5th house. Evidently some pages had fallen out of the archetypal MS. The final chapter discusses the signification of the Moon when it is with the Lot of Fortune.[171]

Book IV says that Firmicus has derived his material from those things that Mercury (Hermes) and Hanubius handed down to Aesculapius, which Petosiris and Nechepso explained, and which Abram, Orpheus, and Critodemus wrote in their books. And first he gives the significations of the separations and applications of the Moon, including the case when the Moon is void of course. Then he explains how to calculate the Place of Fortune and its effects and the Place of the Daemon. First he gives what

---

Hermeticum (see below) in the Discourses of Hermes to Tat: ``Moreover, there are other stars also which travel in heaven and obey the Decans, namely the so-called Liturgi, whom the Decans have under their command as servants and private soldiers.'' (Scott's translation). This nine-fold division of the signs is the origin of the navāmśas in Hindu astrology.

[169]Again, from Hermes to Tat, op.cit., "From the Liturgi come the destructions of other living beings that take place in this or that region, and the swarming of creatures that spoil the crops." (Scott's translation)

[170]And these significations relate to the original Sign-House system of house division, not to the Equal House system that he explained in Book II. See, for example, the signification of the Sun in the 1st house, where he gives two different significations—one for the Sun in the 1st house *by day* and another for the Sun in the 1st house *by night*—positions only possible in the Sign-House system.

[171]He does not mean when Fortuna is in conjunction with the Moon in the modern sense, but rather when it is in the same sign, and hence in the same celestial house.

must be the original method: count the signs from the Sun to the Moon (or in reverse order by night), then count the same number from the 1st house to the House of Fortune; then he gives the method to which we are accustomed in which the measurements are made to the degree, and he says it is the one we should use. He mentions Achilles and Abram. In the next chapter he talks about the Place of the Daemon, but as the text has come down to us (and perhaps as he wrote it), the instructions for finding it are reversed and therefore the same as those for finding the Place of Fortune. "This place," he says, "is called the substance of the soul; from this place we seek all [the native's] actions and increaseses in his personal property; and it shows what sort of affection a woman may have around a man. But this place and its squares also represent in manifest fashion the [native's] fatherland."

Next Firmicus tells us how to determine the ruler of the chart. The method "universally accepted" is this: it is the ruler of the next sign after the Moon sign,[172] but neither the Sun nor the Moon can be the ruler, so if the natal Moon is in Gemini, then the "next" sign will be Virgo, and Mercury will be the ruler. Then he explains in detail what each planet signifies when it is the ruler, and he adds the special signification of the Sun in conjunction with the ruler and the Moon in conjunction with the ruler. In Chapter 20 he discusses the climacteric or dangerous years indicated by the seven and nine-year cycles, in particular the 63rd year of life. Next comes a chapter on actions or occupations. These are indicated by that one of the three planets Mars, Venus, or Mercury which is most powerfully related to the MC. This is from the early tradition, as it is also followed by Ptolemy.

Chapter 22 is on "empty and full places," which, we learn, are the degrees not occupied or occupied by the [stars of the] decans. He gives a table listing the decans in each sign. Their Egyptian names are badly distorted by having passed from Demotic into Greek then into Latin and perhaps miscopied by the scribes. The "full" degrees, which are favorable, and the "empty" degrees, which are unfavorable, are the origin of the "bright" and "dark" degrees found in the lists later given by the Arabian astrologers.[173]

Chapter 23 gives a list of masculine and feminine degrees in the signs based on some as yet undiscovered scheme.[174] Finally, Book IV closes

---

[172]This rule probably results from the injunction to look at the Moon on the "third day," which means the second day after birth. In most cases the Moon would then be in the next sign after its natal sign.

[173]The "full" degrees are evidently the degrees occupied by the decanal asterisms in some early star catalogue and are therefore referred to the fixed zodiac used by the Alexandrian astrologers.

[174]A similar list is given by al-Bîrunî, *The Book of Instruction*, Sect. 457. While it does not agree in detail with Firmicus's list, it shows sufficient similarities to indicate that both it and Firmicus's list go back ultimately to the same

with two short chapters on configurations of the Moon.

Book V, most of which is lost, opens with a chapter delineating the influence of the signs on the four angles—Aries on the ASC, Capricorn on the MC, Libra on the DSC, and Cancer on the IC—and similarly for the remaining eleven signs on the ASC. This amounts to a detailed delineation of each sign when it is in the ASC. The chapter concludes with the statement that the *Myriogenesis* of Aesculapius contains very specific delineations for the individual minutes of the ASC degree and that these are sufficient to characterize the native's future life without even considering the placement of the planets in the chart. Firmicus promises Mavortius that he will write twelve books for him containing these delineations. He may have done so, but the book has not come down to us; nor does any other author give us this information.[175] Chapter 2 gives delineations of the ASC degree in the terms of each of the planets along with the variations due to the presence of a planet or luminary in the same terms. Chapter 3 originally gave the influence of each planet in each sign, but only Saturn in the signs and Jupiter in Aries through Capricorn remains. This was followed by chapters giving the influences of the planets in the terms of the other planets, but of these only the chapters on Mercury and the Moon remain.[176] The book closes with some helpful hints on how to interpret a horoscope.

Book VI opens with a review of the houses; the following chapter lists the "royal stars" in Taurus, Leo, Scorpio, and Aquarius, and closes with another mention of the *Myriogenesis* and his translation of it. Chapters 3-28 give delineations of the mutual aspects of the planets and luminaries. Chapters 29-31 contain many short excerpts from actual horoscopes that were taken to be indicative of some facet of the natives' lives. Among

---

Greek source. Vettius Valens, *Anthology*, i. 11, has a simpler scheme in which sex is assigned to the dodecatemories of the signs.

[175]The delineations in the *Myriogenesis* must have been entirely theoretical, since a minute of the zodiac rises on the average in 4 seconds of time, and the ancients could scarcely measure time much closer than the nearest half hour. The book must have been rare, since no one but Firmicus mentions it. Presumably the classical astrologer who possessed a copy of the *Myriogenesis* merely started at the calculated ASC degree and ran his eye up and down the list of delineations until he found one that seemed suitable to the native. This is what some Indian astrologers do today with a similar set of interpretations of fractional parts of a degree that are called *nadi*. In both cases, these delineations are used to produce an instant outline of the native's destiny without requiring the astrologer to expend any time or effort on interpreting the complete horoscope.

[176]Not to be outdone by the defects of the MSS, Pescennius Franciscus Niger, the editor of the Aldine edition of the *Mathesis*, filled up the gap (and all the other gaps that he detected in the *Mathesis*) either by writing the missing chapters himself or by copying similar passages from other authors. Hence the Aldine edition has many spurious passages that were taken as genuine by Renaissance and early modern astrologers.

these are the invented horoscopes of Oedipus, Paris Alexander, Demosthenes, Homer, Plato, Pindar & Archilochus, Archimedes, and Thersites. The charts for Demosthenes, Homer, Pindar & Archilochus, and Archimedes are schematic, i.e. they have the same house positions, but the signs are different. Firmicus says of several of these that so-and-so "is *said* to have had such a chart."

But some of the other excerpts can possibly be dated.[177] Among them are the one in Chapt. 31.1, which has Saturn in Libra in the terms of Jupiter and the ASC in the same degree, with Venus in Aries, Mars conjunct the Moon in Cancer, the Sun and Mercury in Gemini, and Jupiter static retrograde in Aquarius. These positions occurred at about 2 PM on 23 May 139 B.C. except that Saturn was not in the terms of Jupiter and the Moon was a few degrees past Mars and in early Leo. This horoscope, we are told, denotes the most powerful command of a kingdom or the emblems of a powerful dignity. If the date just given is correct, the chart might be that of Ptolemy IX, or, less likely, Antiochus VIII or Antiochus IX. Another possibility is the Roman dictator Sulla (138-78 B.C.), who is known to have had his horoscope cast.

And in Sect. 55 of the same chapter we are told that Jupiter, Mars, Mercury, and Venus on the ASC in Virgo, with Saturn in Pisces, the Sun in Libra, and the Moon in Aquarius, with all planets in their own terms, shows the "decree of a most powerful emperor." Again, the sign positions occurred on the 27th and the 28th of September in 96 B.C., but only Mars was in its own terms.[178] If this date is correct and the chart refers to a king rather than to an emperor, it might be the chart of Ptolemy XI Auletes, who was born about 95 B.C.

Probably Firmicus or his Greek source took these examples from a collection of horoscopes, such as that of Antigonus.

Chapter 32 gives instructions for determing the houses (or rather, the lots) of the father, the mother, the brothers, the spouse, children, afflictions and illnesses, etc. In all, 19 or more lots are given, along with instructions for interpreting some of them. Chapters 33-40 give the influences of the planets and luminaries when they are chronocrators or rulers of one of the 10-year and 9-month time periods of the native's life.

Book VII begins with an exhortation to Mavortius not to reveal the teachings of astrology to anyone who is not pure in soul. Thereafter, Firmicus gives special instructions for judging various topics: exposed infants, twins, slaves, the number of masters a slave will have, parents who are slaves, monsters, physical infirmities, which of the parents will die first, children who are inimical to their parents, royal horoscopes, violent

---

[177]In attempting to date these charts, care must be taken to use the Alexandrian fixed zodiac rather than the tropical zodiac.

[178]There was a partial recurrence on 20 September 142, but the Sun was in Virgo and Saturn in Aries, and only Jupiter was in its own terms.

death, condemnations, sex, etc. Again, we see what appear to be many excerpts from actual horoscopes.

Book VIII begins with an another pious statement to the effect that the study of astrology will strengthen our souls, so that we may approach the vicissitudes of life, both the good ones and the evil ones, with philosophic calm. Then Firmicus explains the technical matter of the seeing and hearing signs, which he says rather surpringly is derived from the Barbaric Sphere, which is the non-Greek constellations. But first he says to look at the 90th degree from the ASC degree and the 90th degree from the Moon. If these degrees are aspected by benefics, the native will be fortunate, but the reverse if they are aspected by malefics. He criticizes Petosiris for not explaining this matter very well. Chapter 3 sets forth the seeing and hearing signs. Chapter 4, which is taken from a book by Abram, lists by degrees the parts of the body of the zodiacal figure that are found in each sign. For example, in Aries: 1-2, the horns; 3-5, the head; 6-7, the face; 8-10, the mouth; 11-12, the breast; 13-15, the shoulders; 16-17, the heart; 18-19, the right arm (!); 20-22, the left arm (!); 23-25, the belly; 26-27, the feet; 28-29, the kidneys; 30, the tail. These are evidently intended to specify the location of the fixed stars that are in the specified part of the figure, but they do not correspond to the usual descriptions of the constellational figures.

Chapters 5-17 are devoted to the fixed stars of the extra-zodiacal constellations that rise and set with the individual signs of the zodiac. Chapters 18-30 give interpretations from the Barbaric Sphere for the ASC in each individual degree of the zodiac. Unfortunately, 50 or more degrees are missing due to lacunae in the Latin text. Chapter 31 mentions nine bright fixed stars and gives delineations for those who have their ASC on these stars. Chapter 32 states that all the different elements of the horoscope must be taken into account in preparing an overall reading of the chart. And Firmicus ends the book by reiterating that astrological doctrine should be reserved for the pure of spirit and withheld from profane persons. He has, he says, written this book for Mavortius alone, and he urges him to hand it down to his sons and to his most trusted friends.

Like the *Tetrabiblos*, which made no immediate impact upon the astrological community but seems to have remained in a private collection for more than two centuries, the *Mathesis* evidently never came to the attention of those few later astrologers of the Classical Period whose works have survived in whole or part. Of course it was in Latin, and that must have reduced its appeal to a largely Greek readership. In fact, the earliest notices of the *Mathesis* appear around 1125 in books by Honorius of Autun and William of Malmesbury. William mentions that Gerbert (c.940-1003), who reigned as Pope Sylvester II (999-1003), in his younger days in Spain had studied "Julius Firmicus on fate." The oldest MSS of the *Mathesis* belong to the 11th century.

Around the year 346, while he was still working on the *Mathesis*,

Firmicus wrote a short and rather violent pro-Christian book, the *De errore profanarum religionum* [The Error of Pagan Religions].[179] However, there is no conflict between the two books. In the *Mathesis* Firmicus never mentions Christianity, and in the *De errore* he never mentions astrology. It is interesting to note that the *De errore* survives in a single defective MS, while there are 34 MSS of the *Mathesis* and 9 more are known to have existed but are now lost.

Paul of Alexandria

In the year 378 **Paul of Alexandria** wrote an *Introduction*[180] to astrology for his son Cronamon. The second edition of it has come down to us (and also a 6th century *Commentary* ascribed to Heliodorus[181]). The preface says that Paul is writing a second edition of his book because his son had complained that the first edition did not give the rising times of the signs according to Ptolemy. However, although Paul mentions Ptolemy's chapter on the length of life (*Tetrabiblos*, iii. 10) and the *Handy Tables* at the end of Chapter 15 and the beginning of Chapter 28, his own statement of the rising times in Chapter 2 repeats the traditional rising times that go back to Hypsicles (2nd cent. B.C.). The reason for this discrepancy is uncertain.

Despite its late date, Paul's book was based on much earlier material. For example, it contains a lengthy excerpt from the lost *Panaretos* of Hermes, in which the seven lots are discussed.

23. THE SEVEN LOTS ACCORDING TO THE PANARETOS.

The first lot[182] is the Lot of Fortune, which for those who are born by day it will be necessary to count from the solar degree to the lunar degree; and it is necessary to cast the resulting number from the ASC, counting by degrees, giving

---

[179]This is another reason why Mommsen wanted to believe that Firmicus wrote the *Mathesis* in 334-337.

[180]The Greek text was edited by Emilie Boer, *Pauli Alexandrini elementa apotelesmatica* (Leipzig: B.G. Teubner, 1958). My translation, *Introduction to Astrology*, was completed in 1985 and circulated privately. I have recently (1995) revised it and again circulated it privately, but it has not yet been published.

[181]Edited by Emilie Boer, *Heliodori, ut dicitur, in Paulum Alexandrinum commentarium* (Leipzig: B.G. Teubner, 1962). It has been conjectured that the true author of the *Commentary* was a certain Olympiodorus, but the authorship is uncertain.

[182]The word 'lot' is a translation of the Greek *klēros*; the corresponding Latin word is *sors*, which means the same thing. Both referred originally to small numbered balls that were selected at random to decide some issue or to allocate something to one or more people. Hence, the word 'lot' acquired the figurative meaning of 'luck' or 'fate' or 'destiny'. In the earliest times the astrological lots were determined on a whole sign basis, so Firmicus, for example, calls them *loci*

30 degrees to each sign, and wherever the resulting number leaves off, say that the Lot of Fortune is there. But for those [who are born] by night, the reverse, i.e. [count] from the lunar degree to the solar. Similarly, it is necessary to cast the number from the degree of the ASC.

The second lot is the Lot of the Daemon, which you will count in diurnal births from the degree of the Moon to the degree of the Sun; and it is necesaary to cast the resulting number from the degree of the ASC, again similarly allotting 30 degrees to each sign, and wherever the number leaves off, there is the Lot of the Daemon. And thus by day, but by night the reverse.

The third lot is the Lot of Love, which you will count for those who are born by day from the Lot of the Daemon to the degree of Venus and an equal [number of degrees] from the ASC. But for those [who are born] by night, the reverse.

The fourth lot is the Lot of Necessity, which you will also reckon for those who are born by day from the degree of Mercury to the Lot of Fortune and an equal [number of degrees] from the ASC. But for those [who are born] by night, the reverse.

The fifth lot is the Lot of Boldness, which you will work out from the degree of Mars to the Lot of Fortune for those who are born by day, and an equal [number of degrees] from the ASC. But for those [who are born] by night, the reverse.

The sixth lot is the Lot of Victory, which you will count for those who are born by day from the Lot of the Daemon to the degree of Jupiter, and an equal [number of degrees] from the ASC. But for those [who are born] by night, the reverse.

The seventh lot is the Lot of Retribution, which you will count in diurnal births from Saturn to the Lot of Fortune, and an equal [number of degrees] from the ASC. But by

---

'places.' Later, when astrologers began to determine them by degree, the lot was found to lie in a certain degree, and the Latin word for degree is *pars* 'part'; hence we speak of the Part of Fortune, and all the numerous lots are called 'parts.' The ones under discussion here are apparently the oldest, since they are attributed to Hermes Trismegistus. They have all fallen out of use with the exception of the first two, the Lot of Fortune and the Lot of the Daemon, which Ptolemy combined into what is called today the Part of Fortune. (By the ancient definition, Ptolemy's Lot of Fortune was the Lot of fortune by day but the Lot of Daemon by night.)

night, the reverse.

As is reasonable, the lots have the same origin, since the Moon naturally becomes Fortune, the Sun Daemon, Venus Love, Mercury Necessity, Mars Boldness, Jupiter Victory, and Saturn Retribution. And the ASC presides in the midst of these, the established *Basis* of the universe.[183]

And [the Lot of] Fortune signifies everything concerning the body and the actions of life; and it was instituted to be indicative of ownership and honor and authority.

The [Lot of the] Daemon is the ruler of the mind and the disposition and intelligence and all power; sometimes too it has to do with the matter of action.

The [Lot of] Love signifies the desires and longings, [and] things done by choice; it was also instituted [to be] the cause of affection and charm.

The [Lot of] Necessity makes subordinations and anxieties and conflicts and battles, also enmities and hatred and condemnations and all other violent things befalling men in the course[184] of life.

The [Lot of] Boldness was instituted [to be] the cause of boldness and treachery and strength and all criminal acts.

The [Lot of] Victory was instituted [to be] the cause of faith and good hope, and of contest and all fellowship, and, in addition, of enterprise and luck.

The [Lot of] Retribution was instituted [to be] the cause of the spirits of the underworld and all things concealed, also of exposure and inactivity and flight and destruction and mourning and of the kind of death.

The [Lot of] Basis, which is the ASC, was instituted [to be] the cause of life and breath because at the time of birth all that which is generated from the breathing of air draws forth the breath of life at the moment of the water clock[185]

---

[183]The ASC was the prime point in the horoscope. The other houses were counted from it, and the (astronomical) MC degree, if it was wanted at all, was calculated from the ASC. Hence the ASC was legitimately called *Basis* because it was the foundation of the horoscope.

[184]The Greek text has *en gennai* 'in the coming forth' where 'coming forth' is a technical term for one of the Moon phases. I have assumed that this is an error for *en geneai* 'in the course'.

[185]*Stalagmiaîa hōra*, lit. 'dripping hour.'

81

that was appointed at birth, which is indicative of all things.[186]

Paul's *Introduction* is rich in tables and contains two different tables of *monomoiriai* or planetary rulers of individual degrees. These are found nowhere else in the earlier literature, although they must certainly go back to earlier books that are now lost. The second table, which depends upon the triplicity rulers, is said to be useful for rectifying the ASC degree.

Paul gives an example of progressing the ASC degree to the aspect of a planet for a certain year in the native's life.[187] The planetary positions mentioned enable us to identify the native's birthdate as 19 March 353. It seems likely that this was in fact a direction he calculated for his son Cronamon.[188]

The *Commentary on Paul of Alexandria* is ascribed to **Heliodorus** in the MSS, but some have argued that it was really written by a certain Olympiodorus. Whoever wrote it did us a service, for it forms a useful companion work to Paul's *Introduction*. Some things that are not clear in Paul's work are explained in the *Commentary*. It is also notable for containing an extensive list of lots (pp. 53-61 of the Greek text).

The Astrologer of the Year 379

The next year after Paul wrote, an unknown astrologer wrote a short treatise *The Effects of the Position of the Fixed Stars* [in nativities]. The author mentions the year in which he wrote, so for want of his actual name he is called **The Astrologer of the Year 379**.[189] Ptolemy's books had become known by his time, for the longitudes of the stars are derived from Ptolemy's Catalogue of Stars, and the planetary natures of the stars are taken from the *Tetrabiblos*. Here is how his treatise begins:

The Effects of the Position of the Fixed Stars.

> If then you find that in a nativity the Moon is lying alongside one of the bright and notable stars, i.e. it is in about equal degrees of [one of] those, and especially if the Moon has the same direction of latitude that the bright star has which is quite near to the degrees of it, they make the nativities great and illustrious and eminent and wealthy. And similarly if one of the bright stars is in the ASC or it is rising at the natal hour or it is vertically in the MC or even in one of the other angles, it denotes persons who are honored

---

[186]Following this, Paul gives an example of the calculation of some of the lots using the planetary positions in his son's horoscope.

[187]A zodiacal primary progression in modern terms.

[188]See my paper "The Horoscope of Cronamon" in the AFA *Journal of Research*, vol. 5, no. 1 (1989):7-10.

[189]The Greek text was edited by Franz Cumont, CCAG V.1, pp. 194-211.

and energetic and commanding and very busy and holding much property and known and a terror to cities or countries; and especially the natives are honored in those countries in which the bright stars lie or rise simultaneously, when someone is born as is shown below in the table. When they are in the ASC then or the MC, they grant good fortune in their own cities almost from the age of youth; but if one of these bright stars is found in the DSC angle at the natal hour, it especially denotes happiness abroad and around middle age, and it gives a brilliant marriage, and it gives exceptional inheritances of riches, in particular through the agency of female persons. And if one of the bright stars is found in the underearth angle (IC) at the natal hour, it will grant the native good fortune and happiness in his old age; and they will meet with good fortune from large trusts—for this house is invisible—and their deaths are notable and well-known; for from this house we apprehend the wrapping of the body after death. And we have stated these things in the [section] about luck in dignities; for in general, in the case of all men, the one who is born at the rising of a bright star, or when one is angular, and when the Moon, as we said previously, is alongside one of the bright and notable stars at the natal hour—that one will have a bright and famous life.

Hephaestio of Thebes

Hephaestio of Thebes (b. 380) wrote an important book called *Apotelesmatics*[190] about 415 A.D. It summarizes Ptolemy and Dorotheus and includes valuable material from several other earlier writers, some of whom are mentioned by name. It is in three books, of which the first is drawn in part from the *Tetrabiblos* and the third in part from the *Pentateuch*. Like all the other books that have survived from the classical period it contains unique material. For example, it offers detailed interpretations of the influences of the individual decans when they are in the Ascendant; and it also gives the significations of the 144 dodecatemories for use in what is called "the divination of thoughts"—that is, what was in the querent's mind that prompted him to ask the astrologer a question.

As an illustration of the significations of the decans, we may cite that of the second decan of Cancer, whose name according to Hephaestio is Sit:

---

[190]Edited by D. Pingree, *Hephaestionis Thebani Apotelesmaticorum libri tres* (Leipzig: B.G. Teubner, 1973) and a supplementary volume of epitomes *Hephaestionis Thebani Apotelesmaticorum epitomae quattuor* (Leipzig: B.G. Teubner, 1974). Pingree's edition gives cross-references to the corresponding passages in Ptolemy's *Tetrabiblos* and Dorotheus's *Pentateuch*.

And the one born in the second decan will be reared richly and of better parents, and he will see the deaths of his brothers; and he will be a public man[191] and he will be held in honor by the common people and entrusted with laws; but he will be unstable in things regarding his wife, and he will suffer grief because of his children. And the [physical] indications [are these]: small in stature, swarthy, his beard thin, small-chested. A black mark will be found around his navel, [and he will be] cheering up men with his speech, but not at all with his action. And his climacteric years [are these]: the 4th, 7th, 12th, 23rd, 42nd, 54th, 62nd, 73rd, [and the] 88th.

And here are the significations of the dodecatemories of the sign Cancer when ascending in a horary chart:

III 4.26. And the first dodecatemory of Cancer signifies authority or the high-priesthood or a religious service; and the second, some great affair and honor and priesthood; and the third, fear because of something he did with his wife; and the fourth, credit or loss or a claim; and the fifth, a secret deposit or treasure or something entrusted; and the 6th, a trip or a voyage or foreign persons; and the 7th, a quarrel with feminine persons and jealousy; and the 8th, a loss or a theft or damages or refusals [to return something of the querent's]; and the ninth, marriage, partnership, and things relating to benefits; and the 10th, authority and honor and priesthood and something similar to these; and the 11th, theft or something lost or refusals [to return] things entrusted; and the 12th, partnership and friendly actions or some joint matter.

Proclus

Proclus the Philosopher (412-485)[192] was the last important classical philosopher. A *Paraphrase of Ptolemy's Tetrabiblos* is attributed to him,

---

[191]Reading *dēmosieuthēsetai* 'he will be a public man' rather than *dēmosiothēsetai* 'he will be published, confiscated, converted to public use, or registered.'

[192]His horoscope is preserved in the biography by Marinus. See Neugebauer and Van Hoesen, *Greek Horoscopes*, pp. 135-136. He was born at Constantinople on 8 February 412 at about the middle of the 3rd hour of the day or about 9:15 AM LAT. The biography says he had 8°19' Aries rising with 4°42' on the MC (but these figures correspond to Rhodes, not to Constantinople). The planetary positions were evidently calculated from the *Handy Tables* (the longitudes of Jupiter and Saturn are very close to the HT positions), but the received text contains errors.

but its actual authorship is disputed. Nevertheless, it is a valuable work, since it adheres closely to the text of the original and is based on an earlier MS tradition than the surviving MSS of the *Tetrabiblos*. The modern translations of the "*Tetrabiblos*" made by astrologers have mostly been translations of the *Paraphrase* rather than of the *Tetrabiblos* itself. And in fact, most of them are translations of the Latin version of the *Paraphrase* that was made by Leo Allatius (1586-1669).[193] But J.M. Ashmand states explicitly that his translation[194] is from the Greek text of the 1635 edition, although he says he has compared the Greek text of Proclus with the older editions of the *Tetrabiblos* and with Allatius's Latin translation of the *Paraphrase*.

Rhetorius the Egyptian

Rhetorius the Egyptian seems to have lived around 505 A.D.[195]; he compiled a valuable compendium of the works of Antiochus and Porphyry, with excerpts from Vettius Valens and some other earlier writers. His book seems to have been entitled *From the Treasury of Antiochus, an Explanation and Narration of the Whole Art of Astrology.*[196] A number of chapters are nearly identical to chapters in Porphyry's *Introduction*. This probably indicates that both Rhetorius and Porphyry independently borrowed those chapters from Antiochus of Athens.

There is much material in Rhetorius's book that is found nowhere else. In addition we get the impression that Rhetorius himself was a competent astrologer. One particularly notable section in his book is Chapter 54 "Topical Examination of the Chart," which contains the only systematic method of chart reading that has come down to us from the classical period.[197] The anonymous compiler of the *Book of Hermes* copied this into

---

[193] *Procli Diadochi Paraphrasis in Ptolemaei libros iv. De siderum effectionibus.* 'Proclus Diadochus's Paraphrase of Ptolemy's Four Books on the Effects of the Stars' ed. by Leo Allatius (Leiden: Elzevir, 1635); Greek text with Allatius's Latin translation in parallel columns. The *Paraphrase* was translated into English three times in the 18th and 19th centuries — by John Whalley (1701), James Wilson (1820), and J.M. Ashmand (1822). The translation most commonly used by 19th and 20th century English-speaking astrologers is that of Ashmand.

[194] *Ptolemy's Tetrabiblos or Quadripartite, being Four Books of the Influence of the Stars....* (London, 1822; London: W. Foulsham & Co., 1917. repr.).

[195] Pingree dates him a century later on the basis of his determination of the date (24 February 601) of a horoscope at the end of the work, but this seems doubtful. The rest of the book indicates a date at the beginning of the 6th century.

[196] Edited by D. Pingree but not yet published. Most of the text has been edited and published previously in the CCAG, but Pingree's edition would be a welcome improvement.

[197] The chapter is too lengthy to be cited here in its totality, and to cite only a portion of it would give a false impression of the whole. Suffice it to say that it is very detailed and embraces almost every technique employed by the Greek astrologers of the Classical Period. Whether it is by Rhetorius or by one of his sources is unknown.

his work as Chapter 16 and the medieval Latin translation is useful for emending the text of Rhetorius and for supplying portions of the text that are now missing in the Greek.

Chapter 57 contains the most elaborate set of interpretations of the planets in the twelve houses that has come down to us. Actually, it is a double set, for Rhetorius evidently had two separate sources for this material. One of them is the same source used by Firmicus in Book 3 of the *Mathesis*. The other one is different. Rhetorius also gives the signification of the nodes in the houses, and he gives many significations for the ruler of one house being located in another house (e.g. when the ruler of the 5th is in the 3rd).

To give the reader an idea of the wealth of detail found in this chapter, here is the section dealing with the 8th house:

The Eighth House.

The eighth house is called *idle* and *epicataphora* of the ASC and *epikatadysis* and *dimming*.[198] It is the sign that is turned away from the ASC; because of this, and because of its meaning of death, it signifies the turning away of life.

If then the Lot of Fortune chances to be there, and its lord, and the lord of the ASC, it makes misfortunes and irregularities. And if these [lords] are malefics, the evil is worse, for it makes unfortunate persons, and if [they are] under the Sun beams, short-lived persons. Mercury being lord of the [Lot of the] Daemon, [and] being present in the 8th, [makes] unintelligent, and illiterate, and lazy persons. Mercury being lord of the 8th or of the 12th or of the 6th, being present in the 8th under the Sun beams with Saturn and Mars, [makes] deaf and dumb persons. The Moon there by night adding to her numbers[199] and light, especially if Jupiter is in the 11th, [the native] will profit from matters having to do with the dead and with inheritances. The ruler of the 4th in the 8th, he dies abroad. The lord of the 8th makes these same things when it is cadent. Venus in the 8th makes miserable and shameful persons. The lord of the 8th in the 10th or the 11th or the 5th, [the native] will grow rich from matters having to do with the dead, especially if it is in its own domicile or exaltation and not under the Sun beams and if it is adding to its numbers. But if it is under the Sun beams, it makes an inheritance, but he imme-

---

[198]The two names I have left in Greek mean respectively 'falling down upon the ASC' and 'falling down upon the DSC.' The reasoning behind the phrase 'epicataphora of the ASC' is that the DSC is opposite the ASC.

[199]Swift.

diately squanders it. The lord of the 3rd in the 8th destroys the brothers first. The lord of the 5th being there causes childlessness. The lord of the 12th or of the 6th being there [makes] the deaths of enemies and slaves.[200]

Mars there injures the vision, especially if the Sun or the Moon is in the ASC. Saturn [and] Mars there without Jupiter [and] Venus make [the natives to be] banished. Jupiter there in its own domicile or exaltation, adding to its numbers, [the native] profits from matters having to do with the dead, and especially without Saturn and Mars. Mercury and Mars there [make] forgers.

Saturn, lord of the 8th beholding [the eighth] destroys him [in some fashion involving] water or abroad, especially in a water sign or impedited in another [sign]; but if Saturn is in an earth sign, it destroys [him] on a mountain. In a word, examine the ruler of each sign of the 8th, in what sign it is, for that one becomes the [significator of] death. The Sun ruler of the 8th impedited in the sign of another, if the 8th house itself is impedited, it destroys [by a fall] from a height according to the nature of the sign. Mars lord of the 8th, with the house impedited, makes those dying violently; sometimes too, huntsmen.[201] Mars aspected by the Sun makes a violent death [caused] by kings or enemies. Venus ruler of the 8th impedited, and the 8th impedited, makes violent death from [too] much wine or from poisoning by women. Mercury ruler of the 8th impedited, and also the 8th itself, makes death [caused] by slaves or by writings. Jupiter ruler of the 8th impedited along with the house makes the death [to be caused] by kings or magnates, and, if [it is] in its own domiciles or triplicity or exaltation, in the same country, but if in other [signs], abroad. If the Ascending Node happens to be in the 8th with the Sun, Mars, Mercury, [and] Saturn or if they aspect the house, it makes a bad death or a short-lived person. If Jupiter and Venus [are] in the 8th alone, [it makes] an easy death and great good fortune. If the Descending Node happens to be in the 8th and Jupiter, Saturn, Venus, and Mars [are] there, they make those dying violently.[202]

---

[200]As J.B. Morin points out in *Astrologia Gallica*, Book 21, the 8th house is only the house of death for the native, so some of these aphorisms are inconsistent with the doctrine of derived houses.

[201]Literally, '(hunting-) dog leaders.'

[202]This paragraph is a condensed version of Chap. 77 of the book.

Saturn there by day denotes those acquiring [assets] with the passage of time, in order to assist others, but some [other natives] acquiring [assets] from death. Being there by night, it makes those who are banished, consumptives, and those dying a bad death.

Jupiter there by day and by night denotes acquisition and inheritance with the passage of time.

Mars in the 8th by day makes needs and disorders and dangers.

The Sun in the 8th makes the early death of the father, and some [of the natives] are madmen;[203] the stars that are with it or in aspect to it show the cause. But the Sun opposing the Moon, with the bond not yet broken,[204] injures the one that was born.

Venus by day in the 8th [makes] those who marry late and those who have intercourse with lower-born women or widows or young girls. And it destroys the natives through gonorrhea[205] or spasms or apoplexy. But by night, it denotes wealthy and rich persons and those who benefit from the death of women. And it makes the death [of the native] quick and painless and easy.

Mercury in the 8th vespertine by day [makes] ineffective, unsuccessful, lazy, toilsome persons; but vespertine by night, those inheriting from unrelated persons, those deserving of windfalls, fortunate, but passive and who easily become sick. Matutine in the 8th, it makes increases of money and those who aim at great actions, and some who share in responsibilities or fiduciary relationships or managing or legal documents or even those inheriting from unrelated persons.

[The influence of the Moon in the eighth house is missing.]

In the latter part of the book, there are several short chapters devoted to the astrological indications of specific occupations.

Towards the end of the main part of his book[206] Rhetorius gives the

---

[203]In Greek, *phrenētikoús*, a variant spelling of *phrenitikoús*, means someone suffering from inflammation of the brain. Here it refers to the noisy type of dementia—the raving madman.

[204]He means 'with the technical condition of "bonding" still in effect.'

[205]That is, through some sort of venereal disease, not necessarily the one we call gonorrhea.

[206]Chapter 113.

horoscope of the poet Pamprepius of Thebes (440-484) who associated himself with some insurgent Byzantines and rose to a high position but perished when their rebellion collapsed. In another chapter he gives the horoscope of a short-lived child of the emperor Leo I (c.400-474).

In Chapt. 12 of what Pingree calls Epitome IV of Rhetorius[207] there is an explanation of how to calculate what we would call modified Alchabitius cusps using an unidentified nativity of 8 September 428 as an example. The modification consists of trying to follow Ptolemy's precept of beginning the houses 5° before the normal cusps. The basic principle is the same as Alchabitius cusps—the arc of right ascension between the RAMC and the RAASC is trisected. However, Rhetorius makes a small error in his calculations. Still, this shows that the principle of the Alchabitius cusps goes back at least to the time of Rhetorius and perhaps to his source in the 5th century. It was a logical development from the Porphyry system, which trisects the zodiacal arc from the MC to the ASC.

Rhetorius was the last major astrological writer of the Classical Period. There are a few other short treatises preserved from the Classical Period, but the ones just mentioned are the major works that have survived. Much to be regretted is the loss of the earliest works of the Alexandrian astrologers.

Hermetic and Pseudepigraphal Writings on Astrology

There were once some substantial books on astrology attributed to Hermes Trismegistus. They are lost except for excerpts in the books of later writers. For example, Paul of Alexandria gives a lengthy extract from a book of Hermes entitled *Panaretos* on the seven lots (the Lot of Fortune and its six associates). This perhaps indicates that a Hermetic writing originated the idea of the lots. Pingree thinks that another tract containing the significations of the planets in the twelve celestial houses was ascribed to Hermes. Several sets of such interpretations are found in the works of Vettius Valens, Firmicus, Paul of Alexandria, and Rhetorius. They differ considerably, and no study has yet been made to try to determine whether they all stem from a common origin that has been modified separately by each of the individual astrologers.

The Christian writer Clement of Alexandria (c.150-c.220) mentions forty-two books of Hermes that were carried by Egyptian priests in a religious procession. Of these, ten dealt with the laws, the gods, and the training of priests; ten more dealt with Egyptian religious practices; two contained hymns to the gods and rules for the king; six were on medicine,

---

[207]See the paper by David Pingree, "Antiochus and Rhetorius" in *Classical Philology* 72 (July 1977):203-23. The received text of Rhetorius consists of 117 chapters of what might be called the main series plus four epitomes. Some chapters translated into Latin appear in the *Book of Hermes* (for which, see the note to the Section "Degree Symbolism" below).

"treating of the structure of the body and diseases and instruments and medicines and about the eyes and the last [of these] about women [and their diseases]"; four were on astronomy and astrology; and another ten dealt with miscellaneous matters. Possibly some of the medieval tracts ultimately descend from these, although some of the tracts may be falsely ascribed to Hermes.

Aside from these, a number of short writings remain, some of them perhaps excerpts from other lost books. Among them are: (1) a *Centiloquy*; (2) a tract on *The Desert Stars* (*De stellis beibeniis*); and (3) one on *The Fifteen Stars*. But one or all of these may be apocryphal.

In addition to the writings that relate more or less directly to what we might call the main stream of horoscopic astrology, there are a number of writings attributed to Hermes that give lists of plants, animals, diseases, stones, planetary images, etc., ruled by the signs, the decans, or the planets. These obviously attempt to provide celestial rulerships for nearly everything on earth and are thus astrological; but they are also somewhat magical in nature. And at any rate, except for the medical indications, they do not deal directly with natal astrology but are perhaps useful for the other branches of astrology.[208]

The reader who wishes to venture into this Hermetic maze can refer to Lynn Thorndike's discussion in HMES 1, pp. 287-292, HMES 2, pp. 221 ff., and to A.J. Festugière's *La révélation d'Hermès Trismégiste*, vol. 1 "L'Astrologie et les sciences occultes" (Paris: J. Gabalda et Cie., 1950) (in French). For a list of Latin astrological and magical MSS that are attributed to Hermes, see Francis J. Carmody, *Arabic Astronomical and Astrological Sciences in Latin Translation*, hereinafter cited as AAASLT, (Berkeley and Los Angeles: The University of California Press, 1956), pp. 52-70.

Also, a fairly extensive collection of philosophical and religious texts called the *Corpus Hermeticum* has come down to us,[209] but it contains little information relating to astrology except for a short discourse on the decans[210] and a few references to them in other parts of the corpus. From this we gather that the decans loomed large in Egyptian religious thought in the Ptolemaic period during which horoscopic astrology was invented, and that they were still thought to be important in the first centuries of the present era.

Some treatises on astrology are ascribed to **Zoroaster** (7th cent. B.C.?), **Hippocrates** (468-377? B.C.), and **Galen** (131-c.200 A.D.). But

---

[208]See David Pingree, *The Yavanajātaka of Sphujidhvaja*, vol. 2, pp. 429-433, for a discussion of the astrological writings attributed to Hermes.

[209]See the edition and translation by Walter Scott, *Hermetica* (Oxford: The Clarendon Press, 1924; repr. in facs. London: Dawsons of Pall Mall, 1968. 4 vols.). A cursory scanning of this Hermetic material will convince the reader that it has nothing to do with horoscopic astrology.

[210]*loc. cit.*,vol. 1, p. 411 ff. "From the Discourses of Hermes to Tat."

there is no reason to suppose that any of these men ever wrote on astrology. The two physicians may have left something on "critical days," but the treatises on medical astrology ascribed to them must be as apocryphal as are the astrological treatises ascribed to Zoroaster, who lived before anything other than omen astrology existed.

In addition to these, there were astrological writings ascribed to **Orpheus** and **Achilles** of which some fragments remain. These certainly have no connection with the semi-legendary figures who bore those names.

Some Special Features
of Greek Astrology

Several features of this original system of horoscopic astrology are unfamiliar to modern astrologers. Some of these are:

- The point of prime importance in the horoscope was the rising sign and specifically the ASC degree. The (astronomical) MC degree was a later development and was little used.
- The triplicities and their planetary rulers were important. Each triplicity had a set of three rulers: Fire—Sun, Jupiter, Saturn; Earth—Venus, Moon, Mars; Air—Saturn, Mercury, Jupiter; and Water—Venus, Mars, Moon. These were the rulers by day; by night the rulers were the same but the sequence was different—the first two in each set reversed their positions. For example, the night rulers of the Fire triplicity were Jupiter, Sun, Saturn. Dorotheus uses them to determine the native's viability at birth, his fortune (or infortune) in life, etc. The triplicity rulers of the ASC and the Light of the Time[211] were especially important. Each was also considered to rule a third of the life in sequence, and the quality of those thirds of life were indicated by the triplicity ruler and its position and aspects in the horoscope.
- The importance of the signs as houses or domiciles of the planets. The original concept was that each sign was like a household presided over by a ruler or master of the house. The dividing line between adjacent signs was like the wall that divides one house (or one apartment) from its neighbor on that side. This had important consequences for the reckoning of the celestial houses, aspects, and the various lots (what we mistakenly call the "Arabic parts").
- Special relations of the signs were important. Perhaps that most often used was the pairs of signs that were equidistant from the solstices, what we would call the 0 Cancer–0 Capricorn line. But the solstices were first considered to be in the middle of Cancer and Capricorn,[212]

---

[211]The Sun for diurnal nativities, and the Moon for nocturnal nativities.

[212]Probably following the lead of Eudoxus (4th century B.C.) who placed the solstices and equinoxes at 15° of the cardinal signs (referred of course to some fixed zodiac).

so the sign pairs were originally Gemini and Leo, Taurus and Virgo, Aries and Libra, Pisces and Scorpio, Aquarius and Sagittarius. Much later, after the Ptolemaic tables which put the solstices at the beginning of the signs Cancer and Capricorn became standard, these pairs were altered to Gemini and Cancer, Taurus and Leo, Aries and Virgo, Pisces and Libra, Aquarius and Scorpio, and Capricorn and Sagittarius. These are the signs that were *antiscia* 'opposite shadows' or *antiscions* of each other, since their distances from the solstitial line were the same and the pairs were both north or both south. This realtionship eventually led to what is now called the *parallel* in declination, which goes back at least to Placidus (see below), and which substitutes equal distances from the equator for equal distances from the solstices.

Another special relation between signs was the "seeing and hearing signs." These were pairs of signs equidistant from the equinoctial line, what we would call the 0 Aries–0 Libra line. Originally the line was considered to pass through the middle of Aries and Libra, so the pairs were Taurus and Pisces, Gemini and Aquarius, Cancer and Capricorn, Leo and Sagittarius, and Virgo and Scorpio. Much later, after the Ptolemaic tables which put the equinoxes at the beginning of Aries and Libra became standard, these pairs were altered to Aries and Pisces, Taurus and Aquarius, Gemini and Capricorn, Cancer and Sagittarius, Leo and Scorpio, and Virgo and Libra. These would now be called *contrantiscions*, and their modern derivative the *contraparallels* in declination (having the same declination, but one north and the other south).

There were other special relations, but these were the most important.

- The Greek astrologers put great emphasis on the terms[213] and the rulers of the terms. There were several sets of terms—Ptolemy mentions three, that "according to the Egyptians," that "according to the Chaldeans," and his own, that he claims to have found in an old MS. Vettius Valens mentions another set that was used by Critodemus. But the set that was almost universally used by the Greek astrologers (and most of the medieval astrologers) was the terms "according to the Egyptians," which probably means that they were devised by the founders of horoscopic astrology, who, as we have seen, lived in Alexandria, Egypt.

According to this set there were five terms in each sign, ruled by

---

[213]The name *terms* is derived from the Latin *termini* 'limits or boundaries' and is an exact translation of the Greek *hória* which means the same thing. It refers to the boundaries of the areas ruled by the individual planets; hence, it is properly plural. We should say "Jupiter is in the terms of Mars," not "Jupiter is in the term of Mars."

the five planets. Generally Mars and Saturn came at the end of the sign, but not always. The sums of the terms ruled by the planets were important: Saturn 57, Jupiter 79, Mars 66, Venus 82, Mercury 76—all of which add up to 360. The individual totals were considered to be the standard length of life in years granted by each planet when it was the "ruler of the nativity." The years of life could be augmented or diminished or in extreme cases reduced almost to nothing by various configurations in the horoscope, but these were the base from which the actual years could be determined. (If the years of the Sun and the Moon were required, they were separately stated to be 120 for the Sun and 108 for the Moon.) These figures are often referred to as the "major years" of the planets.

In general, a planet in its own terms was considered to be in its own domicile, just as if it were in a sign it ruled. And a planet in its own terms in its own sign was doubly fortified. A malefic planet (Mars or Saturn) was rendered less malefic if it was posited in the terms of a benefic planet (Venus or Jupiter). Conversely, a benefic was rendered less so if it was posited in the terms of a malefic. And if a profection or progression put a planet or the ASC degree in the terms of a malefic, it was considered to be a portent of some evil occurrence. In short, in reading the ancient texts one gets the impression that the ruler of the terms of a planet or of the ASC degree was almost more important than the sign ruler.

- Other subdivisions of the signs were also used but were evidently considered to be less important than the terms. The *dodecatemories* or twelfths of the signs ranked second in popularity. They are frequently mentioned by Dorotheus, and Firmicus continually exhorts the astrologer to take note of the *dodecatemory* occupied by a planet. Paul of Alexandria gives two different sets of *monomoiriai* or single-degree rulers, one of which he recommends as a useful tool to rectify a birthtime.
- Aspects were originally conceived as belonging to the signs, not the planets. In other words, Taurus was square Leo; hence, any planet in Taurus was square any planet in Leo, irrespective of the degree positions of the planets within the two signs. Again, this reflects the basic concept of signs as 'houses' or 'domiciles' of the planets. The idea was that the household we call Taurus was at variance with the household we call Leo, much as if the Smith household were at odds with the Jones household. Consequently, a visitor (planet) in one of those houses would automatically become at odds with a visitor in the other house. One consequence of this is that a planet in say the 1st degree of one sign would not be considered to be in conjunction with a planet in the 29th degree of the preceding sign even though they were only two degrees apart. Why? Because there was a wall between them, just as a person standing next to the dividing wall be-

tween two apartments cannot see another person who may be standing on the other side of the wall in the adjacent apartment. Aspects (except the opposition) were also either "right" or "left"—thus, a planet in Aries is in right trine to a planet in Sagittarius, but in left trine to one in Leo. The "right" or *dexter* aspects were considered to be more favorable than the "left" or *sinister* aspects.

The concept of the *orb* of an aspect was not part of the original system of horoscopic astrology for the reason just stated. So long as astrologers were content to make their charts on a whole sign basis, there was no need for an orb. After a century or so, when some astrologers sought more precision and took the degrees of the planets into account, a few of them began to think about orbs. Ptolemy mentions (*Tetrabiblos*, iii. 10) that Jupiter and Venus exercise a protective influence if they aspect the anaeretic place within 12° in the case of Jupiter and 8° in the case of Venus. However, we should note that these numbers are simply the minor years[214] of those planets. The only clear statement is in Porphyry, *Introduction*, Chapt. 55, which gives the orbs: Sun, 15°; Moon, 12°; Saturn & Jupiter 9°; Mars, 8°; and Venus & Mercury 7°. But this chapter may actually be from Zahel (see below), where the same numbers are found, and not from Porphyry.

- The celestial houses, which were called *tópoi* 'places' in Greek were originally conceived to be a *sequence* of houses, just like houses along a street or apartments down a hall in a block of apartments. This was the original system of houses. It had no name in antiquity, but I have referred to it as the "Sign-House" system.[215] It was very simple: the ascending sign was the 1st house, the next sign was the 2nd house, the next sign after that was the 3rd house, etc. The 10th sign was called *mesouránēma* or 'midheaven'. No calculation was necessary; once you knew the rising sign, you knew the signs that occupied all twelve of the celestial houses. Thus the ancient astrologers often speak indifferently of the "5th sign" or the "5th place," where we would say the "5th house." This has confused some modern astrologers and astrological historians.

The first variation of the Sign-House system departed from the neat logic of that system. It consisted of measuring 30° arcs of zodiacal longitude from the ASC degree. This is what we call the Equal House system. It is perhaps important to point out that Ptolemy specified the use of the Equal House method of house division, or rather a slight variation of it—he put the cusp of the first house 5° above the ASC degree and said that the remainder of the house extended for 25°

---

[214]See below.
[215]See my paper "Ancient House Division" in the AFA *Journal of Research*, vol. 1 (1982):19-28.

below the ASC degree, with the other houses at 30° intervals.[216] It was probably the system most in vogue in the 2nd century or at least the one that seemed most logical to him.

- Celestial houses could be counted from any point in the zodiac. The original and always the primary set of houses was counted from the ASC, and they are frequently so designated throughout the classical literature (e.g. "the 3rd house from the ASC"). But some of the ancient astrologers made a subsidiary horoscope by counting houses from the Lot of Fortune. This is explained by Manilius and also by Dorotheus and Vettius Valens, to mention some of the early writers whose works have been preserved. An especially favorable house was the 11th house from the Lot of Fortune because the name of the 11th house was Good Fortune, so when measured from the Lot of Fortune it became a place of double good fortune.

Dorotheus mentions counting houses from the Moon[217] or other planets. And a century later Ptolemy gives instructions[218] for making extracted horoscopes for the father or the mother or brothers by considering the house of the relative as an ASC and counting houses from it "just as though it were a nativity."

This is properly called the technique of "derived houses." It is a fundamental technique of horoscopic astrology, but one that much later became embroiled in controversy because it was mistakenly thought to be a technique peculiar only to horary astrology.

- At some time after the 2nd century B.C., a few mathematically-minded astrologers began to insert the astronomical Midheaven degree into horoscopes. In lower latitudes it fell either in the 9th house or the 10th house. It was considered to be what we would call today "a sensitive point"—something like the so-called Vertex. It was not originally conceived to be the "cusp" of the 10th house. It was probably two centuries after the invention of horoscopic astrology before someone got the idea that it should be considered to mark the beginning of the 10th house and came up with

---

[216]*Tetrabiblos*, iii. 10. He actually states that the 11th, 10th, 9th, and 7th houses are in aspect to the 1st house, which he had defined specifically with reference to the ASC degree. This of course could only be the case if he had in mind equal houses measured from the ASC degree. The notion held by so many later astrologers that by "aspect" he was referring to aspects in something besides zodiacal arc is plainly false. It is inconceivable that the premier astronomer of antiquity would have envisioned some elaborate trignometrical system of house division and never bothered to mention or explain it. He simply considered house division to be one operation and primary directions another—entirely independent of the method of house division.

[217]*Pentateuch*, i. 12, where he says to take special note of the 10th house from the Moon.

[218]*Tetrabiblos*, iii. 4 and 5.

the so-called Porphyry system of house division.

Ptolemy mentions the "Midheaven" several times in the *Tetrabiblos*, but the only place where he means the *astronomical* Midheaven is in iii. 2 "The Degree of the Horoscopic Point," where he says that if the selected ruler is closer to [the degree of] the Midheaven than it is to [the degree of] the ASC, it should be used to establish the Midheaven [degree] and from that the other angles. Elsewhere, by "Midheaven" he simply means the 10th house of the Equal House system.

• An important distinction was made between diurnal births (when the Sun was above the horizon) and nocturnal births. The Sun ruled diurnal nativities and the Moon ruled nocturnal nativities. The ruling luminary was called the Light of the Time, a term that has become obsolete in modern astrology. Planets were also classified as diurnal (Saturn, Jupiter, Sun) or nocturnal (Mars, Venus, Moon). Mercury could go either way depending on its circumstances in the chart. A diurnal planet in an angle in a diurnal chart was favorable, but a diurnal planet in an angle in a nocturnal chart was unfavorable. And similarly for the nocturnal planets. This distinction of the *sect* was carefully observed, but is unknown to modern astrologers.

• Another important feature of Greek astrology was the Lot of Fortune (now generally called the Part[219] of Fortune) and the proper method of calculating it. Originally it seems to have been calculated on a whole sign basis without reference to the individual degrees occupied by the Sun and Moon or to the ascending degree. Its original name was the Place (we would say 'House') of Fortune. Also, it was calculated by finding the distance from the Sun to the Moon and measuring an equal distance from the ASC, but only for diurnal births. If the native was born at night, then the measurement was from the Moon to the Sun and an equal distance from the ASC. This rule was observed by all the astrologers of the classical period and by most of the medieval astrologers. (But Ptolemy used the diurnal method for both diurnal and nocturnal nativities.)

A century or two after the invention of horoscopic astrology, some astrologers discarded the whole sign method of measurement and began to measure from degree to degree. In some cases this put the Lot of Fortune in an adjacent sign.

• To predict and time future events the ancients used an elaborate sys-

---

[219]The word 'part' is from the Latin *pars* 'part' or 'degree' (= 'part of a circle'). This is a medieval term meaning the 'degree of Fortune'. The original term "lot" referred to an object that was used to make a random choice, such as a die or a pair of dice that were thrown to see how the numbers would come up—the "casting of lots" as the King James Bible puts it.

tem of profections or what are now sometimes called "symbolic progressions." There were two main systems.

The first system began with the sign of the Light of the Time or with the ASC and counted a whole sign for each year of life, e.g. for a diurnal nativity the Sun sign was the 1st year of life, the next sign the 2nd year of life, etc. If you came to a sign with a malefic in it, then that would be a bad year. If a finer division of time was required, you could start with the sign in which the year-count fell and count months within that year, etc. Obviously the cycle would repeat itself every 12 years, but there were other considerations to be observed that kept the 27th year for example from being an identical repetition of the 15th year.

The second system assigned 10 years and 9 months to each planet (including the Sun and Moon), and began with the sign in which the Light of the Time was posited. For example, suppose the birth was diurnal and the Sun was in Sagittarius. The Sun would rule the first 10 years and 9 months of the native's life, Saturn (ruler of the next sign, Capricorn) would rule the next 10 years and 9 months and also the next 10 years and 9 months after that (because it is also the ruler of Aquarius), etc.

Within each of these 10-year and 9-month periods the time was subdivided among the planets using the following numbers as the number of months: the Sun 19, the Moon 25, Saturn 30, Jupiter 12, Mars 15, Venus 8, and Mercury 20. The subdivision begins with the planet that is ruler of the 10-year and 9-month period. All this is set forth in detail by Valens in Book 4 of the *Anthology* and by Firmicus in Books 2 and 6 of the *Mathesis*. If you add these numbers together, you get 129 months, which is of course 10 years and 9 months. (These same "month" numbers are sometimes referred to as the "minor years" of the planets.[220])

In all cases, judgment of the quality of each period or sub-period was made by considering the nature and circumstances of the planetary ruler in the natal chart.

• Primary directions were also used by some astrologers, but usually only the ASC was directed to the conjunction or aspect of a planet, allowing one degree (of what we would call sidereal time) per year of life. Only Ptolemy gives instructions for calculating interplanetary primaries (according to what is now called the Placidus method).

---

[220]After 19 years the Sun and Moon return to their original places; Saturn's period is a little less than 30 years; Jupiter's is about 12 years; Mars gets back into approximately the same place and the same phase in 15 years; Venus returns to her original place and phase in 8 years; and Mercury returns to his original place and phase in 20 years. These are all approximations of course, and the planets do not return to their exact original places.

- Another technique for forecasting future prospects for a native was to note the transits to the natal planets when the Sun returned to its natal position each year. However, no chart was erected. The ruler of the year was determined by the 12-year symbolic direction described above, taken either from the Light of the Time or from the ASC. This was the origin of what the medieval astrologers developed into "the revolution of the years of the nativity" and what we call "the Solar return."

- The decans, which had provided the original basis for the rising sign and the celestial houses, do not seem to have played any great role in astrological practice thereafter. With the sole exception of Manilius, who assigns the decans to the signs of the zodiac, they were assigned rulers in the usual astrological order beginning with Mars as ruler of the first decan of Aries.[221] They are sometimes mentioned in the papyrus horoscopes that have been found, but even there they seem to be mentioned more as a curiosity than as an important astrological factor. Rhetorius thought better of them, for he points out that the three decans of the sign Aries, which are ruled by Mars, the Sun, and Venus, have quite different characteristics (which he describes); and in another chapter he tells us which decans are lewd and indecent. Firmicus Maternus lists their names[222] and their actual extents in the zodiac, while Hephaestio of Thebes lists their names[223] and gives detailed significations for each of them, but neither of these writers makes any further use of them. Rhetorius gives very brief interpretations—half a dozen words or so for each of them. But most of the other ancient astrologers either ignored them altogether or were content to mention their existence and let it go at that.

- Finally, we may mention the planetary hours. The planetary sequence Saturn, Jupiter, Mars, Sun, Venus, Mercury, Moon was called in Greek the *heptazone* 'seven-zoned'. At some unknown date, possibly in the 2nd century B.C., some astrologer decided that he would assign the first hour of the Jewish Sabbath to the planet Saturn and the succeding hours to the succeding planets in the order of the heptazone. Since there are 24 hours in a day and night, the planet assigned to the first hour of each succeeding day was three steps

---

[221]Late 20th century astrologers have generally adopted the rulerships invented by the Hindus, which assigns the first decan to the sign itself and the second and third to the succeeding signs of its triplicity. This scheme is found in the Greek text of Achmat the Persian (9th century?). However, it seems to have been first introduced into Western astrology by Alan Leo at the beginning of the 20th century.

[222]In a garbled and Latinized form.

[223]Also rather garbled and seemingly drawn from an eclectic Egyptian source. See O. Neugebauer & Richard A. Parker, *Egyptian Astronomical Texts* (Providence: Brown Univ. Press, 1960-1969. 3 vols.), vol. 3 (text), pp. 170-171.

down in the heptazone series. For example, if we start with the day whose first hour is ruled by Saturn, the next day will begin with the first hour ruled by the Sun, the day after that with the first hour ruled by the Moon, etc. This is the origin of the Saturday, Sunday, Monday day-of-the-week sequence.

Who did this and when did he do it? No one knows. The earliest known mention of a named weekday is by the Roman poet Tibullus (d. 19 B.C.). I believe the first astrologer to mention the weekdays is Vettius Valens, who, in *Anthology*, i. 9, explains how to calculate the day of the week corresponding to a given Alexandrian date (he uses what is probably his own birthdate for an example). Once the day of the week is known, the planetary hours follow in sequence.

Both the planetary hours and the weekday names are obviously of astrological origin. The Jews at that time had no names for any of the days, except Sabbath, which means "rest." The other days were merely numbered—1st day, 2nd day, 3rd day, etc., although the 6th day (Friday) was sometimes called by a Hebrew word meaning "preparation." The Jews would certainly not have named the days of the week after foreign gods.

The only one of the ancient astrologers who paid any great attention to the weekday and the planetary hours was Paul of Alexandria (fl. 378 A.D.). Chapters 19-21 of his *Introduction* explain how to calculate the day of the week and the planetary hour.

Some Important Points

- Horoscopic astrology was invented by Greeks (or at least by Greek-speaking persons whose culture and philosophy was Greek) in Alexandria, Egypt, in the 3rd or 2nd century B.C. The characteristics assigned to the planets are those of the Greek gods. Orbital astronomy and the first application of trigonometry to astronomical calculation were developed by Greeks in the same time period, although the Alexandrian astrologers adopted the system of arithmetical rising-times of the signs that had been developed by the Babylonians and adapted to the clime of Alexandria by the mathematician Hypsicles (2nd century) in his *Anaphorikos* 'Ascension'.[224] This probably indicates that the invention of horoscopic astrology preceded the invention of trignonometry and the determination of more accurate rising times by its use.

- The Greek astrologers used a fixed zodiac until the Ptolemaic *Handy Tables* became available in the 4th century. However, their zodiac differed by about 3 degrees from the Babylonian zodiac (which is

---

[224]See the ed. and trans. (into German) by V. De Falco and M. Krause with an Introduction by O. Neugebauer, *Hypsikles, Die Aufgangszeiten der Gestirne* 'Hypsicles, The Rising-Times of the Stars' (Göttingen: Vandenhoeck & Ruprecht, 1966)

close to the 20th century Fagan-Bradley "sidereal" zodiac).[225]
- Greek horoscopic astrology passed to the Hindus in the 2nd century. The earliest known Sanskrit work on horoscopic astrology is the *Yavanajataka* of Sphujidhvaja (269/270 A.D.),[226] which says it is a versification of a prose translation (from Greek) of a work written in 149/150 A.D. by *Yavaneśvara* the 'Lord of the Greeks'. The very title of the versification—*Yavanajātaka* 'Greek Horoscopy'—shows its source. Like all later Indian astrological works it contains a number of fundamental technical terms transliterated from Greek: Here are some examples: ASC Gk. *hōra* (an older term than *horoskópos*), Skt. *hora*; IC Gk. *hypógeion*, Skt. *hipaka* or *hibuka*; DSC Gk. *dynon* or *diámetros*, Skt. *dyuna* or *jamitra*; MC Gk. *mesouránēma*, Skt. *mesurana*; angle Gk. *kéntron*, Skt. *kendra*; succedent Gk. *epanaphorá*, Skt. *panaphara*; cadent Gk. *apóklima*, Skt. *apoklima*.[227] But despite this and other scholarly evidence, most Hindu astrologers cling to the mistaken belief that both astronomy and astrology were invented by or revealed to Indian sages five or more thousand years ago, and they deny that there was any borrowing at all from the Greeks.
- It is known that Ardashir I, King of Persia 222-237, sent emissaries to surrounding countries to bring back works of science, which were lacking in Persia.[228] This evidently dates the introduction of Greek horoscopic astrology into Persia. An example of this is found in the Arabic version of Dorotheus (translated from the Middle Persian or Pahlavi version), where a Persian horoscope for 381 A.D. has been interpolated into the text of Book iii of the *Pentateuch*.[229] The Persians also obtained books on astronomy and astrology from India in the period between the 3rd and the 6th centuries. Most Persian literature was destroyed by the Muslim invaders in the 7th century, but some astrological and astronomical writings must have survived at least into the 8th century. And some of the eighth and 9th century astrologers who wrote in Arabic were Persians who may still have possessed Persian astrological treatises.

---

[225]A fixed zodiac which is approximately equivalent to that used by the Babylonians. It was promoted by 20th century "siderealist" astrologers as a substitute for the standard tropical zodiac, but it did not catch on.

[226]Edited and translated with an elaborate and valuable commentary by David Pingree.

[227]See David Pingree, *The Yavanajātaka of Sphujidhvaja*, vol. 2, pp. 218-219 and elsewhere.

[228]See *The Fihrist of al-Nadim* ed. and trans. by Bayard Dodge (New York & London: Columbia University Press, 1970. 2 vols.), vol. 2, p. 575.

[229]Not *two* Persian horoscopes, as Pingree will have it. The chart he has dated to the 3rd century really belongs to the 1st century. See above in the entry for Dorotheus.

- Astrology in the classical period was a Greek science. The principal books and tables were in Greek. (Educated Romans and other West Europeans knew Greek as well as Latin, so this caused no problem.) But when the Western Roman Empire fizzled out in the 5th century and knowledge of Greek died out in the West, would-be astrologers who knew only Latin were deprived of astrological literature and tables.

- Knowledge of horoscopic astrology virtually died out in Western Europe with the collapse of the Western Roman empire. Public education ceased; libraries vanished because of loss of financial support and public indifference; booksellers closed up shop; knowledge of Greek generally died out; the Latin language of the Western empire broke up into the early forms of the Romance languages; the public became generally illiterate. Even for those few who could read, writing materials became increasingly scarce and expensive. Papyrus continued to be manufactured in Egypt, but with the decline in trade and the impoverishment of the Western Europeans, its availability became restricted, and its cost increased considerably.[230] Four centuries passed before things began to pick up a bit in the West.

- In the Eastern Roman Empire, astrology survived at a low ebb despite some opposition from the Church. Visits from Arabian book collectors in the 8th and 9th centuries may have sparked some interest in astrology and the other sciences. And in the 10th century Greek translations of Arabic books began to be made. By the year 1000, astrology had begun to revive a little. Astrologers sought out old books on astrology and made copies or excerpts of them. For the first time in many centuries some astrological books and tables became available. Thus revived, interest in astrology continued to increase slowly until it entered a period of vigorous revival in the 14th century.

The libraries of Constantinople and other cities in the Greek-speaking East had originally contained a fairly good selection of astrological and astronomical texts. But much was later lost due to accident, neglect, and the sacking of Constantinople and other cities by the Crusaders in 1204 and by the Turks in 1453. The upsurge of interest in Greek literature and culture that began in Italy in the 14th century and was in full tide in the 15th century came just in time to

---

[230]The only available writing materials were papyrus, which was manufactured exclusively in Egypt, and vellum, which was very expensive. But Egypt fell into Muslim hands in the 7th century, which caused a disruption in trade with Christian Europe. Papyrus sheets undoubtedly became difficult to obtain and very expensive. Paper as we know it was a Chinese invention that became known to the Arabs in the 8th century. But its use was restricted initially to the Arab world (which included southern Spain). The lack of affordable writing material must certainly have contributed to the low level of literacy in Christian Europe during the Dark Ages.

permit Westerners to acquire some Greek books before they were lost forever. Much of the surviving Greek literature owes its present-day existence to the Medici Family and the other Italian book collectors.

The Third Period

Medieval Astrology

Arabian Astrology

In the 8th century the Arabs[1] developed a thirst for knowledge. They became aware that the Byzantines, Persians, and Hindus knew things that they did not—particularly the Byzantines. They invited learned foreigners to come to Islamic territory and especially to Baghdad. They also sent emissaries into the other countries to obtain books, while at home they eventually set up both private and government bureaus to translate foreign books into Arabic.

Among the books they acquired in this way were books on astrology and astronomy. It must be remembered that while much of the classical Greek literature on all subjects had already been lost by the 8th century, a fair amount still remained—much more than remained by the 15th century when the Medici and other (mostly) Italians frenziedly gathered up a selection of what little was left and brought it back to Italy before the Turks sacked Constantinople and the other Greek cities and destroyed most of what remained. (Remember that the loutish knights of the Fourth Crusade had sacked Constantinople in 1204 and undoubtedly destroyed a great deal of the ancient literature that was still extant at that time.)

The earliest important astrologer among the Arabs of whom we have any information was **Nawbakht the Persian** (c.679-777), who was court astrologer to the Caliph al-Mansur (d. 775). He does not seem to have written any books, but history records that he was selected to head up a group of astrologers and astronomers to make the

---

[1]Here and elsewhere I use the term Arabs and Arabian to refer in general to those persons of whatever race who wrote in the Arabic language. Thus, the term Arabian astrologers includes Māshā'allāh, who was a Jew, and Nawbakht, who was a Persian. However, in some cases I have identified either an individual's race or nationality.

election[2] for the refounding of the city of Baghdad on 31 July 762 at about 2 PM (Sagittarius is rising in the election chart). One of his assistants was the young Jewish astrologer Māshā'allāh (see below). Nawbakht retired some years before his death and was succeeded as court astrologer by his son **Abū Sahl ibn Nawbakht** (d. 786), one of whose sons, **Abū Sahl al-Fadl ibn Nawbakht** (c.735-c.815), was court astrologer to the Caliph Hārūn al-Rashîd (reigned 786-809) and supervisor of the royal library. He wrote at least seven books on astrology, but only fragments of them remain. Two of his grandsons were court astrologers to the Caliphs al-Ma'mun (813-833), al-Wāthiq (842-847), and al-Mutawakil (847-861). And a sixth generation descendant of Nawbakht the Persian, **Mūsā ibn Nawbakht** (c.840-c.940) was the author of an extensive work on astrological history,[3] following in the footsteps of Albumasar (see below).

Theophilus of Edessa

The first notable astrological writer among the Arabs was a Greek, **Theophilus of Edessa** (c.695-785), who in his old age became court astrologer to the Caliph al-Mahdî (d.785).[4] This account of him appears in the Syriac *Chronicle* of Bar-Hebraeus (1226-1286)[5]:

> Theophilus served the Caliph al-Mahdî, who esteemed him very much because of his superiority in the art of astrology. It is said that one day the Caliph wanted to take a trip into one of his provinces and to take his court with him. The Caliph's wife sent someone to say to Theophilus: "It is you who have advised the Caliph to take this trip, thereby imposing upon us the fatigue and boredom of the journey, which we don't need. I hope therefore that God will make you perish and disappear from this world, so that, rid of you, we may find some peace." Theophilus replied to the servant who had brought him this message: "Return to your

---

[2]See the chart in al-Bîrunî's *The Chronology of Ancient Nations* (London, 1879; repr. Frankfurt-am-Main, 1984), p. 263. Al-Bîrunî says it was Nawbakht, who drew the chart. See also my paper "The Foundation Chart of Baghdad" in *Today's Astrologer* Vol. 65, No. 3 (March 2, 2003): pp. 9-10 and 29.

[3]The Arabic text of his book has recently been edited from the unique MS in the Bibliothèque Nationale in Paris, translated into Spanish, and provided with a learned preface by Ana Labarta, *Al-Kitāb al-Kāmil/Horóscopos históricos* (Madrid: Instituto Hispano-Árabe de Cultura, 1982).

[4]See the discussion by David Pingree in the *Oxford Dictionary of Byzantium* (New York: Oxford University Press, 1991. 3 vols.). The notes that follow are mainly taken from that source, but I have revised some of the book titles and added a note from CCAG V.1, p. 230.

[5]CCAG V.1, p. 230 n.5, which contains a French translation by Rubens Duval of the original Syriac.

mistress and say to her: 'It is not I who have advised the king to take this trip; he travels when it pleases him to do so. As for the curse that you have cast upon me for God to hasten my death, the decision about it has already been taken and affirmed by God; I shall die soon; but do not suppose that I shall have died so that your prayer might be fulfilled; it is the will of my Creator that will accomplish it. But you, O Queen, I say to you: "Prepare a lot of dust for yourself; and when you learn that I am dead, pile all that dust on your head." When the Queen had heard these words, she was seized with a great fear, and she wondered apprehensively what the result would be. A little while afterward, Theophilus died and twenty days after him the Caliph al-Mahdî also died. That which Theophilus had determined came to pass.

Theophilus wrote four treatises on astrology in Greek (some excerpts from which are edited in the CCAG):

> *Works on Elections for Wars and Campaigns and Sovereignty* addressed to his son Deucalion.

This is a work on military astrology, partially based on Indian astrology; it is the only medieval Greek astrological treatise devoted entirely to military astrology. It begins like this:[6]

> The nature of the stars is specific, O most excellent Deucalion; their energy does not have a single dwelling-place but a variegated one and diverse [characteristics] suitable for every type of astrological influence, and each one of these things is especially made known in one generality for the active [planet] with regard to the disposition and characteristic emphasis alloted to it, for example in wars Mars and in speech Mercury, and in agricultural matters Saturn, and in matters of love Venus; for while these have [their nature] thus, not only does Mars activate war, but Saturn also accomplishes the ruin of kings and the taking of cities, as it is found in the mundane astrological influences. But Mars also makes arsons and pestilential sicknesses and droughts and scarcities of fruits. Similarly too, Mercury [makes] armed robberies and disorders and irregularities in life, or else it is called "the messenger," and it awards peace.

> Similarly too, in genethliacal astrological influences, we find the stars acting one way and another and signifying

---

[6]The Introduction is edited by F.Cumont in CCAG V.1, pp. 233-234.

in accordance with their configurations and their alterna-
tions of houses—[sometimes] indeed the malefics acting as
benefics and the benefics being inactive, but still the astrological influences are activated in accordance with the
chart and the determination of their individual degrees.
And in view of this, the wise men of astrology made use of
the stars by a mixture of their natures—not only distin-
guishing [them] in their most individual [significances]
and according to [the nature of] each but also in those
[significances] that are the most general and specialized—for example, about war; and they used all the stars
and also the lights for working with a single chart.

And I kept this in mind because I know that military
methods are seldom found in [the books of] the ancients,
other than that from the mundane astrological influences
[we can see that] there is going to be war and captivity in
this or that land, neglecting of course the more particular
things, and in particular the expeditions or counter-expedi-
tions that are made, [the rise of] tyrants, and those actions
that are done in season and are provoked, I say, by two armies when they are encamped facing and attacking each
other, of which it was difficult to find accurate day-by-day
accounts in the books of the ancients.

And, having turned my mind to this, I thought it necessary to make a change and to draw from the genethliacal
and horary systems some elections for war that have plausi-
bility together with the truth, since I had also really had the
proof of these in many [instances]—having been forced, as
you knew, by those ruling at that time to take these things in
hand, at the time when we made the expedition with them
into the eastern regions in the country of Margiane,[7] and
[there] we suffered successive military calamities, with
much cold and an inclement winter, as well as with much
fear and countless controversies.

But, while arranging these elections into some physical
conformity of order, I have neglected none of the things
that are needed and required in connection with military affairs, and I have composed a book entirely for this [pur-
pose], having the military elections along with those for

---

[7]The Greek name for Khorāsān (today a province of NE Iran). Cumont thinks
this campaign probably took place in the winter of 757-758, when the local ruler
raised an insurrection, and troops were sent by the Caliph al-Mansūr to put down
the rebellion.

information about tyrants and cities that are being besieged and such like.

But it is necessary [that] you approach this treatise with great care and diligence, and by [using] the meager theory make for yourself a combination of the influences of the signs and the stars, I mean of the planets and the fixed stars, and the luminaries, and the lots that are there and their rulers, and you will not err, if God is willing.

A "second edition" of this work contained matter ascribed to Zoroaster and Julian of Laodicea in Chapters 24-41; a recension of that edition was made about the year 1000 and still another by the Byzantine astrologer John Abramius in the late 14th century, when Eleutherius Eleus incorporated excerpts from this work in the compendium he issued under the name Palchus (see below).

Astrological Effects.
addressed to his son Deucalion.

It contains some Indian astrological material and is also partly dependent on Rhetorius's compendium of astrology.

Various [Kinds of] Elections.

A treatise on elections related to the matters ruled by each of the 12 houses. It depends mainly on Dorotheus and Hephaestio of Thebes.

Collection on Cosmic Beginnings.

This is a treatise on mundane astrology that explains how to make annual and monthly predictions. It contains a section that discusses the beginning of the year according to the Egyptians, Greeks, Persians, and Arabs.

These books have been preserved more or less intact, along with fragments of their Arabic versions. Some selections from the Greek texts have been published in the CCAG.[8] We may hope for critical editions of the texts by David Pingree.

Indian Astrologers at Baghdad

During the last half of the 8th century a number of Indian astrologers visited the court at Baghdad bringing with them Hindu books on astronomy and astrology. The best known of these was **Kankah**, who came to Baghdad during the reign of the Caliph al-Ma'mūn (754-775). Here is what al-Nadîm[9] says about him and a few of the other Indian scholars:

Kankah the Indian

---

[8]See CCAG, vols. 1, 4, 5.1, 8.1, 11.1.
[9]Muhammad ibn Ishaq al-Nadîm lived in Baghdad in the latter years of the 10th century. He was the head of a bookselling establishment and compiled what

Among his books there were:
Calculations for Nativities, about periods of time
Secrets of Nativities
Conjunctions, a large book
Conjunctions, a small book.

Judar the Indian
Among his books there was *Nativities*, in Arabic.

Sanjahil the Indian
Among his books there was *Secrets of the Questions*.

Naq (Nahaq) the Indian
Among his books there was *Nativities*, a large book.

With the Indian astrologers came their astronomical theories and tables, which were based upon the false concepts of a grand conjunction at some remote epoch and of an integer number of revolutions of the planets in a certain time period. Furthermore, unlike Ptolemy's tables, the Indian tables gave positions in a fixed zodiac. These principles had already passed to the Persians two centuries earlier. The result was a set of tables, such as the *Zīj al-Shāh* or *Tables of the King*, which were similar but not identical to the Indian tables. Both Māshā'allāh and Albumasar utilized these or similar tables (Albumasar is said to have constructed a set of his own based on a 360,000 year time period) in preparing their "astrological World histories." Fortunately, these aberrations were confined to a few Arabian astrologers.

Nevertheless, from the Indian astrologers listed above (and perhaps from a few others) a small amount of Indian astrology entered into Arabian astrology. But their greatest contribution was to make known to the Arabs the marvelous Indian invention of special signs for the numerals—what we call *Arabic* numerals because it was through Arabic writings that Western Europeans became aware of them. Prior to this, the Arabs, like the Greeks, had used the numerical values assigned to the letters of the alphabet, so that the Arabic letter *dal*, like the Greek letter *delta*, had to serve not only as the letter *d* but also as the numeral *4*. Better still, the Indians had invented a symbol for zero, which was lacking in the Arabic and Greek alpha-numerals.

Confusing as it must have been, with Persian and Indian influences intermingling in the Greek mainstream, the hundred and fifty year period from about 775 to 925 was the golden age of Arabian astrology. Its leading figures were:

---

amounts to a general catalogue of the books that were available in the Arabic language in his day. As mentioned in an earlier note, this extremely valuable book has been translated into English as The Fihrist of al-Nadîm. The current reference is to Fihrist, vol. 2, pp. 644-645.

Māshā'allāh

Māshā'allāh (c.740-c.815), known in the West as **Messahalla**, was a Jew from Basra who was the leading astrologer of the late 8th century. His original name was either Jethro or Manasseh (the authorities differ); Māshā'allāh is an Arabic phrase that means 'what has God done'. As a young man he participated in the founding of Baghdad. Māshā'allāh was the author of more than two dozen astrological treatises that were considered to be authoritative by both the Arabs and the Western Europeans.[10] Among his books were *The Revolution of the Years of Nativities* [Solar Returns], *The Revolutions of the Years of the World* [Aries Ingresses], *Conjunctions, Letter on Eclipses, Reception of the Planets or Interrogations*, and a book on *The Construction and Use of the Astrolabe*. Two lists of his known works have been published.[11] There is an English translation of the four chapters of Māshā'allāh's *Book of Nativities*[12] and a modern Spanish translation of the books on *The Revolutions of the Years of the World, Conjunctions*, and *Reception of the Planets or Interrogations.*[13] Here is an extract from the latter work:

> You have to know that reception is formed through the exaltations and the domiciles, but either way, it is the same thing: for example, if any one of the seven planets is found in the exaltation of another or in its domicile, and the same thing if it unites with another by important aspects; or if they are both in one sign, and one of them is in the exaltation of the other in union with it, when it unites itself with it

---

[10]One of his short works is available in English—see Kennedy, E.S. & Pingree, David, *The Astrological History of Māshā'allāh* (Cambridge, Mass.: Harvard University Press, 1971).

[11]*See* Lynn Thorndike, "The Latin Translations of the Astrological Works by Messahala" in *Osiris* xii (1956): 49-72; and Pingree's article on Māshā'allāh in the *Dictionary of Scientific Biography*. No. 15 in Pingree's list is the *Kitāb tahwīl sinī al-mawālīd* or *Book of the Revolution of the Years of Nativities*. Pingreee says the Arabic text is lost, but it is partly preserved in the work of a later writer. It seems likely to me that this book and *The Revolutions of the Years of the World* may have contained the earliest instructions on how to cast and interpret what are now called "Solar Returns" and "Aries Ingresses." The invention of these two techniques may therefore be credited to Māshā'allāh, although it is possible that he found them in the now lost books of some earlier writer or writers.

[12]In Appendix 2 of *Abu 'Ali al-Khayyat: The Judgments of Nativities*, trans. by James H. Holden (Tempe, Az.: A.F.A. Inc., 1988), pp. 86-91.

[13]Translated by Demetrio Santos in *Textos astrológicos medievales* (Madrid: Editorial Barath, 1981) in two parts (Part 1: Māshā'allāh; Part 2: Ibn Ezra). Māshā'allāh's book contains six horary charts, five from the year 791 and one from 794 (see the list in Neugebauer & Van Hoesen, *Greek Horoscopes*, p. 172. One of these, the chart for 11 April 791 is quoted by Guido Bonatti in *Treatise* 6, Sixth House, Chapter 4.

by body (Conjunction).

For example, Saturn in 20° Aries and Mars in 15° Aries; in this case, Mars unites with Saturn by body, and Mars receives Saturn in its domicile, but the latter is not in reception with Mars.

This occurs when there is not any planet in notable aspect that is found closer to the conjunction with Saturn, that is, with a value of a few degrees before Mars; then the true union is in the same degree, as well in conjunction as in aspect.

Another example is of connection and reception: when Saturn was in 20° Aries, and Mars in 10° Capricorn, and none of the other planets is closer to Mars in union with Saturn, that is within a few degrees. If Mars is united with Saturn within a degree, in such case they are found to be in mutual reception by domicile, since Mars receives Saturn because it is in its domicile, and Saturn receives Mars because it is also in its domicile.

Also, for the same reason, the exaltation is like the domicile: but the exaltation is of greater importance in the kingdom; i.e. if the question is about the king [because] the lord of the exaltation is stronger than that of the domicile. Hence, when the Sun is in 10° Aries and Mars in 10° Capricorn, the Sun is united to Mars, and Mars receives the Sun because it is in its domicile; but the Sun does not receive Mars because it is not in its domicile. Likewise, each of the other planets can be united to its companion by domicile or by exaltation, by important aspect, or by being in the same sign, and if it projects or sends its disposition and the former receives it over the one that sends it, the action [of the question] takes place, by the will of God. [And in the present example] the Sun in this aspect does not receive Mars because it is not found in its domicile or exaltation, but the same Mars does receive the Sun that is in its domicile.[14]

If the Sun were in 1° Libra and Saturn in 25° Aries, and no other planet were in Aries nor in any aspect closer than the Sun with relation to Saturn, and Saturn does not leave

---

[14]Note by Demetrio Santos: "The exaltation or the reception by domicile, or whatever, requires, to be effective, that an aspect or union be formed between the planets. The planets can be in good or evil signs, in reception or not, but only when the planets located there activate their connection by forming aspects is the deed realized."

Aries before the Sun unites with it in the same degree, then when the Sun exactly aspects Saturn, the Sun receives Saturn, and Saturn receives the Sun. Therefore, each one of them receives its companion in that place by exaltation. And if it is found in opposition and square, [it signifies] an evil error, difficulty, worry, and disappointment; and in trine or sextile, rapidity and sharpness. And when the Sun unites with Saturn and Saturn receives the Sun, and the same was received by the Sun, that is in its domicile or exaltation, they will balance and will realize the action by the will of God.[15]

Masha'allah was familiar with Persian and Indian astrology and is said to have used the Persian *Zīj al-Shāh* mentioned above, a set of astronomical tables compiled for Shah Khusrau Anushirwan in the 6th century. These were based on an earlier Indian set and therefore were referred to a fixed zodiac. A later summary of his book *On Conjunctions, Religions, and Peoples* has been published, translated into English by E.S. Kennedy, and provided with an extensive commentary by David Pingree. It is an outline of World History (from the Middle Eastern point of view) on a framework of Aries Ingress charts (referred to a fixed zodiac) and Jupiter-Saturn conjunctions.[16]

In Masha'allah's later years an Arabic translation of Dorotheus's *Pentateuch* became available to him, and he used it as a basis for his *Book of Nativities.*[17] His best known pupil was Abū ʿAlī al-Khayyāt (see below).

Omar Tiberiades

Abū Hafs ʿUmar ibn al-Farrukhān al-Tabarî (d.c.815), known as **Omar Tiberiades**, was of Persian descent. Around the year 800 he translated the Pahlavi version of Dorotheus's *Pentateuch* into Arabic.[18] Pingree says he completed a paraphrase of Ptolemy's *Tetrabiblos* in the

---

[15]Translated from the Spanish version of Demetrio Santos, *Textos astrológicos medievales*, Book I, pp. 14-15.

[16]Kennedy, E.S., and Pingree, David, *The Astrological History of Māshā'allāh*. Also, see the entry for Albumasar below. Those who wish to study these elaborate astrological historical schemes can consult the books cited (including the *Kitāb al-Kāmil* by Mūsā ibn Nawbakht mentioned above).

[17]A short tract (No. 14 in his list) edited by Pingree from Paris MS 7324. His edition is printed in Appendix 3 to *The Astrological History of Masha'allah* cited above. The text (but not the comments on the example horoscopes) is translated into English by Holden as mentioned above. See Holden's translation for his comments on the charts.

[18]See p. XIV of the Preface to David Pingree's edition of the Arabic version of Dorotheus, *Dorothei Sidonii Carmen astrologicum* (Leipzig: B.G. Teubner, 1976).

summer of 812, presumably from a Pahlavi version.[19] His *Book on Nativities* was translated into Latin by John of Seville as *De nativitatibus secundum Omar* (Venice: J.B. Sessa, 1503; etc.). Not surprisingly, it relies heavily on Dorotheus. This book was often quoted by Western astrologers.

Albohali

Abū ʿAlî al-Khayyāt (c.770-c.835), known as **Albohali**, was a pupil of Māshāʾallāh and the author of ten or more books on astrology.[20] His work on natal astrology was strongly influenced by Dorotheus's *Pentateuch*, which was available to him in an Arabic translation. Albohali's book contains three example horoscopes from the *Pentateuch* and seven more from some unidentified Greek source with charts of the 4th and 5th centuries (one of which is also found in Rhetorius). See James H. Holden, *Abu ʿAli al-Khayyat The Judgments of Nativities* (Tempe, Az.: AFA Inc., 1988), an English translation of the 1546 Nürnberg edition by Joachim Heller of John of Seville's 12th century Latin translation. Here is an extract from Albohali's book:

Chapter 35. Friends.

Decide the condition of friends from the 11th house and its lord, and from the planets that you find in it, and from Venus, and from the Part of Friends.[21] If most of these are fortunes, it signifies that the native will have many friends and companions, and especially if there is an application between the lord of the 11th and the lord of the ASC. And if you find fortunes in the 11th sign,[22] or in square or opposite aspect to it,[23] it signifies that the native will have many friends and associates, and that they will be fortunate. And

---

[19]See David Pingree's article on Omar in the *Dictionary of Scientific Biography*. The article contains a verified list of the books written by Omar. (Pingree says the lists of Omar's works and those of his son Abū Bakr Muhammad ibn ʿUmar given in al-Nadîm's *Fihrist* are confused.)

[20]See the list in the *Fihrist*, vol. 2, p. 655.

[21]Albumasar, al-Bîrûnî, Leopold of Austria, and Guido Bonatti give the formula Mercury - Moon + ASC by day and by night. (Ibn Ezra gets it backwards by mistake.) This part also appears in the list given in the oldest MS of Heliodorus's *Commentary on Paul*, but it says to reverse it by night. However, the same MS in a different place contains a scholium on Hephaestio of Thebes which says that in the fourth book [of the *Pentateuch*] of Dorotheus he takes the Lot of Friendship with the same formula 'by day and by night', which agrees with Albumasar.

[22]Albohali used the Sign-House system of houses, so the 11th sign = the 11th house.

[23]Note that these are aspects to the 11th sign itself whether there are planets in it or not. This was a common procedure of the Greek astrologers (and following them, the Arabs), but one usually ignored by modern astrologers.

if you find evil [planets] in it, or in square or opposite aspect to it, it signifies few friends and associates and that their assets will be scanty.

And if the planet that has the most dignities in the house of friends is Saturn, it signifies that most of his friends will be old men, slaves, and captives. But if it is Jupiter, many of them will be nobles and rich people of great worth and repute. And if it is Mars, most of them will be [military] leaders and princes and warlike men. But if it is the Sun, most of them will be [military] leaders and princes, kings, and nobles. But if [it is] Venus, they will be women and effeminate men. But if it is Mercury, they will mostly be writers and businessmen and wise men and artisans. But if it is the Moon, most of his friends will be nobles, but many [others] will be commoners. And so every star signifies according to its own nature; and according to its strength and fortunate or unfortunate [condition], the native will have advantage or disadvantage.

Besides all this, look at the lord of the ASC and the lord of the 11th, and the application that is between them and their mutual reception, and how much one of them makes the other fortunate or unfortunate, and their places in the circle. For if they are in mobile signs, it signifies that the native's friends will seldom be constant in their attitude towards him. But if [they are] in common signs, it indicates that sometimes there will be friendship and at other times it will break up. But if they are both in fixed signs, it signifies firm and lasting friendship of the friends towards the native.

But where the lord of the ASC impedites the lord of the 11th, the friends will suffer some impediment from the native. But if the lord of the 11th impedites the lord of the ASC, the native will receive some harm from his friends. And if each of them makes the other fortunate, the friends and the native will have mutual good and benefit among themselves. But if the lord of the 11th does not aspect his own house and Venus does not aspect the lord of her domicile, and the lord of the Part of Friends [does] not [aspect] the Part, it signifies that the native will be odious to men, nor will he delight in their company, being a lover of solitude. But when the house of friends is made fortunate and is essentially good, it signifies good circumstances and good fortune for the friends. [But] if it is made unfortunate, conversely it threatens them with bad luck and poverty.

Zahel

Sahl ibn Bishr (1st half of the 9th cent.), another Jew, was a master of horary astrology. He is very often cited by later astrologers as **Zael** or **Zahel**. The Latin versions of his five short treatises, *Introduction to Astrology*, *The 50 Precepts*, *Judgments of Questions*, *Elections*, and *The Book of Times* appear to be the principal medieval source of rules for Horary Astrology and Elections.[24] There is a modern Spanish translation by Demetrio Santos.[25]

The first treatise contains a chapter entitled "The 16 Modes that Signify the Accomplishment or Destruction [of the Question]." These are the particular aspects or configurations that give the necessary indications in horary astrology. They are: Perfection, Deterioration, Conjunction, Separation, Translation [of Light], Collection, Prohibition, Reception, Non-Reception, Void of Course, Return, Giving Virtue, Giving Disposition, Fortitude, Debility, and Conditions of the Moon. This is followed by separate chapters defining each of these modes in detail.

Guido Bonatti lists these modes (along with their badly corrupted Arabic names) in the 4th of his "146 Considerations."[26] Ibn Ezra discusses some of them in detail in Chapter 7 of *The Beginning of Wisdom*. And William Lilly explains those that he considers most important: Application, Separation, Prohibition (and Refrenation), Translation of Light, Reception, Void of Course, Frustration, Hayz, Combust, and Collection.[27]

The second treatise contains *The 50 Precepts* [of Horary Astrology], of which the first three are these:[28]

> First Chapter. Know that the significator, which is the Moon, whose circle is nearer the earth than those of the other planets, more than all the other planets is the one most like the things of the earth. Do you not see that a man begins by being small and then increases until he attains full growth? The Moon does the same thing. Therefore, take it to have the signification of all things, because its good state is the good state of everything, and its bad state is the bad state of everything. And it strikes, that is it commits, its disposition to that one on which it casts its rays, and to that one of the planets to which it is joined, and it sends its light to that same planet; and that planet is termed the receiver of

---

[24]First printed together by Bonatus Locatellus at Venice in 1493/1494 along with books of five other astrological authors (Abū Bakr, Bethem, Hermes, Māshā'allāh, and Rāzî).

[25]*Textos astrológicos Zahel-Hermes-Bethen-Almanzor* (Collección Mirach).

[26] He also uses one of Zahel's charts (set for 5 July 824) as an example in *Treatise* 6, First House, Chapt. 4.

[27]*Christian Astrology*, pp. 107 ff.

[28]Translated from my unpublished edition of the Latin version.

the disposition because it receives that which was committed to it. Therefore, the Moon itself is the informer of these planets; and it pacifies them, and it carries from some of them to others.

Second. The evil planets signify a bad state and evil on account of excess or superfluity. The force of cold or heat in those things that are overcoming and impediting. But if there is a planet in the domicile of a malefic or in its exaltation, it receives it and restrains its evil from it. Or if there is an aspect of the malefics by trine or by sextile aspect, it is restrained, and by the fact that it is an aspect of friendship without any enmity to fortune; but because they are of a temperate nature and an equable configuration—that is, because they are tempered by heat and cold—they always perform and advance [the matter], whether they receive another planet or not. But reception between these is more useful and better.

Third. The stars have two modes: namely good and evil. Wherever, therefore, you see malefics, i.e. evil planets, pronounce evil; and wherever you see the fortunes, pronounce good.

Albumasar

Of all the Arabic writers on astrology, the most imposing is **Ja`far ibn Muhammad Abū Ma`shar al-Balkhî** (c.787-886), known in the West as **Albumasar**. He began his career as a student of the Hadîth or traditions of the Prophet Muhammad, but in his 30's or 40's he gave that up and turned his attention to astrology (see the entry for al-Kindî). Thereafter, he became famous not only as the leading authority on astrology but also as a court astrologer and a professional astrologer. His knowledge of the subject was encyclopedic. Some fifty books are credited to him,[29] of which the best known are *The Great Conjunctions* and *The Great Introduction*. The *Great Introduction* or the *Introductorius maior* was translated by John of Seville—his translation was never printed but is preserved in numerous MSS. An inferior translation by Hermann of Carinthia was published by Erhard Ratdolt at Augsburg in 1485 and again in 1489. The *Great Introduction* is exactly what its title implies—an elaborate and comprehensive treatise of astrology. *The Great Conjunctions*, or *De coniunctionibus*, translated by John of Seville, ed. by Johannes Angelus (Augsburg: Erhard Ratdolt, 1489) is an elaborate treatise on mundane astrology with special reference to the conjunctions of Saturn and Jupiter.

---

[29]See the detailed list by David Pingree in his article on Abū Ma`shar in the *Dictionary of Scientific Biography*.

Book 1, Chapter 3 discusses the conjunctions that signify the advent of prophets or violent men [tyrants] and their characteristics. A short extract from it will give some idea of the great depth of detail to be found throughout the work:

> The knowledge of their garments is received from the planet which was in the tenth house from the ruler of the ASC at the time of the mutation[30] and the conjunction. But if there was no planet in the tenth, the planet is accepted that is the ruler of the tenth house from the ASC. If Saturn is the significator, it signifies that the greater part of the clothing of the citizens of that sect will be black clothes, sc. of rough and dirty hair. And if it is Jupiter, the clothing will be that of religious persons, such as wool for example, and such like. And if it is Mars, the clothing will be colored with red and pale shades. And if it is the Sun, silk clothing. And if it is Venus, clean clothing and similar to that of women. And if it is Mercury, the clothing will be decorated with embroidery. And if it is the Moon, the clothing will be white and such like.

> And the knowledge of their mounts is received from the planet which is in the fourth [house] from the ruler of the ASC at the time of the mutation conjunction. But if there is no planet in the fourth from it, the ruler of the fourth [house] from the ASC will be the significator. And if it is Saturn, it signifies that the greater part of the mounts of that sect will be broken-down horses; and if it is the Sun, [fine] horses; and if it is Mercury, asses; and if it is Venus, camels; and if it is the Moon, bulls and cows.

Albumasar's pupil and assistant **Sa`îd Shādhān** wrote a lengthy account of his master's sayings and some of his interesting cases. It is preserved in Arabic and in Greek and Latin versions (the Latin is only a short extract). Thorndike examined the Latin version and wrote an interesting article on it.[31] He cites several interesting anecdotes, of which the following are samples:

> Said Albumasar: Once with some travelers I went to Baldac [Baghdad] and I stayed with a friend of mine who knew a little astronomy [astrology], and he asked me how the Moon would be the next day, and I said, "In quartile aspect with Mars." And he said to me, "Then don't you

---

[30]A mutation occurs when the conjunctions of Jupiter and Saturn change from one triplicity to another, which occurs every 238 years.

[31]"Albumasar in Sadan" in *Isis* 45, Pt. 1 (May 1954):22-32.

leave''; and I said to him, "I have no intention of departing on such a day, but the other passengers [travelers] won't listen to us." He said, "Let's test them." So I said to them, "Tomorrow is an unfavorable day, wait, and I'll feed your animals." They would not acquiesce, so I let them go and stayed on with my friend. When they would be leaving, I observed the horoscope [ASC] and it was Taurus and Mars in it. And the Moon was in Leo in quartile aspect to Mars. I said to them, "For God's sake don't go at this hour," but they laughed at me and went off. I said to my friend, "I'm sorry for those senseless men." And we sat down and ate and drank. While we were still drinking, there came in some of the company who had been saved. For they had fallen among thieves and some were slain, others wounded, and the thieves made off with whatever they carried. Moreover, those who had escaped came at me with sticks and stones, saying, "These things happened because of your superstition, in order to confirm what you said." And I barely escaped. And then and there I swore that I would never discuss the science of astronomy [astrology] with the man in the street.

Said Albumasar, "We were with the army of the Cumans and many of us astronomers [astrologers] were sitting in a tent and someone was approaching. One of the astronomers [astrologers] said, 'Let's see what he is going to say.' So we observed the ascendant which was Sagittarius in the terms of Mercury. And the Moon was there at that hour void of course. And I said, 'He is full of idle talk and a useless fellow.' And we questioned him when he arrived and he talked a lot of nonsense. And all the astronomers [astrologers] marvelled at my great experience.

"Aposaites [Abu Sa`îd Shādhān] said that, although [his master] Albumasar was very rational and supreme in science, whenever the moon was diametrically opposite to the Sun, he fell down and shook. He had no record of his nativity[32] but had made a universal interrogation. Virgo was the horoscope [ASC] of the interrogation, while the Moon was in Scorpio diametrically opposite to the Sun and configured with Mars. And such a figure signified epilepsy. He had the custom of having fruit and anything he liked set be-

---

[32]This would seem to negate Pingree's contention that the horoscope in Book 3, Chapter 1, of Albumasar's *The Revolutions of Nativities*, which is set for 10 August 787, is that of Albumasar himself.

fore him, and ate once a day and drank wine for the rest of the day, and he had a marvelous thirst. "He told me, 'If I could stop drinking wine for one year, I would be cured of epilepsy.'"

Thorndike cites another anecdote of Albumasar that was recorded by the Arabic historian Ibn Khallikān (13th century): "[Albumasar] was singularly fortunate in his divinations," and he gives this example. "An official who had gone into hiding to escape arrest and who knew that the prince would ask Albumasar to discover his place of retreat, tried to hamper the investigation by sitting for days on a golden mortar placed in a vessel which contained blood. Albumasar, on consulting the stars, reported that the fugitive was on a mountain of gold in a sea of blood, but that he did not know of any such place in the world, and the prince was able to lure the official from his hiding-place only by a promise of amnesty. When the official returned and told of the trick he had employed, the prince marveled both at the artifice and the skill of Abû'l-Mashar in making the discovery."[33]

One of Albumasar's books which is unfortunately lost was the *Kitāb al-uluf* or *Book of the Thousands*. This book contained Albumasar's outline of World History on a framework of Aries Ingresses and conjunctions, but also with an elaborate system of profections.[34] Pingree has been able to restore a substantial portion of this work from citations by later Arabic writers. In his book *The Thousands of Abū Ma`shar* (London: The Warburg Institute, 1968), he discusses Albumasar's theory in great detail. This gives us an interesting look at the developed form of this branch of mundane astrology. An earlier and somewhat different version is found in a book by Ibn Hibinta that summarizes a lost work of Māshā'allāh, *On Conjunctions, Religions, and Peoples*.[35] See also a later treatment in the *Kitāb al-Kāmil* by Mūsā ibn Nawbakht (see above).

A book of more general interest is Albumasar's short book, *Flores astrologie* or *Liber florum*, 'The Flowers of Astrology' or 'The Book of Flowers', which was also translated by John of Seville (Augsburg: Erhard Ratdolt, 1488. repr. 1489 and 1495). It is an anthology (whence the title) of Albumasar's larger works on mundane astrology with special reference to the "Revolutions of the Years of the World" or Aries In-

---

[33]*Ibn Khallikan's Biographical Dictionary*, English translation by Baron William MacGuckin de Slane, (Paris, 1842-1843. 4 vols.), vol. 1, p. 325.

[34]These are generally unknown to modern astrologers and are referred to by academic scholars by their Arabic or Persian names: The Tasyîrât (four profections moving at $1°$ per thousand years, per 100 years, per 10 years, and per year respectively); the Intihā'āt (four profections moving at 1 *sign* per year period); and the Fardārāt, a mixed bag of profections related to planets and signs. See David Pingree, *The Thousands of Abu Ma`shar*, pp. 59ff, for details.

[35]See the book by E.S. Kennedy and David Pingree, *The Astrological History of Māshā'allāh*. (Cambridge, Mass.: Harvard University Press, 1971).

gresses[36] as modern astrologers call them—that is, charts set for the moment when the Sun enters the sign Aries. This book was very popular in the late Medieval and Renaissance periods. There is an unpublished translation by James H. Holden, *The Book of Flowers* (Dallas: The Translator, 1985, privately circulated). It begins as follows:

[Chapt. 1. Finding the Lord of the Year.]

Albumasar said: First, you ought to know the lord of the year; and the knowledge of this thing is known from the hour of the entrance of the Sun into the first minute of the sign Aries. Know, then, the ASC in that same hour as most certainly as you will be able; verify the cusps of the twelve houses of heaven because error falls in this if it is neglected. And when you have done this, look at the lord of the ASC along with the rest of the planets—the one then who has more strength from the testimonies of the circles of the angles.

And whichever planet you have found in the ASC, the 10th, the 7th, or the 4th angle, afterwards the 11th, the 9th, [and] finally the 5th. And you shall not prefer the MC to the ASC, nor the 5th house to the 9th, but let it be done according to the aforesaid scheme. And if you have found a planet in the ASC, you shall not seek another one of those which were in the houses of the planets. Similarly, if there was no planet in the ASC, and there was one in the MC, you should not look at the other houses of the planets. Similarly, if there was no planet in the MC, but [there was one] in the seventh [house], you should not look at the other houses. Similarly, if not in the seventh, but in the fourth, you shall not pay attention to the other houses of the planets. And the one which you have found in these houses, that one will be the dispositor of the year if he has any dignity, sc. of domicile, or exaltation, triplicity, terms, or face. But if there is in the ASC a planet that has no dignity in it, and there is in the MC having [dignity of] terms and face, [then] because it has doubled its dignity, that is the one that is sought, and you shall not seek another. And if there is after them a planet in the seventh which has [the dignities of] domicile, exaltation, terms, triplicity, or face, [then] that is the one sought.[37]

---

[36]An Aries Ingress is obviously a horary chart set for a time certain, for which the question is, "What sort of year will it be for the people, animals, and crops in this particular location?"

[37]Presumably in the case where it has three or more dignities, while the one in the MC has only two.

Another of Albumasar's books is a general treatise on the *Revolutions of Nativities* or what are now called solar returns. The Arabic text is preserved, as is a Byzantine Greek translation[38] and a Latin translation made from the Greek.[39] Still another book of his with a similar title but a different text is known in Latin; it begins, *Omne tempus breve est operandi.*[40] These would seem to be the oldest books on solar returns known in the West. The latter work begins thus:

All time for working is short, and the work of [making] the revolution of years is drawn out. It is necessary for us to copy out a few things from many, so that from the fruit of so great a work we may not slight everything negligently. And before everything else it must be stated what utility we can gain from the revolution of years or what reason there is to revolve the years, since in the ASC of the nativity there is signified everything that is going to happen to the native, as some of those who argue against revolutions have said. To which the reply is that the wisdom of the philosophers testifies to the fact that the signification of human events cannot be understood from a single significator, but [rather] from two or more because the testimony of one thing in so great a matter cannot suffice; therefore, according to the authority of the greater [philosophers], we ought to revolve the years because in the revolution of years there are planets in other places in which they were not [found] in the nativity; and it is necessary that their significations in the figure be commingled with the signification of the revolution, so that both the quantity and the quality of the accident[41] may appear more openly.

For example, if a planet in the nativity signifies that anything good or evil will happen in the future, the quantity of it cannot be known in any particular year except through

---

[38]Edited by David Pingree, *Albumasaris De revolutionibus nativitatum* (Leipzig: B.G. Teubner, 1968), but the Greek translation covers only Books 1-5 and Book 9, Chapter 7, of the nine books of the Arabic text. Book 3, Chapter 1, contains a horoscope set for 10 August 787, "Someone was born in the 4th clime in a city whose latitude is 36°, and the ASC was Taurus 2 degrees and 54 minutes, etc." Since this is close to the year Albumasar was born, Pingree thinks it is his horoscope. But see the remark of Albumasar's disciple Shādhān above, p. 113 n.32.
[39]Falsely attributed to Hermes when it was printed in the 16th century: *Hermetis philosophi de revolutionibus nativitatum libri duo incerto interprete* 'Two Books of Hermes the Philosopher on the Revolutions of Nativities, translator unknown' (Basel: H. Wolf, 1559).
[40]See Lynn Thorndike, HMES 1, p. 651 n.1.
[41]The word "accident" in the older astrological literature simply means "occurrence" or "event."

the revolution because when the years are revolved, if the planets in the revolution signifiy the same thing [as those in the nativity], there will be a great accident in [those] times, either good or evil. but if the planets of the revolution did not signify anything about this, that evil will be happening moderately, i.e. it will be neither entirely good nor entirely evil, for the good is natural, and from its signification natural, but the accident will be evil and [this is] from the signification of that same year.

Again, if the planets of the nativity signified to the native anything of evil in every year, it will happen. And [if] the planets of the revolution signify [something] to the contrary, [then] that natural evil from the natural signification would [actually] be good, and it would [also] be good from the signification of that same year. Of which an example is that if the planets of the nativity signified to the native that in each year the native might acquire wealth, and the planets of the revolution signified the loss of that same wealth, [then the native] will acquire wealth from that same source from which it will be expected and in which he may have trust, so that this would be a natural signification. But losses will happen to him from adversity or [from] men who disturb his acquisition or they will make expenses for him, and so, in some way or other he would lose what he had acquired or he would acquire less.

Again, if the planets of the nativity signified evil, and the planets of the revolution signified good, he would find in that same year loss or evil. But he would find some friends who would restore the loss to him in part and would help him or he would find advice by means of which he might evade those evils. And this would be done because it would not be undertaken and because he had no faith in it. But if there were good signification in both [charts], then he would find many good things in what will be undertaken and in what will not be undertaken, and he would find helpers who would help him and from whom advice would be forthcoming.

Similarly, understand about evil the other way around. And he would find many evils, and there would not be anyone who might help him, and he would not find advice by means of which he might evade this. And, to say it briefly, a single significator will not suffice, just as we have said above, because there is [such a thing as] much good and moderate good, and similarly with evil; and the planets of the nativity signify the native's accidents universally, i.e. those past, those present, and those in the future. And this signification is not sufficient because what it signifies about the future it signifies potentially, but in the revolution it signifies something in actuality because then it signifies only the present [occurrence] of the thing signified, i.e it will signify that particular thing absolutely happening in that same year, distinct namely from other significations. And already [we are able] in the revolution to see more openly and lucidly the quantity and quality of the signification of the nativity, and it should not be passed over that some have said that the revolution of the years is unnecessary and that the sign of the profection would suffice.[42] To which it might be replied that because even though we may look at the sign of the profection, still it is necessary for us to know its house and the house of its ruler in the circle at the time of the revolution, and, according to those houses of the time, their significations. For, just as the Sun, when it has passed through the four seasons of the year, returns to its original place and begins to be renewed another time, so should the accident be renewed, so that through it the strength or debility of the planets may more perfectly be demonstrated at that present time and their significations might be better understood.

Accidents also are due to the houses of the planets through that very book in which the substance of the nativity is equated, and not through a variety of books can they be generated by the judgments of individual actions.[43] For this reason our predecessors established revolutions. And in fact the utility of a revolution is that the astrologer can see in advance what may be proper for the native [to do] in that same year, and he may do that thing or whatever is proper in order to abstain from [doing] it. For example, if someone wishes to travel, the astrologer can look to see whether the planets in that same year signify travels for him and whether he will be fortunate in that or not, and then he

---

[42]The classical Greek astrologers relied on profections (and direction of the ASC degree) and did not use solar returns. Evidently in Albumasar's time some astrologers still followed the older procedure. We can infer from this that solar returns were then a relatively recent invention.

[43]This sentence is not altogether clear. Perhaps some words have fallen out of the text. In any case the word "book" seems to be an error either of translation or of copying.

can travel. But if he sees it otherwise, [then] he can abstain from it.

For all the rich and wise men of the Babylonians, Persians, and Egyptians, as well as the Indians, when they wished to do any particular thing, were always careful to consider their own revolutions, in which if they found the signification to be useful for that thing which they wished to do, [then] they did it. But if it was otherwise, then they abandoned [the idea]. Their kings too, when they wished to send their military commanders to [wage] war, if they saw that the revolution of the year of him whom they wished to send signified for him [that he would have] victory over their own enemies in that same year, [then] they sent him. But if not, they sought out another one for whom his revolution signified victory, and they sent him, and doing thus in all their actions, they attained success. And so they did in everything.

The work and the sequence of the revolution is [to be done] just as I shall tell [you] in the present book. When, with the return of the year, the Sun has gone around the whole circle and has returned to that very [degree and] minute and second in which it was [placed] at the hour of the nativity and has taken up the position from which it departed, [then] you may know that that is the hour of the revolution. Therefore know thus what the hour is and what sign is ascending. And having established the ASC, you shall determine the houses from it, and do just as I shall tell you in the present book.

You shall begin to make the figure of the revolution of the year with all the things that are in it [such as] the planets—namely, you shall make the figure round or rectangular[44] and divide it into 12 [sections]; [and] you shall divide it according [to the way] men are accustomed to divide it. And know the ASC of the year just as was said above, along with its own degree and minute, and write it in each of the houses; then write the twelve signs in their own succession in each house, that is in each sign; and the houses will be divided by their own degrees and minutes according to how they are equated, that is [by] times through parts of hours and by sections of the direct circle; and write in that [chart] the planets of the revolution of the year in accordance with their status of ascension or descension or

---

[44]Note that both shapes of charts are mentioned.

retrogradation and the other things that go along [with them]. Write also their aspects and their dodecatemories and the dodecatemories of the degrees of the 12 houses and the parts and the head and tail [of the Dragon]; and let each and everyone [of these] be [written] in its own sign in which it was [posited] at the hour of the revolution of the year. After [doing] that, write in it the planets [and] the ASC of the nativity [itself] in accordance with their status and their aspects and their dodecatemories and the dodecatemories of the houses, and the parts and the head and tail [of the Dragon] in their own houses and in the signs in which they were [posited] in the nativity. After this, write in it the location of the ASC of the nativity and the place of the profection of the year from it, i.e. from that same ASC of the nativity; then write in it the location of the profection of the division [of time] and its ruler and its partner in the division, [i.e.] the ruler of the *fardar*;[45] and the one that divides with it and the ruler of cycle—each of these in the sign and in the terms in which it is [posited]. And if in the radix of the nativity there was, in the ASC or in the angle of the MC or with either of the lights or with those of the seven planets which were in the angles, any one of the fixed stars, [then] write that one there.

And when you have done this, there are collected together for you in the figure of the revolution of the year 14 planets and the head and the tail [of the Dragon] in two [separate] places and the aspects of the planets of the nativity and of the revolution in 98 places. Then the twelve degrees of the signs and of the planets of the revolution or of the nativity in 38 places; but the parts will be in accordance with what you have made [of them]—few or many.

And when you wish to describe in any of the houses where some of the planets are [posited]—several in number, you ought first of all to begin with the one that has few degrees[46]; then you will write the one that follows it in its degrees, [and so on] until [you come to] the one with the latest degrees. After this, you will look at the aspects and the parts and the dodecatemories and the faces of the [planets] similarly until you have finished with whatever was in

---

[45]Probably the "small *fardar*"—a Persian profection of 75 years, subdivided as follows—Sun 10 years, Moon 9 years, North Node 3 years, Jupiter 12 years, Mercury 13 years, Saturn 11 years, South Node 2 years, Mars 7 years, and Venus 8 years. See the list in *The Thousands of Abū Ma`shar*, p. 62.

[46]That is, the one that is closest to the cusp or beginning of the house.

the 12 houses according to this method. And when you have done this, then you have put in proper order the figure of the revolution of the year.

The next chapter explains how to judge the solar return chart. It is too long to reproduce here. But what is cited above should be sufficient to demonstrate the high degree of sophistication of this technique as practised by the master astrologers of the Arabian period. Note in particular that Albumasar also takes into account the classical profection (the 12-year one) along with the Persian profection mentioned above. Obviously, a considerable amount of time and effort was needed to construct such a chart. And a skilled astrologer was required to interpret the complex diagram after it was made. Special study and much practice is required to be able to successfully delineate such a chart.

One reason I have cited this passage at length is because it sets forth very plainly several facts about natal horoscopes and solar returns (or any other method of judging future prospects for a particular time). The first fact is that the natal horoscope specifies the whole life of the native and its mixture of successes and failures. The second fact is that the individual solar returns specify what will happen—**within the limits set by the natal horoscope**—in individual years. The quality of the natal chart therefore governs what can happen in any particular year. If the natal chart is totally good and the native lives in a favorable or at least a neutral environment, then no affliction in a subsequent solar return is capable of indicating anything more serious than a minor annoyance. Conversely, if the natal chart is totally bad, then the least affliction in a subsequent solar return will indicate a serious occurrence, while the best indication in a solar return will indicate only a small benefit.

This is nothing more than common sense. The familiar bell curve of statistics applies—there are a relatively few totally miserable people on one end, a relatively few totally fortunate people on the other end, with the great mass of humanity somewhere in between. Nearly all humans live lives in which both good fortune and bad fortune are mixed. Examples are easy. A beloved parent or other relative may die, bringing much sorrow to a native, while at the same time leaving him a nice inheritance—perhaps through a bad aspect of Saturn and a near simultaneous good aspect of Jupiter. A promotion at the office or factory may bring increased income but also increased responsibility and more stress. Many occurrences ("accidents"—to use the astrological term) in life are mixed—partly good and partly bad. Most humans live complex lives.[47] Common sayings such as,

---

[47]This should be plain even to critics of astrology, who frequently state that astrology presents a maze of contradictory indications to the astrologer, who then arbitrarily picks out a few that he likes and ignores the others. Not so! Good and bad indications all operate in some way or other. One would think that even the critics would be able to see that this is the way life is.

"Lucky at cards, unlucky at love" or its reverse find their realization in individuals.

Just as a physician learns through education and experience to sort through various physical indications and determine the probable cause of a patient's illness or condition, so does an astrologer in the same way learn how to predict both the general course of a client's life and its probable course within a given time period.

I believe this tract of Albumasar's, except for its use of the profections, would have been approved 800 years later by the French astrologer J.B. Morin (see below). And since Māshā'allāh's treatise on solar returns, The Revolutions of the Years of Nativities, is lost (see above), Albumasar's books on solar returns are perhaps the earliest that have come down to us.

Al-Kindî

Al-Kindî (c.796-873), the "philosopher of the Arabs." An exceedingly prolific author whose innumerable works included some twenty or more "epistles" on various topics in astrology. According to the *Fihrist*,[48] it was he who first interested Albumasar in astrology. As the story goes, Albumasar was persistently attacking al-Kindî for some of the latter's philosophical opinions and continually causing him to have to waste time by defending himself. So al-Kindî introduced Albumasar to astrology. He promptly fell in love with the subject and gave up philosophical controversy. We can all thank al-Kindî for having played this trick on Albumasar.

Al-Kindî wrote hundreds of books on a variety of topics (he seems to have been the Isaac Asimov of the 9th century). Among those he wrote on astrology, the following are the best known in the West:

> De iudiciis astrorum.
> [The Judgments of the Stars; with works of other writers]
> Venice: Peter Liechtenstein, 1507.

> De pluviis, imbribus et ventis ac aeris mutatione.
> [Rains, Storms and Winds, and Change in the Air; with works of other writers]
> Venice: Peter Liechtenstein, 1507.

Carmody says[49] that al-Kindî's books on meteorological astrology were prime sources for later writers on that branch of the art.

Albubater

Abū Bakr al-Hasan ibn al-Khasîb (late 9th century), known in the West as **Albubater**, wrote an introduction to astrology, a book on the revolutions of nativities (what modern astrologers call "solar returns"), and a

---

[48]al-Nadîm, *Fihrist*, vol.2, p. 656.
[49]Francis J. Carmody, AAASLT, p. 79.

very popular book on natal astrology, which was translated c.1225 at Padua, Italy, by Salio (or Solomon)—the *De nativitatibus*, which was published in an astrological compendium at Venice in 1492 and in another in 1493. There is a modern Spanish translation by Demetrio Santos of the 1492 edition: *Sobre las natividades* (Barcelona: Edicomunicación, 1986). It is divided into 206 chapters ranging in length from a single sentence to several pages. Each one covers a specific topic and gives one or more natal configurations that indicate some tendency or condition that the native will have. Many of these appear to have been taken from actual nativities, while others have a theoretical look.[50] Here are some brief examples:

20. The native's modesty.

Jupiter in the ASC of a nativity without any aspect to Mars indicates that the native will be modest. When the Moon is in the ASC and in the terms of Saturn or in its face [decan] and Mars is in the DSC and Jupiter is in aspect with the Moon, the native will be modest.

85. Natives who are bald.

When the ASC is in Leo, Virgo, Scorpio, or Sagittarius and Mars is in those signs, the native will be bald.

When the ASC is in Cancer and Mars or the Moon is in it, or when Mars aspects it by square or opposition, the native will be bald.

When the Part of Fortune and the Part of Faith and their rulers are in Aries, the native will be bald.

94. Natives who are Carpenters.

When Mars is aspected by Mercury from the house of profession and the sign of that house is one of those of seed and earth, the native will be a carpenter or [a member] of the profession that works with wood and iron.

And if Venus aspects them, the native will be a maker of trumpets, flutes, or citharas, or [other] stringed instruments.

If Saturn aspects them, the native will be a carpenter of houses and of anything that the architects need [to be made] of wood.

---

[50]Many such aphorisms appear in the writings of the classical astrologers, e.g. Firmicus and Rhetorius. Not having the Latin text at hand, I have translated the examples that follow from Santos's Spanish version.

If the Sun aspects them, the native will be a maker of shields and other equipment that are made for kings and for war.

If Jupiter aspects them, the native will be a constructor of instruments that are used by priests and ecclesiastics, or instruments with which stones are raised.

If the Moon aspects them, the native will be a constructor of boats and bridges.

When Saturn, Mars, and Venus are at the same time in a masculine sign of Mars, and especially in Aries, Leo, or Sagittarius, the native will be a carpenter or seller of wood (firewood).

This is only one of a group of chapters that give the astrological indications for various professions, among them weavers, shoemakers, leather workers or harness makers, painters, sculptors, dyers, earth movers, mariners, iron workers, entertainers, etc.

William Lilly, in his "Introduction to Nativities" (*Christian Astrology*, p. 632), mentions "*Albubater* a learned *Arabian Physitian*, out of whose Writings most of our *Astrologicall Aphorismes* are collected."

The Nine Judges

An anonymous compilation of extracts from nine Arabian astrologers was translated into Latin under the title *Liber novem iudicum* 'The Book of the Nine Judges'. The authors cited are Abendaiat, Māshā'allāh, Dorotheus, Jirjis, Aristotle, Albumasar, Omar Tiberiades, al-Kindî, and Zahel. This book was often cited by the later medieval astrologers in Western Europe, and is preserved in several MSS, but it was never printed. Carmody calls this *Liber novem iudicum I*.

Another book of the same sort and with the same title, but with some different authorities cited (e.g. Ptolemy and Albohali) was also popular. It was printed by Peter Liechtenstein at Venice in 1509 (in an omnibus edition with other books). Carmody calls this *Liber novem iudicum II*.[51]

Some other well-known figures of Arabian astrology belong to the later 10th or even the 11th century, of whom the most notable were:

Haly Embrani

`Alî ibn Ahmad al-`Imrānî, a resident of Mosul, Iraq, who died in the year 344 A.H. (955/956 A.D.), was a mathematician, astrologer, and book collector.[52] He was known in the West as **Haly Embrani** and was the au-

---

[51]See Francis J. Carmody, AAASLT, pp. 103-112 for more information and for a list of chapter titles from the printed version.

[52]See al-Nadîm, *Fihrist*, vol. 2., p. 667. Apparently the Arabic texts of his books are lost.

thor of a book on elections *Kitab ikhtiyarat* 'Book of Choices', which was translated into Latin in Barcelona in 1134 by Abraham the Jew under the title *Liber electionum* 'Book of Elections'. This book was a favorite of the late medieval astrologers and was finally printed at Basel in 1572.[53] Haly Embrani was famed as a teacher; one of his students was Alchabitius (see below).

Alchabitius

Abū al-Saqr al-Qabîsî `Abd al-`Azîz ibn `Uthmān (d. 967), known in the West as **Alchabitius** or less commonly as **Abdilaziz**, was the author of a book, *Introduction to the Art of Judgments of the Stars*, dedicated to the Sultan Sayf al-Dawlah (c.916-967). It became one of the most popular astrological treatises in the West. The Latin translation by John of Seville, *Alchabitii Abdilazi liber introductorius ad magisterium judiciorum astrorum*, was printed more than a dozen times. Beginning with Erhard Ratdolt's edition published at Venice in 1503, it was often printed with the commentary of John Danko (14th century).

Carmody says Alchabitius's book contains "a complete presentation of astrological practices and materials, with definitions, distinctions, numerous lists of place names by climates and influences, and many long [passages quoted from] Dorotheus and Māshā'allāh."[54]

The system of house division to which Alchabitius's name is attached was expounded by several other Arab writers of his time, but since his book was very widely read in Europe after its translation in the 12th century, the system was generally ascribed to him. Actually, as we have seen above, it was explained, with an example chart of 428 A.D., by Rhetorius the Egyptian, so it goes back at least to the 5th century. This system was the principal one used in the late middle ages and the renaissance until it was supplanted by the Regiomontanus system, which first became known to most astrologers in 1490.

Nallino gives a mathematical explanation of the house system[55] (since it also appears in the astronomical work of al-Battanî), and he adds an observation of his own followed by a similar one by Delambre:[56]

> In this division of the houses, not only do two unequal series of cusps appear, but the absurdity is also found

[53]See Francis J. Carmody, AAASLT, pp. 137-139.

[54]Francis J. Carmody, AAASLT, p. 144.

[55]An understandable one with diagrams, unlike the abstruse explanation and planispheric diagram given by Neugebauer and Van Hoesen in *Greek Horoscopes*, p. 139.

[56]Carlo Alphonso Nallino (1872-1938), *Al-Battanî sive Albatenii Opus astronomicum* (Milan: Reale Osservatorio, 1899-1907. 3 vols.), vol. 1, pp. 248-249. Arabic text with a Latin translation and commentary. The reference to J.B. Delambre (1749-1822) is to his *Histoire de l'astronomie du Moyen âge* 'History of the Astronomy of the Middle Ages' (Paris, 1819)

which Delambre notes about Alchabitius on p. 502, saying:

> "The last six houses are always diametrically opposed
> to the first six, from which there results a kind of absurdity.
> The quadrant of the equator between the meridian and the
> western horizon is found to be divided according to the
> nocturnal arcs, although it belongs to the day; the quadrant
> between the western horizon and the lower meridian is di-
> vided according to the hours of the day, although it belongs
> to the night. As for the rest, the calculation is extremely
> simple, and it is perhaps this that has enabled it to pass over
> the absurdity that we have just remarked."

This criticism is invalid! In the case of the Alchabitius system, the
twelfth and eleventh house cusps are found by trisecting the arc of right
ascension between the ASC and the MC, while the ninth and eighth house
cusps are found by trisecting the arc between the MC and the DSC. The
same rule is used for both quadrants. Thus, there is no absurdity.
Delambre and Nallino were simply looking at the procedure incorrectly.

However, considering the severe distortion of the quadrants in the
higher latitudes, that can result in double interceptions of signs on one side
of the meridian and tiny houses only a few degrees in extent on the other
side (not to mention that the Alchabitius and all the other quadrant systems
fail completely at and above the arctic and antarctic circles, it would appear that the only reasonable house systems are the original Sign-House
system (still in use in India) and its derivative the Equal House system.

Haly Abenragel

`Alî ibn abî al-Rijāl, Abū'l-Hasan** (d. after 1037), called **Albohazen
Haly** or **Haly Abenragel** in Latin, was court astrologer to the Tunisian
Prince al-Mu`izz ibn Badis (first half of the 11th century). Haly is best
known for his large and comprehensive book on astrology called *The Out-
standing Book on the Judgments of the Stars*, which was translated into
Old Castilian at the court of Alphonso X the Wise (1226-1284) under the
title *El libro conplido en los iudizios de las estrellas* 'The Complete Book
on the Judgments of the Stars', edited meticulously by Gerold Hilty from
MS 3065 of the National Library in Madrid (Madrid: Real Academia
Española, 1954). A Latin translation was made from the Castilian version.
Haly cites his sources (many of whom have not been identified). His book
was very popular with the late medieval astrologers, such as Bonatti and
Leopold. In fact, according to Carmody,[57] most references by later astrol-
ogers to "Haly" refer to Haly Abenragel (and if not to him, usually to Haly
Abenrudian, for whom see below), but there were also a few other
"Halys."

---

[57]Francis J. Carmody, AAASLT, pp. 150-154.

Unfortunately, MS 3065 contains only the first five of the eight books; hence, it is an incomplete MS of *The Complete Book*. However, a Latin version was made from a MS now lost that contained the complete Castilian translation. It was first published as *Praeclarissimus liber completus in judiciis astrorum* `The Very Famous Complete Book on the Judgments of the Stars' (Venice: Erhard Ratdolt, 1485). The printed book proved to be as popular with Renaissance astrologers as MS copies had been with their predecessors. It was reprinted in 1503, 1520, 1523, 1525, 1551, and in 1571 along with *The Book of the Nine Judges*. Carmody says the Latin text of the 1551 edition has been stylistically ``improved.'' William Lilly tells us that all editions other than the Basel edition of 1571 are defective.[58] But since that edition also contains *The Book of the Nine Judges*, Lilly may have thought that it was part of Haly's text, and, not finding *The Book of the Nine Judges* in the earlier editions, he may have judged them to be defective for that reason.

The contents of all eight books are listed in the Castilian text on p. 3 of Hilty's edition:

> Both in the first book and in the second and in the third, he speaks about questions and all the things that are useful for them.
> And in the fourth and the fifth book, he speaks of nativities.
> And in the sixth book, he speaks of the revolutions of nativities.
> And in the seventh book, he speaks of elections.
> And in the eighth book, he speaks of the revolutions of the years of the world.

Al-Bîrunî

Muhammad ibn Ahmad al-Bîrunî (973-1048?) was born in a suburb of Khiva, the capital of Khwarizm, whence his name (al-Bîrunî means literally 'the suburban').[59] He was a sort of universal scholar and thus in some ways like Claudius Ptolemy, although he was an honest, capable observational astronomer, which Ptolemy was not. He spent several years in India, during which time he learned Sanskrit and consulted with leading Indian astronomers and astrologers. He was not favorably impressed either by their knowledge or by their books. In his *India* he characterized their astronomical knowledge as being "a mixture of pearls and dung," and he says that he never met a Hindu who could point out the stars of the

---

[58]William Lilly, *Christian Astrology*, p. 838.

[59]His horoscope is preserved in the MSS and was published by Wright in his edition and translation of al-Bîrunî's book (p. 191). He was born near Khiva, Uzbekistan, on 4 September 973 at 4:58 A.M. L.A.T. with the Sun and Mercury rising in Virgo.

nakshatras in the night sky.

Al-Bîrūnî's own works in Arabic were not translated into Latin by the 12th century translators, but four of them are now available in English translation: *The Chronology of Ancient Kingdoms* trans. & ed. by C. Edward Sachau (London, 1879), *Alberuni's India* trans. by Edward C. Sachau (London, 1888), *The Book of Instruction in the Elements of the Art of Astrology* trans. by R. Ramsay Wright (London: Luzac & Co., 1934), which actually contains introductions to astronomy, mathematics, and astrology, and *Al-Biruni on Transits* trans. by Mohammad Saffouri and Adnan Ifram with a commentary by E.S. Kennedy (Beirut: American University of Beirut, 1959). See the Bibliography for further publication details. Al-Bîrūnî liked to make lists of things,[60] and he had an obvious gift for didactic writing, but at the same time his books contain many odd bits of knowledge on a wide variety of subjects. They are a delight to read.

Haly Abenrudian

'Alî ibn Ridwān (988-1061 or 1067) was called **Haly Abenrudian** in the West. He was the author of a number of short treatises on various astrological and medical topics. His *De revolutionibus nativitatum* 'The Revolutions of Nativities' was edited by Luca Gaurico (1476-1558) and printed at Venice in 1524; his *Tractatus de cometarum significationibus per xii signa zodiaci* 'Treatise on the Significations of Comets in the 12 Signs of the Zodiac' was printed at Nürnberg in 1563; but he was perhaps best known for his commentaries on Ptolemy's *Tetrabiblos* and pseudo-Ptolemy's *Centiloquy.*

After the 11th century, astrology declined in Islamic territory, especially after the sacking of Baghdad and the destruction of its great library by the Mongols under Hulagu Khan in 1258.[61]

Abraham Ibn Ezra

Somewhat later than the Arabs was the great Jewish scholar **Abraham Ibn Ezra** (1089?-1167). In addition to Bible commentaries and a Hebrew grammar, he wrote more than fifty books on astrology and astronomy,

---

[60]He not infrequently displays a wry witticism, as when he says (Sect. 476) "It is impossible to enumerate the lots which have been invented for the solution of horary questions, and for answering enquiries as to prosperous outcome or auspicious time for action; they increase in number every day, but the following 97 different lots, 7 of which belong to the planets, 80 to the houses and 10 to neither are those most commonly in use." He would no doubt shake his head sadly if he could know of the "Part of Plastic" proposed by a 20th century astrologer.

[61]For further details of the books of the Arabian astrologers known in the West through Latin translation and their early printed editions, see Francis J. Carmody, AAASLT. Some additional information is given in the older survey by Dr. Heinrich Suter in his *Die Mathematiker und Astronomen der Araber und ihre Werke* (Leipzig: B.G. Teubner, 1900) and in Bayard Dodge's ed. and trans. of *The Fihrist of al-Nadîm*, vol. 2.

based on Arabic works but containing his own opinions and theories.[62] His best known astrological work is *The Beginning of Wisdom* (*Sefer Reshit Hokmah*) written in 1148. There is a modern edition (by Francisco Cantera) of the Hebrew text and an edition of the Old French translation (made by Hagin le Juif in 1273) with an English translation of the Hebrew by Raphael Levy (Baltimore: The Johns Hopkins Press, 1939). A French translation of *The Beginning of Wisdom* and of *The Book of Reasons* (*Sefer ha-Te 'amim*) has also been published:

> Ibn Ezra, Abraham ben Meïr
> Le livre des fondements astrologiques (précedés de)
> Le Commencement de la Sapience des signes.
> [The Book of the Fundamentals of Astrology (preceded by)
> The Beginning of Wisdom of the Signs]
> Paris: Retz, 1977.

Chapter 8 of the *Beginning of Wisdom* contains 120 "prognostics" for horoscopes, revolutions, and questions. Here are some examples:[63]

> 2. If the Moon is moving by itself [void of course], that indicates any futile thing, and it signifies that anything which the asker requests can not possibly occur.

> 3. The planet which enters into conjunction or into aspect with the Moon prognosticates every future thing and anything which the asker will expect; if the planet is favorable, it will be a boon; if the planet is unfavorable, it will bring harm.

> 4. The separation from the Moon denotes things which have passed; if it separated in conjunction or in aspect with a helpful planet, it was beneficial, and with a harmful planet, it was sinister.

> 8. The planets move in two faces, one helpful, the other harmful; no matter where you find the planet to be favorable, predict good; for the opposite position, predict the opposite.

> 12. The favorable [benefics] always prognosticate a boon, and the unfavorable [malefics] prognosticate harm. Nevertheless if the unfavorable one should be in its exalta-

---

[62]See the short article with bibliographical references in the *Dictionary of Scientific Biography*, the Introduction to *The Beginning of Wisdom*, and the comprehensive study by Raphael Levy, *The Astrological Works of Abraham Ibn Ezra* (Baltimore: The Johns Hopkins Press, 1927).

[63]Raphael Levy's translation.

tion, the effect will be good, although it will involve pain and sorrow.

89. The star [planet] which moves beneath the rays of the Sun [is "under the Sunbeams"] is like a man in prison.

91. The star, which is about to assume a retrograde motion [is "static retrograde"], is like a man bewildered and trembling at the misfortunes which will befall him.

92. The star which retrogrades is like a twitching and rebellious person.

93. The star in its second station ["static direct"] is like a man who expects good luck.

110. The star in the second house is the same as the person who is in the house of his assistants.

114. The star in the sixth house is equivalent to a weak man running away.

115. The star in the seventh house is the same as a man prepared for battle.

116. The star in the eighth house is related to a person beset with fear and terror.

117. The star in the ninth house refers to a man leaving his place to go into exile or a man who has lost his high rank.

Along with some of his other treatises it was translated into Old French and Catalan, from both of which languages Latin versions were subsequently made. One of his astronomical works, *The Book of the Fundamentals of the Tables* explains how to calculate what were later called Placidus cusps[64]—five hundred years before Placidus reinvented them.

The Twelfth Century Translators

The Arabic authors, with the exception of al-Bîrûnî, were translated into Latin by the so-called Twelfth Century Translators—a group of individual translators, most of whom lived in southern Spain or northern Italy, but a few elsewhere. Some of these men knew both Arabic and Latin, so that they could translate directly from one language to the other. Others knew Arabic but did not know Latin. They translated Arabic into Spanish or Italian, and a partner translated the vernacular into Latin. The best

---

[64]See the paper by James H. Holden "House Division II" in the AFA *Journal of Research*, vol. 5, no.2 (1989):33-52. The Latin version of Ibn Ezra's book was edited by José Millás Vallicrosa, *El libro de los fundamentos de las Tablas astronómicas* (Madrid-Barcelona: Instituto Arias Montano, 1947).

known (and most capable) of those who translated astronomical and astrological works was **John of Seville**, who also wrote a short general treatise entitled *The Epitome of All Astrology*.[65]

The Alfonsine Tables

An event of importance to Western astrologers was the publication of the *Alfonsine Tables*, a set of up-to-date astronomical (and astrological) tables prepared under the sponsorship of the Spanish King Alphonso X the Wise (1226-1284). (Publication here means that master sets of handwritten tables were made available to copyists.) These tables remained in use for two or three centuries.

In the 11th century Western Europe began to wake up from its long sleep. And things picked up even more in the 12th century, sparked by the exploits of the Crusaders, who aroused considerable interest in things more exotic than living and dying in illiterate drudgery on a farm or in some miserable village. Scholars multiplied and began to seek knowledge in all fields. Astronomical tables became available again (you can't practice, or even experiment with horoscopic astrology without tables). An interest in astrology arose, despite the occasional efforts of the Church to prevent it.

With books and tables again available, astrology burst into life. Universities were founded, and a number of them had chairs of astronomy and astrology. A demand arose for professional astrologers to counsel rulers and individuals of the middle and upper classes.

Albertus Magnus and Roger Bacon

These two men were not astrologers, but they both wrote favorably on astrology, and their works were widely read. Hence, they have some importance in the history of astrology.

Albert was the eldest son of the Count of Bollstädt. He was born at Lauingen, Bavaria, some time between 1193 and 1206. He is said to have died in 1280. He entered the Dominican Order of the Catholic Church at 16 and studied for a few years at Padua in Italy. Returning to Germany with a head full of knowledge (he was one of those fortunate individuals with a near perfect memory), he held teaching positions at Hildesheim, Freiburg, Strasbourg, and Ratisbon. Thereafter, from 1245 to 1248 he was in Paris, where he signed the condemnation of the *Talmud*. Thorndike[66] says Albert was in Rome in 1256, but he spent more time at Cologne than anywhere else. He is the sole learned man of the 12th and 13th centuries to be called "the Great."

---

[65]*Epitome totius astrologiae* ed. by Joachim Heller (Nürnberg: Montani & Neuber, 1548). In his translations John used the Latin word *cuspis* 'point' or 'sharp end' as the equivalent of the Arabic *watad* 'peg' or 'pin', which was used to designate the point at the beginning of a celestial house. This is the origin of the English term 'cusp'.

[66]Lynn Thorndike, HMES 2, Chapter 59.

Albert was a theologian, so he had to come to grips with the fate vs. free-will question, but he resolved this in favor of astrology. Thorndike cites a passage from one of his numerous books in which he says: "There is in man a double spring of action, namely nature and the will; and nature for its part is ruled by the stars, while the will is free; but unless it resists, it is swept along by nature and becomes mechanical." And in another place he states that the astrologer who understands the virtues of the signs of the zodiac and of the stars situated in them at the moment of birth can prognosticate so far as lies within the influence of the sky concerning the entire life of the person born.[67] But his principal claim to fame in astrological history is his *Speculum Astronomiae*.[68]

The *Speculum Astronomiae* or *Mirror of Astrology* was possibly written about 1277. It consists of an introductory defense of both astronomy and astrology as proper subjects for scientists and Christians to study, a chapter on astronomical books, and a lengthy chapter on astrological books. In a way it is a sort of annotated catalogue of books known to Albert (and he was evidently familiar with nearly all the books available in Latin in his time). He is careful to divide all the books into two categories—licit and illicit (from an ecclesiastical point of view). Along with the purely astrological books, he lists books on astrological images, some of which he condemns, although he says that even the books of necromancy should be preserved and not destroyed, for they might be useful sometime. Finally, he mentions the existence of "experimental" books on various other "ancies"—geomancy, hydromancy, aerimancy, pyromancy, and chiromancy. He says that these arts, in his opinion, do not deserve to be called sciences, but "babblings."[69] He also cites Albumasar to the effect that the Virgin Birth of Jesus Christ was prefigured in the sky, and regards this assertion as a notable confirmation of the true Faith, not that the Lord of all things was under the stars but that what God had decreed was signified by the stars.[70]

The *Mirror of Astrology* is therefore a very valuable book for the history of astrology, since it not only provides a classified bibliography of the books available in the latter part of the 13th century, but it also contains the comments of one of the leading scholars of the age.

Roger Bacon was born of an aristocratic family somewhere in England around 1210. In his younger days he joined the Franciscan Order. He was a student of philosophy and science and by 1267 had written a large work on these subjects entitled *Opus Maius* [The Larger Work]. The existence of this work had come to the attention of Pope Clement IV (d. 1268), who sent a letter to Bacon requesting a copy. Bacon also wrote a shorter

---

[67]Thorndike, *loc. cit.*, pp. 585-586.
[68]Edited in the general collection of Albert's works. There is an improved partial edition by Franz Cumont in CCAG V.1.
[69]Thorndike, *loc. cit.*, pp. 701-702.
[70]Thorndike, *loc. cit.*, p. 703.

version, called *Opus Minus* [The Smaller Work], and some years later another book called *Opus Tertium* [The Third Work]. All of these books were popular in the 13th century. In them he accepts astrology as a valid science and supports his acceptance with a battery of philosophical observations and arguments. Thorndike says:[71]

> Bacon was especially attracted by the doctrine of Albumasar concerning conjunctions of the planets, and he derived comforting evidence of the superiority of the Christian faith to other religions from the astrological origin of religious sects according to the successive conjunctions of the other planets to Jupiter. He was pleased by the association of Christianity with Mercury, which he calls the lord of wisdom and eloquence, of oracles and prophecies; it is dominant only in the sign Virgo, which at once suggests the Virgin Mary; and its orbit, difficult to trace because of epicycle and eccentric, typifies well the Christian creed with its mysteries that defy reason.

The reference to Albumasar is to his book *The Great Conjunctions*, Book 1, where the advent of prophets (and their religions) is discussed along with the planets typifying each of the major religions of Albumasar's time.

As mentioned above, Bacon's importance in astrological history is that he offered what were considered to be powerful arguments in favor of astrology, thereby countering the arguments against it put forward by others.

Bonatus

Perhaps the best known astrologer of the late Middle Ages was the Italian **Guido Bonatti**, called **Bonatus** in Latin.[72] In his youth he was one of the astrologers attached to the court of the emperor Frederick II (1194-1250). In middle life he seems to have been a professor at the University of Bologna. In his later years he retired to Forlì, Italy, where he practiced astrology and wrote a massive and comprehensive textbook *Liber introductorius ad iudicia stellarum* 'A Book of Introduction to the Judgments of the Stars', which is actually a collection of ten separate treatises on various phases of astrology[73] dedicated to his nephew Bonatus:

---

[71]Thorndike, *loc. cit.*, p. 672. The whole Chapter 61 discusses Bacon's remarks about astrology and the other sciences.

[72]For an account of his career, see Lynn Thorndike, HMES 2, Chapter 67. The dates of Bonatti's birth and death are unknown, but he evidently lived from about 1210 to about 1295.

[73]The first page of the first edition has the title *Guido bonatus de forlivio: Decem continens tractatus astronomie* 'Guido Bonatus of Forlì: containing Ten Treatises of Astrology' and at the end the book is described as *Liber astronomicus* 'A Book of Astrology' (Augsburg: Erhard Ratdolt, 1491). Bonatti often uses the

Author's Preface

1. General Introduction
2. The Fundamentals of Astrology
3. The Natures of the Planets
4. Conjunctions
5. The 146 Considerations
6. Interrogations
7. Elections
8. Revolutions of the Years of the World and Conjunctions
9. Nativities
10. Storms and Changes in the Weather

He was obviously familiar with most of the Arabic treatises that had been translated into Latin by the Twelfth Century Translators, since he continually cites them as authorities for various astrological techniques. For example, just in *Treatise* 3, Part 3, Chapter 5, which contains descriptions of the celestial houses, he mentions Adila, Alezdegoz, Alchabitius, Albohali, al-Kindî, Albategnius (al-Battanî), Albuas, Argapholon, Mansur, the Master (Māshā'allāh), [Omar] Tiberiades, Vuellius (Vettius Valens), and Zahel (Sahl ibn Bishr). His citations from these and other Arabic astrologers are often helpful in correcting the printed texts of those writers.

Bonatti was evidently prominent enough to have become the target of clerical attacks from time to time. Thorndike[74] notes that he says of them "astrologers know vastly more about the stars than the theologians do about God, 'Of Whom they none the less preach daily.'" Bonatti might also have added that astrology is an experimental science, while theology rests upon speculation and belief. Thorndike cites another instance:

> Bonatti then mentions "some silly fools, of whom that hypocrite, John of Vicenza, of the Order of Preaching Friars was one, who said that astrology was neither an art nor a science." Guido scarcely thinks it worth while to notice such men. This John of Vicenza mentioned by Bonatti was the well-known friar of that name to whom manifold miracles were attributed and who in the Alleluia year of 1233 had been made duke of Vicenza, but so abused his power that he was soon imprisoned and discredited. Bonatti complains that no one had ever seen a single one of the eighteen men whom John was said to have raised from the dead, and

---

Latin word astronomia 'astronomy' to mean 'astrology'. The title is often cited in modern literature as 'Ten Treatises of Astronomy (or Astrology)', which is actually the publisher's description rather than the true title.

[74]Lynn Thorndike, HMES 2, Chapter 67. This chapter contains an excellent survey of Bonatti's book.

affirms that he himself long sought in vain for anyone who had either been cured by John or had himself witnessed one of John's miracles.

However, Bonatti seems to have had clerical clients, for "Among the interrogations which Bonatti lists are whether a bishopric or abbotship or cardinalate, or other clerical dignity, rank, or order, even up to the papacy will be attained by the inquirer.[75] In this connection Guido grants that it may not seem honorable to seek ecclesiastical offices, but that the fact is that many clergy do it and that it is necessary for the astrologer to be prepared to answer them, if they consult him as to their prospects."

Bonatti gives rules for investigating many different types of questions. Some of them obviously relate more to medieval European society than they do to that of the modern day, although they might still arise on occasion. Here are the last four questions listed under the twelfth house[76]:

> 6. When Someone is Invited to a Banquet: Whether it will be Held or not and what Foods there will be.
>
> 7. Whether the Banquet will Consist of One Kind of Food or More.
>
> 8. Knowing why the Banquet is being Held:
> How Long the Banquet is Going to Last.
> When the Banqueteers will be Quarrelsome.
> How the Food will be Served at the Banquet.
> When One Should Beware of the Food at the Banquet.
>
> 9. Which House Signifies the Cause of the Banquet and Things Related to it.

It is perhaps indicative of the suspicion with which Bonatti's contemporaries evidently viewed an unexpected invitation to dine that these questions are listed under the House of Enemies rather than under the House of Friends.

As an example of Bonatti's methods, the following horary chart is cited[77]:

> If anyone has asked you whether there is going to be a battle between two armies or not, then look at the first [house] and its ruler and the Moon and the seventh [house] and its ruler, and see whether they are joined together by body in any one of the angles, since that signifies that there will be a battle between them. But if they were not joined

---

[75]*Treatise* 6, Ninth House Questions, Section 10.

[76]*Treatise* 6, Twelfth House, Sections 6-9, copied from Zahel.

[77]*Treatise* 6, Chapt. 28.

by body, see whether they were joined by opposition or square aspect, since that similarly signifies that there will be a battle. And if neither of these [configurations] exists, then see whether any planet transfers the light between them by opposition or square aspect, since that signifies that there will be a battle if there is no reception [between them]. But if the heavier one of them receives the one which transfers their light between them, it signifies that there will not be a battle, but if there is, that they will be pacified either during the engagement or in a little while after the engagement. And if [the indications] were different [from those mentioned], viz. that the significators of the armies, viz. the ruler of the first [house] and the ruler of the seventh were not conjoined anywhere [in the chart], nor did they meet [by aspect], nor was there any [planet] that to transfer the light between them as was mentioned, it signifies that there will not be a battle.

And this was an example of that. When Count Guido Novello was the Podestà[78] of Florence, and we were with the army above the district of Lucca, and the men of Lucca were holding [the territory] in the heart of it with their own army of close to one thousand, then a veteran asked a man whether there would be a battle between those armies or not. I looked at this question, whose ASC was the 4th degree of Sagittarius and the MC the 24th degree of Virgo; Mars in 13 degrees and 30 minutes of it; Venus 17 degrees and 6 minutes; Mercury 17 degrees and 13 minutes, [all of them] in the 9th [house] cadent from an angle. And the Sun [was] in the same [sign] 26 degrees and 4 minutes in the angle of the tenth house. Libra the 11th house 18 degrees; the Tail [of the Dragon] in it at 3 degrees. Scorpio the 12th house 14 degrees. Capricorn the 9th house 9 degrees; Jupiter in it at 13 degrees. Aquarius the 3rd house 13 degrees. Pisces the 4th house 24 degrees. Aries the 5th 18 degrees; the Head [of the Dragon] in it at 3 degrees; Saturn in it retrograde at 13 degrees; the Moon in it at 21 degrees. Taurus the 6th house 14 degrees. Gemini the 7th house 4 degrees; the Part of Fortune in it at 29 degrees. Cancer the 8th house 9 degrees. Leo the 9th house 13 degrees. And [the time of] this was the 658th year, the 9th month, and the 16th day from the Era of the Arabs approximately. The altitude of the sun before noon

---

[78]Guido Novello, Count of Poppi, was Podestà [Mayor] of Florence 1261-1266.

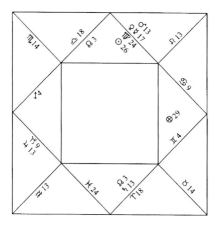

Fig. 8 Question about A Future Battle

was about 48 degrees,[79] Monday, the 12th of September.[80]

Therefore, I looked at the ASC of this question and its ruler, which was Jupiter, and the seventh [house] and its ruler, which was Mercury, of which one was in the second [house] in Capricorn, sc. in its own fall, which seems to signify small capability on the part of the querent when he would seek [to engage in] battle, but because it was in the second [house], it signifies some strength for him. then I looked at the Moon, which was in Aries void of course, which signified a similar debility and small capability on the part of the querent. Then I looked at Mercury for his adversary, which was in Virgo, combust and cadent from an angle, which even though it was in its own domicile (just as

---

[79]Measuring the Sun's altitude, probably with an astrolabe, was Bonatti's standard method of finding the time of day. Unfortunately, this method is particularly inaccurate between 11 AM and 1 PM, since the Sun's altitude does not change more than 2 degrees in 1 hour that close to noon, and it is doubtful that the astrolabe could be read any closer than to the nearest degree, which would cause a margin of error of 30 minutes or more in the determination of the time. Here, Bonatti reports an observed altitude of 48°, but the maximum solar altitude at Lucca on that date was 47°28'. A sundial would have given the time more accurately.

[80]This date corresponds to 15 Shawwal 659 A.H. or 12 September 1261. It was actually 658 years 9 months and 14 days after 1 Muharram 1 A.H. The house cusps (which are according to the Alchabitius system) and the planetary positions are reasonably accurate, the largest error as usual being in Mercury's position (17°13' Virgo instead of 21°43').

141

they[81] were in their own land), signified its own weakness, so that they would not seek [to engage in] battle. From [these considerations] I judged the question for him, and so it turned out because they did not position themselves at the battleground; and so afterwards both armies dispersed, just as it will be related in the chapter below on the hidden camp.

Bonatti's Latin style is simple and straightforward and a delight to read. He was sufficiently well known in Italy to be mentioned by his younger contemporary Dante (1265-1321) in *Inferno*, XX, 118, "Vedi Guido Bonatti . . ." [I saw Guido Bonatti], where he is represented as being among those spirits of the dead who had tried to pry into the future and were therefore condemned to look backwards with their heads turned.

Bonatti's book was very popular and is found in many MSS, including a deluxe parchment copy of it and some other astrological treatises that was made for Henry VII of England (1457-1509), whose picture appears in the middle of Bonatti's text.[82]

Bonatti was a master horary astrologer.[83] In fact, William Lilly was accused by a jealous rival of having merely "Latinized Bonatus" in his *Christian Astrology*. This was not true, since Lilly himself was a master of that branch of astrology, but he certainly used Bonatti's book. Later, at Lilly's suggestion, Henry Coley (1633-1695?) translated the 146 Considerations which make up the fifth treatise of Bonatti's *Book of Introduction to the Judgments of the Stars*.[84] These make rewarding reading for anyone interested in horary astrology.

See below under "Astrological Images" for an interesting story about Guido Bonatti.

Leopold of Austria

Another astrologer of the same sort was Bonatti's contemporary **Leopold of Austria**, who also wrote a compendium of astrology (contain-

---

[81]The army of Lucca.

[82]Thorndike, HMES 2, p. 827 & n.3. The MS is Arundel 66, membr. folio maximo; Bonatti's text is on fols. 48-249.

[83]Horary, as mentioned above, is the branch of astrology that deals with individual questions put to the astrologer by a client seeking counsel. A horoscope is erected for the moment when the question is asked, and an elaborate set of rules is used to answer the question. This branch of astrology was especially popular during the Middle Ages, when many clients did not know their own birthdate and birthtime.

[84]*Anima Astrologiae, or a Guide for Astrologers* (London, 1676). Reprinted with notes and a preface by Wm. C. Eldon Serjeant (London: George Redway, 1886). The 1886 edition was republished in typescript with a new short preface (Washington: The National Astrological Library, 1953); reprinted 2005.

ing two short introductory treatises on astronomy).[85] In the eighth treatise there is a horary chart that can be dated to 17 December 1278 at 11:20 A.M. This indicates the approximate date of composition of the work. Both Bonatti and Leopold depended on the Latin translations of the Arabian astrologers made by the Twelfth Century Translators. In general, Bonatti is wordy and Leopold is concise. They often cite the same authorities, and sometimes offer better readings than the published texts of those authorities.

Two Byzantine Astrologers

John Abramius was a physician and astrologer to the Byzantine Emperor Andronicus IV (reigned 1376-1379 and d. 1385). He seems to have been active in the period 1370-1390. Several Greek astrological MSS that are now in Western libraries were written by him, and others were written by his associates or pupils; some of the MSS contain horary charts for the moments of important political events, e.g. one set for Constantinople on 12 August 1376 at about 8:40 A.M., the moment when Andronicus entered the city to besiege his two brothers Manuel II and Theodore in their palace.[86]

In the year 1388 the Byzantine astrologer **Eleutherius Eleus**, an associate or pupil of John Abramius, completed his *Apotelesmatic Book*, the last important Greek astrological work—consisting of a compendium of material he had gathered from old books. He issued his book under the pseudonym **Palchus**, a name derived from the Arabic *al-Balkhî* 'The Man from Balch'. This was perhaps a reference to Albumasar, who came from there. Some extracts have been edited in the CCAG. Pingree has prepared an edition of the entire work, but it has not yet been published. He says that along with translations from Arabic it contains many fragments of the works of the classical Greek astrologers, but some of the latter are attributed to the wrong authors, so that the work "must be used with extreme caution."[87]

Two English Astrologers

Several astrologers of the thirteenth and fourteenth centuries specialized in mundane predictions. One example is the Englishman **John of Ashendon** (fl. 1350), who seems to have been an Oxford scholar.[88] And it is quite obvious that **Geoffrey Chaucer** (c.1340-1400)

---

[85]*Compilatio Leupoldi ducatus Austrie filii de astrorum scientia* (Augsburg: Erhard Ratdolt, 1489). Carmody, AAASLT, p. 171, says the reprint (Venice: Melchior Sessa, 1520) is defective. There is also an early 14th century French translation. Carmody edited the first three of the ten treatises as *Li compilacions de la science des estoilles* (Berkeley, Calif.: University of California Press, 1947).

[86]See David Pingree, "The Astrological School of John Abramius" in *Dumbarton Oaks Papers*, vol. 25 (1971): 189-215.

[87]See the reference cited for John Abramius.

[88]He wrote a 'Summary of Judicial Astrology Related to Mundane Occur-

was an accomplished amateur astrologer, since astrological references are scattered throughout his works, and he also wrote a treatise on the astrolabe.[89] Perhaps his best known astrological reference is in *The Wife of Bath's Prologue* (Lines 605-620) in *The Canterbury Tales*:

As help me God! I was a lusty oon,
And faire, and riche, and yong, and wel bigon;
And trewly, as myne housbondes tolde me,
I hadde the best quoniam myghte be.
For certes, I am al Venerien
In feelynge, and myn herte is Marcien.
Venus me yaf my lust, my likerousnesse,
And Mars yaf me my sturdy hardynesse;
Myn ascendent was Taur, and Mars therinne.
Allas! allas! that evere love was synne!
I folwed ay myn inclinacioun
By vertu of my constellacioun;
That made me I koude noght withdrawe
My chamber of Venus from a good felawe.
Yet have I Martes mark upon my face,
And also in another privee place.

Campanus

An Italian mathematician, astrologer, and papal physician whose name is still familiar to astrologers is **Campanus of Novara** (1233-1296). He invented a system of house division which found few adherents at the time but which has been revived in the 20th century. Its principle is the trisection of the prime vertical, the great circle which passes through the east and west points on the horizon and the zenith and nadir. Great circles are drawn through the north and south points on the horizon and the points of trisection on the prime vertical. Where these latter circles intersect the ecliptic, there are the cusps of the houses. The division of the heavens is thus rather like the segments of an orange lying on its side. It suffers even more from disparity in the size of the houses in higher latitudes than does the system of Regiomontanus.

Maurice Wemyss spoke favorably of the Campanus system and published tables of houses for the latitudes of London and New York in Vol. 1 of his book, *The Wheel of Life*.[90] Later advocates of this system include Dane Rudhyar and Cyril Fagan (see below).

---

rences' Summa astrologiae iudicialis de accidentibus mundi... (Venice, 1489. folio).
[89]The text of this work, which is dedicated to Lewis Chaucer, is to be found in complete editions of Chaucer's works.
[90]See the entry for Wemyss below in Section 5 "Modern Astrology."

A complete set of Campanus tables of houses was published in *The Occidental Table of Houses* (Occidental, Ca.: Occidental D.A.T.A., 1972. paper. xvi,135 pp.) and another set to tenths of minutes, *Campanus System Tables of Houses* (Tempe, Az.: A.F.A., Inc, 1977).

Summary

The principal emphasis during this period was on horary astrology and elections, for many clients did not have sufficient birthdata to enable the astrologer to make a natal horoscope. Also, most clients wanted advice on specific questions relating to current problems rather than a character reading or a generalized life forecast. The next most popular branch of astrology at this time was mundane astrology, which gave general predictions for specific towns or countries.

Technical Procedures

How did a medieval astrologer make a horoscope for his client? Fairly easily if the client knew his birthdate in whichever calendar the astrologer's tables were based upon. Otherwise, the calendar conversion problem arose. The astrologer would need to have some knowledge of the Western calendar (the Julian calendar) and of the eras used by Western Europeans and the Greeks, as well as the Muslim calendar used by the Arabs and the rest of the Islamic countries.

A set of planetary and ascension tables was a prerequisite, since ephemerides were not generally available. In Arabic-speaking countries there were a number of such sets of tables available, most of them based on the tropical zodiac, but a few based on a fixed zodiac (favored by those influenced by Indian or Persian astrological traditions). Planetary tables were of two types: (1) those that required calculation of the positions from tables of the elements of the orbits; and (2) those that in effect contained abbreviated ephemerides for certain periods of years for each body, which could be used to obtain approximate positions for other years by adding or subtracting recurrence periods from the required date to bring it within range of the tables. The latter type was the most popular.

The Arabic tables of the Cordovan astronomer al-Zarqālî (c.1029-1100), called **Arzachel** in Latin, were translated into Latin under the name *Toledan Tables.* These were arranged to be convenient for European users; they give the Sun's positions for 4 years, Mercury's for 46 years, Venus's for 8 years, Mars's for 79 years, Jupiter's for 83 years, and Saturn's for 59 years. The Sun's position is given to degrees and minutes for each day; the planets' positions are given to degrees only—Mercury, Venus, and Mars at 5 day intervals, Jupiter and Saturn at 10 day intervals. The Moon's position has to be calculated from some short tables. These tables were frequently used by medieval astrologers. We see a reflection of this in Chaucer's *Canterbury Tales* (c.1385), where, in the *Franklin's Tale* we read of the Clerk, "His tables Tolletanes forth he brought/Ful wel corrected . . . ."[91] The *Toledan Tables* remained in use for two or three centuries, but were eventually supplanted by the *Alphonsine Tables,* prepared c.1272 by order of the Spanish King Alphonso X the Wise (1226-1284), who was a great patron of astronomy and astrology. However, the latter tables apparently did not become well-known until the middle of the 14th century and did not immediately displace the older tables as we see from Chaucer.

By using these tables, an astrologer could calculate approximate positions for a given date without too much effort. The positions were generally accurate to within a few degrees (the Sun positions were of course closer), except for Mercury, which might be ten degrees off. The tables of ascensions enabled him to determine the ASC and MC fairly easily and Alchabitius house cusps without too much effort. There were tables for latitudes up to 48°24', which covered the Arab states and southern and central Europe. The large number of MSS that have been preserved show that these tables were much used.

If the astrologer was very careful, he would also need to know the longitude and latitude of the birthplace. The longitude would be "so many hours east or west of the prime meridian of his tables," and the latitude might still be the "clime" for rough work, but the actual degrees of latitude for more precise calculations. An up-to-date astrologer would have an astrolabe, which, combined with his knowledge of the solar position, would enable him to find the time of day or night and also to calculate the ASC and MC and even Alchabitius house cusps for the intermediate houses. If he could not afford an astrolabe or lived in a region where they were not available, he would employ a sundial to tell time by day.

The use of a diagram to display the horoscopic data seems to have become fairly common. The Arabic writers used a rectangular chart that was wider than high and which put the ASC at the top center. In most cases the astrologer used either the Sign-House system or the so-called Alchabitius system for the celestial houses.

Arabian astrology is basically Greek astrology with a small admixture of Persian and Indian techniques. From the Persians came the concept of cyclic periods of time correlated with the conjunctions of Jupiter and Saturn, which occur every twenty years. This was developed into an elaborate system best exemplified in the works of Albumasar and Māshā'allāh. In addition to the conjunctions (usually in mean longitude rather than in geocentric longitude), various profections were applied to the conjunctions.

Another technique that became very popular among the Arabs and later the Western European astrologers was that of the Aries Ingress—the

---

[91]See José Millás Vallicrosa, *Estudios sobre Azarquiel* (Madrid-Granada: Escuelas de Estudios Árabes de Madrid y Granada, 1943-1950), which contains the tables, instructions for their use, and an extensive commentary.

horoscope erected for the moment each year when the Sun enters the sign Aries. Unfortunately, from our vantage point we are bound to notice that both Māshā'allāh and Albumasar used solar tables that yielded positions in a fixed zodiac; hence, a chart drawn for the moment when the Sun had zero longitude was not the moment when the Sun reached the vernal equinox.[92] And even in the case of those astrologers who used nominally tropical tables there was a sizable error in their determination of the moment when the Sun reached the vernal equinox due to errors in the tables. The sad truth is that none of their charts were correct. And in fact astronomers did not produce tables that gave tropical longitudes of the Sun with an accuracy of plus or minus 1 minute of arc or better until the 18th century! Thus, the only elements of the older Aries Ingress charts that were reasonably accurate were the placement of planets in signs and the mutual aspects of the planets. The house positions were entirely wrong.

A similar technique in natal astrology became very popular—the revolution of the years of a nativity, or as we would say, the solar return. It is important to note that errors in the solar tables had little effect on the accuracy of solar returns, in contrast to their disastrous effect on Aries Ingresses. The reason is this: one of the errors inherent in a solar table is cyclic, i.e. it has almost the same value every time the Sun comes back to the same place in the zodiac and another is constant. Hence, if we calculate the natal Sun for a particular nativity, and the solar position is in error by 45 minutes of arc, when we calculate, say, the 20th solar return, the error in the solar position will again be close to 45 minutes, so we will have found very nearly the true time when the Sun has returned to its original position, and the house positions will be approximately correct. However, in the case of an Aries Ingress, we are expecting the error in the solar position to be zero; and if it is 45 minutes of arc, then the time of the ingress will be approximately 18 hours in error, which will of course completely vitiate the chart.

Another difference between Arabian astrology and 20th century astrology is that the Arabian astrologers continued to use the terms, the full and empty degrees, and various other features of Greek astrology, plus the Mansions of the Moon. Nineteenth and 20th century astrologers, not finding those features in Ptolemy's *Tetrabiblos*, supposed them to have been invented by the Arabs, and therefore invalid. It is still not generally recognized by modern astrologers that Ptolemy did not invent astrology, nor did he give a full exposition of the Greek astrology of his day (he admits as much). The Arabs also used many lots, or "parts" as they are now called,

---

[92]Despite the protestations of the 20th century "siderealists," it is difficult to see how bringing the Sun to the beginning of Aries in a fixed zodiac that has been arbitrarily bolted onto the stars can have any significance. By contrast, when the Sun reaches either equinox it comes to a point where something definite happens—it moves from one hemisphere to the other.

and they inherited dozens of them from the Greeks, although they did invent some new ones (al-Bîrûnî says waggishly[93] that "their number increases daily," and he lists 97 for nativities, 19 for mundane charts, 24 for crops, and 18 for horary charts).

In general, Arabian astrology tended to be more concerned with mathematical precision than the older Greek astrology had been. Also, the Arabs had recognized that Ptolemy's tables, which in Albumasar's time were already 700 years old, were no longer as accurate as they once were. New tables were prepared, and astronomers began the process of reviewing the accuracy of their tables every generation or so. This process was continued in the West once the accumulated Arabic knowledge became available in Latin translation. However, the best of the tables had errors of from 1 to 10 degrees in calculated positions. Usually the Sun was within 1 degree of the truth; the Moon, Jupiter, and Saturn within 2 degrees; and Venus and Mars within 3 degrees; but Mercury could be as far as 10 degrees off one way or the other. Things did not improve much until Kepler published his *Rudolphine Tables* in 1627.

It should of course be noted that all civil time was what is now termed Local Apparent Time (LAT), sometimes called "sundial time." Mean time such as we are accustomed to did not come into use until the 19th century except in one or two cities that began to keep mean time in the late 18th century. There were no clocks in ordinary use, so people mainly kept track of time by means of sundials. At night they guessed at the time or perhaps estimated it by burning candles. Water clocks seem to have fallen out of favor.

In the late middle ages some churches and monasteries began to ring bells at fixed times during the day or night, which helped people to estimate the time. And, finally, in the 14th century public and church clocks began to be erected, which helped the astrologers because those who lived within seeing distance or within hearing distance of striking clocks became aware of the time of day and might be able to tell their children what time of day they were born or they might recall the time when someone took to his bed because of sickness[94] or when they noticed that some event had occurred about which they later posed a question.[95]

Astrology continued to flourish, fighting a running battle with the

---

[93]*The Book of Instruction...*, Sect. 476 (p. 282).

[94]A chart erected for the moment when a sick person took to bed was used by astrologers and physicians for diagnosing the ailment and determining proper treatment and prognosis.

[95]We must also be aware that someone had to set the church clock, and his means of doing this were the same as those available to the individual astrologer. Thus, the church clock might well be wrong. Or, to put it more precisely, it was almost always wrong, with the error varying from a few minutes to a half hour or so. Still, for those who could not afford a sundial or some other means of keeping the time, it was better than nothing.

church. The percent of the population that was literate also grew, which helped because birth records began to be kept in the great families and gradually in the upper middle class families. Astrologers need books, tables, timepieces, and clients who can furnish dates and times. All of these things were on the increase in western Europe. In the Byzantine territory astrology enjoyed a renaissance during the 14th and early 15th centuries. But it seems to have declined substantially in Islamic lands, perhaps due to religious interference.

Astrological Images

Although mainstream astrology has nothing to do with magic, there was a secondary branch of the art that dealt with the production of amulets and talismans, generally called "astrological images." The idea behind the demand for these was that if one could procure a "lucky piece" and keep it, he would enjoy good fortune. These objects usually consisted of a small stone or piece of metal engraved with some sort of magic symbol representing a planet or a fixed star or else a ring. They are also sometimes called "seals."

To judge from the number of MSS that contain instructions for making these images, the demand was considerable and longstanding. Astrology entered the picture by supplying information as to an appropriate time to make the image. Thus, the making of astrological images was a branch of electional astrology. They could be made for special purposes, for which the astrologer would choose planetary positions that would be favorable to such a purpose. At the chosen time he would then manufacture the image.

Those who would like to read a concise introduction to this practice will find it in Vivian E. Robson's *The Fixed Stars and Constellations in Astrology* (Philadelphia: J.B. Lippincott, 1931. 3rd ed.), Chapter VII "Stars and Constellations in Mediaeval Magic." Some of the images of the fixed stars are shown on p. 233.

There are many medieval tracts on planetary images, rings, etc. A number of these are attributed to **Hermes** and some are said to have been translated by Belemith (Apollonius?). For details see Thorndike, HMES, Vols. 1 and 2; also, Carmody, AAASLT.

Thorndike[96] cites an interesting story about Guido Bonatti and an astrological image:

> One of the stories told of Bonatti may be noted in conclusion, since it conerns an astrological image. Pitying a poor apothecary with whom he used to play chess, Guido gave him a wax image of a ship, telling him to keep it hid in a box in a secret place and he would grow rich, but that if he

---

[96]Lynn Thorndike, HMES 2, p. 835. His source for this story is Muratori, *Rerum Italicarum Scriptores*, rev. ed., Fasc. 20, 1903, p. 105.

removed it, he would grow poor again. True enough, the man became wealthy, but then he began to fear lest the image be the work of witchcraft. So, having made his fortune, he decided to save his soul and confessed concerning the image to a priest who bade him destroy it. But then, as Bonatti had predicted, he rapidly lost his entire fortune. He then begged Guido to make him another image, but Bonatti cursed him and told him that the image had been no magic one but had derived its virtue from constellations which would not recur for another fifty years.

The Mansions of the Moon

In ancient times the Arabs had established a circle of twenty-eight asterisms in the sky. The Moon's mean period is 27.321 days, so each day the Moon moved into the next asterism in the circle. In the Arabic language these asterisms were called *manāzil* (sing. *manzil*), a word derived from the verb *nazala* 'to dismount, to stop for a rest, etc.'; hence, the *manāzil* were 'stopping places', in Latin translation, *mansiones*, whose root meaning is the same. They were also sometimes called "stations" from the Latin *stationes*, lit. 'standing still [places]' or 'stations'.

Al-Bîrûnî tells us[97] that the lunar mansions were invented by the early Arabs to keep track of the seasons of the year. They observed the one that rose before the Sun every morning, and by means of memorized verses passed down from father to son they knew what weather they might expect and when to plant their crops, etc. Al-Bîrûnî rightly points out that it is the Sun's position in the tropical zodiac that controls the seasons and the general trend of the weather, not its position with regard to the asterisms of the lunar mansions. But the country folk were of course unaware of this.[98] Originally, then, the Mansions of the Moon had only a meteorological significance. But al-Bîrûnî notes that some astrologers have ascribed astrological significations to them. He adds that in his own time (early 11th century) the series was considered to begin with *al-Sharatān* 'the two signs' consisting of the two stars β and γ Arietis, which are the two horns of the Ram. And he adds "Other nations begin with the Pleiades. I do not know whether they do this because the Pleiades are more clearly and easily visible without any study or research than the other Stations, or because, as I have found in some books of Hermes, the vernal equinox coincides with the rising of the Pleiades."

---

[97]The *Chronology of Ancient Nations*, Chapt. XXI, translated by Edward Sachau.

[98]Since the fixed stars of the Mansions of the Moon appear to drift slowly with respect to the equinoxes and solstices, the season of the year indicated by their heliacal risings slowly changes at the approximate rate of one calendar month every 2,100 years.

Al-Bîrûnî gives a description of the stars in each asterism, but he also points out that it is appropriate to measure them at equal intervals of approximately 12°51′26″. from the vernal equinox. As he notes, the Hindus generally reckon twenty-seven mansions, called *nakshatras* which originally consisted of asterisms, but which the Hindu astrologers were accustomed to measure off from the first point of Aries according to their tables, at equal intervals of 13°20′. But their series nominally begins with the one called *Krittika*, which represents the Pleiades; its longitude in the Hindu fixed zodiac is 28°52′ Taurus.

Details of the Arabian *manāzil*, the Indian *nakshatras*, and also the Chinese *sieu* are given in Chapter III of V.E. Robson's *The Fixed Stars and Constellations in Astrology.*

Perhaps influenced by the astrology associated with the Hindu *nakshatras* and by analogies based upon their Arabic names, the Arabian mansions seem to have taken on special characteristics that related directly to ordinary human affairs, rather than being restricted solely to meteorology. These characteristics could be used for elections, but they also began to be associated with the ancient art of geomancy, so that certainly not later than the 10th century books and "boards" began to appear that enabled the user to make (in various ways) a selection of one of the twenty-eight mansions. These were often called "the twenty-eight judges." He then referred to a table which gave standard assessments of present conditions and prognostications of the future. The user then tried to apply these oracular statements to the situation or question he was interested in. It was something like the Chinese *I Ching*, although with fewer standard pronouncements.

Two medieval books that gave the necessary information for practicing this form of divination were the book called *Mathematicus* by **Alhandreus**,[99] which makes the selection of the appropriate "judge" from the numerical values of the letters in the querent's and the querent's mother's names, and Bernard Silvester's *Experimentarius* (12th century).[100] In addition, the book of magic called *Picatrix*[101] gives instruc-

---

[99]See Lynn Thorndike, HMES 1, p. 710 ff. It is found in a Paris MS of the 10th century. Various later versions appear in the MSS, and one reworking of it was printed as *Arcandam doctor peritissimus ac non vulgaris astrologus, de veritatibus et praedictionibus astrologiae* .... 'The most skilled scholar Arcandam and no mean Astrologer, On the Truths and Predictions of Astrology ....' ed. by Richard Roussat (Paris, 1542). It was translated into French (Rouen, 1584, et al.), and an English translation of the French version was published at London in 1626, et al.

[100]See Lynn Thorndike, HMES 2, Chapt. 39 "Bernard Silvester." The names of the "28 judges" are given in a footnote to p. 113.

[101]See Lynn Thorndike, HMES 2, Chapter 66 "Picatrix." There is a modern edition of this work by David Pingree, *Picatrix: the Latin Version of the Ghāyāt al-hakîm* (London: The Warburg Institue, 1986) lxxx,326 pp. illus.

tions for making astrological images for the Mansions of the Moon. The methods of selecting a mansion or "judge" seldom had anything to do with the actual position of the Moon; hence, this was not really an astrological procedure, although it masqueraded as one.

Perhaps the only surviving true astrological use of the Mansions of the Moon is in making elections[102] and in connection with the so-called Prenatal Epoch. E.H. Bailey (1876-1959), in his book *The Prenatal Epoch* (London, 1916; repr. in facs. New York: Samuel Weiser, 1970 and 1973), Chapter 5 "The Paramount Law of Sex," says the Mansions are indicators of sex.

Centiloquies

A collection of 100 astrological aphorisms called *Karpós* 'Fruit' in Greek and *Centiloquium* 'Hundred Sayings' in Latin was attributed to **Claudius Ptolemy** in the Middle Ages. It is certainly not his, but its real author is unknown.

Perhaps spurred on by the popularity of this work, others appeared. The best known are those attributed to **Hermes** and **Bethem**. Both of these were fairly well known as late as the 17th century, but most modern astrologers are only aware of the *Centiloquy* attributed to Ptolemy.

The *Karpós* was early translated into Arabic and is often found in the MSS with a *Commentary* by `Alî ibn Ridwân (Haly Abenrudian). The Greek text has most recently been edited by Emilie Boer in *Claudii Ptolemaei Opera quae extant omnia* (Leipzig: B.G. Teubner, 1961), vol. 3, Part 2. The most familiar English translation is by J.M. Ashmand. It was translated into French by Nicolas Bourdin, the Marquess of Villennes (d. 1670), as *Le Centilogue de Ptolomee* (Paris: Cardin Besongne, 1651). The translation was reprinted along with the Latin version and an extensive commentary in French by J.B. Morin, *Remarques astrologiques* (Paris: Pierre Menard, 1657), one year after Morin's death.

An English version of the *Centiloquy* attributed to **Hermes** is included in Henry Coley's *Clavis Astrologiae Elimata* (London: Ben Tooke and Thos. Sawbridge, 1676), pp. 329-339. A few may be cited as examples:

> VI. Venus is opposite to Mercury. He comprehends Languages and Discipline[103]; she delights and pleasures, Jupiter the like to Mars; this coveteth Mercy and Justice; that, Impiety and Cruelty

> XLII. The Lord of the second House hath the same strength in hurting, as the Lord of the eighth; the Lord of the sixth, the same with the Lord of the twelfth.

---

[102]See Vivian E. Robson, *Electional Astrology* (Philadelphia and London: J.B. Lippincott Co., 1937), Chapter IV "The Lunar Mansions and Aspects."
[103]i.e., 'education', not 'punishment' as we commonly define the word.

XLIV. The best Artist in the world may chance to err when he mistakes a true Significator for a false one.

LXXX. Planets in fixed Signs shew the matter durable; in Bi corporeal Signes, doubtful; in moveable, convertible to good or evil.

Bethem was evidently an Arabian astrologer, but his identity is unknown. Coley also published a translation of his *Centiloquy* (*op. cit.*, pp. 339-345). Most of Bethem's aphorisms deal with horary charts or elections. Some of the earlier ones resemble the corresponding ones in Ibn Ezra's list of precepts. Here are some examples:

II. Thou mayest know, when a Planet is Retrograde, he is as a man infirm, stupified, and sollicitous.

V. If Stationary to Retrogradation, as a healthful man receding from health; yet there is hope of Recovery remaining.

VI. If Stationary to Direct, as a sick man amending.

VII. If Besieged, as a man fearful, between two Enemies: (*i.e.*) when between the two Infortunes.

VIII. A Planet between Jupiter and Venus, is as a man pleasant and free from Want and Trouble.

LVI. The Moon in square of Saturn, is a bad day. Chiefly in meeting with Kings, and great Persons. Let not Noble and Eminent Men then take Journeys; for they will prove ill. The sick man will hardly escape, that is taken sick at such a time.

Some Important Points

- While learning languished in western Europe during the Dark Ages, it survived in the Eastern Roman Empire, and from the 8th through the 11th centuries it flourished in Islamic lands, after which it slowly declined for a century and then was dealt a devastating blow when Baghdad was sacked by Hulagu Khan (1217-1265) in 1258. Astrology followed pretty much the same pattern.
- One by one the classical Greek astrological texts disappeared beginning in the 5th or 6th centuries. This loss paralleled the loss of classical Greek literature, and was due to disinterest and neglect, aggravated by individual losses due to war and pillage. Around the year 1000 there was a revival of interest in astrology among the Byzantines. This slowly increased until it reached its peak in the 14th century, when a number of astrological texts were copied from older MSS and some compendiums of older material (and even of Arabic

material in Greek translation) were prepared. Some of these 14th century MSS (as well as 15th century copies of them and a few still older MSS) were brought to the West before the fall of Constantinople.

- Astrology virtually died out in western Europe after the 5th century, not to be revived until the 12th century. When it did begin to come back to life it depended almost entirely on books and tables translated into Latin from Arabic originals. These books contained Arabian astrology, which was mostly Greek astrology with a small admixture of Persian and Hindu astrology. Hence, the so-called traditional astrology of later western Europe was Greek astrology as transmitted by the Arabs.

- Following the lead of Dorotheus (rather than Ptolemy), the Arabs made considerable use of accidental significators (house rulers), rather than relying almost entirely on general significators as the *Tetrabiblos* directs.

- Adding to the sizable number of lots they inherited from the Greeks, the Arabs added many more. Modern European astrologers, noting that Ptolemy had mentioned only one (the Lot of Fortune) and that the Arabic astrologers used many, concluded that the Greeks had had only one, and the Arabs had invented all the rest. Whence, the lots other than the Lot of Fortune are generally referred to today as the "Arabic Parts."

- The Arabs invented the Solar Return as a predictive technique for natal astrology.

- Horary astrology was in common use and was developed substantially beyond the techniques handed down from the Greeks. The fundamental rules, definitions, and techniques in use today go back to the early 9th century books of Zahel (Sahl ibn Bishr).

- Mundane astrology was developed greatly—the Arabs invented Aries Ingresses and constructed elaborate schemes for judging conjunctions of Mars, Jupiter, and Saturn, and the appearance of comets. Using Persian ideas and planetary tables derived from Persian tables (using a fixed zodiac), they developed outlines of world history tied to astrology.

- The so-called Alchabitius system, which was actually developed by the Greeks not later than the 5th century, gradually became the standard house system. However, some astrologers continued to use the original Sign-House system of the Alexandrian founders.

- Arabian astronomers recognized that Ptolemy's tables were out of date and no longer accurate, so they produced several sets of improved planetary and star tables, some of which became the basis of Western European tables in the 12th century.

- Beginning as early as the ninth century there was an upsurge in magic and divination that was associated with astrology—the making of astrological images, geomancy, and various numerological schemes of divination.

- Sadly, the destruction of Arabic literature in the east in the 13th century was followed by the destruction of Arabic literature in the west which accompanied the Christian reconquest of Spain. There were said to have been seventy libraries in Andalusia containing more than a million Arabic and Hebrew volumes, while that territory remained in Muslim hands. Virtually all of these books were destroyed, so that today only a few thousand volumes in Arabic survive in Spain's libraries. There is no doubt that many books on astrology were among those destroyed. Fortunately, the Twelfth Century Translators had produced Latin versions of some of the most important books while the Arabic originals were still available.

The Fourth Period

Early Modern Astrology

The invention of printing in the mid-15th century ushered in the Fourth Period of astrological history in the west. Coinciding as it did with an upsurge of intellectual and economic activity, astrology gained rapidly in popularity (and inevitably became a larger and more inviting target for the Church). For the first time in a thousand years books became readily available and affordable (at least by the middle and upper classes). Literacy increased. Chairs of astrology were established in many European universities. It was a required subject for most medical students, since it was used both as a diagnostic and a prognostic tool.

Most of the Arabic works translated by the Twelfth Century Translators were printed by the year 1500. Manilius's *Astronomica* (1472) and Firmicus's *Mathesis* (1497) were printed. Ptolemy's *Quadripartite* (its Greek name is *Tetrabiblos*) and (pseudo-) Ptolemy's *Centiloquy*[1] appeared in 1484 (John of Seville's and Plato of Tivoli's translations from the Arabic).

Regiomontanus

Johann Müller (1436-1476), usually known by his Latin name **Regiomontanus**, was a native of southern Germany who was educated at the University of Vienna. He was a capable mathematician and astronomer and was also interested in astrology. After leaving Vienna, he eventually settled in Rome, where he is said to have died of the plague in the summer of 1476. His lasting contribution to astrology was the computation of an elaborate set of house and auxiliary tables for what has since been called the Regiomontanus system of houses[2]:

---

[1] A short treatise containing 100 aphorisms or short statements of astrological techniques. It was universally attributed to Ptolemy during the medieval period, but internal evidence shows that it is actually of later and unknown origin.

[2] The *Dictionary of Scientific Biography* says that Regiomontanus was as-

Tabulae directionum profectionumque...
in nativitatibus multum utiles.
[Tables of Directions and Profections...
Very Useful in Nativities]
Augsburg: Erhard Ratdolt, 1490. 4to.

Regiomontanus either calculated or had calculated for him an ephemeris for the years 1474-1506; it was published by Regiomontanus himself at Nürnberg in 1474. I believe it was the first ephemeris printed in Europe. As such, it ran through eleven editions before 1500, and was succeeded by an ephemeris for the years 1499-1532 published by Johann Stoeffler (1452-1531) and Jakob Pflaum.[3]

The house tables,[4] which were published in 1490, soon caused a change in the standard house system from Alchabitius to Regiomontanus. In the early 1500s there was some interest in the Equal House system[5] following the publication of Firmicus, who explains it in Book II of the *Mathesis*, but most astrologers stayed with the new Regiomontanan tables, which undoubtedly looked more scientific. The Campanus house system, although a century older, never caught on because the calculations were too much for most astrologers and no tables were available. It has become a cliché in the 20th century that the Placidus system later became the 19th and 20th century standard because it was the only one for which affordable tables were readily available. This is partly true, but the same thing could be said for the initial success of the Regiomontanus system. Had the first published book of house and auxiliary tables been according to the Campanus system, there is little doubt that it would have become the standard of the time.

---

sisted in the computation of these extensive tables by Martin Bylica (1433-1493) of Olkusz, Poland, who later presented a MS of the work to the University of Cracow. In addition to the astrological tables, the printed book contains the first printed table of tangents (at $1°$ intervals), although they were not called by that name.

[3]Lynn Thorndike, HMES 5, p. 348.

[4]Astronomical tables that partition the sky into the celestial houses. This is usually done by making trigonometrical calculations that were especially tedious before the invention of logarithms. By using a table of houses, the time required for the erection of a horoscope is substantially reduced. Astrologers have devised several different ways of dividing the sky. Each requires a separate set of trigonometrical formulae or a separate set of house tables. In the calculation of primary directions, auxiliary tables are also very helpful.

[5]One of the systems used in classical antiquity. It did not require calculation, since you simply measured off 30° intervals from the ascending degree. Its simplicity disturbed many astrologers after the invention of trigonometry, since they thought that surely some more elaborate calculation should be required to establish the beginning points (called "cusps") of the celestial houses. (See p. 135 n. 65 for the origin of the term 'cusp'.)

However, Regiomontanus erred in thinking that he had recovered a system of house division that Ptolemy "had in mind" when he wrote *Tetrabiblos*, iii. 10. Actually, as a careful reading of the text will show, Ptolemy had merely a small modification of the Equal House system in mind, along with what we would call Placidus primaries.[6] Later astrologers thought that surely Ptolemy must have based his house division, whatever it was, on his method for primary progressions. But on the contrary, he evidently considered house division and primary progressions to be separate techniques.

Symon de Phares

Symon de Phares was born about 1440 and died not long after 1499.[7] He was well-educated in his youth and later studied at the Universities of Paris, Oxford, and Montpellier into his 30's. Thereafter he visited Rome, Venice, Cairo, and Alexandria. Then he was attached to the court of Louis XI (1423-1483) at Paris, and after the king's death to the court of John II, Duke of Bourbon (d. 1488) at Moulins. When the Duke died, Symon moved to Lyons where he quickly built up a reputation as a good astrologer, which in those days meant one who could successfully predict actual events. He was married and is said to have had four sons and a daughter.

Symon's fame spread to Paris and came to the attention of the new king Charles VIII (1470-1498). The king was so entranced by the stories about Symon's accurate predictions, that he determined to visit him. On All Saints Day 1490 the king met with Symon at Lyons and was much impressed by the astrologer. Thereafter Charles favored Symon, but unfortunately the king did not have full control over the government and the ecclesiastical ministers; and, to make matters worse, he died in 1498, leaving Symon without a prominent protector.

Going back to 1490, one would think that being well thought of by the king was about as much as an astrologer could hope for, but as Wickersheimer observes:[8]

"The favor of great men is not always a good thing. That of Charles VIII was for Simon de Phares the principal

---

[6]See my paper "Jean Baptiste Morin's Comments on House Division in his Remarques Astrologiques" in the AFA *Journal of Research*, vol. 6 (1991):19-35.

[7]Most of the information that follows is from Ernest Wickersheimer's preface to his edition of Symon's book, *Recueil des plus celebres astrologues et quelques hommes doctes faict par Symon de Phares* 'A Compendium of the Most Celebrated Astrologers and some other Learned Men made by Symon de Phares' (Paris: Honoré Champion, 1929). The text, edited for the first time by Wickersheimer, is from what is probably the autograph MS fonds français 1357 of the Bibliothèque Nationale in Paris. It is written in Middle French, which has a certain charm of its own to the modern eye. There is a new edition by Jean-Patrice Boudet (Paris: H. Champion, 1997). See also Thorndike, HMES 4, Chapter 62.

[8]*Ibid.*, p. viii.

cause of his misfortunes, for it excited envy, then slander, and soon the noise was spread abroad that a familiar spirit was whispering his responses to the astrologer."[9]

"The hostilities were opened by the Archbishop of Lyons. . . ."

Shortly after the king's visit, Symon was hauled into ecclesiastical court, tried, and thrown in jail. After some time his case was reviewed by his enemies, and, in order to get out of jail, Symon was obliged to renounce all future efforts to predict the future by any means whatsoever. He was released, but his astronomical instruments and his books were seized and sent to Paris to be examined by masters of theology and law. Symon naturally wanted to get his books back, so he moved to Paris and engaged in fruitless legal wrangling to reclaim them. This only irritated his accusers, who added to his annoyance (and to that of other astrologers) by issuing a general prohibition against the printing or selling of astrological books.

Having exhausted the legal approach without success, Symon got the idea of writing a book on astrology addressed to King Charles. It was to be in three parts, of which the first would be a history of astrology, and the other two an exposition of its technical side. Only the first part was ever written, possibly because Charles died unexpectedly on 7 April 1498. Thereafter, Symon passes from history. The last notice of him is from the Archives of Lyons, which contain a notice dated 1499 that he was living in Paris.

His book remained uncirculated and unpublished until 1929. It is a remarkable work, full of a mixture of fact and fancy, but always interesting to read. Wickersheimer says of it:[10]

The author proposes in effect to prove the excellence of astrology by the quality of the men who cultivated it, "holy patriarchs, prophets, popes, cardinals, archbishops, bishops, emperors, kings, dukes, counts and many other noble men, sages, serious persons and great teachers, philosophers and clerics." He has assembled for this purpose several hundred biographical notices, relevant, as he says

---

[9]The Catholic Church, being unwilling to admit that an astrologer could read the future in the stars, fell back on the dictum of Saint Augustine (354-430) that astrologers could not predict anything truly from their charts but that demons knew something of the future and would sometimes give their knowledge to astrologers. It is amusing to note that modern scientists opposed to astrology also believe that astrologers cannot predict the future, but since they don't believe in the existence of demons, they ascribe the astrologers' successes to vagueness, or failing that, to coincidence.

[10]*Op. cit.*, p. XI.

when he addresses Charles VIII, to "the very noble, excellent and great personnages, who from the time of the first man Adam down to the present, which is the XVI year of your reign, who have devoted themselves to the study and practice" of astrology.[11]

The first twelve and a half pages of the printed edition contain Symon's prologue. Then he begins his list with Adam and his children. He rehearses many famous names from the Bible and from ancient history, mixing the knowledge of his day with his own speculations. A few of his notices may be of interest:

3346.[12] Chiron, the doctor was around this time—a very just man and a very wise philosopher, the which was very well educated in the science of the stars and also in the science of medicine. It was this one who first sought out and investigated the virtue, nature, and property of herbs through the celestial course, and he demonstrated it to many people and also the science of astrology, especially to Aesculapius, who was then a sovereign physician. . . .

4524. Nycepsus was in this time, a virtuous philosopher, physician and great astrologer, the teacher of the sons of King Celestes of Greece. This one predicted and prognosticated many things, both on the great conjunctions and on the revolution of the years of the world, and, among other things, he predicted the destruction of Babylon and the great battle that was then between the Greeks and the Barbarians, and also that which was between the Greeks and those of Alexandria....This one did not write anything, with the exception of a few particular judgements that I have seen.

[1486]. Johannes Miller,[13] physician and great astrologer. This one made the table of the book of Guido Bonatti, very curiously and well arranged, employed by Erath Radolt, a printer in Augsburg.

[1487]. Johannes de Monte Regio, German, excellent

---

[11]Wickersheimer notes that Charles died in the fourteenth year of his reign, so evidently Symon had planned to have his book ready to present to the king in late 1498 or early 1499.

[12]Symon used an era for dating that apparently began some six thousand years before the birth of Christ, so his year 3346 is equivalent to about 2654 B.C. The date is of course entirely fanciful.

[13]Note that Symon did not realize that Johann Müller (Miller, as he spells it) is the same person as Johannes de Monte Regio (Regiomontanus).

astrologer, the most profound in the theory of the planets that has been demonstrated in the last hundred years, and was held to be the flower of the Germans and the Italians and, because of his excellence, was sent for by Pope Sixtus [IV] to enlarge upon the Easter [calculations] of the abbot Denis,[14] of whom mention was made above, . . . He made before going to Rome, the great almanac for many years, made an astrological calendar of very great utility, [and] died around the age of 34 years, when he had made his directions, which are very useful. May God receive his spirit!

Symon's biographical notices improve with quality as he approaches his own time. The early ones, as can be seen from the samples above, are entertaining but not factual. But some of the later information is valuable. He was at any rate the first astrological biographer/historian of the Renaissance, as well as a notable victim of religious bigotry.

Astrology on the Continent after 1500

Astrology was in a boom as the new century opened, and it continued to flourish for half a century before the first signs of a slow-down appeared. Curiously enough, it seems to have ultimately been a victim of the Protestant Reformation, not because of a conflict with religion, but because the Reformation signaled a fundamental revision in European thinking. Before, men were accustomed to taking things on ancient (or at least medieval) authority. There were interminible squabbles over details but ancient authority was generally accepted. But when men began to gain the courage to reject thousand year old religious beliefs, they also began to look at everything associated with the past as not necessarily being valid merely because it was in all the books. This diverted a certain amount of scholarly effort from finding more old opinions to back up what was already believed to viewing things as they are and to looking for new information on everything. Probably the discovery of the New World by Columbus also had some lasting impact upon patterns of thought in general, rather than just upon geography.

These changes did not necessarily bode ill for astrology, but they did increase scepticism of it as of everything else. What was worse for astrology was the constant publication of prophecies of disasters and the demise of prominent persons, especially the popes. The former increased scepticism, since not all of them were fulfilled, while the latter aroused the ire of powerful persons who resented being pushed into their graves ahead of time. It took a century and a half for these things plus the change in thinking to have their ultimate effect, yet by the end of the century the tide had turned and was running out. But more of this below.

---

[14]The Christian chronographer Dionysius Exiguus (fl. 532).

Mundane Astrology

While the main occupation of astrologers continued to be with natal horoscopes and horary charts, a number of astrologers busied themselves with mundane predictions. These consisted mainly of judgments on Aries Ingresses, eclipses, and Jupiter-Saturn conjunctions. As we noted above, the Aries Ingresses they calculated were actually invalid, since their times could not be obtained with accuracy from the available tables and ephemerides, although something might be made out of the mutual aspects of the planets. With eclipses the astrologers were on safer ground. The average error of timing for eclipses was perhaps an hour or an hour and a half. Thus, about half the time they might get the rising sign right.

Conjunctions were another matter. The inherent errors in the Jupiter and Saturn positions might well throw the calculated conjunction dates off by a month. The modern procedure of erecting a chart for the exact time of the conjunction was therefore inapplicable. More commonly, judgment was made by considering the sign position of the conjunction and also judging the nearby Aries Ingress and any eclipses that might be close. With the cost of printing affordable, many mundane predictions were published. We cannot review them here,[15] but we will say something about the Conjunction of 1524, which sparked a tremendous outburst of astrological predictions. Thorndike cites a paper by G. Hellman that mentions 133 different publications by 56 different authors.[16]

From modern astronomical data we can see that the conjunction occurred on the morning of 1 February 1524 in 10 Pisces. Mars was in 6 Pisces applying to the conjunction. The occurrence of the conjunction in the water sign Pisces caused many astrologers to predict a deluge or flood. Had they known that the as yet undiscovered planet Neptune was in 8 Pisces, they would undoubtedly have been even more certain that some watery disaster impended.

Thorndike says the rash of predictions can be traced back to a statement made by **Johann Stoeffler**[17] (1452-1531) in his *Almanach nova plurimis annis venturis inserviens* 'A New Almanac Serving for Many Years to Come' (Ulm, 1499). Thorndike translates the passage as follows:

> In this year we shall see eclipse neither of sun nor moon.
> But in this year will occur positions of the planets well worthy of wonderment. For in the month of February will oc-

---

[15]See Lynn Thorndike, HMES 5 & 6, for many citations of such predictions, and in particular HMES 5, Chapter XI ``The Conjunction of 1524.''

[16]"Aus der Blütezeit der Astrometeorologie" 'From the Heyday of Astrometeorology' with the sub-title "J. Stoefflers Prognose für das Jahr 1524" 'J. Stoeffler's Forecast for the Year 1524', No. 1 in the series *Beiträge zur Geschichte der Meteorologie* 'Essays on the History of Meteorology (Berlin: Behrend, 1914).

[17]Stoeffler was a professor of mathematics at the University of Tübingen.

cur twenty conjunctions, small, mean, and great, of which sixteen will occupy a watery sign, signifying to well night the whole world, climates, kingdoms, provinces, estates, dignitaries, brutes, beasts of the sea, and to all dwellers on earth indubitable mutation, variation and alteration such as we have scarce perceived for many centuries from historiographers and our elders. Lift up your heads, therefore, ye Christian men.

This almanac proved to be very popular. It was reprinted at Venice seven times—the latest issue in 1522, just two years before the fateful year. Reading Stoeffler's prediction apparently inspired many mundane astrologers to investigate the configurations for 1524 and to publish their own predictions of floods, but some astrologers opposed the idea. Brother Michael de Petrasancta, Th.D., professor of metaphysics at the University of Rome, published a *Defense* of mundane predictions,[18] although with reasonable restrictions, and concluded that "no educated astrologer believes that there will be a universal deluge [in 1524]", but "that the coming conjunctions of February, 1524, signify a great amount of rain and snow."[19]

Some later critics of astrology scoffed at the aqueous predictions and stated that in fact the year 1524 was unusually dry, but Thorndike cites a contemporary record which states that while February was mostly fair in northern Italy, the remainder of the year saw periods of much rain, heavy and damaging thunderstorms and hail that killed livestock.[20]

Predictive almanacs remained popular, and probably contained enough hits to offset the misses. At any rate, they offered the public something interesting to read and kept astrology in the public mind. Natal and Horary astrology benefitted from the publicity.

But now let us mention some of the most prominent continental astrologers of the 16th and 17th centuries:

Gauricus

Luca Gaurico (1476-1558) was a Roman Catholic bishop and court astrologer to the popes and to Catherine de' Medici (1519-1589), Queen of France. He was the second modern astrologer to publish a collection of horoscopes of notable persons (along with the foundation charts of a number of cities): *Tractatus astrologicus, in quo agitur de praeteritis multorum hominum accidentibus per proprias eorum genituras ad*

---

[18]*Libellus in defensionem astrologorum iudicantium ex coniunctionibus planetarum in piscibus M.D.xxiiii...* (Rome: Marcellus Silber alias Franck, 1521. 32 fols.).

[19]Thorndike's summary, HMES 5, p. 199. See *ibid.*, p. 197 n.45, for the book title and publication data.

[20]HMES 5, pp. 231-232.

unguem examinatis... 'An Astrological Treatise, in which the Principal Accidents of Many Men are Carefully Examined along with their Genitures...' (Venice: C.T. Navò, 1552). The book contains 20 foundation charts and 141 natal horoscopes with comments. All of his works may be consulted in his *Opera Omnia* (Basel, 1575).

Schöner

Johann Schöner (1477-1547), a professor of mathematics, wrote several astrological works, of which the best known is his *De judiciis nativitatum libri tres* 'Three Books on the Judgments of Nativities' (Nürnberg, 1545). William Lilly says of it, "a good Book, but immethodicall." See the Bibliography for a new translation.

Melanchthon

Philip Schwarzerd (1497-1560), who translated his surname into the Greek **Melanchthon**, was the leading religious scholar of the Reformation and a close friend of Martin Luther (1483-1546). He was the first to edit and translate Ptolemy's *Tetrabiblos* directly from Greek into Latin (Basel, 1553); with it was included Giovanni Pontano's Latin version of pseudo-Ptolemy's *Centiloquy*. Unlike many other theologians, Melanchthon saw no conflict between astrology and religion.

One of his principal interests was Luther's horoscope. Many had thought that Luther was born in 1484, one reason being that there was a Jupiter-Saturn conjunction in November of that year. Melanchthon seems to have believed that in the beginning, for Peuckert cites a passage from a letter he wrote to Andreas Osiander (1498-1552) in 1539, "We are in doubt as to Luther's birthdate.[21] The day is entirely certain, also very nearly the hour, midnight, as I myself have heard from the mouth of his mother. 1484, I say, was the year... Gauricus approved the chart for 1484."[22] But Melanchthon later changed his mind and stated that the year was 1483. (It is now generally agreed that Luther was born between 11 PM and midnight on 10 November 1483.)

Cardan

Jerome Cardan (1501-1576) was a famous physician, mathematician, astrologer, and miscellaneous writer. His astrological works include an edition of the *Quadripartite* (the Latin version of Ptolemy's *Tetrabiblos*) with an elaborate commentary, *Seven Segments*, a large collection of astrological aphorisms (containing a number of horoscopes as

---

[21]Melanchthon says *Geburtszeit*, lit. 'birth time', but he plainly means the birth *date*, since he only brings the year into question.

[22]Will-Erich Peuckert, *Astrologie* (Stuttgart: W. Kohlhammer, 1960), pp. 119-120, who reproduces Gaurico's chart from his *Tractatus astrologicus* (Venice, 1552). It is set for 22 October 1484 at 1:10 PM with a quintuple conjunction of Sun, Mercury, Venus, Jupiter, and Saturn in the 9th house—obviously a speculative chart erected on an incorrectly reported birthdate.

examples of the rules), a collection of 100 nativities *De exemplis centum geniturarum* 'Examples of One Hundred Genitures' (Nürnberg: Johannes Petreius, 1547), and a smaller collection of twelve nativities. Cardan was in fact the first Western astrologer since Antigonus of Nicea to publish a collection of nativities. Most of his published horoscopes are drawn using the Equal House system, although he occasionally used the Regiomontanus system, and, in the case of his own chart, he says the "old style houses" [Alchabitius] seemed to him to give more appropriate house placements.

Cardan was generally fortunate in his horoscope interpretations, but he had one famous failure. In 1552 he was summoned as a physician to treat John Hamilton (c.1511-1571), the Archbishop of St. Andrews. From the reports it appears that the Archbishop was suffering from an allergy to feathers. Cardan told him to change his pillow and undertake some other revisions in his regimen. The Archbishop recovered and begged Cardan to stay, but he chose not to. On his way home, he was introduced to the young King Edward VI (1537-1553). Cardan examined him and also cast his horoscope. It looked promising, he said. Unfortunately, the king had contracted consumption, and he died in July 1553. Cardan was chagrined at his failure to see that in the chart. He therefore reviewed his calculations and published the king's chart as the first in his *The Book of Twelve Genitures*.[23] The chart is set for 12 October 1537 at 1:26 AM. It has 29 Leo rising with Venus in 12 Virgo and Saturn in 16 Virgo below the ASC, while Mars is in the 12th house. Cardan mentions that Saturn was ruler of the preceding New Moon, and, since it was in the 17th degree, that should also be the MC degree. Having adopted that, he got 29 Leo for the ASC.

The surviving historical records give the king's birth time as 2 A.M. If correct, it would make 7 Virgo rise rather than 29 Leo as Cardan shows. This is immediately worse, for Mercury is now ruler of the ASC and square Mars in the 12th house. It looks as if Cardan may have been led astray by the Ptolemaic rectification method he employed.

Cardan was perhaps the most famous of the renaissance astrologers. His huge literary output on a variety of subjects was published in a collected edition nearly a century after his death: *Opera Omnia* (Lyons: Huguetan & Ravaud, 1663. 10 vols.; New York & London: Johnson Reprint, 1967. 10 vols. repr. in facs.). Vol. 5 contains most of Cardan's astrological works.

Junctinus

Francesco Giuntini (1522-1590?), known to astrologers as **Junctinus**, was a Catholic priest, and the author of a huge work *The Mirror of Astrology*. It contains the Greek text and a Latin version of Ptolemy's *Tetrabiblos*, Junctinus's commentary on that work, a collection of

---

[23]*Opera Omnia*, vol. 5, pp. 503-508. The chart is on p. 503.

all the sets of aphorisms known to him and his synthesis of astrological theory and techniques from the Arabic writers, the whole illustrated with 400 or more example horoscopes, revolutions, and other charts. This consitituted the largest collection of nativities ever assembled until the publication three centuries later of Alan Leo's *Notable Nativities* (which contains many horoscopes from Junctinus in abbreviated format). Most of Junctinus's text remains untranslated; however, there is a French translation of the section on Solar Returns:

Speculum astronomiae.
[The Mirror of Astrology]
Lyons: , 1573.
Lyons: Symphorien Beraud, 1583. 2 vols in-folio. repr.

Junctin de Florence
Traité des révolutions solaires.
trans. by Charles de Camiade
annotated by A. Volguine
Nice: Éditions de Cahiers Astrologiques, 1962. 206 pp.

Ranzovius

Count Heinrich von Rantzau (1526-1599) studied at the University of Wittenberg, after which he spent seven years at the court of the emperor Charles V (1500-1558). He was a good businessman and money-manager and became very rich. Von Rantzau was also an art lover, a book collector, and a student of astrology. In the latter part of his life he wrote several treatises on astrology, one of which is important for the history of the science:

Catalogus imperatorum, regum ac virorum illustrium,
qui artem astrologiae amarunt, ornarunt et exercuerunt.
[Catalogue of Emperors, Kings, and Illustrious Men,
Who Loved, Honored, and Practiced the Art of Astrology]
Antwerp: Plantin Press, 1580. 8vo. 109 pp. 1st edition.
Leipzig, 1581. 2nd ed.
Leipzig, 1584. 4to. xx,469,vii pp. 3rd ed. enlarged.

Thorndike says the history contains numerous errors but also offers information on many astrologers who are otherwise seldom or never mentioned in the usual reference books.[24] This is the second book of its sort, the first being Symon de Phare's *Recueil*, mentioned above.

---

[24]See Lynn Thorndike, HMES 6, pp. 135-137; Dr. Hubert Korsch, *Grundriss der Geschichte der Astrologie* 'Compendium of the History of Astrology' (Düsseldorf: Zenit, 1935), pp. 68-69; and F. Leigh Gardner, *Bibliotheca Astrologica* (No. Hollywood: Symbols & Signs, 1977. repr.).

Von Rantzau also wrote two books on astrology:

Exempla, quibus astrologicae scientiae certitudo,
doctissimorum virorum veterum et recentiorum
auctoritate astruitur.
[Examples, by Which the Certitude of Astrological
Science is Enhanced by the Authority of the Most
Learned Men, both Ancient and More Recent]
Cologne, 1585

Tractatus astrologicus de genethliacorum thematum
judiciis pro singulis nati accidentibus.
[An Astrological Treatise on the Judgments of Natal
Horoscopes for the Several Accidents of the Native]
Frankfurt, 1593.
Oldenburg, 1594. 2nd ed. 4to. xxxii,601,ii pp.
[reprinted in a smaller size in 1602, 1625, and 1633]

Rantzau, Henri
Traite des jugemens des themes genetliaques pour
tous les accidens qui arriuent à l'homme apres sa
naissance....
[Treatise of Judgments of Natal Horoscopes for
All the Accidents that Happen to Man after his Birth....]
Paris: , 1657. 8vo. xvi,614,xvi pp.
trans. by Jacques Aleaume.
Traité des jugements des thèmes généthliaques....
Nice: Cahiers Astrologiques, 19 . repr. of 1657 ed.

Oestmann, Günther
Heinrich Rantzau und die Astrologie.
[An excellent biographical study of Rantzau and his
contemporaries. Beautifully illustrated in large format in
German.]
Brunswick: Braunschweiges Landesmuseum, 2004. 317 pp.
30 cm

Naibod

Valentine Naibod (1527-1593) was the author of a general treatise on astrology *Enarratio elementorum astrologiae* (Cologne: Arnold Birckmann's Heirs, 1560. 4to.). He advocated a measure of time, now called *Naibod's Measure*, by which $0°59'08"$. (the mean motion of the Sun in longitude) is equated to 1 year of life in calculating primary directions. This was a refinement of Ptolemy's value of exactly 1 degree per year. Naibod's fame rests upon this measure.

Naibod inadvertently came to a bad end. He was living in Padua, Italy, when he deduced from his own horoscope that he was about to enter a period of personal danger, so he laid in an adequate supply of food and drink, drew his blinds, and locked his doors and windows, intending to hole up there until the period of danger had passed. Unfortunately, some burglars, seeing the house closed and the blinds drawn, decided that the resident had gone away. They therefore broke into what they thought was an empty house, and, finding Naibod there, murdered him to conceal their identities. His prediction was right—it had been a period of personal danger.[25]

Stadius

Johann Stadius (1527-1579), a Belgian mathematician and astrologer, was well known to astrologers as an ephemeris-maker. In his *Bergensen Tables* published at Cologne in 1560 he described himself as Royal Mathematician to Philip II (1527-1598), king of Spain, and Mathematician to Emanuel Philibert (1528-1580), duke of Savoy. His *Ephemerides secundum Antwerpiae longitudinem 1554 ad 1606* were published at Cologne in 1581.

Garcaeus

Johann Gartze (1530-1574) was a fine astrologer, called **Garcaeus** in Latin. He wrote a guide to natal astrology illustrated with many example horoscopes, some from his predecessors, Junctinus, Gaurico, and Cardan, but many from his own collection. Unlike many of his fellow astrologers, he resisted the temptation to rectify his published charts. Garcaeus researched several categories of indications in horoscopes, including violent death. His book was entitled *Astrologiae methodus* 'Method of Astrology' (Basel: H. Petrus, 1576).

A Primary Critic

Sixtus ab Hemminga (1533-1584), M.D., was a native of Nijfinne, Friesland, in the Netherlands. He learned astrology along with medicine at the university and was a successful physician. However, he evidently had no success in using primary directions, for towards the end of his life he wrote an extensive critique of that technique based upon a comparison of "accidents" in the lives of thirty mostly notable persons and what he considered to be the corresponding primary directions in their natal horoscopes. He found that the primaries he calculated did not coincide in time with the accidents. Hence he concluded that this astrological technique was worthless.

---

[25]See Lynn Thorndike, HMES 6, pp. 119-123. Dr. Hubert Korsch, *Grundriss der Geschichte der Astrologie*, p. 66, says he was born in 1510 (which is apparently wrong!) and died on 3 March 1593.

Sixtus's criticism is noteworthy, since it alone is based on an actual examination of primary directions in natal horoscopes.[26] Three quarters of a century later, J.B. Morin (see below) challenged Sixtus's conclusions in his *Astrologia Gallica*, Book 22, Section 5, Chaps. 3 & 4. The reader who is interested can read Sixtus's book and what Morin had to say about it and judge the matter for himself. [27]

> Astrologiae ratione et experientia refutatae liber continens brevem quandam apodixin de incertudine et vanitate astrologica et particularium praedictionum exempla triginta....
>
> [A Book on the Refutation of Astrology by Reason and Experience Containing a Brief Demonstration of Astrological Uncertainty and Vanity and Thirty Examples of Particular Predictions. . . .]
>
> Antwerp: C. Plantin, 1583. 4to. xii,303 pp.

Tycho Brahe

Tycho Brahe (1546-1601) became interested in astrology while still in his teens, but he reasoned that the lack of accurate ephemerides was a serious obstacle to correct prediction. Therefore he determined to improve the ephemerides. The obvious need was an extensive series of precise observations. Brahe was an aristocrat and was able to obtain financial support from King Frederick II (1534-1588) of Denmark. He built a castle/observatory and the necessary instruments. After years of observations he began to work out solar, lunar, and planetary theories. He did not live to complete his work, but, from the foundation he had laid, his assistant John Kepler succeeded in making the long-sought improvements.

Brahe spent most of his time working on astronomy, but he did not neglect astrology. Over a period of several years he worked out the probable astrological effects of the great supernova that had first been seen on 6 November 1572. It was in the constellation Cassiopeia in 7 Taurus and north latitude 54. Tycho concluded that it portended vast changes in politics and religion that would begin to appear in 1592 when those who were born in 1572 would reach maturity. In particular he predicted that a princely warrior would be born in the north, not before 1592, that he would conquer Germany, and that he would disappear in 1632. This was fulfilled in the person of King Gustavus II Adolphus of Sweden, who was born in 1594 and was killed in battle in 1632.

---

[26]To learn how rare informed criticism of astrology is, the reader can refer to the two sections entitled "Astronomy and Astrology" and "Science and Astrology" towards the end of the present volume.

[27]Unfortunately, Sixtus's book has never been translated into any modern language, so the interested reader will have to read it in the original Latin. However, Morin's discussion, which includes some excerpts from Sixtus, is now available in an English translation. See the entry for Morin below.

Magini

Giovanni Antonio Magini (1555-1617), was from 1588 professor of astronomy, astrology, and mathematics at the University of Bologna. He wrote several excellent treatises of astrology, and he is said to have explained the theory of the Placidus house division in one of his books. If so, then Placidus presumably got the idea from reading that book.

Ephemerides . . . [1581-1630].
Venice: D. Zenarius, 1582.

Tabulae primi mobilis...
Venice, 1604.

Primum mobile . . .
Bologna: The Author, 1609.

Logarithms—A Revolution in Calculation

The invention of logarithms and the publication of logarithmic tables in the early 1600s proved to be a great boon to astrologers, especially after the year 1633 when the first logarithmic trignonometrical tables were published. In Cardan's time any calculation at all was tedious, and astrologers were largely dependent upon printed tables of houses and auxiliary tables.

Argol

Andrea Argoli (1570-1657), a pupil of Magini's, was a well-known astrologer, who, in addition to writing several worthwhile treatises on astrology, also published house and auxiliary tables and ephemerides that covered the period 1620-1700. Perhaps the best-known of his books was his treatise on medical astrology, but the various volumes of ephemerides were in common use.

De diebus criticis et de aegrotorum decubitu.
[Critical Days and the Decumbiture of the Sick]
Padua, 1639, 1644). 4to.

Ephemerides ab anno 1630 ad annum 1680.
Venice, 1638.
Novae caelestium motuum ephemerides
. . . . ab anno 1620 ad annum 1640.
[New Ephemerides of the Celestial Motions
. . . . from the year 1620 to the year 1640]
Rome: , 1629.

Exactissime coelestium motum ephemerides
. . . . 1641 ad 1700.
[Most Exact Ephemerides of the Celestial Motions

. . . . 1641 to 1700]
Padua: , 1648. 4to. xviii,587,iv pp.
Lyons: , 1659.

Kepler

John Kepler (1571-1630) was an assistant to Tycho Brahe and court mathematician (astrologer/astronomer) to the emperor Rudolph II (1552-1612). The emperor was interested in astrology, so he understood the need for improved astronomical tables. Unfortunately, his successors the emperors Matthias (1557-1619) and Ferdinand II (1578-1637) were not interested in astrology and consequently could not see any reason to waste imperial funds on a useless science like astronomy. Kepler's salary fell into arrears, and in fact this indirectly led to his death, for he undertook a lengthy trip to Ratisbon in the fall of 1630 to try to get a commitment from the government to come across with his back pay. He evidently caught pneumonia while traveling and died.

Kepler carried on a fairly active practice of astrology, especially under Rudolph II, making horoscopes and forecasts for the members of the imperial family and later for the famous soldier Count Wallenstein (1583-1634). His personal papers contain a great number of charts cast for various purposes. He also kept a personal diary in which he noted the dates and often the exact times when significant events occurred in his own life. His personal life was thrown into turmoil in 1620 when his mother was arrested and imprisoned on a charge of practicing witchcraft. Kepler had to go to much trouble and expense to get the charges quashed and his mother released after thirteen months in prison. She survived for a few months and died in early 1622.

One of Kepler's first published astrological works was a short tract *De fundamentis astrologiae certioribus* 'The More Certain Fundamentals of Astrology' (Prague: Schuman, 1602).[28] This was followed by *Judicium de trigono igneo* 'Judgment on the Fiery Triplicity' (Prague?, 1603), which was actually on the mutation conjunction of Jupiter and Saturn that occurred in 9 Sagittarius on the 18th of December 1603. Two other books were his *De stella nova in pede Serpentarii* 'On the New Star in the Foot of Ophiuchus' (Prague: The Author, 1606), referring to the supernova that was first seen on 9 October 1604 in 18 Sagittarius and 2° north latitude near the conjunction of Mars and Jupiter in 20 Sagittarius that occurred on the same date; and his *De cometis, libelli tres* 'Three Tracts on Comets' (Augsburg, 1619), which treated of their astronomical, physical, and astrological natures. His major work was his *Tabulae Rudolphinae ...* 'Rudolphine Tables' (Ulm: J. Saurius, 1627).

Kepler was the first astronomer to recognize that the planets moved

---

[28]There is an English translation, *Concerning the More Certain Fundamentals of Astrology* (New York: Clancy Publications, 1942. pamphlet.).

172

with variable speeds in elliptical orbits instead of moving with constant speeds in circular orbits. His insight into the true nature of planetary motion and his establishment of the constants of the solar, lunar, and planetary orbits based upon Tycho Brahe's careful observations enabled him to construct the first set of astronomical tables to give reasonably accurate positions for the Sun and the planets. His lunar positions were somewhat better than those of his predecessors, but still subject to an uncertainty in the longitude of around plus or minus $0°35'$. This uncertainty was not reduced until lunar tables based upon a gravitational theory were constructed a century later.

Kepler invented several new aspects: $18°$, $24°$, $30°$, $36°$, $45°$, $72°$, $108°$, $135°$, $144°$, and $150°$. Of these, the $30°$, $45°$, $135°$, and $150°$ aspects have been adopted by most astrologers. He is also said to have considered that the number of days after birth that the Sun took to reach a natal planet was equivalent to the number of years of the native's life that would elapse before the indicated influence would manifest itself. This is the earliest instance I have encountered of the use of what we would call a secondary direction.[29]

Morin De Villefranche

In France, the leading astrologer of the 17th century was **Jean Baptiste Morin** (1583-1656), a native of Villefranche. Trained as a physician (M.D., Avignon, 1613), he was also an accomplished astronomer and wrote a prize paper on the determination of longitude at sea. He had begun the serious study of astrology in the mid-1620s and soon acquired a reputation in court circles, that probably led to his appointment to the post of Royal Professor of Mathematics at the Collège de France in 1630, a post he held for the rest of his life. He was in effect court astrologer to Louis XIII (1601-1643). As such he was summoned in 1638 to be present at the birth of the future Louis XIV (1638-1715), so that he could cast the royal infant's horoscope.

Although he was a generation older than Placidus (see below), Morin lived long enough to read Placidus's books. He disagreed entirely with Placidus's methods, both his system of house division and—worst of all, from Morin's point of view—Placidus's rejection of solar returns as a predictive tool. In the end, they both won out. The Placidus method of house division eventually displaced the older Regiomontanus method, but now that computers are available to do the work, solar returns are enjoying something of a revival as a predictive tool.

Morin was a prolific writer, but his earlier astrological works[30] were

---

[29]See Maurice Wemyss, *The Wheel of Life*, Vol. 5 (Edinburgh: The International Publishing Co., n.d.), p. 119. This usage may have been suggested by a common procedure used in horary astrology, where the motion in degrees after the question may be equated to days or to some longer period of time, such as weeks, months, or years.

[30]Perhaps the most notable of these from an astrological point of view are: (1)

overshadowed by his massive *Astrologia Gallica* on which he labored for the last three decades of his life. He had finished it a few years before his death but was unable to get it published. After his death, it was published in 1661 through the patronage of Queen Marie Louise of Poland (1611-1667), a grateful former client.

Morin was the last great French astrologer of the early modern period. The climate turned increasingly hostile to astrology in the last half of the 17th century, culminating with the royal decree prohibiting astrology issued at the instigation of J.B. Colbert (1619-1683). But the "Age of Reason" was starting, and astrology, like religion, was increasingly scorned as superstition.

The *Astrologia Gallica* contains an innovative theory of astrology which departs from the bare-bones techniques of Claudius Ptolemy and relies instead on "analogy," "determinations," and "accidental rulerships." It is the master work of French astrology, but it was not so recognized at the time. One reason is that it was written in Latin, which restricted its readership, and the other is that astrology was already on the decline. Latin never recovered, and astrology had to wait more than two centuries before it came back to life in France.

The AG has never been fully translated into any modern language, but the core principles of Morin's system are now available in English. Book 21 on Determinations was translated by Richard S. Baldwin in 1974 and Book 22 on Primary Directions, Book 23 on Revolutions, Book 24 on Progressions and Transits have been translated by James H. Holden, and Book 18 on The Strengths of the Planets by Pepita Llacer and Anthony LaBruzza.

Morin's system of astrological interpretation cannot be effectively summarized in a few paragraphs, but the essence of it is something like this:

Planets are essentially benefic or malefic. The benefics indicate favorable events or conditions, the malefics indicate unfavorable effects or conditions. Mercury is variable; the Sun and Moon act as potentiators. Morin rejects general significators (such as the Sun for the father, Venus for the wife, etc.), but he retains these general significations as "analogies." The true significators are the accidental significators—the planets posited in a house (or, if a house is empty, the planets posited in the opposite house) along with the ruler of the house.

The planets have two states—cosmic and celestial. The cosmic state is

---

Astrologicarum domorum cabala detecta a Joanne Baptista Morino... [The Cabala of the Astrological houses Revealed by Jean Baptise Morin....] (Paris: J. Moreau, 1623. 8vo. 38 pp.); and (2) Tabulae Rudolphinae ad meridianum Uraniburgi supputatae a Joanne Baptista Morino,... ad accuratum et facile compendium redactae [The Rudolphine Tables Calculated for the Meridian of Uraniborg by Jean Baptise Morin,.... Reduced to an Accurate and Easy-to-use Compendium] (Paris: J. Le Brun, 1650. 4to. 117 pp.).

determined by the sign position. Morin accepts the traditional sign and exaltation rulerships (with their opposites, the detriment and the fall) and the concept of triplicity rulers (although he invented a revised set), but he rejects the terms and the other minor subdivisions of the zodiac. The celestial state of a planet results from its accidental determination to activity in a certain field of human action or existence that is defined by the celestial house in which it is placed and the celestial houses which it rules. The angular houses are viewed as those having the greatest effect upon the native, followed by the succedent and the cadent houses. Aspects (including antiscia) are interpreted as links between planets, whose effects are heavily dependent upon the accidental significations and interrelations of the planets, rather than simply upon the nature of the aspect itself. The linkage between the planets merely acts to combine their individual determinations. Hence, it is not possible to define the influence of an aspect in isolation without relating it to a specific pair of planets in a specific chart.

Morin accepts the traditional house rulerships (which he calls *determinations*) with two main exceptions: he defines the 4th house as ruling both parents and not just one of the two parents; and he defines the 12th house as the house of sickness rather than the 6th (which he restricts to subordinates, etc.). However, he points out that due to the action of planets on the house opposite to their actual position (particularly when the opposite house is empty), planets in the 10th house may indicate something about the native's parents, and planets in the 6th house may indicate something about the native's illnesses.

In making predictions of specific events, Morin relied primarily upon Regiomontanan primary directions and solar returns. As secondary indicators he used lunar returns, and, relegated to third place, transits. But in the case of transits they have to be interpreted in terms of a specific chart. You cannot say, for example, that Saturn square the Moon always indicates a certain type of event or condition. Its actual effect will be "determined" by Saturn's nature, the nature of the square aspect, by its position in the horoscope, and by the determinations of the natal Moon.

There are many fine points to be considered, all of which are dealt with extensively in the *Astrologia Gallica*. Perhaps the main distinction that can be drawn between the Morin system and that of traditional Western astrology as it is generally practiced by modern astrologers is the distinction between using general significators (the Ptolemaic method) and accidental significators (the Morin method). Morin's method is similar in some respects to the method commonly used in horary astrology and thus goes back to the Dorothean or mainstream of Greek astrology. It is thus much more specific than the traditional method that uses general significators.

An example may make this clear. If we take Venus to be the (general) significator of love and marriage and the wife in a man's horoscope, then every man born within an approximately 10 to 12 day period when Saturn is conjunct, square, or opposite Venus would have unhappy love affairs, a bad marriage, and a severe, unloving wife. Experience, says Morin, teaches us that this is not the case. To determine love and marriage prospects in a particular chart, we must look primarily at the 5th and 7th houses, the planets posited in them, their rulers, and the aspects. Thus, on a day when Saturn afflicts Venus (cosmically), that aspect may fall in other houses and therefore be determined to money, health, travel, worldly status, friends, or something else, and have no effect upon love or marriage.

This will perhaps give the reader some idea of the Morin method. But to understand it fully, he should read the following books:

Morin, Jean-Baptiste
The Morinus Method of Horoscope Interpretation.
Astrologica Gallica Book Twenty-One.
trans. by Richard S. Baldwin
Washington: A.F.A., Inc., 1974.

Morin, Jean-Baptiste
Astrologica Gallica Book Eighteen.
trans. by Pepito Llacer and Anthony LaBruzza
Tempe, Az.: A.F.A., Inc., 2003.

Morin, Jean-Baptiste
Astrologica Gallica Book Twenty-Two Directions.
trans. by James Herschel Holden
Tempe, Az.: A.F.A., Inc., 1994.

Morin, Jean-Baptiste
Astrologica Gallica Book Twenty-Three Revolutions.
trans. by James Herschel Holden
Tempe, Az.: A.F.A., Inc., 2002.

Morin, Jean-Baptiste
Astrologica Gallica Book Twenty-Four Progressions and Transits.
trans. by James Herschel Holden
Tempe, Az.: A.F.A., Inc., 2004.

Schwickert, F. & Weiss, A.
Cornerstones of Astrology.
Dallas: Sangreal Foundation, 1972.

Tobin, Patti
Planetary Powers. The Morin Method.
Dallas: The Author, 1980.

The first five books contain the essence of Morin's method in his own words. The next to last book introduces the reader to the Morin method with some modifications made by the two authors. It contains a number of example horoscopes that are used to illustrate the various rules. It is an English version of a German-language original, *Bausteine der Astrologie* 'Building-stones of Astrology', vol. 2 *Die astrologische Synthese* 'Astrological Synthesis' (Leipzig, 1925; since reprinted). It has also appeared in a Spanish version. The book by Tobin is a small book (probably difficult to obtain) that gives the essential rules and illustrates them very effectively with small inset charts. It contains more modern examples than those in Schwickert and Weiss. French readers can learn fundamentals of the method from the translation by Henri Selva, *La Théorie des déterminations astrologiques de Morin de Villefranche* 'The Theory of Astrological Determinations of Morin de Villefranche', and from Jean Hieroz's book *L'Astrologie selon Morin de Villefranche* 'Astrology according to Morin de Villefranche' (for both, see below).

In the last years of his life, having despaired of ever seeing the *Astrologia Gallica* in print, Morin wrote a commentary on the *Centiloquy* of pseudo-Ptolemy in French, *Remarques astrologiques . . . sur le Commentaire du Centiloque de Ptolomee . . . par Messire Nicolas Bourdin . . . Marquis de Villennes . . .* 'Astrological Remarks . . . on the Commentary on Ptolemy's Centiloquy . . . by The Most Honourable Nicolas Bourdin . . . The Marquess of Villennes' (Paris: Pierre Menard, 1657), but even this was published posthumously. Actually, as the title clearly states, it is a commentary on another commentary[31] as well as on the original *Centiloquy* itself. But it also contains miscellaneous remarks on astrology and references to the unpublished *Astrologia Gallica*. There is a fine modern French edition of this work by Jacques Halbronn, *Les remarques astrologiques* (Paris: Retz, 1976) and a recent Italian translation of that edition by Jolanda Boyko, *Commenti astrologici* (Padova: MEB, 1990). Also, see my paper "Jean Baptiste Morin's Comments on House Division in his *Remarques Astrologiques*" in the AFA *Journal of Research* 6 (1990):19-35, which translates and discusses Morin's defense of the Regiomontanus system of house division.

Unfortunately, Morin is best known to 20th century English-speaking astrologers not as the inventor of a superior method of chart delineation and prediction, but only as the inventor of the Morin system of house division, which in fact he only proposed as a supplement to the Regiomontanus system for use in the polar regions, in which the Regiomontanus system fails like all the other quadrant systems. But since

---

[31]Nicolas de Bourdin, *Le centilogve de Ptolomee* 'Ptolemy's Centiloquy' (Paris: Cardin Besongne, 1651). The author was the Marquess of Villennes, a former secretary of state, who died in 1670. Morin generally disagrees with the Marquess's commentary.

Morin apparently never calculated any charts for persons born in the far north, he never used the Morin system, but instead relied entirely on the Regiomontanus system. The only person who has used the Morin system to any extent is the 20th century English astrologer Edward Lyndoe (see below).

Placidus

Undoubtedly, the best known Italian astrologer of the 17th century was **Placido de Titis** (1603-1668), generally known as **Placidus**. A member of the noble house of Titi, he joined the Olivetan Order and was professor of mathematics at the University of Pavia 1657-1668. He also served as an astrological consultant to the Archduke Leopold William of Austria (1614-1662). Placidus was the author of a revolutionary treatise, *Quaestionum physiomathematicarum libri tres* 'Three Books of Physiomathematical Questions' (Milan, 1650)[32] on house division, primary directions,[33] and secondary directions[34] (of which he seems to have been the first major user, although Kepler is said to have used secondary solar progressions[35]). Seven years later he published a further elucidation of his theories in his *Tabulae Primi Mobilis . . .* 'Tables of the Prime Mobile' (Padua: Paulo Frambotti, 1657).[36] Placidus firmly rejected the solar return,[37] which was a favorite method of prediction used by many astrologers (including J.B. Morin).

Placidus had studied the *Tetrabiblos* carefully and believed that the methods set forth in his book were in agreement with those given by Ptolemy in the *Tetrabiblos*. He was partly right. He had understood Ptolemy's

---

[32]Reprinted by his students a quarter century later under the title *Physiomathematica sive coelestis philosophia . . .* (Milan: Francesco Vigoni, 1675).

[33]Placidus equated arcs of direction by adding the arc to the Sun's natal right ascension (RA) and then inspecting the ephemeris to see when the Sun would attain the value of RA that was equal to the sum. Having found the date and time, he further equated it to years, months, and days by using the standard 1 day = 1 year measure. This is the RA version of what is now called "the solar arc."

[34]Secondary directions are based on the assumed equivalence of 1 day to 1 year of life. (On the analogy that the Sun has rotated once in the sky in 1 day and once in the zodiac in 1 year.) Thus, for the astrological indications for the year that begins with the 25th birthday, we consult the ephemeris for the day that is 25 days after the birthdate.

[35]See the entry for Kepler above.

[36]Translated rather ineptly into English by Manoah Sibly as *Astronomy and Elementary Philosophy* (London, 1789) and *A Collection of Thirty Remarkable Nativities...* (London, 1789). The standard English translation is by John Cooper, *Primum Mobile . . .* (London, [1820?]); it was repr. in facsimile with an intro. by Michael Baigent (Bromley: The Institue For the Study of Cycles in World Affairs, 1983).

[37]A chart erected annually for the moment when the Sun returns to its exact natal longitude. It is judged by special rules. This procedure goes back at least to Māshā'allāh, but Placidus believed it to be ineffective.

method of primary directions where Regiomontanus had failed to do so. However, Ptolemy had apparently favored a slightly modified version of the Equal House system rather than a system for the intermediate cusps based on 1/3 or 2/3 of a cusp's semiarc. He evidently saw no reason why house positions had to be consistent with his criteria for primary progressions, which were in essence a method of determining "similar appearances." Nevertheless, Placidus's system was consistent with Ptolemy's primary directions.

Placidus explained a method of calculating the intermediate house cusps that used "poles,"[38] and this method was faithfully followed by his successors.

The suggestions made by Ptolemy for another method of directions most likely referred to what are now called profections or symbolic directions (which were in common use by the Greek astrologers but which are not based on the actual motion of the planets following birth), rather than to the "day for a year" method of directions invented by Placidus, which he called "secondary progressions." However, Placidus's innovations came too late for most astrologers on the Continent,[39] but they were adopted enthusiastically by John Partridge (1644-1715), the last major figure of 17th and early 18th century English astrology.

It is important to note that while Placidus calculated secondary directions and took them into account, they were definitely considered to be *secondary* to primary directions—in other words, an adjunct or supplement. This was understood by his 17th, 18th, and 19th century readers, and the emphasis remained on primary directions, but, as we shall see below, things changed when Alan Leo came on the scene.

Despite the fact that astrology continued to be studied and practiced in Italy for another half century or more, Placidus was the last major figure of the early modern period.

Tattoni and de Bonattis

Towards the end of the 17th century Italy produced two notable astrologers. **Antonio Tattoni,**[40] City Physician of Terni wrote an elaborate trea-

---

[38]Poles are pseudo-latitudes that can be used to calculate the intermediate cusps of a horoscope. However, while they give an exact trignometric solution for Campanus and Regiomontanus cusps (of course, using different values for the poles), they do not give an exact solution for Placidus cusps, but only an approximate one. Placidus must have recognized that the use of an iterative process was necessary to find the true position of the cusps, but he only explained their calculation by means of poles, perhaps because the astrologers of his day were accustomed to use poles to calculate Regiomontanus cusps. The failure of subsequent astrologers to recognize that the poles only gave approximate values for the Placidian cusps caused a certain amount of confusion that lasted for three centuries.

[39]J.B. Morin had evidently read Placidus's book, as he denounces Placidus's system of house division and views with horror his dismissal of solar returns.

[40]See Wilhelm Knappich, *Geschichte der Astrologie*, 168 n.1

tise on medical astrology based on Placidian methods *Il medico astrologo o vera apologia medicofisica astrologo contra il volgo* (1685). **Antonio Francesco de Bonattis**,[41] a professor at Padua, published an important astrological work *Universa astrosophia naturalis* (1687) in which he espoused Placidus's methods, including secondary directions, proposed a new method of rectifying birthtimes using the position of the planet Jupiter, and studied many horoscopes based on data from the public records. He remarks in his book that he had noticed in his own city that different churches struck the hours at different times, sometimes a half-hour different from each other. And since the people had come to depend upon these audible time pieces, it was plain that even accurately recorded birth times might be in error. It was this observation that led him to devise his method of rectification.

The Decline of Astrology

Astrology had flourished in Italy until the latter part of the 16th century. Then the popes began to shut it down, partly driven by religious qualms and partly by annoyance at those astrologers who circulated or published predictions about when the incumbent pope was going to die. Sixtus V (1521-1590) issued a bull against astrology in 1585. Urban VIII (1568-1644), annoyed by the prediction of an astrologer that he would die soon, issued another bull in 1631. In addition, the intellectual tide increasingly turned against astrology. One by one the universities abolished their chairs of astrology (Bologna in 1572),[42] although it continued to be taught as an adjunct to astronomy or medicine for another century.

Papal bulls and the rejection of the past, combined with an upsurge of interest in investigative and experimental science, drew the attention of most students away from astrology. A few hung on, but by 1700 it had sunk to a low ebb where it remained until its revival in the 20th century.

A little-noticed but probably a major reason for the decline of interest in astrology after 1700 was the upsurge of newspapers, novels, and musical entertainment. With these things available, literate people with a little money to spend could find more pleasant ways to amuse themselves than by reading prophetic almanacs. With the decline in public interest, the numbers of persons wanting to consult professional astrologers fell towards zero. The professional practice of astrology virtually died out. No clients, no astrologers! A few individuals read the old books and studied astrology, intrigued by the promise of the art or in some cases merely wishing to delve into something outside of the main stream. But by 1800, outside of England, it would have been difficult to find anyone who really understood astrology sufficiently to be able to cast a horoscope and inter-

---

[41]See Lynn Thorndike, HMES 8, 344-345.

[42]The last university to abolish its chair of astrology was the University of Salamanca in Spain—in the early 19th century! The reason given for its abolition was that there were no longer any students who wished to major in astrology.

pret it. After one more Frenchman, who was a sort of *fin-de-siècle* astrologer, and two German professors, who turned out to be a century before their time, we will transfer our attention to England, where things were somewhat different.

de Boulanvilliers

The last French astrologer of the early modern period, but one who had no impact upon astrology in his own lifetime, was **Henry de Boulainvillers**[43] (1658-1722), the Count of Saint-Saire, who wrote a lengthy book on natal astrology that remained in MS until the mid-20th century, when it was published as *Traité d'astrologie* 'Treatise of Astrology' (Garches, France: Éditions du Nouvel Humanisme, 1947). Saint-Saire says that he based the statements in his book on both traditional astrology and his own personal investigation of more than 500 horoscopes. His most notable additions to astrological techniques are (1) a method of rectifying birthtimes that is not dependent on the accidents of the native,[44] and (2) the use of concurrent heliocentric positions. This is the oldest astrological usage of heliocentric positions that I have encountered.

In France and elsewhere on the Continent, by the middle of the 17th century, many educated people who considered themselves to be modern, up-to-date, rational thinkers had already begun to view astrology as an outdated superstition obviously lacking any scientific basis. It began to fizzle out all over the Continent. The fact that Saint-Saire's book found no publisher for over two centuries is an indication of the low esteem in which astrology was held in France in the 18th and most of the 19th centuries. The situation was pretty much the same in the rest of Europe.

There was, however, a momentary upsurge of interest in astrology in Germany in the early 19th century evidenced by the publication of a textbook of astrology and a translation[45] of the *Tetrabiblos* by a professor of mathematics at the University of Erlangen, J.W.A. Pfaff (1784-1835). Pfaff found a colleague in another Erlangen professor, G.H. von Schubert (1780-1860). The two tried without success to reintroduce astrology into the academic world. Thereafter astrology languished in Germany until it finally revived in the early 20th century.

Astrology in England

There were astrologers in England at least from the 12th century, and as literacy increased in the 13th and 14th centuries, their numbers increased. An Oxford scholar, John of Ashendon, known in Latin as

---

[43]Boulainviller seems to be the correct spelling, but in reference books the name is usually spelled Boulainvilliers. See the introduction to the edition of his book.

[44]He uses the method originated by de Bonattis (see above), of which he seems to have been the only proponent.

[45]*Astrologisches Taschenbuch* 'Astrological Textbook' (Erlangen, 1822-23).

Eschuid was particularly interested in mundane astrology. One of his books was *Summa astrologiae iudicialis* [Summary of Judicial Astrology] (Venice, 1489). And as we have already seen, Geoffrey Chaucer (c.1340-1400) was evidently a skilled amateur astrologer. His works are sprinkled with astrological allusions showing a mastery of the technical terminology, and he wrote *A Treatise on the Astrolabe* for his son Lewis. In the 16th and early 17th centuries a number of astrological books were published in England, although nothing like the number that emanated from Italy and Germany. Perhaps the three most notable astrologers of the time were Dr. John Dee, Dr. Simon Forman, and the Welshman, Dr. Robert Fludd.

Three Doctors

Dr. John Dee (1527-1608) was a very learned mathematician, occultist, magician, alchemist, and astrologer. He is nearly always referred to as "Dr.," although he was an M.A. of Cambridge University and not professionally trained as a physician. For a number of years he was a private confidant and adviser to Queen Elizabeth I (1533-1603), sometimes signing his dispatches to her as "007" with the top of the 7 extended over the zeros to represent the idea that he was the Queen's "eyes." (This is what gave Ian Fleming the idea for the designation of his popular spy character "007.") Dr. Dee's long life was filled with fascinating adventures and incidents.[46] Like his younger contemporary Dr. Forman, he was not primarily an astrologer, but he was an ardent praticioner of astrology. Still, Lilly possessed one book of his, a Latin book of aphorisms *120. Aphorismi* (London, 1558).

Dr. Simon Forman (1553-1611) is usually described as a "quack" or sometimes as an astrologer and a quack. This is unfair, since he seems to have been a capable physician, although his medical education was irregular, and he had difficulty in obtaining a license to practice. The truth of the matter is that by 20th century standards all the physicians of his day were quacks! In actuality he was what we might call a "society doctor and psychologist" as well as an astrologer. He has retained some notice in literary circles by having attended some of the plays of Shakespeare and having jotted down his impressions of them in a notebook that has been preserved. Fortunately, his case-books have also been preserved. They are replete with astrological charts and notes. He did not advance the art of astrology, but, like Dr. Dee, he is too interesting a character to pass over without notice.[47]

Dr. Robert Fludd (1574-1637) was an Oxford-educated physician in

---

[46]Several biographies of Dr. Dee can be found in libraries. And notes that he scribbled in the margins of some of his books were edited by J.O. Halliwell as *The Private Diary of John Dee* . . . (London: The Camden Society, 1842); these contain a number of birthdates and birthtimes of various persons, some well-known and some obscure.

[47]See the very interesting biography of Forman by A.L. Rowse, *Sex and Society in Shakespeare's Age* (New York: Charles Scribner's Sons, 1974).

London, but he was also an occultist and an astrologer. He is considered to have been an important figure in the history of Freemasonry and Rosicrucianism. Lilly says of him "[Fludd] *hath wrote much of Astrologie, he may justly be accounted the mirrour of our times, and of the Welch Nation.*"[48] Fludd's principal astrological work is his *De astrologia* [Astrology]. It has been more appreciated by the French than the English. There is a partial French translation:

> Étude du macrocosme, annoté et traduite pour le premier
> fois par Pierre Piobb.
> [Study of the Macrocosm, Annotated and
> Translated for the First Time by Pierre Piobb]
> Paris: Daragon, 1907. xxii,293 pp.

A Minor but Persistent Annoyance

During the lifetimes of these men, Pope Gregory XIII (1502-1585) was persuaded to change the calendar. Since the calendar year was slightly longer than the tropical year, the date of the vernal equinox had changed since the time of the Council of Nicea (325 A.D.) by about ten days. This meant that the date of Easter, calculated according to the established rules, was sometimes incorrect. To restore the position of the Sun in the calendar to where it was in the 4th century, the Pope ordered ten days to be added to calendar dates beginning with 5 October 1582, which was changed to 15 October 1582. Most Catholic countries adopted the new calendar in 1582 or 1583, but the Protestant countries generally ignored it. Those European countries that were a patchwork of small kingdoms or territories—Germany, Holland, and Switzerland—wound up being a patchwork of calendar styles. This confusing situation lasted until 1700, when many of the recalcitrants adopted the Gregorian calendar. But Great Britain held out until September 1752, and countries where the Eastern Orthodox Church predominated stuck with the Julian calendar into the 20th century.

In addition, some countries did not observe 1 January as New Year's Day, which caused the year count to differ. Great Britain, for example, considered 25 March to be New Year's Day until 1753. These two calendar discrepancies caused a certain amount of confusion among astrologers when they had to erect horoscopes or mundane charts for dates in the past. And this problem still persists to some extent, since it is not always clear what calendar was being observed at a particular place in the 16th century and thereafter, and standard reference books often alter the years (but not the dates) to the New Style without saying so. We will see below some instances of this confusion in the 17th century.

But now it is appropriate to mention the principal English astrologers of the 17th and later centuries.

---

[48]William Lilly, *Christian Astrology*, p. 836.

William Lilly

In England astrology hung on into the early decades of the 18th century despite occasional opposition from Church authorities. In fact the golden age of English astrology was the 17th century, and its leading figure was **William Lilly** (1602-1681). Lilly was the son of an impoverished yeoman farmer. He had a good preparatory education, but when the time came his family was financially unable to send him to college, thereby frustrating his early ambition to become a minister of the Church of England. Having gone to London to seek his fortune, he found it before the age of thirty by marrying the wealthy widow of a London merchant for whom he had worked. After a few years, the death of his wife left him independently wealthy, and thereafter he devoted the rest of his life to astrology.

He had learned Latin so well in school that he could speak it as readily as English. He purchased every book on astrology that he could find (most of them in Latin) and apparently read or at least skimmed through them all. Thus he had a complete knowledge of astrology as it existed in his own day. In addition, he acquired much practical knowledge of the art through his practice of horary astrology. His casebooks containing thousands of horary charts with his marginal notes are preserved in the Ashmolean Library.[49]

Lilly seems to have been a congenial sort of person who had many friends. One of them, Sir Elias Ashmole[50] (1617-1692) became acquainted with him in November 1646 and designed some of the charts for Lilly's *Christian Astrology* in 1647. Ashmole's acquaintance with Lilly soon led to an enduring friendship that later included the two men's wives. It was in fact Sir Elias who eventually prevailed upon Lilly to write his autobiography. The book remained in MS until 1715 when it was published as *Mr. William Lilly's History of his Life and Times*. It contains much information about the astrologers of London and many anecdotes about Lilly's own activities (including one about digging for treasure in Westminster Abbey!).

Lilly wrote a number of smaller works on astrology and prophecies, but his major work was *Christian Astrology/modestly Treated of in three*

---

[49]See the informative but unsympathetic biography by Derek Parker, *Familiar to All* (London: Jonathan Cape, 1975) with some interesting illustrations. However, Parker sometimes gets his facts wrong., e.g. p. 17, Lilly was born on 1 May 1602 OS, not 30 April 1602; and p. 188, Lilly's third wife, Ruth Needham, was twenty-seven years younger than Lilly, not "a year younger."

[50]Sir Elias was also an ardent amateur astrologer. His published autobiographical and historical notes and correspondence, *Elias Ashmole* ed. by C.H. Josten (Oxford: Clarendon Press, 1966. 5 vols.), contain many records of the times of events that Sir Elias noted down for later astrological consideration. There are also many references to his friends the Lillys as well as to other astrologers.

Books[51] (London, 1647; repr. at London, 1659, and repr. at Exeter, 1985). The first part is a general introduction to astrology, very rich in tables of rulerships; the second part is an exceptionally detailed treatise on horary astrology with some 35 or more example charts from Lilly's own casebooks;[52] and the third part treats of nativities. The whole runs to almost 900 pages and includes a valuable bibliography of astrological books (a catalogue of Lilly's own library) and an index (a rare feature of such a book). It is a remarkable astrological work, and Lilly's 17th century English makes it a delightful book to read.

Since *Christian Astrology* has been reprinted and is now available, it would be superfluous to go into further detail about its contents. However, I shall cite one of Lilly's cases[53] as an example of his method of interpreting a horary chart:

Chap. XCIII
A Horse lost or stolen neer Henley, if recoverable or not?

Mercury Here Lord of the twelft signifieth the Horse, whom you see Retrograde, & hastening to a conjunction of the Sun Lord of the *Querent's* House of Substance; forasmuch as Mercury did by his Retrograde motion apply to the Lord of the *querent's* house of Substance, and that the Moon was locally in the second and both Jupiter and Mars Retrograde, neer the cusp of the second, I judged the *Querent* should have his Goods or Horse quickly and unexpectedly, within a day or two from the time of the Question asked; and because the seventh house was afflicted by the Dragon's Tail, I judged the Thief could not keep him.

I was asked, *Which way he went?* I considered the Signe of the twelft was Gemini, *viz.* West; the Signe wherein Mercury Lord of the twelft was in, was Aquarius, *viz.* West; though the quarter of Heaven was South, but much

---

[51]So entitled to indicate that astrology was not anti-Christian. Lilly was a devout member of the Church of England, received a license from the Archbishop of Canterbury to practice medicine, and was buried in his parish church.

[52]Lilly's exposition of horary astrology is the ultimate (but not always acknowledged) source of most of the English language treatises on that subject that have appeared since the 17th century. W.J. Simmonite's *The Prognostic Astronomer* (London, 1851?) owes a considerable debt to Lilly. About the same time, Zadkiel published a revised and abbreviated version of *Christian Astrology* in 1835 (2nd ed., 1852), under the title *An Introduction to Astrology*. It has often been reprinted, and as recently as 1990 it appeared in a fine Italian translation *Grammatica Astrologica*, trans. by Franca Cargnello Ventura, with an Introduction by Grazia Mirti (Padua: MEB, 1990).

inclining to the West; the Moon was in Leo, a North-east Sign. Besides, Mercury as he was Lord of the fourth, was in a West Signe. From whence I concluded, the Horse was gone Westward; but because Mercury was Retrograde, I judged the Horse would not proceed farre, but return again to his proper owner; [*and indeed the Horse did come home three dayes after, and had been full West.*] However, I judged the Horse would have been at home a day sooner; but who shall more exactly consider of the Scheam; shall find, that Mercury *Significator* of the Horse, although he came to the body of Sun Lord of the *Querent's* house of Substance, the same night the Question was asked, yet because the Sun had no dignities where he was, the Horse came not home untill Wednesday or Thursday the 13th or 14th of *January*, at what time Mercury and Venus came to a partill conjunction.

I must confesse, here were many good significations that the *querent* should recover his lost Horse: first, the Dragon's Head in the ascendant: next, Moon in the second, arguing he should be discovered: thirdly, Mercury Lord of the thing lost Retrograde, importing a returning of the thing againe casually: fourthly, two Retrograde Planets upon the cusp of the second, which usually shews quick and unexpected recovery: Jupiter and Mars peregrine,[54] I took them for those that rode away the Horse, Jupiter especially: [*and it was very true.*]

I have taken pity on the reader and drawn the chart in the round form,[55] so that it is easier to read. The cusps and planetary positions are as Lilly calculated them.[56] The reader who wishes to recalculate this chart on computer or from tables should set it for 21 January 1647 NS 3:11 PM LMT at Henley-on-Thames 51N31 0W54. (This date and time is the modern

[53]*Christian Astrology*, pp. 467-468. I have written out the names of the planets and signs where Lilly used symbols. The reader who is unfamiliar with 17th century English prose should note that the rules for spelling, capitalization, and punctuation have changed during the last three and one-half centuries.

[54]A planet is said to be *peregrine* if it has no dignity in the sign it is in. This is a neutral condition between being in a sign in which it has dignity and being in a sign in which it has debility.

[55]Many different chart designs are used in *Christian Astrology* for the sake of variety (Sir Elias Ashmole designed them). However, this one was square and that was the type of chart Lilly commonly used. (See the photo of two pages of Lilly's casebooks facing p. 97 in Parker's *Familiar to All.*)

[56]But I have corrected the MC/IC cusps from 12° to 18° (this was probably a typesetter's error, since the other cusps are correct).

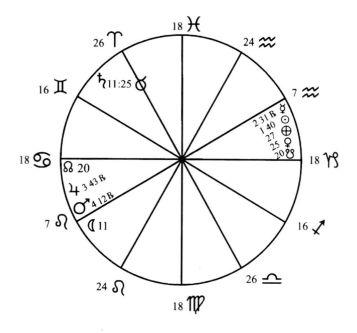

11º Ian 1646 Monday 2 59 PM
a quadrato Saturni ad Vac.
Fig. 9 A Horse Stolen

equivalent of that given by Lilly.) He will find that the planetary positions are reasonably accurate, only the Moon and its nodes being a degree off. The house cusps are of course those of Regiomontanus.

Three years after *Christian Astrology* was published, the Italian astrologer Placidus (1603-1658) published his book *Physiomathematica or Celestial Philosophy*, in which he set forth the Placidus system of houses. Lilly undoubtedly bought a copy and read it, but he was evidently unimpressed because he continued to use the Regiomontanus system.

Christian Astrology is the prime modern sourcebook of horary astrology. Lilly's almanac *Merlinus Anglicus, Junr.*, was first issued in 1644 and survived its author, being continued for a number of years after his death by his younger associate Henry Coley. Astrological almanacs became very popular in England, and their continuing popularity later enabled astrology itself to survive the lean years from about 1700 to 1780.[57]

Finally, we should mention that Lilly was generally supposed to have predicted the Great Plague that visited London in 1665 and the Great Fire

---

[57]For a detailed bibliography of the almanacs, see Bernard Capp, *English Almanacs 1500-1800* (Ithaca, N.Y.: Cornell University Press, 1979).

that burned much of the city in 1666. In his book *Monarchy or No Monarchy in England* (London, 1651), he included some symbolic woodcuts, one of which showed corpses and another two naked twins falling head downward into flames. After the plague and the fire had taken place, these and some more recent remarks in his almanacs were noted by the government committee formed to investigate the fire. Lilly was summoned to testify before the committee. He stated that he had not foreseen the exact year of the fire, but that he was satisfied that it arose from natural causes. The committee discharged him. Whether these were lucky hits he had made or actual mundane predictions that were borne out by subsequent events is unknown.[58]

Culpeper

Nicholas Culpeper (1616-1654) was a physician and medical astrologer. He never had much money and was only able to attend Cambridge University for one year, but he had acquired a good knowledge of Latin and Greek, so that he could read the old medical writers. For a year or so he worked for a druggist and then about 1640 he began practicing as a physician and an astrologer. His medical career was interrupted by the Civil War, in which he supported the Parliamentary side. He received a severe chest wound in 1643 during military service. Returning to his practice, he treated everyone who came to him whether or not they could pay. His office was flooded with patients, and he gained a fine reputation for healing the sick.

Culpeper spent all his spare time writing medical books, so that he hardly had time for sleep. In 1649 he published *A Physical Directory*, an English translation of the Latin pharmacopoeia published by the College of Physicians. They were outraged and never forgave him. The *Directory* was followed by *The English Physician, or an Astrologo-physical Discourse of the Vulgar Herbs of this Nation* (London, 1652), which sold out immediately and was reissued in a revised edition *The English Physitian Enlarged, with Three hundred Sixty and Nine* Medicines *made of* English Herbs. . . . (London, 1653). These books were instantly popular and enjoyed an enormous sale. Unfortunately, the combination of his battle wound, overwork, lack of rest, and a harsh English winter did Culpeper in. He died of pneumonia in January 1654 at age 37. Gadbury later said of him, ". . . by study and practice . . . he hath left a name behind him, which will remain until time will be no longer."

"Culpeper's Herbal," issued repeatedly under various titles during the last two centuries, goes back ultimately to his book, *The English Physician, or an Astrologo-physical Discourse of the Vulgar Herbs of this Nation* . . . (London, 1652. 1st ed.). *Culpeper's Astrologicall Judgment of*

---

[58]See Derek Parker, *Familiar to All*, pp. 223-232; there is a fine full-page plate facing p. 160 with a reproduction of Lilly's "hieroglyphic" of the twins (Gemini—the sign of London) falling into the fire. See also Lilly's autobiography.

Diseases from the Decumbiture of the Sick (London: Nathan Brookes 1655. 2nd ed.), a purely astrological work, has also been popular with astrologers. Both books are still available. Gadbury was right!

Gadbury

John Gadbury (1627-1704) was perhaps Lilly's principal rival. He was a royalist, whereas Lilly had favored the Parliamentary faction during and immediately after the Civil War. They had started out on good terms, but Gadbury was jealous of Lilly's popular acclaim and became increasingly bitter and vituperative towards his one-time friend. Lilly seems to have maintained the attitude of a parent towards an errant child. Their quarrel caused the London astrologers of the time to choose up sides, and the rancor persisted even after Lilly's death, perhaps culminating with the publication of *Nebulo Anglicanus, or the First Part of the Black Life of John Gadbury* by John Partridge (London, 1693).

Gadbury wrote many books and short tracts on astrology and published an annual almanac. His major works were *Genethlialogia, or the Doctrine of Nativities*, which also contained an extensive set of astronomical tables (London, 1658. folio.), and *Collectio Geniturarm* (London: James Cottrel, 1662. folio.), a collection of 153 natal horoscopes ranging from those of Alexander the Great and the emperor Nero (both set for incorrect dates) to several charts of children who had died young. Some of the charts show the difficulties astrologers encountered with the various calendars of the time. The chart for Queen Mary is set for the wrong year (1517 instead of 1516); and he has unaccountably taken Cardinal Richelieu's birthday (9 September) to be O.S. and added ten days to it, making him born on 19 September!

This was the earliest sizable collection of nativities to be printed in England. As a whole, it is marred to some extent by Gadbury's habit of "rectifying" the birthtimes[59] to agree with what he judged to be appropriate arcs of primary direction for important "accidents" in the lives of the natives. This was a fairly common procedure among astrologers of the time. Nevertheless, he has preserved some charts and their associated "accidents" that would be difficult or impossible to find elsewhere.

Gadbury's almanac was continued for a number of years after his death, at first by his cousin Job Gadbury, and later by others.

---

[59]Rectification is a technical term used by astrologers to refer to the process of deliberately altering the stated or "estimate" birth time to agree with arcs of direction or transits to a location (usually the ASC or MC) in a chart, so that the "rectified" birth time produces a chart whose directions or transits give the actual time of events in the native's life. Ordinarily, several important events are used to guide the rectificaiton. Even if theoretically sound, the success of the method obviously depends upon the astrologer's skill. Gadbury sometimes makes us wonder.

Coley

Henry Coley (1633-1707) was a skilled mathematician and astrologer. He published a textbook of astrology, *Clavis Astrologiae* (London, 1669), and a revised and enlarged edition, *Clavis Astrologiae Elimata* (London, 1676). It is an excellent book with an extensive set of astronomical tables at the end. It also includes translations of the three best known centiloquies—those of pseudo-Ptolemy, Hermes, and Bethem. Coley was a personal friend of William Lilly and from 1676 helped him write the annual issues of Lilly's almanac *Merlinus Anglicus, Junr.* Lilly gave him the rights to the almanac, and Coley published it for several years after Lilly's death in 1681. Coley also translated the *146 Considerations of Guido Bonatti* along with selected aphorisms from Jerome Cardan's *Seven Segments*, to which he added "A Catalogue of Fifty of the Most Principal Fixed Stars" for the epoch 1 January 1700. Lilly wrote a one-page preface to the book, which was entitled *Anima Astrologiae: or, A Guide for Astrologers . . .* (London: B. Harris, 1676). However, the title page is so arranged that it implies (perhaps inadvertently) that the translation was made by Lilly himself, although the preface plainly states otherwise. The book has been reprinted at least thrice: first, with notes and a preface by Wm. C. Eldon Serjeant (London: George Redway, 1886), and a reprint of that edition with a brief preface (Washington: The National Astrological Library, 1953), reprinted again by the A.F.A. (Tempe, Az., 2005).

Partridge

Morin had rejected Placidus's system of house division as had most of the English astrologers. However, **John Partridge** (1644-1715) adopted it and published two very technical books using Placidian directions in the waning years of the 17th century, *Opus Reformatum* (London, 1693), and *Defectio Geniturarum* (London, 1697), both in English despite the Latin titles. In them he tried to display the superiority of the new Placidian directions. These books were later to cause the final switchover from Regiomontanus to Placidus houses.

As a mere child, Partridge was apprenticed to a shoemaker, but he had a thirst for knowledge and at age eighteen he began to study astrology (from Lilly's book) and Latin. He subsequently taught himself Greek, Hebrew, and medicine. Partridge began to publish astrological works in 1678. His first major book was a general treatise on astrology:

> ΜΙΚΡΟΠΑΝΑΣΤΡΩΝ [Mikropanastron]
> or an Astrological Vade Mecum. . . .
> with a dedication to Sir George Wharton.
> London: , 1679. 12 mo. xlvi,348 pp.

As its title implies (it means 'Little All Star'), it is a small book, but one packed with much useful material.

Partridge is known to have studied medicine in the Netherlands in the late 1680s and may have received an M.D. there (it is inscribed on his tombstone). At any event, he practiced both medicine and astrology, but principally astrology. In 1680 he published the first issue of what proved to be a very successful almanac, *Merlinus Liberatus*, although its very popularity ultimately made him a convenient target for a practical joke played on him in 1708 by Jonathan Swift (1667-1745) under the pseudonym Isaac Bickerstaff. Swift published a short tract in the guise of an almanac in which he predicted the death of Partridge on a certain date. Subsequently he published another tract in which he stated that his prediction had been confirmed, since Partridge had died on the date predicted. "Bickerstaff" added two lines of verse:

> Weep all you customers that use
> His pills, his almanacks, or shoes.

This was of course false, but it so confused the public that Partridge was obliged to suspend his almanac temporarily until he was able to convince the public that he was still alive.[60] Still, Partridge recovered, resumed publication, and died some years later in comfortable circumstances,[61] honored in his own profession. His death was noted in the scholarly *Miscellanea Lipsiensia* for 1715 with these words "John Partridge, of the order of philosophers, an astrologer and astronomer very famous in England." Swift on the other hand died insane. And, to quote Ellen McCaffery, "[Swift's] greatest satire, which is upon the whole human race,—*Gulliver's Travels*,—is now read by children, who do not know it is a satire. Time has taken its revenge upon the Dean rather than upon astrology."

Whalley

The Irish journalist and astrologer **John Whalley** (1653-1724) published the first English translation of Ptolemy's *Quadripartite* in 1701 (actually it was a translation of the Latin version of Proclus's *Paraphrase*).[62] This was the last major astrological work published in English until the Sibly brothers began to publish in the late 1780s.

> Ptolemy's Quadripartite, or Four Books concerning the Influences of the Stars, faithfully render'd into English from Leo Allacius, Library-Keeper to the Vatican in Rome....by John Whalley.
> London, 1701. 1st ed. 8vo. xvi,168,viii pp.

---

[60]See the account of the affair given by Ellen McCaffery in her *Astrology* (New York: Charles Scribner's Sons, 1942), pp. 327-328.

[61]His estate was valued at more than 2,000 pounds sterling, equivalent in purchasing power to more than $200,000 in today's currency.

[62]See the entry for Proclus above.

The Quadripartite, or Four Books concerning the Influences of the Stars, first written in Greek by Claudius Ptolemy, translated by J. Whalley. Second Edition, by M[anoah] S[ibly] and J. B[rowne].
London, 1786. 2nd ed. 8vo. vi,219 pp.

As mentioned above, beginning in the latter part of the 17th century, public interest in astrology rapidly declined throughout Europe. This trend continued for more than 200 years on the Continent. Only in England did astrology survive at a low level, kept alive by the continuing public interest in annual astrological almanacs.[63] And there the revival of astrology began in the last decades of the 18th century as we shall see presently.

---

[63]See the note on almanacs at the end of the entry for William Lilly above.

The Fifth Period

Modern Astrology

Technical Developments
Calendars and Clocks

One problem that astrologers had had since the invention of the art was inaccurate ephemerides. As has been noted above, the first reasonably accurate solar, lunar, and planetary theories were published by John Kepler in 1627 (*The Rudolphine Tables*). But even these left something to be desired, particularly in the case of the Moon. Ephemerides prepared from these tables with later minor corrections served the astronomical and astrological communities for a hundred years or more.[1] Naturally the accuracy could not be improved beyond a certain point until the gravitational theory of planetary motion had been worked out. This took nearly a century, and it was not until the late 1700s that ephemerides began to appear that were generally accurate to within one or two minutes of arc.[2]

The calendar problems were greatly reduced by the end of the 18th century. Most European countries had adopted the Gregorian calendar with 1 January as New Year's Day. Only those countries that adhered to the Eastern Orthodox religion, such as Greece and Russia, continued to use the old Julian calendar.

However, in the late 1700s the clocks began to change from Local Apparent Time (LAT) to Local Mean Time (LMT). One of the first cities to adopt LMT was Geneva in 1780. It was followed by London in 1792, Berlin in 1810, Paris in 1816, and Zürich in 1832.[3] The changeover from

---

[1] There is an extensive list of ephemerides in the British Museum Catalogue.

[2] See the informative graphs of ephemeris errors in Owen Gingrich & Barbara L. Weller, *Planetary, Lunar, and Solar Positions, A.D. 1650-1805* (Philadelphia: The American Philosophical Society, 1983), p. xx.

[3] See F.K. Ginzel, *Handbuch der mathematischen und technischen Chronologie* (Leipzig: J.C. Hinrichs, 1906-1914. 3 vols.), vol. 3, pp. 334 ff.

LAT to LMT took some 70 years to complete. It was slow at first, but it accelerated with the establishment of railroad lines in the 1830s and more particularly with the building of lines for the electric telegraph in the 1840s. It soon became apparent that railroads needed telegraphic communication, and this spurred the construction of telegraph lines.

When the railroads began to run in and out of major cities on regular schedules (in the late 1830s), it became necessary to adopt some time as standard for the rail lines. Usually the time of the hub city was adopted. Thus, "London time," "Paris time," "Berlin time," etc. became established. By 1880 a crazy-quilt of different times had developed, and the situation became intolerable. Conferences of the European nations in 1883 and a world conference of the principal nations in 1884 agreed to establish a world-wide system of "time zones" at 1 hour intervals of their longitude from Greenwich, England.[4] This system was officially launched in the U.S. and Canada in November 1883, but it was more than 30 years before nearly all countries adopted it.[5] Naturally, during the years of confusion preceding 1883 and the transition period that followed, astrologers were sometimes at a loss to know what sort of time was in use if a client stated that he had been born at 2:30 P.M. at such-and-such a place.

The changeover in civil time from LAT to LMT early in the 19th century caused a change in the time base used in the government ephemerides. The British Nautical Almanac changed from LAT to LMT with the 1834 issue. Astrological ephemerides were usually copied from the official publications. This created a problem for astrologers. In the past they had erected a chart by adding the LAT to the RA (expressed in time rather than in arc) of the Sun to get the RAMC. With the changeover to LMT this procedure was invalid. What was needed was a column in the ephemeris showing the Sidereal Time (ST). Then the formula would be ST + LMT = RAMC. Thus, an astrologer was faced with the problem of deciding whether a past time that had been given to him was LAT or LMT. And if it was LMT, then he needed to know the ST, which might not be in his ephemeris for those years.

The problem could be solved by using a table of time correction containing what is called "the Equation of Time." This shows the difference between LAT and LMT for any day in the year (it can be tabulated as a function of the calendar date). Thus, for several decades, astrologers had to convert past times in LMT to LAT, so that they could use the old formula. This created some uncertainty in the application of the table, an uncertainty which was compounded in the early 1900s when the astronomers decided to reverse the direction of conversion in the table,

---

[4]See F.K. Ginzel, *loc. cit.*, for an account of the various conferences and dates of adoption of the zone time system by individual nations. (The adoption dates are also given in the astrological gazeteers.)

[5]The French held out until 1911 before deciding to give up "Paris Time."

thus reversing the algebraic sign of each figure. Since that time, occasional articles have appeared in the astrological literature stating that all clock times must be corrected by the Equation of Time in order to determine the "true" RAMC, thus demonstrating their authors' ignorance of time keeping systems.

Something should also be said about clocks. Even assuming that a clock runs at a steady rate, how do you set it? In the 17th and 18th centuries clocks were set by obtaining the "correct" time from sundials. Naturally, this was mostly done sporadically, and in periods of extended cloudy weather, it could not be done at all. The mechanical quality of clocks steadily improved during that 200 year period. In the late 1700s the purchaser of a good pendulum clock might receive a sundial and a table of the Equation of Time along with his clock. Then, if he wished, he could keep LMT. Some people did, but most probably did not (since it was extra trouble). Not until the erection of telegraph lines beginning in the late 1840s did "accurate" time become available to railroad stations and other public institutions. Prior to that, clocks had to be set by sundials.

Methods of Calculation

Kepler was halfway through the arduous calculations that enabled him to produce the first fairly accurate astronomical tables when printed tables of logarithms became available (in the period 1614-1627). Astrological calculations were much simpler but still tedious. The astrologers of the early modern period used printed tables to find the cusps of the houses, to convert longitude and latitude to right ascension and declination, and to find oblique ascension. These tables reduced most calculations to simple arithmetic.

Those astrologers who adopted the Placidus system were required to find proportional semi-arcs. They were aided by the use of logarithmic tables. And for those who wished to make their calculations independently for one reason or another, tables of logarithms of numbers and of trignonometric functions were a virtual necessity. All of these were available, if one could afford the cost, by 1630 or so.

Astrological calculations continued to be based on the use of logarithmic tables until the invention of the junction transistor in 1951 and the appearance of the first low-priced (as compared to their mechanical equivalents) electronic calculators in the 1960s. From an initial cost of $250 for a device that would only add, subtract, multiply, and divide, to the little electronic marvel I paid $15 for in 1984 that would do everything you could think of, including sexagesimal to decimal conversions, all to 11 decimal places, took fewer than twenty years.

In the late 1970s the first affordable desktop computers became available. These increased in capability with almost unbelievable rapidity, and, after an initial surge, actually began to slowly decrease in price. Today, the best desktop machines rival the mainframe computers of twenty years ago in many respects. An astrologer with $2,000 to spend can equip himself with a truly marvelous machine. And laptop computers are also available at affordable prices.

All this has had a strong impact upon ephemerides and tables of houses. If you have a computer and the proper software, you do not need any tables. The machine will calculate the positions of the planets and the house cusps according to a dozen different systems—all in a few seconds. It will also display the chart and all sorts of tabular listings on the screen or send them to a printer.

Computers have also obviated the need for gazeteers giving the longitude, latitude, and time zone information for places. Affordable software contains all that information and will look it up automatically when the place-name and date is entered. It is now possible to calculate an accurate horoscope simply by entering the client's name and birthdata—no understanding of the process is required!

It seems likely that the production of printed house tables and ephemerides will slowly decline and perhaps eventually stop altogether, since a growing number of astrologers have computers. Instead of learning the astronomical basis of a horoscope, the owner of a computer now has to learn the rules for entering data into the software and choosing output options. He is thus making a slow but steady transition from being an astrologer to being simply a specialized computer user.

Planets, Planets, and More Planets

For two thousand years or more there were only seven planets (counting the Sun and Moon) known to astrologers. In 1785 Uranus was discovered; in 1801 Ceres, the first of the asteroids,[6] was discovered, followed in 1802 by Pallas, in 1804 by Juno, and in 1807 by Vesta; then no more until Astraea was found in 1845. In 1846 Neptune, the last large outer planet was found. Later, the refusal of the planet Mercury to move in exact accordance with Newtonian gravitation led astronomers to suspect the existence of a planet closer to the Sun than Mercury. Some supposed sightings of such a planet interested the great French astronomer U.J.J. LeVerrier (1811-1877) and later led some astrologers to accept its existence and dub it Vulcan.[7]

Still later, in the 20th century, Neptune's obstinate refusal to run right led to speculation that there might be another large planet beyond it. The French astrologer Fomalhaut stated definitely in 1899 that there was one

---

[6]Amusingly, astronomers called these planetoids "asteroids" for a long time. Then, they decided to call them "minor planets" and looked down their noses at astrologers for using the old term. But in the last few decades the astronomical worm has turned. Astronomers have again begun to call them "asteroids," thus bringing themselves back into synch with the astrologers!

[7]For more information about the supposed planet Vulcan, see the entry for L.H. Weston below.

and that its name would be Pluto. In the early decades of the 20th century other astrologers began to "discover" or simply to postulate "trans-Neptunian" planets. After an intensive search at the Lowell Observatory, the planet Pluto was finally discovered in 1930. However, it proved to be a disappointment to astronomers because it was far too small to account for the irregularities in Neptune's motion. Nevertheless, it was a real "trans-Neptunian" planet to put into horoscopes.

The specialized knowledge and tedious mathematics involved in calculating asteroid orbits with nothing more than logarithm tables and mechanical calculators discouraged all but a few astrologers from investigating the possible influences of the increasingly large number of asteroids.

All of this changed with the advent of electronic computers in the 1950s. Astronomers now found it easy to compute orbits and isolated positions, as well as ephemerides. The planet Neptune continued to move further from the orbits calculated for it by American and French astronomers, and when it became apparent that Pluto could not be held accountable for its irregularity, some astronomers revived the idea that there might yet be a sizable undiscovered trans-Neptunian (now, trans-Plutonian) planet. This naturally interested some astrologers, who began to write articles and books about this supposed outer planet,[8] particularly after one astronomer calculated a hypothetical orbit for such a planet.[9]

The discovery of the asteroid Chiron in 1977 has perhaps aroused the most enthusiasm among astrologers. Its long period of about 50 years (halfway between Saturn's 30 years and Uranus's 84 years) immediately recommended it and sparked a rash of articles, books, and ephemerides, so that it soon became a standard feature of many computer-generated horoscopes. Astronomers subsequently noted that it appears to have a small atmosphere, so they have decertified it as an asteroid and reclassified it as a comet. But this does not appear to have diminished its appeal to astrologers.

In Italy, the astrologer **Fabio Francesco Berti** (d. 1992) thought he had detected the influence of two trans-Plutonian planets. He calculated orbits for them, calling them "X" and "Y," and published ephemerides.

These have not yet been found by astronomers, but during the last few years they have discovered many planetoids in the vicinity of Pluto as well as farther out in the so-called Kuiper Belt Zone. And recently they have made several particularly notable discoveries. (These are discussed in my

---

[8]In Germany, Dr. Theodor Landscheid, *Transpluto Graphical Ephemeris...1878-1987* (Aalen: Ebertin Verlag, 1972); and in the U.S., John Hawkins, *Transpluto or Shall We Call Him Bacchus?* (Tempe, Az.: A.F.A., Inc., 19 .

[9]But the astronomers eventually corrected their orbital calculations for Neptune and gave up the idea.

forthcoming paper, "Distant Asteroids," that will be published in the AFA *Journal of Research,* Vol. 13.)

Perhaps the most surprising is the planetoid Sedna, whose mean distance is 532 astronomical units, or 13 times as far out as Pluto! Its orbit is very eccentric (0.86), and its tropical period is a little more than 8,300 years! It is currently near 18 Taurus and 12 S latitude. Its orbit is so unlike anything else that some astronomers have even speculated that it is not an original part of our solar system, but that it may have been "captured" ages ago from some passing star.

And on July 29, 2005, astronomers Brown, Trujillo, and Rabinowitz announced that they had discovered a planetoid half again as far out as Pluto and somewhat larger than Pluto! It was discussed in my paper, "A Rival for Pluto" in the AFA's *Today's Astrologer,* Vol. 67, No. 10 (October 3, 2005):27-29. As of this writing it has not yet received a formal name, but the astronomers have nicknamed it "Xena" after the warrior princess of the TV show. They have also stated that they expect to find one or two more of that size as they continue their search in coming years.

These discoveries will surely excite the astrological community and may result in the suggestion to name one or more of these larger-than-Pluto planetoids as the rulers of Libra or Virgo. However, since several more may ultimately be discovered, the supply of available signs will run out. And the idea of sign rulership may have to be given up. Since their movement is so slow, they could be treated as points of special significance in the zodiac—rather like the fixed stars. Time will tell.

The availability of calculated positions for hundreds or even thousands of asteroids has claimed the interest of some astrologers. There has even been a recommendation for the individual to claim an asteroid with a name similar to his own as his "personal planet" and to pay particular attention to its position in his natal horoscope, etc.

The comment made by Geoffrey Dean and his collaborators on hypothetical planets is apt:

> To postulate that more planets exist than are known is to imply that deficiencies lie with planets and not with techniques. This is clearly untenable. After all, Hindu astrologers (who probably outnumber all other astrologers combined . . .) claim success despite ignoring three <u>known</u> planets.[10]

A friend and colleague of mine put it more bluntly: "Astrologers who clutter up their horoscopes with hypothetical planets, satellites, and asteroids simply don't know how to read charts!"

---

[10]Geoffey Dean, *Recent Advances in Natal Astrology* (Subiaco, W.A.: Analogic, 1977), p. 241.}

And Another Moon?

In addition to the hypothetical planets, some astrologers have also postulated an additional satellite for the earth. Or, as we shall see, two or more additional satellites. The so-called "Dark Moon," supposedly discovered in 1897 and later discussed by the English astrologer Sepharial[11] (who seems to have given it its name, Lilith), found an American supporter in Ivy M. Goldstein-Jacobson, who published a book on the effects of Lilith containing an ephemeris seemingly based on the principle that Lilith always moves forward in the zodiac at a constant speed of 3°02' per day.[12]

Lilith has since gained some enthusiastic advocates. Books have been written by more recent authors, and articles appear from time to time in the astrological periodicals. However, there are said to be three different "orbits" for this body, that yield entirely different positions. Thus, different astrologers may put Lilith in different places in their charts.

The main split seems to be between the American concept and the European concept. Goldstein-Jacobson constructed her ephemeris by assigning Lilith a constant motion of 3°02' per mean solar day, which gives it a period of 118.68 days. This corresponds to nothing recognized by astronomers. Some, at least, of the Europeans on the other hand have identified Lilith with the lunar apogee, a recognized feature of the lunar orbit with a period of 3231.48 days, which advances only about 0°06'41". per day. Plainly, these are two entirely different "Liliths" with the same name.

The ephemeris most recently published in the U.S. agrees more or less with the "orbit" used by Goldstein-Jacobson.[13]

Availability of Older Books

During the last thirty years many astrological "classics" have been reprinted. This has facilitated the study of "traditional astrology," since most public and university libraries have very few astrology books.[14] A notable example is the 1985 facsimile reprint of William Lilly's *Christian Astrology* by the Regulus Publishing Co. in England. Early books can of course be copied on microfilm (if they can be found), although the cost is

---

[11]Sepharial, *The Science of Foreknowledge* (London: L.N. Fowler, 1918), pp. 39-45.

[12]*The Dark Moon Lilith in Astrology.* [with ephemeris 1860-2000 A.D.] (Pasadena: The Author, 1961. 1st ed.; repr. 1963). There are some errors in the ephemeris.

[13]Delphine Jay, *Lilith Ephemeris 1900-2000 A.D.* (Tempe, Az.: A.F.A., Inc., 1983.)

[14]In general, the university libraries felt no need to acquire books on a discredited subject like astrology. Since there was no astrology department in the universities, there was no faculty demand for astrology books. In the case of the public libraries, many librarians felt that they should not spend their limited funds on "such things," but there was perhaps another reason too. I was once told by a city librarian that "we don't buy many astrology books because people steal them!"

considerable, and the books must either be read on a microfilm reader (another expense) or printed on a special printer. One resource that has appeared is the astrological collection of the Universe Bookstore in Canada, whose Ballantrae Reprint series offers a substantial number of reproductions of older astrological books (mostly in English), some of them from the 17th century. Several publishers have also specialized in bringing out reprints of older 20th century books. And translations of Greek and Latin books are being published.

Astrological Libraries

Many astrological associations maintain libraries of astrological books. The desire to enlarge and enrich these collections has increased considerably in recent years. To mention a few, in England the Urania Trust has been established, originally under the direction of **Charles Harvey** (1940-2000). A notable collection has also been started in Canada. And in the U.S. there is the Library of the American Federation of Astrologers at Tempe, Arizona, and the new Heart Center Library established by **Michael Erlewine** at the Matrix corporate headquarters in Big Rapids, Michigan.

These institutions fill a definite need, since regular public and university libraries rarely contain many astrological books. Back files of astrological periodicals are usually to be found only in the specialized astrological libraries. It is to be hoped that ultimately funds will be found to photograph these items and make them available to astrological researchers through some of the new computerized media that are becoming available.

But now we resume the history with an account of the revival of horoscopic astrology in England in the late 18th century.

Astrology since 1780
The Sibly Brothers

Astrology came back to life rather vigorously in England in the 1780s, sparked by the books of **Ebenezer Sibly** (1752-1799) and his brother **Manoah Sibly** (1757-1840). Ebenezer began to publish *The Complete Illustration of the Celestial Art of Astrology* in 1784, a splendid work that appeared in four parts running to a total of 1130 pages by 1790. It contained a certain amount of occultism in addition to the astrology. This perhaps reflected a predilection of the brothers, for Manoah Sibly eventually became an ardent and prominent Swedenborgian minister. Manoah, in association with J. Browne, also reprinted Whalley's translation of the *Tetrabiblos, The Quadripartite, or Four Books concerning the Influences of the Stars* (London, 1786). Thus, by 1790 a small library of books on horoscopic astrology was available in English in new editions.

Not long after that, there appeared the first issue (August 1791) of *The Conjurer's Magazine*, a periodical at first devoted mainly to parlor magic, etc., but whose astrological content grew steadily until the name was changed two years later to *The Astrologer's Magazine*, of which seven issues were published, the last being for January 1794. This was the first astrological magazine published in any language.[15] Thereafter astrology flourished, despite occasional opposition from the civil authorities. Under the law of the time, astrologers were classified as "vagrants" and were therefore liable to be jailed as public nuisances. An example is the unfortunate **Thomas White**. He had apparently attracted the attention of the law with his book, *The Beauties of Occult Science Investigated; or, the Celestial Intelligencer; in two parts . . . . (London: Anne Davis, 1811. 8vo. 436 pp.).*

Shortly after his book was published, White was arrested, tried and sentenced. He died in prison a year or so later (1813?), a victim of bigotry.

Worsdale

A younger contemporary of the Siblys was the Lincoln astrologer **John Worsdale** (1766-1826). He was a very capable astrologer who specialized in primary directions using the Placidus system. He practiced professionally in Lincoln and at the age of thirty published a very technical work, *Genethliacal Astrology* (Newark, 1796), an enlarged edition of which appeared two years later (Newark, 1798). A third enlarged edition, *Celestial Philosophy or Genethliacal Astronomy*, was published at London in 1828 by his son. It contains thirty nativities from Worsdale's own practice with biographical notes and elaborate tables of primary directions.

Varley and Uranus

The discovery of the planet Uranus in 1781 does not seem to have attracted as much attention among astrologers as might have been expected, perhaps because it is invisible to the naked eye. One of the earliest astrologers to take note of it and to try to establish its influence was the well-known water-colorist **John Varley** (1778-1842), who was also an ardent amateur astrologer. McCaffery cites the following account of his interest in the new planet from a story related by his son Albert[16]:

> "Varley spent much time inserting Uranus in his own and other people's charts, watching carefully to see what kinds of events it provoked when it came into conjunction or aspect with other planets,—also when affected radically by other planets. He had evidently come to the conclusion

---

[15] See Ellic Howe, *Astrology: A Recent History* (New York: Walker and Company, 1968), pp. 23-25. Howe notes that the first issue under the new title contained an editorial statement thanking those "who have enabled us to contribute to the revival of Astrology."

[16] Ellen McCaffery, *op. cit.*, pp. 334-335.

that if Uranus was excited by Mars, there would be sudden or unexpected eruptions. One particular morning he announced to his family that he would stay at home, as something very serious was going to happen and he must be present when it occurred. At noon, part of the house caught on fire. Not one bucket of water did Varley carry, but he sat down to write notes on the effect of Uranus. Let me quote his son Albert who tells the story[17]:

> "He was so delighted at having discovered what the astrological significance of Uranus was, that he sat down while his house was burning, knowing though he did, that he was not insured for a penny, to write an account of his discovery....Although he lost everything in the fire, he regarded that as a small matter compared with his discovery of the new planet's potential."

Truly a dedicated scientific astrologer! Varley later got the idea of publishing a book on astrological physiognomy, which he called *A Treatise on Zodiacal Physiognomy* (London, 1828). With the help of his friend William Blake (1757-1827) he drew illustrations of the physical appearance of persons born with each of the signs rising.[18] Unfortunately, he had only produced the first of four parts (Aries, Taurus, and Gemini) when Blake died, so he never completed the work.

Corfield and Uranus

According to Howe, **John Corfield**, a contemporary of Varley's, provided the prototype statement of the influence of the new planet Uranus. It appeared in his ill-fated astrological magazine *Urania*, of which only a single issue was published in June 1814.[19]

The Asteroids

The discovery of the first four asteroids, Ceres, Pallas, Juno, and Vesta (1801-1807) did not arouse much interest in the astrologers of the time. Not only were they invisible to the naked eye, but the astronomers deduced that they were very much smaller in size than the visible planets. The astrologer James Wilson had this to say about them: "There are also four smaller planets, discovered between the orbits of Mars and Jupiter, viz. Pallas, Ceres, Juno, and Vesta; but their effect can be but trifling, owing to their magnitude, which is very inconsiderable."[20] In fact the asteroids had to wait 170 years before astrologers took much interest in them.

---

[17]Alfred T. Story, *Life of John Varley* (London?: Richard Bentley, 1894).

[18]See the illustration 'The Ghost of a Flea' symbolizing the Gemini type on the plate facing p. 52 of Ellic Howe's, *Astrology*.

[19]*See* Ellic Howe, *op. cit.*, p. 16 n. 2.

[20]James Wilson, *A Complete Dictionary of Astrology* (London, 1819).

And it was not until the advent of affordable desktop computers in the 1980s made the calculation of their positions virtually effortless that they really aroused much interest. In the interval their numbers grew from four to more than 5,000.[21] With continuing discoveries, now approaching 50,000!

Wilson and Ashmand

In 1819 **James Wilson** published *A Complete Dictionary of Astrology* (London: W. Hughes, 1819; Boston: A.H. Roffe & Co., 1885. repr.; New York: Samuel Weiser, 1969. repr. in facs. of the 1885 ed.), followed in the next year by his *Tetrabiblos, or Quadripartite of Ptolemy. . . . [actually a translation of the Paraphrase* attributed to Proclus] (London: W. Hughes, 1820) and *A New and Complete Set of Astrological Tables. . . .* (London: W. Hughes, 1820) Of these, the *Dictionary* has proved perennially popular and is still in print.

Two years later **J.M. Ashmand** published another translation of the *Tetrabiblos* (or rather, of the *Paraphrase*), *Ptolemy's Tetrabiblos, or Quadripartite* (London: Davis & Dickson, 1822). This translation became the standard version used by succeeding generations of English-speaking astrologers.

The year 1795 saw the birth of two men who were to become the leading British astrologers of the first part of the 19th century: R.C. Smith and R.J. Morrison.

The First Raphael

Robert Cross Smith (1795-1832), a native of Bristol, with the assistance of the famous balloonist, G.W. Graham (b. 1784), published his first astrological tract in 1822. Two years later he became editor of a new weekly periodical *The Straggling Astrologer*. It only endured through October of that year, but after another two years he was invited to become the editor of a new annual almanac, *The Prophetic Messenger*, for which he adopted the pseudonym **Raphael**. It contained predictions for every day of the year. This time he had a hit. Sales were good from the outset and increased steadily throughout his lifetime, which unfortunately came to an end in February 1832. During the years 1828-1831 he had found time to write a half dozen books on astrology and fortune-telling. After Smith's untimely death, the publisher promptly hired **John Palmer** (1807-1837), who thus became **Raphael II**. And under a succession of "Raphaels," the almanac has survived until the present time. In the astrological world Raphael's name became a household word because of his publication of the annual *Raphael's Ephemeris*. It has been in print longer than any other

---

[21]The Institute of Theoretical Astronomy in St. Petersburg publishes an annual list of the orbital elements of the asteroids. And software prepared by Russian astronomers that contains orbital data for 5,000 or more asteroids is now commercially available. Also, on-line sources offer ephemerides.

such publication. It is still available for single years from 1832 to the present.

Zadkiel I and II

Richard James Morrison (1795-1874) was a retired Naval Lieutenant who adopted the professional name **Zadkiel**. He came from a well-to-do family, and, encouraged by his friend R.C. Smith's success, he began to publish *Zadkiel's Almanack* in 1830, an annual that eventually outsold its rival and like it was continued into the present century. During his long life Zadkiel published several astrological manuals, including *The Grammar of Astrology* (London, 1833) and *An Introduction to Astrology* (London, 1835),[22] both of which were frequently reprinted. Howe gives an interesting account of his career.[23] One event in his life is especially notable:

> In his 1861 almanac (written in the summer of 1860) he predicted that 1861 would be an "evil year" for the Prince Consort (Queen Victoria's husband). And in fact Prince Albert died quite unexpectedly of typhoid fever on 14 December 1861. As not infrequently happens, this apparently successful prediction outraged certain parties, among them a writer for the London *Daily Telegraph* and Sir Edward Belcher (1799-1877). The latter wrote a scurrilous letter attacking Morrison, who promptly sued Sir Edward for libel. The case was repeatedly delayed by the defendant's attorneys, but, when it was finally heard in 1863, the jury found in favor of Morrison but awarded him only 20 shillings [about $100 in today's money]. The Lord Chief Justice refused to assess costs against Sir Edward, so Morrison was vindicated but at considerable cost and annoyance to himself. It did, however, substantially increase the subsequent sales of his almanac.[24]

The year after the death of Zadkiel I, he was replaced by **Zadkiel II**, who was **A(lfred) J(ohn) Pearce** (1840-1923), a medical assistant, who thereafter turned his attention wholly to astrology. Pearce edited the almanac for nearly fifty years and also found time to write an excellent general treatise, *The Text-book of Astrology*.[25]

---

[22] A much cut-down version of parts 1 & 2 of Lilly's *Christian Astrology* (1647), with some alterations and additions by Zadkiel himself.

[23] See Ellic Howe, *.op. cit*, pp. 33-52. There is a nice picture of Zadkiel facing p. 52.

[24] Ellic Howe, *op. cit.*, pp. 43-46.

[25] It was first published in parts: Part 1, London, 1879; Part 2, London, 1889; and then in a combined rev. ed., London, 1911, repr. in facs. (Washington: AFA, 1970), reset and reprinted (Tempe, Az.: AFA, 2006).

W.J. Simmonite

In Sheffield **Dr. W(illiam) J(oseph) Simmonite** (c.1800-c.1860) was headmaster of a private school, but he also practiced herbal medicine. Whether he had actually received a degree in medicine is unknown. However, he had received a good education. Dr. L.D. Broughton (1828-1899), who had perhaps known him in England, says that he "spoke, wrote, and taught eight different languages, besides being a thorough scholar and mathematician."[26] His astrological works show the hand of the schoolmaster. They contain a very thorough treatment of the mathematics and astronomy necessary to the astrologer.[27] His emphasis throughout is on primary directions, but secondaries are mentioned. His best known books today are:

> Complete Arcana of Astral Philosophy
> or the Celestial Philosopher.
> ed., corr., and augmented by John Story
> London: W. Foulsham, 1890.
> [a revision of the 2nd ed.]

> Horary Astrology: the Key to Scientific Prediction.
> [new edition by John Story]
> London: W. Foulsham, 1896. 6th ed.

Dr. Broughton says of the latter book, "His *Horary Astrology* I kept on my desk for reference for over 30 years." And he adds, "His book on Revolutions is one of the best that has ever been published, and his *Botanic Practice of Medicine*[28] is also an excellent little volume; I carried it in my pocket for years, and committed to memory his descriptions of diseases."

Ackroyd and Neptune

One of Pearce's contemporaries, **"Professor" John Ackroyd**, wrote the prototype formulation of the astrological influence of the planet Neptune.[29] It appears as a letter to John Story, the editor of the 1890 edition of W.J. Simmonite's *Complete Arcana of Astral Philosophy* (London: Foulsham, 1890).[30] However, Ackroyd expresses uncertainty about the sign ruled by Neptune, stating (incorrectly) that according to Ptolemy's

---

[26]Luke D. Broughton, *The Elements of Astrology* (New York: The Author, 1898).

[27]His formulae are of course adapted to the use of logarithms and are therefore old-fashioned today.

[28]This is probably Simmonite's *Medical Botany, or Herbal Guide to Health* (London, 1848?).

[29]See Ellic Howe, *op. cit.*, p. 17.

[30]Reprinted as *The Arcana of Astrology* (Hollywood: Newcastle Publ. Co., 1974. repr. in facs.).

theory it should rule Aquarius, "but Scorpio or Taurus might answer well, as they are both of an obscure and mystical nature."

Alan Leo

Towards the end of the 19th century the famous **Alan Leo** (1860-1917) abandoned his career as a traveling salesman and started a magazine, *Modern Astrology,* and a publishing business, both of which met with great success and rapidly popularized the art. Leo and his wife, Bessie (Phillips) Leo (1858-1931) were Theosophists, and they strove to interest their fellow Theosophists in astrology. This injected a note of esotericism into English astrology, which had not been there previously, and which is still present to some extent.

Leo is the leading figure in the revival of European astrology from the 1890s until World War I. His magazine was read both in England and abroad and his principal books were read world-wide in English and were translated into several European languages. Many people had their interest in astrology aroused by ordering a "horoscope" from Leo. The less expensive versions were assembled from standard delineations of planets in signs, houses, etc., while individually delineated charts were available for a higher fee. (In fact it was through one of these that he met his future wife, Bessie Phillips.)

Similar delineations are found in his book *Astrology for All,* which also contains the Solar-Lunar Polarities.[31] Later interpretations of the Solar-Lunar Polarities appear in Grant Lewi's *Heaven Knows What* (see below) and Robert A. Hughes's *The Sun and Moon Polarity in Your Horoscope* (Tempe: A.F.A., Inc., 1977).

Leo was also responsible for a major shift in astrological predictive techniques. Prior to his appearance on the scene, primary directions had been the favorite tool of the astrologer. But primaries are bothersome to calculate by hand and require some knowledge of spherical astronomy and trigonometry if the astrologer is to understand what he is doing. Even with the aid of the specialized tables developed for that purpose, calculating a series of primaries is a tedious job. Placidus's secondary progressions are much easier to calculate, since they are simply taken from the ephemeris. The only difficulty is converting their time from the nativity in days into time from the nativity in years, months, and days (using the measure: one day for one year).

Leo's solution to the problem was to produce what he called "the progressed horoscope." This is a mixed bag of secondary directions and zodiacal primaries. Secondaries are calculated as just mentioned, while the chart is rotated to bring the ASC and MC (and the other cusps if desired) into conjunction or aspect with the zodiacal longitudes of the planets. This is much easier to do than to calculate primary directions to both mundane

---

[31]Chapter xviii in the fourth edition reprint (London: L.N. Fowler, 1969).

and zodiacal positions. Leo devoted an entire book to this procedure and included "standard" readings for the progressed aspects (based upon general significators). His technique was soon adopted by most Western astrologers, since it was easier and quicker. Thereafter, the use of primary directions rapidly declined to a low level from which it has never recovered (despite the recent advent of computers to do the hard work).

There is no doubt that without Leo's astrological skill, his organizational ability, energy, and enthusiasm, the revival of astrology would have been slower and less vigorous. Among his seven "big books," his *Art of Synthesis, How to Judge a Nativity,* and *The Progressed Horoscope* have served as fundamental guides for many astrologers. Leo also published the first extensive modern collection of horoscopes of notable persons, *A Thousand and One Notable Nativities* (London: Modern Astrology Publ. Co., 1910). It was apparently compiled by one of Leo's assistants, **H.S. Green** (1861-1937).

In the midst of his success, Leo was hauled into court in May 1914 on the charge of "fortune-telling," but was acquitted on a legal technicality. In July 1917 the law was after him again, and this time he lost the case and was fined 25 pounds sterling (about $2,500 in today's currency).[32] His lawyer advised him that the prediction of psychological tendencies rather than specific events would not be considered to be "fortune-telling." This was perhaps the turning point in horoscope delineation. Thereafter, what has more recently been called "event-oriented astrology" gradually receded in favor of character analysis and vague descriptions of possible areas of psychological harmony or stress, sometimes degenerating into what has been termed "psycho-babble."

Sepharial

A younger contemporary of Leo's was the well-known **Sepharial**, whose real name was Walter Richard (*later*, W. Gorn) Old (1864-1929). Although he was interested in occult subjects and in the Cabala and numerology, Sepharial, unlike Leo, was not inclined towards "esoteric" astrology, since he regarded astrology rightly as an empirical science with definite rules. He knew many languages and took some interest in Hindu astrology, but he did not mix Eastern and Western methods. Sepharial wrote more than forty books, some of which are still available. Among them were *Prognostic Astronomy* (London: L.N. Fowler, 1901), an excellent manual of primary directions (which also discusses the parallax of the Moon and gives tables for computing it); *The New Manual of Astrology* (London, 1898); *Eclipses* (London: L.N. Fowler, 1915); *The Science of Foreknowledge* (London: L.N. Fowler, 1918); and *Transits and Planetary Periods* (London: W. Foulsham & Co., 1928).

In his book *The Science of Foreknowledge* (London: L.N. Fowler,

---

[32]See Ellic Howe, *op. cit.*, pp. 63-64.

1918), Sepharial mentions the supposed discovery of a "Dark Moon" of the earth by a German astronomer, for which Sepharial suggested the name Lilith. This did not arouse much interest at the time, but the hypothetical satellite was adopted by some European astrologers and by the American astrologer Ivy M. Goldstein-Jacobson (see below). It has since gained some popularity.

Charles Carter

Charles E.O. Carter (1887-1968), B.A., MAFA, D.F.Astrol.S., was trained as a lawyer and served in the British military during World War I. Prior to the war, he had become interested in astrology and had made the acquaintance of Alan and Bessie Leo and the other leading British astrologers in Leo's circle. From the time of his assumption of editorship of *Astrology, The Astrologers' Quarterly* at its inception in 1926, his reputation grew steadily until he came to be considered the dean of British astrologers. His many magazine articles and books are still considered to be prime authorities in their fields. Carter was president of the Astrological Lodge of the Theosophical Society from 1920 to 1952 and first principal of the Faculty of Astrological Studies (founded in 1948). He continued to edit the astrological quarterly until 1959. Some of his most popular books are: the *Encyclopedia of Psychological Astrology* (London, 1924); *The Principles of Astrology* (London, 1925); *Symbolic Directions in Modern Astrology* (London, 1929); *Astrological Aspects* (1930); *The Astrology of Accidents* (1932); and *An Introduction to Political Astrology* (1951?). In the latter book he defines his subject in this way:

> Mundane Astrology...comprised, one may say, all that concerned many people rather than a single person.
>
> Thus under Mundane Astrology came not only the rise and fall of dynasties, and wars, but also earthquakes, droughts, epidemics, the founding and destiny of cities.
>
> The term Mundane Astrology is still in use, but the tendency seems to be to use more precise terms to determinate its several branches, and to speak of Political Astrology, or the science concerned with politically organized groups, Racial Astrology, or the science as concerned with blood-communities, Astro-Meteorology, Astro-Seismology, and so forth.
>
> - - - - - -
>
> Our subject here is Political Astrology, or the study in the light of Astrology of politically organized and significant communities, from groups of allied nations such as might be represented by Western Union, through the Nation, down to political parties of sufficient importance to justify study.

In the course of the book, Carter explains the various techniques that have been used in making mundane predictions. He offers some interesting comments on the Aries Ingress charts that are commonly used for this purpose, and especially on the ones of 1914 and 1939 which preceded the two world wars. In particular he notes that the 1939 chart hardly seemed at the time to indicate the outbreak of war, and this led him and other astrologers astray in their predictions for that year. Like all of his books, his clear and objective presentation of his material leads the reader through the methods and encourages independent research.

R.H. Naylor, Edward Lyndoe, and Newspaper Astrology

R(ichard) H(arold) Naylor (1889-1952) was the first British "newspaper astrologer." He was asked in August 1930 to write an article for the London *Sunday Express* on the horoscope of the newly born Princess Margaret Rose. The article was so well received that the paper asked Naylor for more articles. The first of what was to become a weekly feature appeared on 5 October 1930. In it Naylor predicted that British aircraft were soon to be in serious danger. That very day the British dirigible R-101 crashed and burned in Beauvais, France. Naylor's reputation was made.[33]

Not long afterward, *The Sunday Express*'s rival newspaper *The People* employed another well-known British astrologer, **Edward Lyndoe** (b. 1901), to write a weekly column for its readers. A few years later newspapers began to publish daily guides for the twelve signs of the zodiac. These journalistic innovations soon spread to the U.S, where they also gave an impetus to the founding of popular astrology magazines.

Lyndoe was later the author of *Everyman's Astrology* (London: Neville Spearman, 1959), which was published in the U.S. as *Astrology For Everyone* (New York: E.P. Dutton, 1960). In this book, Lyndoe espoused the almost forgotten Morinus system of houses, apparently because it is simple and can be printed in little space. He is its only prominent advocate (even Morin didn't use it!).

Brig. Firebrace

Brigadier R(oy) C. Firebrace (1889-1974), British soldier, interpreter, and astrologer. He was a convert to "siderealism" and worked closely with its originator, Cyril Fagan (1896-1970). In 1961 he founded the periodical *Spica* as a review of sidereal astrology and served as its editor until his death (after which it was discontinued). Firebrace was the author of *An Introduction to the Sidereal Zodiac, New Directions in Astrology, Tertiary Directions*, and *Wars in the Sidereal*, all published by Firebrace (London, 1960).[34]

---

[33]See Ellic Howe, *op. cit.*, pp. 68-69.
[34]He was also joint author of: C. Fagan and R.C. Firebrace, *A Primer of the Sidereal Zodiac.* (London: R.C. Firebrace, 1961. 1st ed.).

Robson

Vivian E(rwood) Robson (1890-1942), B.Sc., was a librarian and a scholarly traditional astrologer who was familiar with modern European as well as medieval astrological literature. Several of his books are considered to be standard authorities on their subjects. He was a staunch advocate of the Placidus system of house division. He also advocated a careful examination of symbolic progressions (including tertiary progressions). He is the author of:

A Student's Textbook of Astrology.
London: Cecil Palmer, 1922. 1st ed.
Philadelphia: J.B. Lippincott, [1940]. repr.

The Fixed Stars and Constellations in Astrology.
London: Cecil Palmer, 1923. 1st ed.
London, 1931. 3rd ed.
Philadelphia: J.B. Lippincott Co., [1940]. repr. 264 pp.
New York: Samuel Weiser, 1969. repr.
New York: Samuel Weiser, 1976. repr.

The Radix System.
London: The Stallex Publishing Co., 1930
Philadelphia: J.B. Lippincott, [1940?]. repr.
Toledo, Ohio: Darr Publs., 1974. repr.

Electional Astrology.
Philadelphia: J.B. Lippincott, 1937.

Astrology and Sex.
Philadelphia: W. Foulsham & Co., 1941.

Marguerite Hone

Marguerite E. Hone, D.F.Astrol.S. (1892-1969), revived the Equal House system of houses in her popular courses of instruction in astrology. She was the principal of the Faculty of Astrological Studies in London from 1954 to 1969. Her teachings are embodied in her comprehensive textbooks: *The Modern Textbook of Astrology* (London: L.N. Fowler, 1951. 1st ed.) and *Applied Astrology*. (London: L.N. Fowler, 1953. 1st ed.).

Wemyss

Maurice Wemyss (1892-1973) was in private life Duncan McNaughton, a Scots archaeologist. He had a deep interest in astrology and compiled a remarkable amount of data on "degree areas" in the zodiac that were prominent in horoscopes exemplifying persons with different temperaments, occupations, and medical conditions. His findings are given in the five volumes of his work, *The Wheel of Life or Scientific Astrology* (London & Edinburgh: various publishers, 1927-1952). Vol. 5 contains an astrological commentary covering diseases from A to Gout; but why he never published any more after that is unknown. Upon learning of his death, London colleagues immediately tried to obtain his notes, but they were informed by his family yhat they had all been destroyed after his death.[35]

Although in general Wemyss's work is praiseworthy, he disagreed with some of the traditional sign rulerships, and he also succumbed to the idea of postulating new planets.[36] In Appendix VII to vol. III of his *The Wheel of Life or Scientific Astrology* (c. 1929), he "unhesitatingly" assigns Uranus as the ruler of Scorpio, Neptune as the ruler of Libra and the asteroids as a group to Pisces. Then he assigns Sagittarius, Virgo, Leo, and Cancer to four new planets he had postulated—Jason, Dido, Hercules, and Pluto. And he meant "Wemyss-Pluto," not "Lowell-Pluto," as he later called it. Of these, Jason was first announced to the astrological world in 1922; it was said to have had a period of 45 years. Dido, a period of about 360 years; Hercules, a period of about 654 years; and Pluto, a period of about 1,366 years. In the second edition of vol. III, Wemyss took note of the discovery of Pluto in 1930, declared that it was misnamed, assigned it as co-ruler of Virgo, and suggested calling it "Lowell-Pluto" to distinguish it from his own Pluto, which he considered to be the true Pluto.

Wemyss issued two collections of birthdata drawn from the published volumes of the *Wheel of Life*; these are sometimes published with Alan Leo's *Notable Nativities* (NN) and are usually referred to as *More Notable Nativities* (MNN) and *Famous Nativities* (FN), comprising 200 and 204 nativities respectively. As in *Notable Nativities*, planetary positions are given for each case and the ASC and MC for timed data.

Tucker

William J(oseph) Tucker (1896-1981) was an English astrologer who aimed to remove the "occult" aura from astrology and to establish it on a strictly scientific basis. He was the author of more than two dozen books and pamphlets, some of which are still available. In the mid-1930s he started a periodical, *Science and Astrology,* that ran for a year and a half. Some of his works are:

Astro-Medical Diagnosis. The Principles of Scientific
Medical Astrology.
Cuyahoga Falls, Ohio: Schary Publ. Co., 1959. 1st ed.
Sidcup, Kent: Pythagorean Publs., 1962. 2nd ed.

---

[35]Mentioned in a letter from Charles Harvey to the present author.
[36]Possibly motivated by Alfred Witte's announcement of his "discovery" of Cupido.

Autobiography of an Astrologer.
Sidcup, Kent: Pythagorean Publs., 1960.

Ptolemaic Astrology. . . A Complete Commentary on the
Tetrabiblos of Claudius Ptolemy.
Sidcup, Kent: Pythagorean Publs., 1961.

Gleadow

Rupert S(eeley) Gleadow (1909-1974), B.A., was educated in the
classics and oriental languages. He took an early interest in astrology and
later became a convert to "siderealism" He was an articulate exponent of
Cyril Fagan's "sidereal" zodiac. Two of his books on the subject are *The
Origin of the Zodiac* (New York: Castle Books, 1968) and *Your Character in the Zodiac* (North Hollywood: Wilshire Book Co., 1971. repr. of
1968 ed.).

Davison

Ronald C(arlyle) Davison (1914-1985). A prominent astrologer who
succeeded Charles E.O. Carter in 1952 as president of the Astrological
Lodge of the Theosophical Society, serving in that position until 1982. He
was also editor of the *Astrologer's Quarterly* from 1959 to 1983. Davison
was well-known as a lecturer both in Britain and abroad. Gettings cites
with approval Davison's view of one field of modern astrological activity:

> "In a perceptive comment on the modern penchant for
> astrological 'research', the astrologer Davison writes of
> those who eagerly follow up every new method suggested,
> in the hope that at last they will find the solution to all their
> problems, 'not realizing that most of these problems spring
> from an imperfect acquaintance with the ordinary pro-
> cesses of astrology. There would be far less dissatisfaction
> with existing methods if students took the trouble to master
> them thoroughly before turning their attentions further
> afield'."[37]

Olivia Barclay

Olivia Barclay (1919-2001) worked hard to revive interest in horary
astrology. She arranged for the reprinting of William Lilly's *Christian Astrology*, teaches classes in horary astrology, and has written a book, *Horary Astrology Rediscovered* (West Chester, Pa.: Whitford Press, c.1990),
in which she advocates the use of Regiomontanus houses, apparently reasoning that if they were good enough for Lilly, they are good enough for
20th century horary astrologers.

---

[37]Fred Gettings, *The Arcana Dictionary of Astrology* (London: Arkana (Penguin Group), 1990), Introduction, p. xi.

Addey and Harmonics

A different approach to astrology was proposed by **John Addey** (1920-1982), M.A., D.F.Astrol.S. He joined the Astrological Lodge in London and served as its vice president from 1951 to 1958. In 1958 he joined with other British astrologers to found the Astrological Association, of which he was president from 1961 to 1973. Addey is best known for his discussion of "harmonics," the theory of which is set forth in his books *Astrology Reborn* (London?: The Astrological Assn., 1971) and *Harmonics in Astrology* (London: L.N. Fowler, 1976). The results of a similar investigation were set forth by the Swiss astrologer Karl Ernst Krafft thirty years earlier, but Addey was probably not aware of Krafft's work.[38] Addey's theory excited some enthusiasm when it was first announced, but it has not found favor with most astrologers, and interest in it has waned since Addey's death, although most horoscope-making computer software will calculate harmonics on demand. The Japanese astrologer H.M. Ishikawa (see below) has investigated harmonics and extended Addey's theory.

Psychological Astrology

Since about 1980 there has been an upsurge of interest in psychological astrology. At present, we could say that the astrological public, or at least the buyers of astrological books, can be divided into three or four groups: (1) traditional astrologers, or those who are interested in straightforward analysis of charts and delineating future trends using traditional techniques and technical terms; (2) psychologically oriented astrologers who are interested in astronomically guided psychoanalysis; (3) esoteric or mystically-minded astrologers, who like a generous portion of religion, mythology, and philosophy combined with a small amount of astrology; and (4) event-oriented astrologers, who are interested in predicting specific events at specific times. The latter category also includes those astrologers whose principal business is providing advice and counsel to clients through the use of horary astrology or other predictive techniques.

In England the best-known psychological astrologers are Dr. Liz Greene and her late American collaborator Howard Sasportas (1948-1992). Their books have evidently hit a responsive chord among those readers who fall in Category (2). Some of them are:

Greene, Dr. Liz
Saturn: A New Look at an Old Devil.
New York: Samuel Weiser, 1977. paper. 200 pp.

---

[38]For a detailed discussion, see Geoffrey Dean, *Recent Advances in Natal Astrology*, pp. 137 ff. and 324 ff. See also the entry for Krafft below.

Greene, Dr. Liz
Relating: An Astrological Guide to Living With Others on a
Small Planet.
York Beach, Me.: Samuel Weiser, 1978. paper. 289 pp.

Greene, Dr. Liz & Sasportas, Howard
The Development of the Personality.
York Beach, Me.: Samuel Weiser, 1987. paper. 336 pp.

Greene, Dr. Liz & Sasportas, Howard
Dynamics of the Unconscious.
York Beach, Me.: Samuel Weiser, 1988. paper. 384 pp.

Astrology and Statistics

Spurred on by the statistical studies of astrology initiated by Michel
Gauquelin (see below), several astrologers and academics in England organized a research association to make similar investigations and to see if
astrological techniques other than those studied by Gauquelin could be
subjected to statistical analysis. They founded a "Journal of Research into
Astrology," *Correlation* (1981-), under the editorship of Simon Best. Associate editors included John M. Addey, Prof. J. Bruce Brackenridge, Patrick M. Curry, Geoffrey A. Dean, the Gauquelins, Charles E.W. Harvey,
Nicholas Kollerstrom, Arthur C.M. Mather, Michael J. Startup, and
Beverly A. Steffert. The London University psychologist Prof. H.J.
Eysenck (1916-1997) also worked with the group. This group and their
later associates served as an intermediary between academics who wished
to investigate some features of astrology and astrological researchers.
One of its goals was to institute rigorous statistical procedures into astrological research. The published papers often provoked lively comments
both pro and con from the readership.

House Division

House division became a topic of controversy in the 20th century. The
Australian astrologer Zariel, dissatisfied with the existing systems, all of
which had been invented by astrologers living in the northern hemisphere,
invented a new system in the early 1900s. This was followed by an enthusiastic but abortive move by Cyril Fagan to revive the Regiomontanus
system. The Campanus system was dusted off and promoted, first by
Maurice Wemyss, and second by "siderealists" following the lead of Cyril
Fagan, who abandoned the Regiomontanus system he had espoused in the
1920s and switched with equal fervor to Campanus. After World War II, a
new system was introduced in Germany by Walter Koch with the claim
that it alone used the natal geographical latitude for **all** the cusps—the
so-called "Birthplace System" of Houses. About the same time, a movement began in England to return to the Equal House system. It was recommended by Margaret Hone and has enjoyed some success. South of the

equator, two Argentine astrologers, A.P. Nelson Page and Vendel Polich, invented a new system that they named "Topocentric." All of these are mentioned below in connection with their authors or promoters. The majority of astrologers have clung to Placidus, but a few have defected to Koch or Equal House.

The best books on the subject of house division are those by Ralph William Holden (b. 1934), *The Elements of House Division* (Romford: L.N. Fowler & Co., 1971) and Dona Marie Lorenz, *tools of astrology: HOUSES* [*sic!*] (Topanga, Calif.: Eomega Press, 1973). Holden discusses the traditional significations ascribed to the houses, their historical development, and all the major systems that have been proposed, beginning with the Equal House system.[39] His descriptions of the spherical bases for the various systems are excellent, and each description is accompanied by a nicely drawn diagram. He also provides a lucid and well-balanced survey of the strengths and weaknesses of the various systems. Lorenz's book contains descriptions of the several systems, diagrams, and many useful tables, including tables of houses (to the nearest degree) for the Alchabitius, Campanus, Placidus, Porphyry, Regiomontanus, Morinus, and Zariel systems.

Degree Symbolism

Another feature of astrology that has enjoyed increased popularity in the 20th century is the characterization of individual degrees of the zodiac, or, as it is usually termed, degree symbolism.[40] The basic idea is that, just as each sign has a specific influence, so also the individual degrees may have their own specific influences. This idea is attractive for two reason: (1) it may enable the astrologer to read details that might not otherwise be apparent; and (2) it may eliminate the necessity of learning how to read a chart and permit the astrologer to make an instant "delineation" without expending any real time or effort.

Both of these ideas are old. We have seen above that **Firmicus Maternus** (4th century) gives the significations of the individual degrees in Book 8 of the *Mathesis*. These, he says, are from the Barbaric Sphere, i.e. from the fixed stars in non-Greek constellations. But he also notes that the *Myriogenesis* of Aesculapius (which is unfortunately lost) contained the significations of the *individual minutes* of each degree of each sign!

---

[39] But he omits the earliest system, the Sign-House system of the Alexandrian inventors of astrology.

[40] Degree symbolism is not the same thing as "degree area" influences, which are often derived by tabulating the degrees in which planets are placed in the horoscopes of individuals who share some common characteristic, accident, or affliction. Degree symbolisms are often derived psychically, while the influences of degree areas are more often derived from investigation. However, there is some overlap, since some writers have given symbolic names to degree areas. See the discussion by Geoffrey Dean, *Recent Advances in Natal Astrology*, pp. 449 ff.

This would constitute 60 x 360 = 21,600 separate and distinct character-izations. It seems doubtful that the book can actually have been that spe-cific. Perhaps it contained some individual minute readings but grouped others, so that the total was much less (but still much more than 360!). At any rate, these characterizations would have been entirely theoretical (which is perhaps a nice way of saying "speculative").

But in the case of the degree readings from the Barbaric Sphere, we know that they relate to the longitudes of the fixed stars in the zodiac, and these longitudes, taken from some lost work, were probably referred to the fixed zodiac of the Alexandrian astrologers. Except for Firmicus's ex-cerpts, that book has also perished. But here is what he gives for the first four degrees of Sagittarius:[41]

> 1. Whoever has the ASC in the 1st degree of Sagittarius will be noble, religious, just, and one on whom the greatest distinctions of glory are conferred. But if a benefic star is found in that degree, it will make kings or those who are next to kings, who accomplish everything effectively.

> 2. Those who have the ASC in the 2nd degree of Sagit-tarius will be madmen, perjurers, sacrilegious.

> 3. Those who have the ASC in the 3rd degree of Sagit-tarius will lose one eye in some fashion.

> 4. Those who have the ASC in the 4th degree of Sagit-tarius will be custodians of monuments.

Another early but very incomplete source is the *Book of Hermes*,[42] which contains some individual degree characterizations here and there, mingled with interpretations of the terms and the significance of some of the fixed stars. There is no individual degree characterization in early Sag-ittarius, but for degree areas we find:

> 1-5. From the 1st degree of Sagittarius up to the 5th arises the point of Sagittarius's arrow.[43] This makes ar-chers or those experiencing losses of money.

> 1-7. From the 1st degree up to the 7th is called a sign of

---

[41]Firmicus, *Mathesis*, 8. 27.1-2.

[42]This book was apparently a 6th century compilation from various Greek sources, including Vettius Valens, Paul of Alexandria, and Rhetorius the Egyptian. Little of it could be called "Hermetic." The Greek original is lost, but a medieval Latin translation is extant edited by Wilhelm Gundel from the unique MS Harleianus 3731 discovered by Lynn Thorndike, *Neue astrologische Texte des Hermes Trismegistos* (Munich: Verlag der Bayerischen Akademie der Wissenschaften, 1936). The degree characterizations are scattered through Chapter 25.

[43]The star Gamma Sagittarii, which in Ptolemy's catalogue was in 4°30' Sagit-tarius.

disturbance because [the natives] live and acquire [possessions] intemperately, but they live their lives in traveling, frequently having many adversities in life.

Next we find the curious work of **Pietro d'Abano** (1250-1315), who characterized each degree with a few Latin words. Two centuries later, these were illustrated by symbolic woodcuts inset in 360 horoscope figures in the old square form in the book by **Johann Engel** (1463-1512), *Astrolabium planum in tabulis ascendens....* (Augsburg: Erhard Ratdolt, 1488)[44] The individual degrees of the zodiac appear as the ASC degree of the charts, and Alchabitius house cusps are given,[45] so that each chart (which is otherwise blank) could be copied or filled in to provide a sunrise chart for the day when the Sun was in a particular degree. These degree characterizations fall in the symbolic category. For the first four degrees of Sagittarius, the pictures are:

1. Three well-dressed but headless men.
2. An archer about to shoot an arrow.
3. A man riding a goat? past the Sun?
4. A man carrying a pitchfork.

Four centuries later we find the so-called "Theban Calendar," a French version of which is contained in the book on onomantic astrology by **Ély Star** (1847-1942), *Les mystères de l'horoscope* (Paris: Durville, 1887), pp. 60-78. It is arranged by calendar days, but the degrees of the zodiacal signs are also given, so it can be used either way. Here are the characterizations for the first four degrees of Sagittarius:

1. An association which produces only paltry results. Dangers.
2. Agressive character. Danger of wounds by the hand of man.
3. Procreative power. Love of family. Sweetness.
4. Prudence and security. Bellicose nature. A taste for arms.

In the 20th century, a number of writers have published degree symbolisms or interpretations. Among them are the following.

---

[44]Johann Engel was a humanist scholar and editor of Latin texts for some of the early printers. His book *Astrolabium planum in tabulis ascendens...* contains a series of 360 horoscopes in the square form with a symbolic picture in the center. These are beautifully reproduced in the book by Grazia Mirti, *Astrolabio 1994* (Turin: The Author, 1993). (See also the drawings from a German MS reproduced on the plate facing p. 112 of Knappich's *Geschichte der Astrologie*.) The symbolic pictures represent the degree interpretations, such as a figure of "a man plowing." Subsequent writers who felt inspired by these pictures have added brief commentaries to each one to represent actions or situations that the pictures might be supposed to symbolize.

[45]For about 45° North latitude.

Alan Leo's book *Astrology For All*, p. 245,[46] offers these readings for the same degrees:

1. An intuitive and prophetic nature, gifted with keen insight: an explorer.
2. A practical visionary, carrying ideals into execution: success in subordinate positions.
3. Sensitive and poetical, with literary talent: marriage to a cousin or some relative.
4. Affectionate and demonstrative, fond of home: danger by water.

The Welsh seer **Charubel** (John Thomas, 1826-1908) gives these symbols for the degrees[47] (I omit his comments):

1. A serpent in the shape of the letter S.
2. A stupendous waterfall.
3. A man at a table with drawing instruments and paper before him.
4. A man walking on the edge of a precipice.

Sepharial translated a work *La Volasfera* by an Italian writer whom he calls once Antonio Borelli and a second time Antonio Bonelli (perhaps a misprint in his book). Carelli (see below) could not identify the writer under either spelling of the name nor could he find the Italian original. We have only Sepharial's English version. Again, for early Sagittarius (the symbols only):

1. A man lying on a heap of stones by the roadside.
2. A man standing with drawn sword.
3. The Goddess of Mercy enthroned.
4. A soldier, holding a crossbow, stands behind an embrasure.

Isidore Kozminsky wrote a book entitled *Zodiacal Symbology and its Planetary Power* (Washington: A.F.A., Inc., 1991. repr.) in which he sets forth symbols and interpretations for each degree. Here are the symbols (I omit the interpretations) for early Sagittarius:

1. A woman in the dress of a religious order struggling through a dark and storm-swept valley, a luminous anchor

---

[46]First published 1904. The page reference is to the reprint ed. (London: L.N. Fowler, 1971).

[47]*The Degrees of the Zodiac Symbolized* (London: L.N. Fowler, 1898). I have used a later edition, (Chicago: Aries Press, 1943) — a reprint of Alan Leo's Astrological Manuel No. VIII.

above her.
2. A woman of angry countenance holding a dagger in her hand.
3. A man of scornful face with a big sword in one hand, carrying a child.
4. Two arrows crossed and surrounded by zones of glistening violet light.

E.C. Matthews (1892-1977) published a new set of degree interpretations in 1947, *Fixed Stars and Degrees of the Zodiac Analyzed* (St. Louis: Sign Book Co., 1968. 2nd ed.) He was aware of some previous sets, but he says his own are based on actual degree positions in his collection of horoscopes, not on "psychic revelation," and he gives many references to horoscopes of notable persons. He usually gives a key word and then expands upon it before offering examples. Here is how Sagittarius begins:

1. ENTERPRISE....always in search of knowledge. . . .
2. PRECISION The mark of a good mechanic where accuracy is required. . . .
3. SYMPATHY Much like the preceding degree only the men are more apt to go in for athletics.
4. DIFFERENTIATION An affectionate and home loving degree. . . .

The next entrant in this field was **Marc Edmund Jones**'s *The Sabian Symbols*,[48] which were first obtained by psychic means in 1925. They were circulated amongst interested astrologers, issued as lessons for students in 1931, and revised into more or less their present form in 1948. They are stated to be applicable to any point in the horoscope, not just to the ASC degree. For the first four degrees of Sagittarius, the symbols are (with interpretations omitted):

1. A Grand Army of the Republic campfire.
2. The ocean covered with whitecaps.
3. The garden of the Tuileries.
4. A little child learning to walk.

In 1951 a new set of degree interpretations by the Italian astrologer and occultist **Adriano Carelli** was published.[49] The author says he reviewed

---

[48] *The Sabian Symbols* (New York: Sabian Publishing Society, 1953). I have used the 3rd ed. (Stanwood, Wash.: Sabian Publishing Society, 1969).
[49] Adriano Carelli (1908-1998), *The 360 Degrees of the Zodiac* (Washington: A.F.A., Inc., 1951). I have used a later reprint (Tempe, Az.: A.F.A., Inc., 1977). The original Italian version is, I believe, still in print in Italy.

219

the degree interpretations of Pietro d'Abano, Christian,[50] Charubel, Leo, Sepharial, and Matthews, but he had not seen those of Isidore Kozminsky and Henry J. Gordon[51]. He dismisses Matthews because he had stated flatly that his interpretations were not psychically derived. Carelli says he produced his own series through meditation. Here are first parts of his interpretations (only the 4th degree has a symbol) for the early Sagittarius degrees:

1. This degree confers an unruly imagination that may run away with the native at times. . . . Freedom is for him a proud and jealous possession. . . .
2. A warlike and agressive nature. . . .
3. A self-contradictory character: on one hand gentle and sensitive, on the other mettlesome, combative, and even agressive. . . .
4. A grated window in a medieval manor. The native's warlike and impulsive nature will stay hidden till drawn out and revealed by circumstances. . . .

During the last forty years, a number of additional sets of interpretations have been published. In view of the wide disparity in the interpretations and symbols, it does not seem that much credibility can be given to any of them, even to those (of Jones, Matthews, and Carelli) for which examples are given from actual horoscopes; for, without a careful study of the charts from which the examples were drawn, we cannot be sure that the particular degree in question was aptly chosen as a significator of the characteristic described.

Key Words

In a sense, astrology is a "word science" like psychology. That is, there are definite factors that make up its field of activity, and their characteristics are described in words. Hence, from the outset, astrological textbooks contained descriptions of signs, houses, planets, aspects, etc. Those associated with the signs were descriptive of the figures represented by the signs, while those associated with the planets were generally the epithets applied to the Greek gods whose names they bore. For example, the sign Leo had some of the characteristics of the lion—proud, dominant, etc., while Venus had the characteristics of Aphrodite—love, beauty, etc. The houses and aspects had epithets that described their sphere of influence or their typical manner of interaction. Thus, the 10th house, being the Midheaven of the chart, represented the culmination of action and status in the world, while the square aspect represented divergences and action at cross-purposes.

---

[50]The occultist Paul Christian, pseudonym of J-B Pitois (1811-1877). See Ellic Howe, *op. cit.*, p.74.
    [51]In his book *Rectification of Uncertain Birth Hours*. I have not consulted that book.

The early books, and indeed most astrological texts, contain lists of these epithets. Many of the epithets have become standard and are still in use 2,000 years after their first mention. The beginning astrologer, having mastered the names of the signs, planets, houses, and aspects, must then commit to memory some of these epithets or "key words" as they are usually called today. From time to time astrologers have devoted entire monographs to these key words. Three American examples are:

Johndro, L. Edward
The Astrological dictionary and Self-Reading Horoscope.
San Bernardino: The Author, 1929. 1st ed.
[key words of planets and aspects]
Washington: A.F.A., Inc., n.d. repr.

Hall, Manly P.
Astrological Keywords. (1st ed. 1931?)
Los Angeles: Philosophical Research Society. 1958.
New York: Philosophical Library, 1959. 229 pp.

Bills, Rex E.
The Rulership Book.
Richmond: Macoy Publ. & Masonic Supply Co., 1971. vii,428 pp.

The latter book filled a need and encouraged the writing of similar works, especially since 1990, when powerful, affordable computers and easy-to-use software made the compilation of such a work much easier. In the U.S. some recently published books on rulerships are *The Astrological Thesaurus*, vol. 1 House Keywords (St. Paul: Llewellyn Worldwide, 1992) by **Michael P. Munkasey** (b. 1938) and *The Book of Rulerships: Keywords from Classical Astrology* (1992) by **J. Lee Lehman** (b. 1953). There are similar publications in the other major languages.

History of Astrology

In the 1980s there has been an upsurge of interest in the history of astrology. Some of the European astrologers who have worked in this field are Patrick Curry, Annabella Kitson, Nicholas Campion, Derek Appleby, Nicholas Kollerstrom, and Zoe Starr in England; Jacques Halbronn and Olivier Rimbault in France; Giuseppe Bezza in Italy; and Demetrio Santos in Spain. A series of seminars has been held in England, and individual conferences have been held in England and on the Continent. New historical studies have also begun to appear. This coincides with the revival of interest in translating the older books of astrology into modern languages.

Astrology in America

American astrology generally followed the lead of English astrology. The principal early figures were Dr. Broughton and Professor Chaney.

Dr. Broughton

Dr. L.D. Broughton (1828-1899), a transplanted Englishman settled first in Philadelphia around 1854, where he studied medicine and received his M.D. from the Eclectic Medical College of that city. He practiced homeopathic medicine the rest of his life, using astrology as an aid to diagnosis and treatment. Unlike most other physicians, he advertised that if his treatments failed to cure the patient, there would be no charge!

In 1860 he began to publish his *Monthly Planet Reader and Astrological Journal*. This was one of the earliest astrological periodicals in the U.S. Later that year he predicted that Lincoln would lose the 1860 election to Stephen A. Douglas. The November returns gave Lincoln 39.7% of the vote to Douglas's 29.3%, with the remaining 31% divided between two other candidates. Lincoln won with 180 of the 303 electoral votes.

> Broughton stated following the election that he had taken the evil aspects in Lincoln's nativity (he used a speculative chart with Saturn rising in Sagittarius) to refer to his prospects for gaining the presidency, whereas he should have realized that they referred to what would take place after the election.[52]

In 1861 anti-fortune telling legislation was passed by the Pennsylvania legislature. Dr, Broughton stuck it out for two years, but in 1863 he suspended publication of his periodical and moved to New York City. There he resumed publication in 1864 and continued to publish until 1869, when he was forced to stop during a violent outbreak of anti-astrology agitation in that city.

> "When time came for the next election, the Oct-Nov-Dec 1864 issue of his *Monthly Planet Reader and Astrological Journal* led off with an article by Broughton entitled 'The Nativity of Abraham Lincoln President of the United States' in which he correctly forecast the reelection of Pres. Lincoln, but added 'I might here state, that shortly after the election is over, Mr. Lincoln will have a number of evil aspects afflicting his Nativity (I do not think that any of them will begin to be felt until the election is past.) they will be in operation in Nov. and Dec. of this year. During these months, let him be especially on his guard against attempts to take his life; by such as fire arms, and infernal machines.'"

---

[52]Holden & Hughes, *Astrological Pioneers of America* (Tempe, Az.: A.F.A., Inc., 1988), p. 21. That volume is dedicated to the memory of Dr. Broughton. His horoscope and picture (reproduced from his book *The Elements of Astrology*) are on pp. 4-5 of the introductory material.

"In the spring 1865 issue he added the further prediction: 'Some noted general or person in high offices dies or is removed about the 17th or 18th day [of April].' As it turned out, Lincoln was shot on April 14 and died the next morning. This prediction enhanced Broughton's reputation considerably, but may well have hurt him eventually. For, by putting him in the public eye, it made him an obvious target for opponents of astrology and culminated four years later in attacks against his lecture hall, the sacking of his home by a mob, and the suppression of his magazine, as mentioned above."[53]

While Dr. Broughton's predictions for Lincoln were fairly accurate, he did not do so well with his predictions for King Alphonso XIII (1886-1941). In his *Elements of Astrology* (New York: The Author, 1898. 1st ed.), pp. 332-335, he stated that "He has what we call a very fortunate horoscope, I think equally as fortunate as Queen Victoria's....Spain will be very prosperous under his reign. . . . there is no doubt he will live to be an old man.'' In general, this turned out to be wrong. During his minority the Spanish-American War took place (1898). The king's popularity was never very great, and he was the target of assassination attempts in 1905, 1906, and 1913, and of a conspiracy in 1925. In 1931, when the Republicans won the election, he was outlawed and forced to flee the country. He never regained his throne, although in 1939 Francisco Franco (1892-1975) restored his property, which had been seized by the Republicans in 1932. Two years later Alphonso died in exile at age 54. Spain had not been prosperous under his reign, and it slid into a disastrous civil war in the 1930s.

For the Emperor of Germany, William II (1859-1941), Dr. Broughton's predictions came closer, although he says "His nativity does not indicate a long life. . . ." However, he predicted a good marriage and fortunate children, with one of his sons being almost certain to succeed him to the throne. His marriage was good, and one of his granddaughters[54] became Queen of Greece, but his son did not succeed him, nor did the monarchy itself survive 1918. "He will be unfortunate in war, and will have to pay indemnities . . . [but] The Emperor is almost certain to die a natural death, and not be killed in battle." "This horoscope is quite the reverse of Jay Gould's, who had Jupiter and Venus in the 2nd house, the house of money. He began with nothing, and died worth seventy-two millions; whereas the Emperor of Germany, having his 2nd house so much afflicted by Saturn, will either die poor or the nation will be heavily in debt at his death." Actually, the former Emperor lived in much reduced but comfortable circumstances until the end of his long life. But Germany it-

---

[53]Holden & Hughes, *op. cit.*, p. 21.
[54]Frederika-Louise of Hanover (1917-1981), who married Paul I (1901-1964).

self suffered a financial collapse in the early 1920s.

Dr. Broughton fought a running battle with bigotry all of his adult life, but he refused to bow to the forces of ignorance and intolerance. Towards the end of his life he found some consolation in the fact that the overall acceptance of astrology by the public had increased significantly during that period.

In retrospect, Dr. Broughton was undoubtedly the foremost American astrologer of the 19th century. He established the first major astrological journal, he achieved considerable fame, he was an effective teacher, and he wrote an excellent treatise on astrology. He is also said to have been the first to call attention to the "20-year cycle" of U.S. presidents dying in office.[55]

Professor Chaney

"Professor" W.H. Chaney (1821-1903), who was the father of the novelist Jack London (1876-1916) was Dr. Broughton's best known pupil. He had a very colorful career with many ups and downs.[56] But after learning astrology, he did his best to teach it to others throughout the rest of his life.[57] Despite sometimes violent opposition from ecclesiastical sources, bigots, and rowdy elements of the populace, both men did much to advance the teaching and knowledge of astrology in America during the last four decades of the 19th century.

Chaney's best known books were: *Chaney's Ephemeris from 1800 to Date* (Salem, Or., 1877); and *Chaney's Primer of Astrology and American Urania* (St. Louis: Magic Circle Publ. Co, 1890).

Weston and Vulcan

L(ewis) H(erman) Weston, FAFA (1862-1945) was a printer by profession and an astrologer by choice. He and Llewellyn George studied astrology together around the turn of the century. In 1908 he began to publish a short-lived periodical, the *Astrolite*. Weston was especially interested in ancient astrology, financial astrology, and meteorological astrology. But he is principally remembered today as the author of a little book, *The Planet Vulcan* (1920?; Tempe, Az.: A.F.A. Inc., n.d. repr.). This contained reports of the supposed sightings of the intra-Mercurial planet along with deduced elements of its orbit and tables to facilitate calculating its position.

---

[55]Holden & Hughes, ibid. There is a modern book on this subject by Robert A. Hughes, *The Fateful Presidential Cycle* (Tempe, Az.: A.F.A., Inc., 1988).

[56]His youthful ambition was to be a pirate—not surprising for a man with the Sun in partile conjunction with Mars. See his horoscope in Llewellyn George's *A to Z Horoscope Maker and Delineator* (Los Angeles: Llewellyn Publications, 1943. 8th ed.).

[57]For an account of his life and a list of his books, see the entry in Holden and Hughes, *op. cit.* See also the biographical notes in his *Primer*.

Astronomers, beginning with U.J.J. LeVerrier (1811-1877) in France, had noticed that the perihelion of the planet Mercury revolved around the Sun some 35" per century faster than could be accounted for by Newtonian gravitational theory. LeVerrier supposed that there might be an intra-Mercurial planet of sufficient mass to account for the discrepancy, and he thought there was some evidence for its existence. It was this belief that sparked Weston's book, although by the time his book appeared, the discrepancy had already been explained in 1915 by Albert Einstein's new theory of general relativity. Weston evidently chose to ignore this development in celestial mechanics. As of the present writing (1996), despite a careful search, astronomers have still not found any intra-Mercurial planet.

Dr. Cornell and Medical Astrology

Special mention should also be made of the physician, **Dr. Howard Leslie Cornell** (1872-1938?), whose monumental *Encyclopedia of Medical Astrology* (1st ed., 1933) is an inexhaustible compendium of traditional medical astrology. The 2nd edition has been reprinted in facsimile (St. Paul: Llewellyn Publs., New York: Samuel Weiser, 1972. 3rd ed. with a new Introduction by Laurel Lowell) and subsequently in a paper-bound edition.

Max Heindel and the Rosicrucians

Max Heindel (1865-1919), a native of Denmark, whose real name was Max Grashof, studied in Germany under the occultist Rudolf Steiner (1861-1925) and later emigrated to America. In the U.S. he married **Augusta Foss Heindel** (1865-1949) and founded the Rosicrucian Fellowship at Oceanside, California. Although primarily occultists, the Heindels published several books on astrology, the most important of which is their *The Message of the Stars* (Oceanside, Cal.: The Rosicrucian Fellowship, 1944. 10th ed.). This and their other astrological books form an important part of Rosicrucian study.

Evangeline Adams

In the first third of the 20th century the most famous American astrologer was **Evangeline Adams** (1868-1932). She began to practice professionally in Boston, but in 1899 she moved to New York City. There she achieved almost instant fame but nearly lost her life. She arrived at the Windsor Hotel on the evening of 16 March and was given a choice between rooms on the first floor and some on the fifth. She chose those on the first floor, since they would be more convenient for her clients. The hotel proprietor, Warren Leland (1845-1899), showed some interest in astrology, so she unpacked her ephemerides and table of houses and cast his horoscope (NN 813) around eight o'clock that evening. She saw immediately that he would be in great danger the very next day. She also noted that there had been two similar periods in the past. She asked him what had happened at those times, and he recalled that there had been small fires in the hotel. However, Leland did not take her warning very seriously—he joked that the next day would be St. Patrick's Day, and the stock market would be closed, so he couldn't lose any money.

The next morning Leland visited Adams briefly and then took the elevator to the fifth floor. When the door opened, he saw the entire corridor engulfed in flames. The fire spread rapidly, and the hotel burned to the ground. Many guests were killed by the fire or by leaping from windows. Leland himself lost a daughter and other members of his family. He died from shock three weeks later. But the day of the fire he had told a reporter that the disaster had been predicted by a Boston astrologer, Evangeline Adams. The next day her prediction was headlined on the front page of the newspaper. It made her reputation. Thereafter, she set up a studio in Carnegie Hall and became America's foremost astrologer.

Her autobiography *The Bowl of Heaven* (New York: Dodd, Mead & Co., 1926) contains many interesting accounts of her life as a professional astrologer as well as a variety of incidents in the lives of some of her many clients. Adams wrote two popular astrology books that ran through many printings.[58] She also invented a new subsidiary method of judging horary charts (by inserting the natal planets in the horary houses) and evidently intended to write a book explaining it in detail, but unfortunately her untimely death forestalled that project.

Evangeline Adams is also remembered for her legal triumph against the forces of bigotry in the State of New York. In 1914 she was the target of legal action brought against her as a "fortune-teller." The first suit was thrown out of court, but the crusaders were not satisified and initiated a second suit. Miss Adams retained Clark L. Jordan, a prominent New York attorney, and fought the case. She stated to Judge Freschi that astrology was a science that operated according to stated rules and had absolutely nothing to do with magic or the supernatural. She then offered to illustrate her statement by drawing up a horoscope and preparing a reading of it. The judge accepted this offer, and, unbeknownst to her gave her the birthdata of his own son. The horoscope she prepared described the son's character and circumstances so well that the judge was greatly impressed. His decision of 11 Dec 1914, in favor of Evangeline Adams, contains this sentence: "The defendant raises Astrology to the dignity of an exact science." This landmark case settled the question in New York and has served as a precedent since.

Adams was generally successful in her astrological work, but she had a

---

[58]All of her books were published in New York by Dodd, Mead: *The Bowl of Heaven* (1926), *Astrology: Your Place in the Sun* (1927), and *Astrology: Your Place in the Stars* (1930). See the biographical works by Karen Christino, *Foreseeing the Future* (Amherst, Mass.: One Reed Publs., 2002) and *What Evangeline Adams Knew* (Brooklyn Heights, NY: Stella Mira Books, 2004).

notable failure in 1928 when she predicted that Alfred E. Smith (1873-1944) would win the presidential election. He didn't!

Perhaps the astrologers next most widely known to the American public were **Zolar** (Bruce King, 1897-1976), **Grant Lewi** (see below), **Carroll Righter** (1900-1988), and **Sydney Omarr, FAFA** (1926-2003). Three of these men achieved most of their fame through their popular publications, consisting mainly of daily, monthly, and yearly guides for the twelve signs of the zodiac, although Zolar was the author of a popular history of astrology,[59] Righter was also a sought-after astrological consultant, and Omarr was active as a writer, lecturer, and defender of astrology against its critics.[60]

Llewellyn George

Among astrologers themselves, a Welsh immigrant, **Llewellyn George, FAFA** (1876-1951), was perhaps the leading figure. He wrote many books on astrology,[61] most notably his *A to Z Horoscope Maker and Delineator* (1st ed., 1910), published a magazine, the *Astrological Bulletina* (1905? -), and operated a publishing house and bookstore in Los Angeles for three decades prior to his death. George attended astrological conventions, aided individual astrologers, and was a benefactor to astrology in the U.S. His business was subsequently purchased by Karl Weschke and moved to St. Paul, Minnesota, where it continues to be a major publisher of astrological books.

Other leading American astrologers were:

Alice Bailey

Alice A(nne) Bailey (1880-1949), an occultist and not an astrologer, but she published a five-volume set *A Treatise on the Seven Rays*, of which Vol. 3 is entitled *Esoteric Astrology* (New York: Lucis Publishing Co., 1950?). Mrs. Bailey disclaimed any responsibility for its authorship, asserting that it was the work of "The Master D.K." (previously referred to as "The Tibetan"), and that she had merely transcribed it from his dictation. This book has proved to be perennially popular with those who favor "esoteric astrology," by which is meant mystical interpretations of astrological positions or configurations.

Johndro

L(orne) Edward Johndro (1882-1951) was an electrical engineer and later a radio engineer in the 1920s. His professional training in these fields carried over into his astrological work, so that his two books on the

---

[59]*The History of Astrology* (New York: Arco, 1972). xxii,302 pp. illus.

[60]See his interesting book *My World of Astrology* (New York: Fleet Publishing, 1965. 1st ed.; Hollywood: Wilshire Book Co., 1968. repr.).

[61]See a list of 16 titles in Holden and Hughes, ibid., pp. 58-59. But the list does not include all his books.

stars are studded with references to radio and electromagnetism. He was particularly fond of the word *piezoelectric*.[62] In 1929 he published two abstruse books explaining how to localize the influence of the fixed stars. He also introduced the "Electrical Ascendant" or Vertex,[63] which has since become more or less standard, at least in computer-generated horoscopes. In addition, he prescribed a method for erecting a "locality chart," which can also be used where the birth time is not known, and postulated an elaborate scheme of planetary rulership. His books are: *Astrological Dictionary and Self-Reading Horoscope* (San Bernardino: The Author, 1929; Washington: A.F.A., Inc., n.d. repr.); *The Earth in the Heavens* (San Bernardino: Doherty, 1929. 1st ed.; New York: Samuel Weiser, 1970. 2nd ed. repr. in facs. of the 1st ed.]; and *The Stars: How and Where They Influence* (San Bernardino: Doherty, 1929. 1st ed.; New York: Samuel Weiser, 1970. 2nd ed. repr. in facs. of the 1st ed.).

C.C. Zain and the Church of Light

C.C. Zain is a pseudonym used by the occultist and astrologer Elbert Benjamin Williams (1882-1951). He joined the Brotherhood of Light in 1900 and eventually became one of the members of its Council of Three and president of the Church of Light from its founding until his death in 1951. Zain wrote an extensive series of twenty-one books covering all branches of astrology. They were first used as training material for The Brotherhood of Light Lessons, but were later published and made available outside of the course. Many astrologers in the U.S. and other countries learned astrology from these books.

Marc Edmund Jones

Marc Edmund Jones (1888-1980), Ph.D., FAFA, became well-known to all astrologers for his *Guide to Horoscope Interpretation* (Philadelphia: David McKay, 1941), which introduced his theory of "shapings"—patterns of planetary distribution within a horoscope; for his *Sabian Symbols* (New York: Sabian Publ. Society, 1953), a book of degree interpretations based on psychic revelation and illustrated by references to the elements of the horoscopes of 1,000 notable persons; and for his *Problem Solving by Horary Astrology* (Philadelphia: David McKay, 1943). Jones wrote many other books and was a frequent lecturer at astrological meetings.

Wynn

Sidney K. Bennett (1892-1958) was a prominent professional astrologer and astrological magazine publisher from the 1920s through 1940s; he

---

[62]An electrical term relating to the generation of an electrical potential by the application of pressure to a crystalline substance.

[63]The American astrologer Charles A. Jayne (1911-1985) later claimed that he had invented the Vertex independently of Johndro.

wrote under the pseudonym **Wynn**. He is remembered for his prediction (made in the *New York Daily News* in 1932) of a week of financial turmoil to come early in March 1933. President Franklin D. Roosevelt (1882-1945) was inaugurated on 4 March 1933, and one of his first official acts was to declare a "bank holiday," closing all the banks in the U.S. Many of them did not reopen, and their depositors (including the present author) suffered a total loss. This abrupt and unprecedented act shocked the nation and demoralized the financial markets. Wynn became famous for this prediction. Also in the 1930s he developed a variation of the solar return, which is fully set forth with examples and tables in the book *The Key Cycle* (Tempe, Az.: A.F.A., Inc., n.d.)

Goldstein-Jacobson

Ivy M(artha) Goldstein-Jacobson, FAFA (1893-1990) was a prominent professional astrologer, teacher, and author of a dozen or more books on various phases of astrology. She was an early proponent of the "Dark Moon Lilith." One of her books sets forth her personal system of horary astrology, which was adopted by one of her students, **Gilbert Navarro**. He has established a very successful business as a horary astrologer, is a popular lecturer on Horary Astrology, and also offers a correspondence course in the subject.

Some of Mrs. Goldstein-Jacobs's books are:
The Dark Moon Lilith in Astrology.
[with monthly ephemeris 1860-1999][64]
Pasadena: The Author, 1961.

Simplified Horary Astrology.
Pasadena: The Author, 1960.

The Turn of a Lifetime Astrologically.
Pasadena: The Author, 1964.

The Way of Astrology.
Pasadena: The Author, 1967. iv, 233 pp.

Ernest and Catharine Grant and the AFA

Ernest A. Grant, FAFA (1893-1968), a Congressional consultant and speech-writer, and his wife **Catharine T. Grant, FAFA** (1896-1988) joined with other prominent astrologers in the Washington area and elsewhere to found the American Federation of Astrologers (A.F.A.) in

---

[64]Said to be calculated with a constant daily motion of exactly 3°02' per mean solar day. But there are apparent errors and inconsistencies in the ephemeris. It wobbles around a degree or so and sometimes has jumps of 5° or more. Also, she did not realize that February 1900 had only 28 days, not 29. So there is a 3°02' discontinuity there.

Washington, D.C., in 1938. They later founded The National Astrological Library, which specialized in reprinting out-of-print and foreign books of merit. It was later merged with the AFA. Both of the Grants worked tirelessly to promote astrology in general and the AFA in particular. But they found time to write a four volume astrological course. Mrs. Grant moved to Arizona in 1975, when the AFA relocated its national headquarters to Tempe in that state. She remained active in astrology until a few years before her death, and she left her estate in trust to the AFA.

Grant Textbook series.
vol. I. Elementary Astrology.
vol. II. Analysis of the Horoscope.
vol. III Synthesis of the Horoscope.
vol. IV. Predictive Astrology.
Tempe, Az.: A.F.A., Inc., 1988. 1st ed.

The AFA eventually grew to be the largest astrological organization in the U.S. In 1975 its headquarters was moved to its present location in Tempe, Arizona, a suburb of Phoenix. In addition to its worldwide membership activities, the AFA is a major publisher of astrological books and operates a large mail-order business, carrying in stock almost 900 titles of its own and of other publishers, and acting as agent for the leading astrological software houses.

Dane Rudhyar

Dane Rudhyar, FAFA (1895-1985), pseudonym of Daniel Chennevière, a native of France, was trained as a musician and composer. He emigrated first to Canada and then to the U.S. Like Marc Edmund Jones, Rudhyar was an occultist as well as an astrologer. He was active as a lecturer and was also a prolific author who promoted what he called "humanistic" astrology. His best known books are:

Astrology of Personality
New York: Lucis Publ. Co., 1936

Humanistic Astrology (series)
Lakemont, Ga.: CSA Press, 1970-71. 6 vols.

The Astrology of America's Destiny
[the horoscope of the United States]
New York: Random House, 1974

Cyril Fagan and Sidereal Astrology

Cyril Fagan, FAFA (1896-1970), was a leading Irish astrologer who lived in the U.S. during the last twenty-five years of his life. Fagan was an articulate and convincing writer on a variety of astrological topics. In the

1920s he was a passionate advocate of the Regiomontanus system of house division. Later, in the 1940s he determined that the customary tropical zodiac was ineffective and that it was the fixed stars in the zodiacal constellations that were astrologically significant. He therefore launched the so-called "siderealist" movement. He also abandoned the Regiomontanus house system and switched to the Campanus system with equally passionate arguments.

Fagan attracted two strong supporters in England, Brig. R.C. Firebrace (1889-1974) and Rupert Gleadow (1909-1974), and one, Donald A. Bradley (1925-1974), in the U.S. Initially his ideas gained favor among a number of other astrologers in English-speaking countries, but most astrologers remained unconvinced. Following Fagan's death in 1970, and especially after the fateful year 1974, in which Bradley, Firebrace, and Gleadow all died, the movement declined rapidly.

Fagan was a prolific and impressive writer, especially of magazine articles (a long series of articles entitled "Solunars" appeared in *American Astrology* magazine). His principal books are the *Fixed Zodiac Ephemeris for 1948* (Washington: Nat. Astr. Library, 1948), *Zodiacs Old and New* (Los Angeles, 1950), and two posthumous publications, *Astrological Origins* (St. Paul: Llewellyn Publs., 1971)[65] and *The Solunars Handbook* (Tucson: Clancy Publs., 1976). He was also a joint author with Firebrace of *A Primer of the Sidereal Zodiac* (London: R.C. Firebrace, 1961).

Grant Lewi

Grant Lewi (1902-1951), M.A. An English instructor and novelist turned astrologer. Lewi learned astrology from his mother-in-law, Athene Gale Wallace (b. 1883). In the 1930s he became editor of *Horoscope* magazine, which was one of the two leading astrology magazines in the U.S. Around 1950 he left *Horoscope* and started his own magazine, *The Astrologer*, but he succumbed to a cerebral hemorrhage in July 1951. Lewi developed his own system of interpretation, which was based on equating sign and house influences and blending some psychological considerations with the astrology. He ignored Pluto. He used a conventional chart with Placidus houses. He did not use progressions of any kind, but utilized transits exclusively for prediction. His unique method of using transits was set forth in his book *Astrology for the Millions* (Garden City, N.Y.: Garden City, 1940) and further developed in subsequent magazine articles. His first astrology book *Scorpio's Horoscope Book*, called *Heaven Knows What* in later editions, (New York: Doubleday, 1935), contains his

---

[65]Fagan's effusive writings on ancient astronomy and astrology are a hodge-podge of information and misinformation, all presented as fundamental truths. The reader who has no knowledge of these matters should look elsewhere for instruction. For a detailed critique of Fagan's statements, see Colin James III, *The Relative Strength of Signs and Planets* (Denver: Colorado Astrological Society, 1978), App. II "The Alleged Sidereal Zodiac of Cyril Fagan."

own interpretations of the 144 Solar-Lunar Polarities and the planetary aspects. Both books contain unique tables of planetary positions of Lewi's own devising, so that the reader does not require any other book to use the material in the text; they are now available from Llewellyn Publications in updated editions.

Doris Chase Doane

Doris Chase Doane. B.A. MPAI, FAFA (1913-2005) In 1944 she received the Hermetician Certificate of the Church of Light in Los Angeles and taught classes from 1944 to 1968. She married the Rev. Edward Doane (1892-1970) of that organization and became an ordained Minister herself in 1946.

Mrs. Doane was closely associated with the work of the Church of Light from the early 1940s until 1972, when she moved away from Los Angeles. During that period she served as its Secretary (1949), Director of Astrological Research (1952), Editor of the Church of Light *Quarterly* (1951-1969), and taught classes (1944-1968). She began to write for publication in 1945, and since that time more than 1,500 of her articles and books have been published. A number other books have become standard authorities in their fields, on such diverse subjects as the *Index to the Brotherhood of Light Lessons,* the series on Time Changes, Tarot Card reading (written jointly with King Keyes), and *Horoscopes of the U.S. Presidents.*

Rev. Edward Doane passed away in 1970, and Mrs. Doane married the astrologer John Lawson Ahern (1922-2004) the following year. She served as President of the AFA from 1979 to 2004. She was also Co-Founder (1968) and President Emeritus of Professional Astrologers, Inc., a charter member of the Athena Astrological Society, a long-time member of the Astrologers Guild of America, and a member of several other astrological organizations, m 1988 she was awarded fellowship in the AFA. Mrs. Doane traveled widely, lecturing and conducting seminars and workshops, and was the recipient of many awards from both American and foreign astrological groups. Throughout her career, she was a strong advocate of professionalism and certification in astrological practice.

Friends of the Asteroids

Interest in the possible effects of the asteroids surfaced in the 1970s. Among the astrologers who wrote on their effects were: **Esther Leinbach, Eleanor Bach** (b. 1922), **Zipporah P. Dobyns, Ph.D.** (1921-2003), and **Emma Belle Donath** (1930-1992). Leinbach and Dobyns published ephemerides and wrote on the effects of the first four asteroids. Donath published an abbreviated but more extensive ephemeris and detailed information about the effects of the asteroids in the signs and houses. The late **Al H. Morrison** (1916-1995) took a special interest in the asteroid (now, comet) Chiron upon its discovery in 1977, as did **James Neely** and **Eric Tarkington**, *Ephemeris of Chiron* (Toronto: Phenomena Publications, 1978; 2nd ed. 1982) all of whom published ephemerides. The advent of affordable computer facilities made all this possible. Some of their books are:

Bach, Eleanor & Climlas, George
Ephemerides of the Asteroids Ceres, Pallas, Juno, Vesta 1900-2000.
Brooklyn: Celestial Communications, 1973.

Leinbach, Esther
Planets and Asteroids.
Seattle: Vulcan Books, 1976.

Pottenger, Rique
The Asteroid Ephemeris 1883-1999.
Preface by Eleanor Bach;
Introduction by Z.P. Dobyns
Los Angeles: TIA Publs., 1977.

Donath, Emma Belle
Asteroids in Synastry.
Tempe, Az.: A.F.A., Inc., 1977.

Asteroids in the Birthchart.
Tempe, Az.: A.F.A., Inc., 1979.

Donath, Emma Belle
Approximate Positions of Asteroids: 1851-2050.
Tempe, Az.: A.F.A., Inc., 1981.

Asteroids in Midpoints.
Tempe, Az.: A.F.A., Inc., 1982.

Nolle, Richard
Chiron: The New Planet in Your Horoscope.
Tempe, Az.: A.F.A., Inc., 1983.

Some more recent books on asteroids are: *Asteroid Goddesses* (San Diego, Calif.: Astro Computing Services, 1990) by **Demetra George** (b. 1946), *The Ultimate Asteroid Book* (West Chester, Penna.: Whitford Press, 1988) by **J. Lee Lehman, Ph.D.** (b. 1953), *Personal Name Asteroids* by **Nona Press**, *Chiron* by **Maritha Pottenger**, and *View from Chiron* by **Zane Stein**. The latest and most comprehensive book on this subject is:

Schwartz, Jacob
Asteroid Name Encyclopedia.
St. Paul, Minn.: Llewellyn Publs., 1995.

Many of the horoscope-calculation computer programs now commercially available include positions for the first four asteroids and for Chiron. A few offer positions for additional asteroids, and specialized calculation of thousands more is available on demand. The Russian software that is now available is designed for amateur astronomers and does not give the asteroid positions in the usual astrological format. No doubt an astrological version will soon be offered by one of the astrological software houses.

An effort has even been made to assign "standard" symbols to the asteroids. With tens of thousands already discovered, this seems to be a waste of time, since inventing thousands of distinctive "glyphs" as they are now stylishly termed would be impossible, and no one could remember more than a few dozen at best. The astronomical custom of mentioning the name of the asteroid and its assigned number (or perhaps simply a star symbol and the number) would seem to be more practical.

It is difficult to believe that the majority of these bodies have any noticeable astrological influence. Their comparatively insignificant size and the sheer multitude of them would seem to create a muddle from which individual influences could scarcely be distinguished. My remarks on this subject, made some years ago, still seem to me to be appropriate:[66]

> Here we are on planet earth, nearly at the midst of a giant celestial pudding composed of planets, satellites, planetoids, comets, space vehicles, and who knows what else. How shall we determine which objects in our solar system have a sensible astrological influence? And how shall we determine what that influence is?

> Ideally, the influence of a celestial object would be determined from its observed effects in many charts. But the method most in vogue is to suppose that the name of the object is the key to its influence. This may sometimes be the case. But are we prepared to assume that among the asteroids Oceana influences sailors, Hygiea sanitation

---

[66]The extracts that follow are from my paper "Lumps in the Pudding" in *Today's Astrologer* 40, No. 5 (5-6-1978): 31-32. I might add that while the asteroids vary considerably in physical appearance—a few being dazzlingly white, a few red, and a few coal-black, while the majority are rather greyish like the earth's Moon—these differences might merely reflect variations of planetary material from different regions of a primordial planet.

workers, Limburgia cheese-merchants, and Fanatica pro-
testers and terrorists? And what shall we suppose to be
the significance of Beagle, Brambilla, Esperanto, Fanny,
Jean-Jacques, Li, Rusthawelia, Tynka, and Wrubel?

Perhaps the theory is true that the asteroids are the shat-
tered remnants of a small planet that once existed between Mars and Jupiter. If that be true, then one asteroid
has pretty much the same intrinsic nature as the next. And
the larger ones are in fact merely lumps in the pudding.

- - - - - -

It is also worthwhile to point out that our predecessors
did good work with the major planets, indeed for 2,000
years with only the visible major planets. At best, the
smaller members of our solar system can exert only a minor influence. At worst, they are lumps in the pudding.

Charles Emerson and the NCGR

A(lfred) Charles Emerson (1923-1992), A.B., was a founding member of the National Council for Geocosmic Research (NCGR) in 1971,
and, with some assistance from **Robert W. Cooper, FAFA** and the
American Federation of Astrologers, was instrumental in reconstituting
that organization in the fall of the following year. He was particularly interested in medical astrology and the astrology of the Hamburg School.[67]
Emerson wrote *Case Book of Medical Astrology* and *Rectification by Uranian Techniques*. The NCGR has grown steadily and currently has more
than 2,000 members.

Donald Bradley

Donald A. Bradley (1925-1974), who also wrote under the pen-name
Garth Allen, was a research astrologer and a leading American exponent
of "siderealism." His unpublished study of disasters yielded the definitive
value of the "ayanamsa" or difference between the tropical and "sidereal"
zodiac. This value very nearly put the fixed star Aldebaran in 15 Taurus of
the "sidereal" zodiac, so that was the final value adopted by Cyril Fagan
(who had first put Spica in 0 Libra, and later moved it to 29 Virgo). It put
Spica in 29°03' Virgo, so, despite all the previous arguments advanced in
its favor, Spica was abandoned as the "fiducial star" and replaced by
Aldebaran.

Earlier in his career, Bradley was the author of a book *The Parallax
Problem in Astrology* (Los Angeles: Llewellyn Publs., 1947) advocating
the use of the apparent position of the Moon (as affected by parallax)—a

---

[67]For the Hamburg School and Uranian Astrology, see the entry for Witte and
the Hamburg School below.

position that he later abandoned, since Fagan did not favor it. He also made a statistical study of the birthdates of "2,492 Eminent Clergymen," published as *Profession and Birthdate* (Los Angeles: The Llewellyn Foundation, 1950). Bradley asserted that the latter book demonstrated the validity of Fagan's "sidereal" zodiac.[68]

Holden

James Herschel Holden, M.A. FAFA (b. 1926) has been Research Director of the American Federation of Astrologers since 1982 and is a foreign correspondent of the Italian astrological association C.I.D.A. In 1970 he calculated what was probably the first lunar horoscope, set for the moment when Neil Armstrong stepped onto the Moon. It was published in the article "Lunar Astrology" in *Horoscope Magazine* Vol. 36, No. 4 (April 1970): 43-47, 128.

Holden has been especially interested in the history of astrology and astronomy and has written numerous papers on those subjects. In addition, he has published a biographical dictionary of astrologers and a history of western astrology. He has also translated several classical and medieval astrological works from Latin and Greek and nine books of Jean Baptiste Morin's massive *Astrologia Gallica*. He is currently assisting Robert Corre of New York in his dissemination of the Morin Method of Horoscope Interpretation. Some of Holden's books are:

Abu 'Ali al-Khayyat
The Judgments of Nativities.
Trans. from the Latin by James H. Holden
Tempe, Az.: A.F.A., Inc., 1988.

Astrological Pioneers of America.
Tempe, Az.: A.F.A., Inc., 1988.

A History of Horoscopic Astrology
From the Babylonian Period to the Modern Age.
Tempe, Az.: A.F.A., Inc., 1996.
Tempe, Az.: A.F.A., Inc., 2006. 2nd ed. revised

Morin, Jean Baptiste
Astrologia Gallica.
Books 13-17 and 22-25
Trans. from the Latin by James H. Holden
Tempe, Az.: A.F.A., Inc., 1994-2007.

---

[68]But Michel Gauquelin (see below) later stated that Bradley's statistical analysis was invalid.

T(helma) Pat(rick) Davis

T. Pat Davis (1927-2001) was a well-known astrologer and the leading American exponent of the use of heliocentric positions in natal horoscopes. She wrote and lectured extensively on this subject. Two of her books are:

Revolutionizing Astrology with Heliocentric.
Windermere, Fl.: The Author, 1980.

Interpreting Geo-Helio Planets.
Windermere, Fl.: The Author, 1982.

Lois Rodden

Lois M. Rodden (1928-2003) was the best-known astrological data collector in the U.S. She published five valuable books of horoscopes of notable persons based on carefully researched data with the birthtimes rated according to a system she devised for that purpose. She also published an astrological data newsletter and was the chief adviser of the computerized database RID, maintained by the International Society for Astrological Research (ISAR), which presently contains more than 20,000 data items.

Rodden's data books, which are considered as standard and reliable resources, are:

Profiles of Women.
Tempe, Az.: A.F.A., Inc., 1979.

The American Book of Charts.
San Diego: Astro Computing Services, 1980. 1st ed.

Astro-Data II.
[a revised edition of *The American Book of Charts*]
Tempe, Az.: A.F.A., Inc., 1988. 2nd ed. revised

Astro-Data III.
Tempe, Az.: A.F.A., Inc., 1986.

Astro-Data IV.
Tempe, Az.: A.F.A., Inc., 1990. 1st ed.

Astro-Data V.
Hollywood: Data News Press, 1992. 1st ed.

Michelsen

Neil F. Michelsen (1931-1990) was one of the first astrologers to set up a computer data system to calculate horoscopes with a mini-computer.

His calculating services were offered to the public at a very reasonable price and proved popular. He later established a publishing business, which has printed a variety of ephemerides as well as a number of other worthwhile books, e.g. *The American Ephemeris 1931 to 1980* (Pelham, NY: Astro Computing Services, 1976), *The American Ephemeris 1900 to 1930* (Pelham, NY: Astro Computing Services, 1977), *The American Ephemeris 20th Century* (San Diego, Astro Computing Services, 1991), and *Uranian Transneptune Ephemeris 1850-2050* (Franksville, Wis.: Uranian Publications, 1989).

In 1980 Michelsen offered the use of his computer facilities free to Michel and Françoise Gauquelin for American birthdata that they proposed to collect. The processed data was published two years later as: *The Gauquelin Book of American Charts* (see below under Gauquelin).

Michael Erlewine and Matrix

Michael Erlewine (b. 1941) is a pioneer in astrological software. He is the head of the astrological software house, Matrix, in Michigan. He has also written a computer programming manual for astrological software *Manual of Computer Programming for Astrologers* (Tempe, Az.: A.F.A., Inc., 1980), with Margaret Erlewine a valuable fixed star catalogue *Astrophysical Directions* (Ann Arbor, Mich.: Heart Center, 1977), and a book (with ephemeris) on heliocentric astrology *The Sun is Shining: Helio 1653-2050*. In addition, Erlewine offers training sessions and occasional seminars at his business headquarters, where he has established The Heart Center Astrological Library to serve as an information source for the entire astrological community. His company also publishes an astrological periodical.

Astro*Carto*Graphy

Jim Lewis (1941-1995) originated a system of charting relocated horoscopes described in his book ASTRO*CARTO*GRAPHY (San Francisco: ASTRO*CARTO*GRAPHY, 1976) He was the author of other books and of computer software to display and print the charts. His last book, with Ariel Guttman, was *The Astro*Carto*Graphy Book of Maps* (St. Paul: Llewellyn Publs., 1989). It describes his method of charting relocated horoscopes and explains how an individual can find a favorable location on the earth's surface. His technique has proved to be particularly popular in Europe.

Robert Hand

Robert Hand (b. 1942) is the author of popular astrological treatises and the head of the Astrolabe astrological software house. Hand has embraced the concept of composite horoscopes in which two individual horoscopes are blended into a single chart by averaging the positions of each.[69] This has proved to be a popular technique with many younger as-

---

[69]Since this procedure is supposed to be extensible to three or more individuals,

trologers, and his book on the subject (listed below) has become the standard handbook on composite charts.

Hand is a popular author and lecturer, making frequent appearances at astrological conferences. He has recently sponsored a large-scale translation program, Arhat Publications, which aims to translate all important Latin (and perhaps some Hebrew and Arabic) astrological treatises into English on a subscription basis.

Some of Hand's own books are:

Planets in Composite.
Gloucester, Mass.: Para Research, 1976. xii,366 pp.

Planets in Transit.
Gloucester, Mass.: Para Research, 1976. xii,528 pp.

Planets in Youth.
Rockport, Mass.: Para Research, 1978. repr. of 1977 xii,367 pp.

Horoscope Symbols.
Rockport, Mass.: Para Research, 1981.

Schmidt

Robert Schmidt has undertaken the task of translating all the Greek astrological texts into English. His Project Hindsight has published these on a subscription basis. So far translations of Ptolemy, Vettius Valens, Hephaestro of Thebes, and others have appeared. He also offers a course in The System of Hermes.

Zoller

Robert Zoller (b. 1947) is a student of the late Medieval and early modern Latin texts of astrology and is also interested in Hermetic philosophy. He worked on Project Hindsight as a Latin translator and has also taught classes and lectured extensively on some of the astrological techniques that were popular among the earlier astrologers but are now mostly unknown. One fruit of his studies is his comprehensive book on the lots or Arabic Parts:

The Arabic Parts in Astrology/The Lost Key to Prediction.
Rochester, Vt.: Inner Traditions International, [c.1989] 245 pp.
illus. 23 cm.
[rev. ed. of The Lost Key to Prediction c.1980]

---

it is surprising that no one has yet advanced the idea of calculating a composite horoscope for a large group, a nation, or even the entire world population, all of which could be approximated by a statistical analysis and kept up-to-date by adjusting for recorded birth-rates and death-rates.

Financial Astrology

One very specialized branch of astrology is intensely studied by a small number of astrologers and traders. It is the application of astrological techniques to determining the time to buy and sell in the stock, bond, and commodity markets. The user of these techniques is a trader rather than an investor. Fortunes can be made and lost on changes of a few points (or even fractions of a point) within a single day's trading. Any technique, astrological or otherwise, that can tip the ratio of wins to losses to the positive side is valuable. The techniques do not need to be infallible. A stockbroker once told me, "If you can be right just fifty-five percent of the time, you can get rich."

A number of astrologers have developed astrological systems to pin-point the exact time to make trades. In Belgium, **Gustave Lambert Brahy** (see below) was interested in financial astrology and wrote upon the subject in the 1930s. Some of these systems utilize techniques that are unknown to regular astrologers. A few have become rich using these methods. Perhaps the most successful was the legendary **W.D. Gann** (1878-1955), who combined astrological and numerological methods. Gann is said to have made millions in the markets and as a lottery winner (similar techniques can be used for lottery entries). He wrote six books on stock and commodity trading, published market newsletters and forecasts, and taught trading courses. His book *The Tunnel Through the Air* (New York: F.G. Publishing Co., 1927) is said to contain some obscure astrological allegories. Computer software that claims to embody certain of Gann's trading techniques is currently available.

Some other American names that can be mentioned in this connection are **George Bayer** (1892-1949), who wrote *Turning Four Hundred Years of Astrology to Practical Use and Other Matters*; **L.E. Johndro** (1882-1951); **James Mars Langham**, *Planetary Effects on Stock Market Prices* (Los Angeles: Maghnal, 1932); and **Louise McWhirter**, author of the *McWhirter Theory of Stock Market Forecasting* (New York: Astro-Book Co., 1938 1st ed.; 2nd ed. edited by Henry Weingarten, New York: ASI Publications, 1977). **Lcdr. David Williams, FAFA** (1897-1993) studied business cycles and published his findings in his *Financial Astrology* (Tempe, Az.: A.F.A., Inc., 1982). **Lloyd Cope** (1922-2000) for many years wrote a monthly financial astrology column for Dell *Horoscope* magazine. **Donald A. Bradley** and **Michael P. Munkasey** have both written on fluctuations in the stock market averages. **David McMinn** of Australia has written several papers on the 56-Year business cycle[70] and more recently three books on business cy-

---

[70]The following were published in the A.F.A. Journal of Research: "The 56-Year Cycles and Financial Crises" vol. 4, no. 1 (1987):27-46; "Business Cycles and the Number 56" vol. 7, no. 1 (1991): 27-43; and "The 56-Year Cycle in western Europe: 1600 to 1760" vol. 7, no. 2 (1995): 17-22. A related paper by

cles, *Financial Crises and the 56-Year Cycle* (Blue Knob, Austral.: Twin Palms Publishing Co., 1995), *Market Timing by the Number 56*, and *Market Timing by the Moon and Sun*.

Some other books in this field are:

Mull, Carol S.
750 Over-the-Counter Stocks.
Tempe, Az.: A.F.A., Inc., 1986

Mull, Carol S.
Standard & Poor's 500.
Tempe, Az.: A.F.A., Inc., 1984

Long, Jeanne[71]
The Universal Clock/Forecasting Time and Price in the Footsteps of W.D. Gann.
Fort Lauderdale, Fl.: P.A.S. Publs., Inc., n.d.

Meridian, Bill
Planetary Trading.
New York, NY: Cycles Research, 1994.

Since the techniques used in financial astrology are intricate and time-consuming to calculate, computer software, some of it selling for more than $1,500, has been developed to prepare lists of precise times (to the minute) when the "turns" in the markets should come. The trader then establishes a real time link with a broker, takes his list in hand, and makes his trades.

Skeptics may dismiss these procedures as valueless, but experience shows otherwise. Some astute users of these techniques have done very well.

Data Collection

Spurred on by the example set by Michel Gauquelin (see below) and by the availability of affordable computers beginning around 1980, astrologers in the U.S. and abroad began to collect birthdata and store it in computer databases. Today, there are a number of such databases maintained by astrological groups and individual astrologers with large numbers of records, some of them exceeding 40,000 in number. Some of the software houses have also made data available on diskettes and the new CD-ROM disks that can store enormous amounts of data on a single small disk.

Major encyclopedias, such as the *Encyclopedia Britannica* and the *En-*

James H. Holden, "Tables of Conjunctions of the Sun with the Mean Node of the Moon" in vol. 4, no. 2 (1988):19-26, provides tables for 1760-2025 useful for studying the cycles mentioned in McMinn's 1987 paper.

[71]Long also offers astrological software.

cyclopedia Americana are now also available on CD-ROM, which makes it possible to retrieve the birthdates of many famous persons. No doubt the day is not far off when hundreds of thousands or even millions of birthdates will become available and be in an electronic format suitable for various research projects. Of course, the growth of data banks with *timed* birthdata will be much slower, since timed data is increasingly difficult to come by.[72] Still, the amount of timed data is growing steadily.

Whether such data will prove to be useful in improving astrological techniques is uncertain. Statistical investigations of occupational groups can scarely lead to much, for people may adopt an occupation for a variety of reasons—talent or skill being only one of these. Many people have the ability to follow a particular profession but lack the desire, the opportunity, or the financial resources to do so. Conversely, some people may adopt a profession because a parent or other relative is a professional in that field. And in this day of large-scale layoffs and lack of job security, many people may have to change jobs several times during their lives. (This, of course, is not true of academics and specialists such as architects, engineers, and physicians.)

There is also the question of the degree of skill. Each group is subject to the familiar bell curve, with the barely competent on one end, the majority in the middle, and the experts on the other end. Even Gauquelin found that some of the "Mars effects" he noted in the charts of sports figures were only significant in a group restricted to the best players.

To look at a thousand plumbers or a thousand certified public accountants will give us some statistics, but what will they really mean? And how will they help us to read a horoscope? One American researcher[73] diligently typed in the birthdates of over 50,000 psychologists (later extended to 75,000) and analyzed the corresponding planetary positions. The results were not particularly enlightening.

Traditionally, astrology is supposed to be able to analyze a person's personality, his capabilities, his desires, and his prospects for the future. This must be done on an individual basis, taking into account not only the horoscopic indications but also the "integration factors" as I have called them[74] which describe the individual's physical characteristics and his place in society, as well as the nature of the society itself. Sudying large groups of people may help us to refine some of our astrological techniques, but careful study of individuals and small groups will undoubtedly be more rewarding. After all, some occupational statistics are obvious

---

[72]Some countries do not record birth times on birth certificates and others, such as the U.S., may have local restrictions that deny access to the records to casual researchers. In the U.S., the desire of some adoptive parents to prevent their children from discovering their biological origins has led to legislation restricting access to birth records.

[73]Gary Duncan (1931-1988). So far as I am aware, his study remains unpublished.

without research: a short man can scarcely hope to become a basketball player, but being tall does not necessarily confer either the desire or the ability to play basketball professionally.

Computer databases offer much hope for the furtherance of astrology if they are used correctly, since without adequate data each astrologer is reduced to using what data he can accumulate himself. But studying a group of sailors to see if a statistically significant number of them are born with the Sun in a "water sign" will probably not help much.

But now we return to the the main scene of astrology.

Linda Goodman and Sun Signs

In the latter half of the 20th century the most popular astrology books have undoubtedly been those of Linda Goodman (1925-1995): *Sun Signs* (1968), *Love Signs* (1978), and *Star Signs* (1981). The first of these came on the market at the time of a rebellious upsurge of interest in astrology by younger people. All three are of course non-technical, so the information in them is readily comprehensible by anyone. There seems little doubt that the sales of her books have exceeded the total sales of all other English-language astrological books combined.

Sun sign astrology has often been deprecated both by non-astrologers and by astrologers themselves. But there is no denying that it has served to keep astrology alive in the public mind, and many astrologers first became interested in the subject through reading Sun sign material or daily guides based on the Sun signs. A frequent criticism by skeptics is that Sun sign astrology divides all humanity into just twelve classes, "which cannot possibly be true." This is a silly argument! The analytical psychology of Carl Jung (1875-1961) divides all humanity into just two classes: introvert and extrovert. And the even more elaborate scheme that he later proposed postulates only eight classes. Of both the Sun signs and the psychological classes it might be said that they are valid as fundamental classifications.

The European Revival of Astrology

On the Continent, French astrology revived in the 1880s with the publication of works on cabalistic astrology,[75] of which the book *Les Mystères de l'Horoscope* by **Ély Star** (Eugène Jacob) (Paris, 1888) is an outstanding example. These were followed in the 1890s by books on standard astrology. A book[76] published in 1897 by **Fomalhaut**, the Abbé

---

[74]See my paper "Integration Factors" in the A.F.A. *Journal of Research* 5, No. 2 (1989): 7-17.

[75]More a sort of numerology than true astrology, since the positions of the planets, other than the Sun, are not astronomical. Most of it is a strange hodge-podge of numerology, Tarot symbolism, and astrological terminology.

[76]*Manuel d'astrologie sphérique et judiciaire* 'Manual of Spherical and Judicial Astrology' (Paris: Vigot Frères, 1897), p. 316. "The planet beyond Neptune exists. It is called Pluto. Pluto (nature of Mars) would rule Aries." A nice instance

Charles Nicoullaud (1854-1925), predicted the discovery of a new trans-Neptunian planet and even predicted that it would be called Pluto. The French revival of horoscopic astrology was sparked to some extent by the revival of astrology in England.

Julevno

Jules Eveno (1845-1915), a French revival astrologer, who wrote under the pseudonym **Julevno**, was the author of a much used French-language textbook of astrology, *Traité théorique et pratique de l'astrologie généthliaque* 'A Theoretical and Practical Treatise of Natal Astrology' (Paris, 1900. often reprinted).

Selva and Morin de Villefranche

Henri Selva (1861-1952) is the pseudonym of another important French revival astrologer, A. Vlès. He unearthed the great work of J.B. Morin (1583-1656) and published a partial paraphrase and exposition of the central points of Morin's astrological theories, *La théorie des déterminations astrologiques de Morin de Villefranche* 'Morin de Villefranche's Theory of Astrological Determinations' (Paris, 1897. often reprinted). Unfortunately, his book remained little known to English-speaking astrologers, although it was read with interest by the French and Germans.

Col. Caslant

Col. Eugène Caslant (1865-1940), a graduate of the L'École Polytechnique and an officer of the Legion of Honor, was a leading figure in French astrological organizations in the 1930s. Viscount Charles de Herbais de Thun says of him: "Colonel Caslant was one of the great figures of the renovation of astrology into a scientific path. However, he has not restricted his activity to investigations in this domain; he is also interested in the Conjectural and Philosophical Sciences."[77] Two of the colonel's books illustrate the viscount's statement:

Ephémérides perpétuelles.
[explanatory text and tables enabling the user to find planetary positions from 1000 B.C to 2000 A.D.]
Paris: Chacornac, 1906.
Paris: Chacornac, 1932. 224 pp.

Traité élémentaire de Géomancie.
[An Elementary Treatise of Geomancy]
Paris: Librairie Vega, 1935. 180 pp.

---

of prediction for those who do not believe it is possible to predict the future! (But Fomalhaut missed the rulership, since most astrologers agree that Pluto rules Scorpio.)

[77]*Encyclopédie du mouvement astrologique de la langue française* (Brussels: Éditions de la revue Demain, 1944), p. 246.

Choisnard and Astrological Statistics

Paul Choisnard (1867-1930) was an engineering graduate of L'École Polytechnique and a major in the Field Artillery. He acquired an interest in astrology as a young man and wrote a number of books under the pseudonym **Paul Flambart**. Choisnard was the pioneer of astrological statistics. His grasp of that subject was later severely criticized by Michel Gauquelin (see below), but, whether the criticism was justified or not, Choisnard still deserves credit for being the first astrologer to make an attempt to use statistical analysis to extend astrological knowledge. His best-known books are:

Flambart, Paul
Influence astrale.
[Astral Influence]
Paris, 1901.

Flambart, Paul.
Langage astrale.
[Astral Language]
Paris, 1903. 1st. ed.

Flambart, Paul
Étude nouvelle sur l'hérédité.
[A New Study of Heredity]
Paris, 1903.

Flambart, Paul
Calcul des probabilités appliqué à l'astrologie.
[Calculation of Probabilities as Applied to Astrology]
Paris: Chacornac, 1914.

Picard

Eudes Picard (1867-1932) wrote an important treatise on derived houses, *Astrologie judiciaire* 'Judicial Astrology' (Paris: Leymarie, 1932; 1981. repr. in facs.). In it he sets forth in great detail the significations of the derived houses along with a discussion of the triplicities and their rulers, the dodecatemories, and a large number of lots (or parts, such as the Part of Fortune). He illustrates his method of interpretation with the charts of thirty-seven famous persons. Finally, he gives instructions for finding the cusps of the houses and includes seven tables of Placidus houses (calculated with "poles") for latitudes ranging from 22° N. to 56° N. This book was commended by the English astrologer Vivian Robson.[78]

---

[78]Vivian E. Robson, *Astrology and Sex* (Philadelphia: W. Foulsham Co., 1941), Chapt. XVII "How to Read Details."

Here is an excerpt from Picard's foreword to the significations of the derived houses:[79]

Derived Domifications

The domification of the radix uniquely represents the 12 traditional houses. It is that which, in terms of domification, one could call "the major mode of the houses." There are some minor modes constituting a series of secondary cycles of houses that we shall designate under the term "derived domifications." As their name indicates, they are derived from and are dependent upon the radical [houses]. One understands them by means of certain aphorisms. They appear in germ, in a form and under some fragmentary aspects. But the astrologer has acted quickly in seizing the thread of it. When, for example, one says of Saturn that it menaces the life of children if it occupies the sign of Leo in the 10th, one evokes in the name of this sign the 5th house, which is attributed to children. Furthermore, Leo in the 10th is found in the 6th house from the 5th taken from the ASC, and it concerns sicknesses. If one wants to know about the wife's dowry, it is necessary to consult the 8th house, quite simply because it is the 2nd from the radical 7th, which is attributed to the spouse, and consequently the house of her money.—These keys are sufficient—for one could cite many analogous examples—to establish as a principle that each radical house can be considered to be the ASC of a distinct duodenary cycle, and it is that cycle that we shall call "a derived domification." The set of these minor cycles forms 11 domifications, which, added to the radical set, give a total of 144 houses. The radical domification will de designated D.R. and the derived domification D.D.

Thus, 4th D.D. signifies: the 4th derived domification, that is the one that will have for its 1st house the 4th house of the radical [chart]. See also the the table giving the division of all the houses on the zodiacal circle (Fig. V).[80]

The Mechanism of the Derived Domifications (D.D.) and the Rules that Determine their Significations in a Reasonable Manner.

The nomenclature that one is going to read represents only a part of the significations attributed to the derived domifications (D.D.). The reader will understand that it is

---

[79]Picard, *op. cit.*, pp. 60-62.
[80]On p. 61 there is a large circular diagram showing the numeration of the derived houses, but I have omitted it here because the numeration is obvious.

impossible to stop a definite work of this order of ideas because of the complexity of its nuances. We have, therefore, tried to treat the question under the most extended form of its appearance, but sufficiently at length to permit the practicioner to seize upon the mechanism of the processes of deduction. He will then be able to appreciate by what means and in what measure he will be able to find at his own convenience whatever signification is appropriate in a particular case. The essential thing consists of working in an orderly and methodical manner.

First off, one will study the radical cycle of the houses according to the traditional rules. It is only after this analysis that one will enter upon the study of the D.D. The 11 houses that follow the first radical [house] will then be taken in turn as the origin of a particular duodenary cycle. This will be the root of each D.D. The first house of each D.D. will preserve as its essential signification that which is conferred upon it in the D.R. Thus, the 4th D.D. will have for its 1st house, the 4th [house] of the D.R., that is to say the one that especially represents the [native's] father. The 11 houses which will follow it will have significations relative to the father. With regard to that first house, they will preserve the same [sort of] attributions and prerogatives as [the corresponding] houses of the D.R. with regard to the ASC, which is the first house of the radical cycle. Thus, the 5th radical house, which will be the 2nd house of the father, will have to do with the money acquired by the father; the 6th radical, or the 3rd D.D. of the father, will represent the father's brother; the 7th radical, or the 4th D.D. of the father, will correspond to the father's father. There is no difficulty in this. To apprehend it better, it will suffice to look at the figure of the 12 cycles.

Here is a rule of the greatest importance and one whose strict observance will prevent every error of diagnosis. It is necessary to fix once and for all the order in which the qualitative elements of the two houses must be considered, and which is the one of these two elements which outweighs the other in the specification of the determind sense. It is necessary to take as a basis for the first element that which is found in every other house as the first [element], and to refer its signification to the essential signification of the first house.

In many cases, the application of this rule will give imprecise results which do not give back a neat solution to the astrologer because the signification found will not have a concrete sense. Then, it will suffice to transpose this signification into the plan of analogies in order to find its rational correspondence there; but under no pretext should the astrologer yield to the temptation to invert the order of the terms, which would result in a deformation of the analysis.

Picard continues with a number of illustrations of the various combinations, followed by seventy-five pages of detailed significations of the individual derived houses. This is an ancient method, going back at least to Vettius Valens (see above). It has been denounced by a few astrologers as a "horary method" that should not be applied to natal astrology,[81] but this attitude results from their following the narrow channel of Ptolemaic astrology, which did not mention horary astrology. Those astrologers who have applied this method to natal astrology have been pleased with it. Vivian Robson has this to say in the chapter "How to read Details" in his book *Astrology and Sex*[82]:

> ... This process may be continued indefinitely and will be found to cover the smallest trivialities with extraordinary accuracy. To take a ridiculouly extreme case, the fifth house would furnish any details that might be be required about a cat owned by the daughter of a charwoman employed by the wife's sister-in-law! This is arrived at as follows:—The seventh house is the wife; the ninth (third from seventh) is her brother; the third (seventh from third from seventh) is his wife or her sister-in-law; the eighth (sixth from seventh from third from seventh) is the sister-in-law's charwoman; the twelfth (fifth from sixth from seventh from third from seventh) is the charwoman's daughter; and finally the fifth (sixth from fifth from sixth from seventh from third from seventh) is the required cat.

> If we refer this to the accompanying map (Fig. 7)[83] we find Saturn in Aquarius on the cusp of the fifth house and we should therefore be justified in assuming that the cat in question was a black one which had probably a weak leg due to a fall from a height, all of which is a free rendering of Saturn in Aquarius.

> This may be considered far-fetched, ludicrous, and suggestive of the House that Jack Built, and perhaps the exam-

---

[81]A.J. Pearce (Zadkiel II), for example.
[82]Robson, *op. cit.*, pp. 143-145.
[83]A chart set for London 1 July 1903 11:58 AM with 5 Libra rising.

ple is so, but anyone who takes the trouble to use this method and check the results will find that it is thoroughly reliable and unbelievably accurate.

There is much more of interest in Picard's book, and every astrologer who reads French should acquire it.

Jean Hieroz

Jean Hieroz (1889-1979) was the pseudonym of a scholarly French astrologer whose real name was Rozières.[84] He studied with H. Selva and adopted the methods of J.B. Morin. Hieroz became a frequent contributor to the periodical *Les Cahiers Astrologiques*, and the author of several valuable books, among which we may cite the following:

L'Astrologie selon J-B Morin de Villefranche.
[The Astrology of J-B Morin of Villefranche]
Paris: Payot, 1941. paper. 216 pp.

L'Astrologie mondiale selon Morin de Villefranche.
Paris: Payot?, 1943. 200 pp.

L'Astrologie selon Morin De Villefranche, quelques autres/ et /
Moi-même.
[The Astrology of J-B Morin, Some Others, and Myself]
Paris: Les Éditions des Champs-Élysée, 1962. paper. 248 pp.
[a second and enlarged edition of the 1941 volume]

Henri Gouchon

Henri Gouchon (1898-1978) was the author of an excellent encyclopedic astrological dictionary, *Dictionnaire astrologique* (Paris, 1936-1940. 3 vols.) A supplementary vol. 4 was published after World War II. The work has since been reprinted in a single volume (Paris: Dervy Livres, 1975; Éditions Dervy, 1992. latest printing) and translated into other languages, e.g. *Dizionario di astrologia* (Milan: Armenia Editore, 1980).

Alexandre Volguine

Alexandre Volguine (1903-1977), a Russian immigrant who lived at Nice, was considered by some to be the greatest French astrologer of the 20th century.[85] He wrote a number of astrological books, several of which

---

[84]His pseudonymous surname is properly written without an accent (witness his personal signature on a letter to the A.F.A.), but the first ed. of the book cited below has Hièroz, while the second ed. has Hiéroz. It is derived from the Greek adjective *hierós* 'sacred' or 'holy'.

[85]The judgment of the editors of the *Larousse Encyclopedia of Astrology* (New York: McGraw-Hill, 1980), p. 303.

have been translated into English. He was also the founder (in 1937) of the scholarly French astrological periodical *Cahiers astrologiques*. A few of his books that are available in English translation are mentioned below:
The Solar Revolutions.
Kent, England: Pythagorean Publs., 1969.
The Ruler of the Nativity.
New York: ASI Publishers, 1973.

The Technique of Solar Returns.
[trans. from the 3rd French ed. (1972]
New York: ASI Publishers, 1976.

André Barbault

André Barbault (b. 1921) is probably the best known French astrologer of recent years. He has been active in the astrological organization Centre International d'Astrologie, serving as its vice president from 1953 to 1967. Barbault specialized in psychological and mundane astrology. In 1967 he initiated the computerized horoscope service, Astroflash, the first of its kind. He also began publishing the astrological quarterly, *L'Astrologue*. Some of his books are:

De la psychanalyse de l'Astrologie.
[Astrological Psychoanalysis]
Peris: Éditions du Seuil, 1961.

Traité pratique d'Astrologie.
[A Practical Treatise of Astrology]
Paris: Éditions du Seuil, 1961. 360 pp.

Les astres et l'histoire.
[The Stars and History]
Paris: J.-J. Pauvert, 1967.

L'Astrologie mondiale.
[Mundane Astrology]
Paris: Fayard, 1979. 331 pp.

Astres royaux/ Horoscopes des têtes couronnées.
[Royal Stars/ Horoscopes of Crowned Heads]
Monaco: Éditions du Rocher, 1995. 514 pp. 23 cm.

The Gauquelins and Astrological Statistics

Michel Gauquelin[86] (1928-1991) was a French psychologist, who, with his wife **Françoise Schneider Gauquelin** (b. 1929), collected timed

---

[86]See also the Section above entitled "Data Collection."

birthdata from 50,000 or more birth certificates and performed the most extensive astrological research on natal horoscopes that has yet been done. Unfortunately his work was very narrow in scope, since most of his research consisted of tabulating planets in houses in occupational and family groups. (He had concluded from previous studies that the signs of the zodiac and the planetary aspects had no discernible influence on profession or heredity.) His latest work was on words describing the "character traits" of some of the occupational groups he had studied. Here his findings generally agreed with the "key words" traditionally assigned to the planets.

In his first book, *The Influence of the Stars*, Gauquelin reviewed the statistical work of his predecessors, Paul Choisnard and Karl Ernst Krafft and found fault with everything they had done.[87] He stated unequivocally that all of their conclusions were based on a faulty discussion of their data and were therefore totally worthless. (This sweeping judgment has not been verified.)

Since Gauquelin applied standard statistical procedures to a large volume of data, his conclusions that seemed to demonstrate an undeniable correlation between planetary house positions and profession were immediately denounced as invalid or even fraudulent by academics opposed to astrology. His own university was not pleased with his efforts and refused to accept his doctoral thesis. For the remainder of his life he fought a running battle with academic critics, whose attitude can best be described as: "My mind is already made up. Don't try to confuse me with the facts." One academic went so far as to state, "If statistics prove astrology, then I shall cease to believe in statistics."

Gauquelin had begun his studies with the evident intention of disproving astrology by scientific means, and in his younger days he was very critical of astrology and astrologers. He said, for example, "Whoever claims to predict the future by consulting the stars is fooling either himself or someone else."[88] But as the years went by and he encountered nothing but skepticism and derision from most of the academic community, his attitude gradually changed. Determined movements were launched against him impugning both his statistical skill and his honesty. The only people who were prepared to accept him at face value were astrologers[89] and a few psychologists. He wrote several popular accounts of his studies, some

---

[87]He also dismissed the studies made in Germany by Baron von Kloeckler and those made in the U.S. by The Church of Light and Donald A. Bradley.

[88]*The Cosmic Clocks*, p. 89.

[89]Not all astrologers by any means, for many felt that he took too narrow a view of astrology and had contributed little more to the art than assembling an unparalleled data source. It should also be mentioned that he left the lasting impression among the statistically poorly-informed that astrological research could only be undertaken with massive amounts of data, thus undoubtedly discouraging many would-be researchers.

aimed directly at those interested in astrology, and he eventually became a frequent lecturer at astrological conventions. He also participated in the activities of the English group that produced the journal *Correlation*. Gauquelin published most of the birthdata he had laboriously collected from the civil records of France and other countries, amounting to more than 50,000 timed birthdates. His data books constitute an unparalleled resource for astrological researchers. This, and the impetus he gave to collecting large amounts of reliable data and subjecting it to valid statistical analysis, is his principal legacy to astrology.[90] A few of his many publications are:

L'Influence des astres.
[The Influence of the Stars]
Paris: Éditions du Dauphin, 1955. paper. 347 pp.

Les hommes et les astres.
[Man and the Stars]
with a preface by Prof. H. Bender
Paris: Éditions Denoël, 1960. paper. 268 pp.

Gauquelin, Michel and Françoise
Birth and Planetary Data Gathered Since 1949.
(Coordonnées natales et planétaires rassamblées depuis 1949.)
[text in English and French]
Series A.
[this series contains more than 16,300 records of notable members of professional groups]
Vol. 1 Sports Champions (Champions de Sport)
Vol. 2 Men of Science (Hommes de Science)
Vol. 3 Military Men (Hommes de Guerre)
Vol. 4 Painters and Musicians (Peintres et Musiciens)
Vol. 5 Actors and Politicians (Acteurs et Politiciens)
Vol. 6 Writers and Journalists (Écrivains et Journalistes)
(1971)
Paris: Laboratoire d'Étude des Relations entre
Rhythmes Cosmiques et Psychophysiologiques, 1970-1971.

---

[90]Gauquelin had studied astrology since his teen-age years and had convinced himself that the zodiac, the aspects, and most other features of traditional astrology, such as transits, were insignificant. He therefore confined his studies mainly to house positions. In his later years he investigated the "character traits" normally associated with the planets by making lists of words that frequently occurred in biographies of persons notable in a particular vocational field for which his earlier work had shown particular planets to be statistically significant. He found that the traditional key words tallied fairly well with the "character traits" he derived from his occupational lists.

Gauquelin, Michel and Françoise
Birth and Planetary Data Gathered Since 1949.
(Coordonnées natales et planétaires rassamblées depuis 1949.)
[text in English and French]

Series B.
Hereditary Experiment.
[this series contains almost 25,000 records of parents and their children in 6 vols. (vols. 5 & 6, publ. in 1971)]
Paris: Laboratoire d'Étude des Relations entre Rhythmes Cosmiques et Psychophysiologiques, 1970-1971.

Gauquelin, Michel and Françoise
Birth and Planetary Data Gathered Since 1949.
Series C.
Profession-Heredity, Results of Series A & B
[Profession-Hérédité, Résultats des Séries A & B]
Paris: Laboratoire d'Étude des Relations entre Rhythmes Cosmiques et Psychophysiologiques, 1972

The Cosmic Clocks.
New York: Avon Books, 1967. paper. xxi,234 pp.
Gauquelin, Michel and Francoise

The Gauquelin Book of American Charts.
San Diego, Ca.: Astro Computing Services, 1982.
[contains over 1,400 charts and data entries]

Françoise Schneider Gauquelin continued her research efforts after her divorce from Michel Gauquelin and his subsequent death. She published a research journal in Paris for a time and then settled in the U.S.

Guinard

Patrice Guinard Th.D. (Paris, Sorbonne) (b. 1957) has conducted extensive astrological research and has established the Web site C.U.R.A. (University Center for Astrological Research) that contains a large number of valuable papers on astrological subjects by various authors, all of which may be read in French, English, or Spanish. See the Web site http://cura.free.fr. Dr. Guinard is currently working on materials for his "Dictionary Nostradamus Online," which is an exhaustive investigation (biographical, bibliographical, and historical) of all the works published by Nostradamus, or related to Nostradamus, during the 16th century. It contains a lot of material previously unknown even to specialists. For the Introduction and Index to the 25 articles already published (as of July 2006), see his Web sites http://cura.free.fr/602A-intro.html and http://cura.free.fr/602A-index.html. His research on the first editions of Nostradamus's Prophecies is also available on the Web site http://cura.free.fr/dico2pro/606N-pro.html.

Astrology in Belgium
Visc. de Herbais de Thun

Viscount Charles de Herbais de Thun (1862-1946), among other works, wrote a general summary of astrological interpretative techniques, a short treatise on racehorses, and a marvelously detailed bio/bibliographical work:

Synthèse de l'interpretation astrologique d'après les principaux auteurs modernes.
[Synthesis of Astrological Interpretation According to the Principal Modern Authors]
Brussels: Éditions de la revue Demain, 1937.

Astrologie animale. Le cheval de course.
[Animal Astrology. The Racehorse]
Brussels: Éditions de la revue Demain, 1938. 60 pp.

L'Encyclopédie du mouvement astrologique de la langue française au XX. siècle.
[Encyclopedia of the French-language Astrological Movement in the 20th Century].
Brussels: Éditions de la revue Demain, 1944.

Gustave Brahy

Gustave Lambert Brahy (1894-1989) was the founder and first director of the Institut Astrologique de Belgique (Astrological Institute of Belgium) in 1926, and was a leading figure in Belgian astrology. He was particularly interested in financial astrology and also translated two of Bulwer-Lytton's novels into French and wrote a very interesting volume of personal reminiscences:

Contribution à l'étude de l'Astro-Dynamique.
[Contribution to the Study of Astro-Dynamics]
Brussels: Inst. Astr. de Belgique, 1932.

Fluctuations boursières et influences cosmiques.
[Market Fluctuations and Cosmic Influences]
Brussels: Inst. Astr. de Belgique, 1934.

La clef de la prévision des évenements mondiaux et des fluctuations économiques et boursières.
[The Key to Forecasting Mundane Events and Economic and

Market Fluctuations]
Brussels: 1932. 1st ed.
Brussels: Éditions PIC, 1968. 3rd. rev. ed.

Confidences d'un astrologue.
Brussels?: Flandre-Artois, 1946. with photo of the author.

Antarès

Georges Mostade (1900-1988), known to the astrological world as **Antarès** was a native of Malines. He studied the classical langauges and was also fluent in French, Flemish, German, and English. During the years 1935-1938 he was office manager for the Belgian periodical *Demain*, after which he taught astrology for two years under the auspices of the Belgian Institute of Astro-Dynamics. His astrological textbook was very well received when it first appeared and ran through four editions before wartime restrictions set in: *Manuel pratique d'Astrologie* 'A Practical Manual of Astrology' (Brussels: Éditions de la Revue Demain, 1936. 1st ed. 288 pp.; 1942. 4th ed.)

Lescaut

Jacques de Lescaut (1939-1995) specialized in data collection, publishing a series of volumes (in French and English) containing the birthdata of some 7,200 famous persons born with the Sun in the signs: *Encyclopedia [of] Birth Data* (Brussels: Éditions de l'Apotelesmatique, 1978-).

Bessière

Jany Bessière (b. 1944) is a well-known contemporary astrologer and the current president of the Belgian Astrological Federation (F.A.B.).

Astrology in Germany

In Germany, astrology came to life just prior to World War I and sprouted luxuriantly in the unsettled times of the 1920s.[91] Some of the leading figures in 20th century German astrology are these:

Albert Kniepf

Albert Kniepf (1853-1924) of Hamburg was the first of the German revival astrologers. Knappich says of him:[92]

> In 1898/1899 he published some pamphlets[93] on the
> physical basis of astrology, in which he views the action

---

[91]My principal sources for the German-language astrologers are Ellic Howe, *Astrology*, and Wilhelm Knappich, *Geschichte der Astrologie*.
[92]Knappich, *op. cit.*, pp. 311,351.
[93]In German, *Die psychischen Wirkungen der Gestirne. Physikalische Begründung der Horoskopie und Astrologie* [The Psychical Actions of the Stars. The Physical Foundation of Horoscopy and Astrology].

of the stars as electromotive attractions, and he asserts that the human aura is more sensitive by far than a selenium-cell reaction. He considers the celestial houses to be like polarized fields of force corresponding to the iris of geomagnetism.

Kniepf was a critical thinker, who was constantly endeavoring to warn the German students of astrology against unripe efforts at reform and against those who had no desire to know anything about a popularization of astrology.

Ernst Tiede

Ernst Tiede (1863-19?) of Marienwerder (now Kwidzyn, Poland), a building designer by profession, was the author of the standard German-language astrological dictionary *Astrologisches Lexikon* (Leipzig: Theosophisches Verlagshaus, 1920).

Karl Brandler-Pracht

Karl Brandler-Pracht (1864-1945) was a native of Vienna and an actor by profession. He appeared for some years in German-language plays in America but returned to Europe about 1900. In the U.S. he had acquired a working knowledge of both English and astrology. He was a prominent German occultist and astrologer of Austrian birth. He founded the first Austrian Astrological Society in 1907. Subsequently in Germany in 1911 he became the first editor of the magazine *Astrologische Rundschau* (see below under Vollrath). The books he wrote later have been characterized as psychological and wordy.

Glahn

A(lan) Frank Glahn (1865-19?). A German astrologer well-known in his day, author of the "Glahn Method" of horoscope interpretation, an eclectic procedure with some pearls here and there, but expounded in a rather chaotic fashion in his book, *Erklärung und systematische Deutung des Geburtshoroskop* 'Explanation and Systematic Interpretation of the Natal Horoscope' (Bad Oldesloe: Uranus Verlag, 1924). One of Glahn's innovations was the Glahn Life Circle, a symbolic direction that begins at the ASC degree and revolves clockwise around the natal horoscope at the rate of 8°20' per house, thus completing the circle in 100 years, after which it begins a second circuit. This procedure has found favor with some younger astrologers.[94] Glahn was also an early advocate of E.H. Bailey's prenatal epoch theory. One of his younger associates was Christian Meier-Parm (see below).

---

[94]Compare this symbolic direction with that of Bruno and Louise Huber (see below), which begins at the ASC degree and revolves counter-clockwise at the rate of 6 degrees per house, thus completing the circle in only 72 years.

Alexander Bethor

Alexander Bethor, pseudonym of **A. Backmund** (1876-1938), a Munich teacher, founded *Zodiakus* the first German periodical for scientific astrology. It had a three-year run 1909-1912. In it he published a series of articles on the "Scientific Foundation of Astrology."[95]

Vollrath and the Astrologische Rundschau

Hugo Vollrath (1877-after 1937) was a leading figure in the revival of German astrology. In his younger days he studied (from about 1899 on) under the German-American physician and occultist Franz Hartmann (1838-1912), who had embraced Theosophy in 1878 or thereabouts. For a time he accompanied Hartmann on his lecture tours. In 1907 or 1908 he settled down in Leipzig where he established the Theosophical Publishing House, which became a leading publisher of astrological books and magazines. He began to issue a monthly occult publication called *Prana*, but almost at once he employed Karl Brandler-Pracht to edit an astrological supplement, the *Astrologische Rundschau*. The AR was published continually until the Nazis suppressed it in 1938; it was one of the leading German astrology magazines. Vollrath appears in a group photo of some German astrologers facing p. 53 of Ellic Howe's *Astrology*.

Vollrath was the leader of a faction of German astrologers that was opposed to Dr. Hubert Korsch (see below) when the latter came on the scene in the mid-1920s.

Witte and the Hamburg School

Alfred Witte (1878-1941), was an employee of the City of Hamburg and the founder of the well-known Astrologische Studiengesellschaft or Hamburg School of Astrology, which uses a complex system of midpoints (forming what Witte called "planetary pictures"), a set of six horoscope charts (rotations of the natal horoscope drawn in the Equal House system), and eight hypothetical planets. Witte also revised the sign rulerships, assigning Uranus to Sagittarius, Neptune (and later, Pluto, as joint-ruler) to Scorpio, Cupido to Libra, Hades to Virgo, Zeus as joint-ruler to Leo, and Kronos as joint-ruler to Cancer. The four planets of his associate Sieggrün were assigned thus: Apollon as joint-ruler to Gemini, Admetos as joint-ruler to Taurus, Vulkanus as joint-ruler to Aries, and Poseidon as sole ruler to Pisces (based on its name). However, these rulerships seem to have fallen by the wayside, since the modern proponents of the Hamburg School rely mainly on "planetary pictures."

During military service in World War I, Witte detected the presence of

---

[95]In German, "Natürwissenschaftliche Begründung der Astrologie." About this same time, the English astrologer G.E. Sutcliffe (b. 1859) published a paper "The Foundations of Physical Astrology" in *Modern Astrology* V (1908):156 ff. Both of these writers were inspired by the publicity surrounding the publication in 1905 of the special theory of relativity by Alfred Einstein (1879-1955).

a moving body in the sign Leo. From the data he collected, he postulated the presence of a trans-Neptunian planet and named it Cupido. He subsequently "found" three others, Hades, Zeus, and Kronos; and his associate **Friedrich Sieggrün** (1877-1951) added four more (Apollon, Admetos, Vulkanus, and Poseidon) to make a total of eight "trans-Neptunians." None of these planets has been observed by astronomers, and it might legitimately be asked why their astrological influences were sufficiently strong to be detected while the influence of the planet Pluto was not?

Nevertheless, Witte's elaborate system of astrology found a hard core of enthusiastic followers sufficient to keep it alive. The "bible" of the Hamburg School is Witte's *Regelwerk für Planetenbilder* 'Rulebook for Planetary Pictures' (Hamburg: Witte Verlag, 1928. 1st ed.). Witte's younger associate **Ludwig Rudolph** (1893-1982) was responsible for the publication of the first and subsequent editions in Europe. He also founded a periodical *Hamburger Hefte* that is the official organ of the Hamburg School. The fourth edition of the *Regelwerk* was augmented with the addition by **Hermann Lefeldt** (1899-1977) of planetary pictures for the combinations involving Pluto and the four trans-Neptunians of **Friedrich Sieggrün**. From the fifth edition (1959) an authorized English translation was made by **Curt Knupfer** (1907-1978), MAFA, and published by Rudolph (Hamburg: Witte Verlag, 1974). Since Ludwig Rudolph's death, his son **Udo Rudolph** (b. 1921) has succeeded him as the nominal head of the Hamburg School.

Witte's system of astrology was a new departure. Among his innovations was his assertion that the ASC indicated not the personality but rather the persons with whom the native was associated. The psychological ego he assigned to the MC—a curious concept that runs entirely counter to the established tradition. He also emphasized the lunar nodes, and especially the mid-point combinations and the "hard aspects"—conjunction, square, and opposition—and adopted the "solar arc"[96] as the time measure for directions. His system aroused much skepticism and opposition in Germany when it was first announced and failed to receive general acceptance. While it has continued to find a small number of enthusiastic supporters, it has never caught on with the majority of astrologers and remains a fringe method. However, Witte's basic midpoint concept has received a more favorable response, even among the majority of astrologers who reject his system as a whole.

There are photos of Witte, Sieggrün, Rudolph, and Lefeldt facing the Table of Contents in Witte-Lefeldt, *Rules for Planetary Pictures* (Ham-

---

[96]The "solar arc" is simply the actual distance traversed by the Sun in the zodiac between two points in time, usually between the birthdate and a subsequent point, allowing one day of true solar motion to be the equivalent of one year of the native's life. This is a simplified version of the solar arc advocated by Placidus, which measured the arc in right ascension rather than in ecliptical longitude.

burg: Ludwig Rudolph [Witte Verlag], 1974).

In the U.S. **Richard Svehla** (1878-1942) published an authorized translation of the third edition of Witte's book in 1939. An independent and "unauthorized" translation was published in New York in 1959 by **Hans Niggemann** (1891-1985), who as a former pupil of Witte's felt that he had the right to translate the master's book (Rudolph did not agree).[97] But both Svehla in Cleveland, Ohio, and later Niggemann in New York City worked hard to disseminate Witte's techniques in the U.S.

In a letter to the present author, Niggemann claimed that it was he who had dubbed Witte's system "Uranian Astrology"—a term that has gradually won acceptance both in the U.S. and abroad.

Dr. Korsch

Dr. Hubert Korsch, J.D. (1883-1942) was a corporate lawyer by profession with a natural talent for organization. He became interested in astrology in the 1920s, and from 1926 on he was a leading, but controversial, figure in German astrology and astrological organizations.[98] Dr. Korsch was neither an esoteric nor an occultist. He believed it was necessary to rid the professional astrological field of charlatans, incompetents, and muddle-headed esoteric astrologers. Naturally, this attitude aroused much antagonism. He rallied the learned amateur astrologers to his side in opposition to the professional astrologers and those amateurs of esoteric inclinations. In January 1930 he began to publish the astrological magazine *Zenit*, which soon became one of the leading periodicals in its field. It was continued until December 1938, after which it was suppressed by the Nazis. In 1935, Dr. Korsch published a valuable biographical dictionary of astrologers, *Grundriss der Geschichte der Astrologie* 'Compendium of the History of Astrology' (Düsseldorf: Zenit, 1935. 104 pp.).

Brunhübner and Pluto

Fritz Brunhübner (1894-1965), living in the disturbed social conditions of Germany, took an immediate interest in the newly discovered planet Pluto (announced 13 March 1930), viewing it as representative of the trying post-war years in his native country. He stated the prototype formulation of the influence of the newly discovered planet Pluto in the German astrological journal *Zenit* in 1932.[99] And three years later he published a monograph, *Der neue Planet Pluto*, "The New Planet Pluto" (Diessen: Huber, 1935). It was subsequently translated into French and English.

---

[97]During World War II, the U.S. Government voided all German copyrights, thereby removing all restrictions on the reproduction or translation of pre-war German imprints, so Rudolph could not contest Niggeman's action in court.

[98]See Ellic Howe, *Astrology*, for a blow-by-blow description of the fierce internecine war of the German astrologers during the 1920s and early 1930s.

[99]*See* Ellic Howe, *op. cit.*, p. 17 n.

La planète Pluton.
trans. by Alfred Kotulla
[with a photo of Brunhübner and his horoscope]
Saint-Mandé: The Translator, 1937. 144 pp.

Pluto.
trans. by Julie Baum
Washington: Nat. Astr. Library, n.d.

Ephemerides of Pluto were published almost immediately by
Ed(uard) Koppenstätter:
Koppenstätter's Pluto Ephemeride 1840-1940.
Eltville am Rhein: Verlag Ed. Koppenstätter, 1931.

Koppenstätter's Pluto Ephemeride 1600-1960.
Herrsching bei München: Verlag Ed. Koppenstätter, 1936.

These ephemerides were of course based upon preliminary orbits of
Pluto; however, they were quite accurate for the period from 1840-1960
and no more than a degree out as far back as 1775. Before that time the error gradually widened. Still, they gave the astrologers of the 1930s an opportunity to add Pluto to their charts. Other tables of Pluto were published
in the U.S. by **Benjamine** and **Foelsch**:
Benjamine, Elbert
The Influence of the Planet Pluto.
[with an ephemeris for 1840-1980]
Chicago: The Aries Press, 1939

Foelsch, Kuno, Ph.D.
The Tables of Pluto.
[1 B.C. to 2500 A.D.]
Los Angeles: The Pluto Publishing Co., 1941.

Foelsch's tract is actually a set of tables (not an ephemeris) based upon
the preliminary orbit published by the Lick Observatory in 1931. His tables permit reasonably accurate calculation of positions for the years of
the 19th and 20th century, but the error increases in the earlier centuries.

M.E. Winkel

M.E. Winkel was active in the 1920s. He translated Melanchthon's
Latin version of the *Tetrabiblos* (Berlin: Linser Verlag, 1923) and was a
co-founder of the short-lived Deutsche Kulturgemeinschaft zur Pflege
der Astrologie 'German Cultural Association for the Advancement of Astrology' in 1927. Winkel appears in a group photo of some German astrologers facing p. 53 of Ellic Howe's *Astrology*.

Walther Koch and the Birthplace System of Houses

Walther Koch, Ph.D. (1895-1970), educator and astrologer, was the son of a manufacturer and a soldier in World War I. After his discharge from the army, he pursued his education in classics, and following graduation he entered the German civil service. Koch became interested in astrology early and began writing for the German astrological periodicals in 1924. His classical background evidently gave him a fondness for classical or traditional astrology. To the end of his life he was opposed to "novelties" such as Cosmobiology and Cosmopsychology. However, he was also opposed to the idea that the natal horoscope indicated an unavoidable fate or destiny for the native. In the 1930s he published some books on colors and gemstones:

> Koch, Walter und Bressendorf, O. von
> Astrologische Farbenlehre.
> [Astrological Theory of Colors]
> Munich: O.W. Barth Verlag, 1930.
> Die Seele der Edelsteine.
> [The Soul of the Precious Stones]
> (1934)

But thereafter his attention turned to the problem of house division. He published house tables for the Placidus and Regiomontanus system, but, dissatisfied with both of them, he investigated a new approach. And, after he had published tables for the new system, he destroyed his remaining stocks of the older tables.

Today, Koch is best known for his advocacy of the so-called Birthplace system of houses, although he wrote on a variety of astrological subjects. Koch claimed that this system is the only one that uses the latitude of the birthplace for all the house cusps, but his assertion is false.[100] The most that can be said for the Koch system is that it yields different values for the intermediate cusps. Some researchers have claimed that Koch cusps appear to be more valid, but similar claims have been made for all the major house systems. And, like all the other quadrant systems, the Birthplace system fails at the arctic and antarctic circles. See the following works:

Regiomontanus und das Häusersystem des Geburtsortes.

---

[100]He was apparently led to this odd belief by the fact that Campanus, Regiomontanus, and Placidus intermediate cusps are calculated by using pseudo-latitudes called "poles," which are in every case less than the geographic latitude of the birthplace. However, the "poles" are merely an auxiliary angle that is useful for calculating the cusps. And in the case of Placidus cusps the "poles" give only an approximation to the cusp, not a rigorous determination.

[Regiomontanus and the Birthplace System of Houses]
Göppingen: Siriusverlag Dr. W. Koch, 1960.

Koch, Walter & Schäck, Elisabeth
Häusertabellen des Geburtsortes für 45°-56° Nördliche Breite.
Göppingen: Siriusverlag Dr. W. Koch, 1962.
[tables for additional latitudes were published by Schäck in
1965]

von Kloeckler

Herbert, Baron von Kloeckler, M.D. (1896-1950), was a medical
doctor and astrologer. An assiduous investigator of astrological techniques, he tested and discarded many features of "traditional astrology."
He is best known in English-speaking countries for his monograph *Astrology and Vocational Aptitude* (Washington: The National Astrological Library, 1974), which was based on his own studies of actual horoscopes
rather than upon tradition or theory. His *Course of Astrology* and his other
works have unfortunately not been translated into English.

Berufsbegabung und Schiksal.
[Vocational Aptitude and Destiny]
Leipzig, 1928. 1st ed.

Kloeckler, Herbert und Beckerath, Erich
Kursus der Astrologie.
[Course of Astrology]
consisting of:
1. Lehrbuch der astrologischen Technik....
[Textbook of the Technique of Astrology....]
1984. 8th ed.
2. Grundlagen für die astrologischen Deutung.
[Fundamental Principles of Astrological Interpretation]
1984. 7th ed.
3. Solarhoroskop, Transite und aktuelle
Konstellationen in ihrer Bedeutung für die astrologischen
Prognose.
[Solar Returns, Transits, and Current Configurations: their Significance for Astrological Forecasting]
1981. 6th ed.
Freiburg: Hermann Bauer Verlag, 1981-1984.

Kühr

E(rich) K(arl) Kühr (1899-1951). According to a poll taken in 1949,
Kühr was considered to be the best contemporary German astrologer. He
followed the principles of delineation prescribed by J.B. Morin and was a
specialist in Placidian primary directions. His principal books are these:

Berechnung der Ereigniszeiten.
[Calculation of the Time of Events]
Görlitz: Regulus Verlag, 1936. 388 pp.

Die psychologische Horoskopedeutung
[The Psychological Interpretation of the Horoscope]
Vienna, 1948-51. 2 vols.
Aspekt-Analyse.
[Aspect Analysis]
Görlitz, 1929.

Reinhold Ebertin and Cosmobiology

Reinhold Ebertin (1901-1988). Son of the well-known German astrologer **Elsbeth Ebertin** (1880-1944) and founder of the midpoint system known as Cosmobiology, a bare-bones version of the astrology of the Hamburg School. His system, which ignores the houses and does not use any hypothetical planets, is thus much simpler than its predecessor and has consequently enjoyed more widespread popularity. Ebertin wrote some sixty books on Cosmobiology and also issued a periodical, *Mensch im All* (later called *Cosmobiologie*). His fundamental book is *Kombination der Gestirneinflüsse* or *The Combination of Stellar Influences* in its English version (Aalen: Ebertin Verlag, 1972. 3rd ed.), but several others are also available in English. Since his death, his son **Dr. Baldur Ebertin** has succeeded him as the leader of the Cosmobiology school.

Parm

Heinrich Christian Meier (-Parm) (1905-after 1968). A prominent German astrologer who opposed Dr. Korsch's faction of astrologers in the early 1930s. Parm theorized that transits would only be effective when the transiting planets themselves formed patterns similar to those in the horoscope and simultaneously aspected the natal configurations. This led him to classify horoscopes into three basic types: (1) "harmonic," where the planets are scattered around the chart; (2) "opposition," where some planets are on one side of the chart, and the others are on the other side: and (3) "conjunction figure," where all the planets are within one arc of 180° or less. He was also a pioneer in the consideration of asteroid positions in horoscopes, having investigated the influence of the asteroid Vesta (the only one for which tables were available at the time). See his book, *Der Planetoid Vesta* 'The Planetoid Vesta' (Aalen: Ebertin Verlag, 1974).

Troinski

E(dmund) H(erbert) Troinski (b. 1910) was particularly interested in mundane astrology and published some indications of the possible outbreak of a third world war in the 1960s in his book, *1001 weltpolitische Horoskope* '1,001 Mundane Horoscopes' (Warpke-Billerbeck:

Baumgartner Verlag, 1955). Fortunately, his vision of the future was incorrect, and a "cold war" ensued rather than an "atom-bomb war." However, his book is a gold mine of mundane astrological data. Troinski was also a prominent advocate of tertiary directions in natal astrology (see Edward Lyndoe's *Astrology for Everyone*).

Marr

Alexander Marr (1919-2002) was an intelligence officer and a decoder in the German military during World War II. In his astrological work he adopted the Topocentric House system of A.P. Nelson Page and Vendel Polich (see below) and specialized, as its inventors intended, in primary directions to indicate precisely-timed events in a person's life rather than vague psychological tendencies and periods. Marr's books on natal astrology contain many examples of the elaborate calculations that can be made using the Topocentric methods. Some of his books that are available in English are: *Prediction I* (19 82), *Prediction II* (1985), *Prediction III* (1986), all published at Tempe, Az., by A.F.A., Inc., and *Political Astrology* (Buenos Aires: Ediciones Sirio, 1988).

Taeger's Horoscope Lexicon

Hans-Hinrich Taeger is the author of the most extensive collection of horoscopes ever published in book format—6,000 charts with sources and brief comments, *Internationale horoskopisches Lexikon* (Freiburg im Breisgau: Hermann Bauer Verlag, 1991-1992. 3 vols.). This is an excellent set, very well organized and nicely printed, with extensive documentation of sources.

Astrology in Hungary

As in all the eastern European countries, astrology was suppressed from the time of World War II until the fateful year of 1989. With the liberalization of the government and social conditions within the country, astrologers became able for the first time in five decades to practice their art openly and to meet together. One manifestation of this new era was the organization of the Baktay Erwin Astrologiai Egyesület 'Erwin Baktay Astrological Society', which was named in honor of the Hungarian scientist, writer, and astrologer, **Dr. Erwin Baktay** (b. 1890).[101] Dr. Baktay was a native of Dunaharaszti, Hungary, where today the local grammar school is named for him. He told his astrological students that he had had good success in using the Glahn Life Circle. Dr. Baktay was well-known among Hungarian astrologers and was the author of an astrological textbook:

A Csillagfejtes Könyve/
Az asztrológia elmélete és gyakorlata.

---

[101] I wish to thank my friend Theodore Kritza of Budapest for furnishing me the information on Dr. Baktay.

[The Book of the Interpretation of the Stars/
The theory and practice of astrology]
Budapest: The Author, c. 1935. 1st ed.
Debrecen: Szépirodalmi Könyvkiado, 1989.

Astrology in the Netherlands

Dutch astrology came to life about the same time as German astrology. From the outset it was closely allied with Theosophy. Some of its leading astrologers and their works **Dr. A.E. Thierens**, *Elements of Esoteric Astrology* (Philadelphia: David McKay, 1931), **Else Parker**, *Astrology and its Value for Living* (Amersfort: P. Dz. Veen, 1924), and an unidentified astrologer who wrote under the pseudonym, **C.A. Libra**, *Cosmos en Microcosmos* (Amersfort: P. Dz. Veen, 1915).

Hamaker-Zondag

Among the contemporary Dutch astrologers is the well-known Jungian psychologist and astrologer, **Karen Hamaker-Zondag** (b. 1952), whose books have been translated into several languages. A few of the English titles are:

Astro-Psychology.
Amsterdam: Schors, 1980.

Elements & Crosses as the Basis of the Horoscope.
Amsterdam: Schors, 1984.

Planetary Symbolism in the Horoscope.
Amsterdam: Schors, 1985.

Astrology in Austria
Sindbad the Sailor

Austria was the home of several well-known astrologers in the 20th century. The first was **Capt. Friedrich Schwickert** (1857-1930), an officer of the Austrian Navy, who wrote under the pseudonym **Sindbad**. With his colleague **Adolf Weiss**, M.D. (b. 1888), he wrote *Bausteine der Astrologie* [Building-stones of Astrology] (Leipzig, 1925-27) 5 vols. Dr. Weiss fled Austria at the outbreak of World War II and settled first in Spain, where he issued a Spanish version of *Bausteine*, then he removed to Buenos Aires. Vol. 2 of the Spanish version of this series was translated into English and published as *Cornerstones of Astrology* (Dallas: Sangreal Foundation, 1972).

Knappich

Wilhelm Knappich (1880-1970) was a librarian in Vienna and a prominent astrologer. In my opinion, his book *Geschichte der Astrologie* (Frankfurt-am-Main: Vittorio Klostermann, 1967; reprinted with a new preface by Bernward Thiel and some additions to the bibliography, 1988) is the best general history of astrology that has been written so far. It is illustrated with portraits of Kepler, Cardan, Junctinus, Magini, and Placidus, among others. There is a French translation, but unfortunately the book is not yet available in English.

Gustav Schwickert

Capt. Gustav Schwickert (1885-1964) lived at Graz and presided over a large study group. One of his books was translated into English by Eugene Dernay as *Rectification of the Birthtime* (Washington: National Astrological Library, 1954). Schwickert was convinced that only the Regiomontanus method of house division was correct.

Countess Wassilko-Serecki

Zoë, Countess Wassilko-Serecki, (1897-1978) was the leading figure in Austrian astrology during the post-World War II years. She was a dedicated teacher of classical astrology, author of a number of astrological works, and president of the Austrian Astrological Society (Ö.A.G.) for many years from 1947.

Belcsák

Sándor Belcsák (b. 1938), a native of Budapest, emigrated to Austria, where he became the president of the Austrian Astrological Association (Ö.A.G.) and editor of the periodical *Qualität der Zeit*. He edited the special memorial publication dedicated to the life of Countess Wassilko-Serecki in 1987.

Astrology in Switzerland

Jung

The Swiss psychologist **Carl Gustav Jung** (1875-1961), the founder of analytic psychology and the introvert/extrovert characterization of personality, gladdened the hearts of astrologers by taking an interest in their subject. Since he later became interested in what he called "archetypes," he reasoned that the astrological characterizations of planets and signs might be worth investigating. He also performed an experiment in which he studied the horoscopes of marriage couples.

By taking up these studies, Jung lent some academic sanction for his followers to look into astrology. Some have done so, although they do not always make their interest known. Psychology and astrology have a good bit in common, although astrology is a broader science than psychology. Both are what we might call "word sciences," i.e. they work mainly with words rather than with numbers.[102] However, there is a continuing prob-

---

[102]This statement is not altered by the fact that much psychological research is undertaken as statistical "experiments." The purpose of these is to discover correlations and amass psychological data. But the interpretation and practical use of the data is a verbal process.

lem with trying to blend psychology with astrology—the basic elements as well as the established terminology are different. This makes it difficult to convert the concepts of one science into those of the other. Nevertheless, the task appeals to some individuals, especially to those who view astrology mainly as a means for enriching human understanding rather than as a divinatory art.

Jung investigated many things, and astrology was only one of these. Perhaps it would be adequate to say that, unlike most academics, he thought astrology was worth looking into.

Dr. Fankhauser

Dr. Alfred Fankhauser, Ph.D. (1890-1973) was a native of Bern and leading figure in the modern revival of astrology in Switzerland. His books have been characterized as "synthetic but good." The best known are:

> Das wahre Gesicht der Astrologie.
> [The True View of Astrology]
> Zürich/Leipzig: Orell Fussli, 1932.
> Astrologie als kosmische Psychologie.
> [Astrology as Cosmic Psychology]
> Bern: Pestalozzi-Fellenberg-Haus, 1927. viii, 257 pp.

Krafft

Karl Ernst Krafft (1900-1945) was a pioneer in astrological statistics. He collected a large number of timed birthdates from the Swiss civil registers and conducted many statistical studies on these and on other data that he had collected. He tried to interest both Swiss and English universities in a doctorate program that would set forth his data and findings, but they all declined. In the late 1930s he became disgusted with the situation in his native Switzerland and made what turned out to be a fatal tactical error—he moved to Germany. There he pursued his astrological activities and, with the assistance of two colleagues, gathered his studies into a book:

> Krafft, K.E., Budai, Dr. E., & Ferrière, Ad.
> Le premier traité d'astrobiologie.
> [The First Treatise on Astrobiology]
> Paris: Amédée Legrand, 1939.

Krafft offered his astrological services to the German government, but instead of being taken on as a counselor, he was assigned to write astrological and pseudo-prophetic material that could be used by the Propaganda Ministry. He apparently was never trusted, and along with most of the other German astrologers he was "detained" by the government and finally died in custody, probably from poor treatment, not quite four months before the fall of Nazi Germany.

In statistical research, Krafft was the successor to the French astrologer Paul Choisnard, and he himself was succeeded in the post-war period by another Frenchman, Michel Gauquelin.

Kündig

Heinrich Kündig (b. 1909), an expert on Placidian techniques, was the author of three parts of the six-volume work, *Astrologica* (Zurich, 1949-1953), along with A. Rosenberg and N. Sementowsky-Kurilo (see below).

Ring

Thomas Ring (1892-1983) was well trained in both psychology and astrology and was therefore able to translate astrological concepts into psychological terms, which made a good impression on the psychologists with whom he came into contact. In particular, he worked with Prof. Hans Bender (1907-1991) at the Institue for the Border Areas of Psychology at Freiburg im Breisgau.[103] His books are written in Schwyzer Deutsch and have not yet been translated.

Das Sonnesystem, ein Organismus.
[The Solar System, an Organism]
Stuttgart/Berlin: Deutsche Verlagsanstalt, 1939.

Astrologische Menschenkunde.
[Astrological Anthropology]
consisting of:
1. Kräfte und Kräftebeziehungen. 1956. xii,296 pp. with a preface by Hans Bender
[Strengths and Relationships of Strengths]
2. Ausdruck und Richtung der Kräfte. 1959. xii,355 pp.
[Expression and Direction of the Strengths]
3. Kombinationslehre. 1969. 549 pp.
[Effects of the Combinations]
Zürich: Rascher Verlag, 1956-69. 3 vols.

Existenz und Wesen in kosmologischer Sicht.
[Existence and Being from a Cosmological Viewpoint]
Freiburg im Breisgau: Aurum Verlag, 1975.

Der Kosmos in uns.
[The Cosmos Within Us]
Freiburg im Breisgau: Aurum Verlag, 1979. 2nd ed.

---

[103]See Ellic Howe, *Astrology*, pp. 244-245.

The Hubers

Bruno Huber (b. 1930), a native of Zürich, and his German-born wife **Louise Huber** (b. 1924) are the proprietors of the well-known Swiss School of Astrology. Both of them were trained in psychosynthesis by the Italian psychologist Roberto Assagioli and have blended his training with astrological techniques. Students have flocked to their school from all over the world. They have invented the Life Clock, a symbolic progression that begins at the ASC and moves counter-clockwise through the houses at the rate of 6° per house. At the end of 72 years, "things start over." The Hubers have attended many astrological conferences in other countries and are thus well-known throughout the Western world. Some of their books are:

Man and His World
New York: Samuel Weiser, 1978.

Lebensuhr im Horoskop.
[The Life Clock in the Horoscope]
Zürich, 1980-1985. 3 vols.
Life Clock.
York Beach, Maine: Samuel Weiser, 1994. rev. ed. publ. in one volume

Astrology in Italy

Among the better-known Italian astrologers of the 20th century we may mention the following:

Adriano Carelli

Adriano Carelli, B.A. (1908-1998), better known to the European astrological public as **André L'Eclair**, was born in St. Petersburg, Russia, where his father was a music and artistic director employed by Tsar Nicholas II (1868-1918). He returned to Italy with his family before the outbreak of World War I, and, after having obtained his degree in law, entered government service as an archivist. During World War II he served as a translator, after which he resumed his work in the archives until his retirement in 1966.

Carelli was an occultist as well as an astrologer; as such he has published a series of *Nove lettere astrologiche ad un antroposofo* 'Nine Astrological Letters to an Anthroposophist' (Spoleto: Spoleto Libri, 1990). In the first of these he says:

> To know the rising sign is to have determined 40% of the
> subject's temperament; to know the exact degree of the
> ASC permits us to draw a true and proper psychological
> portrait. All the other factors of the chart (i.e. of the map
> of the sky at birth) are not only secondary with respect to

the sign and the degree of the ascendant; but indeed, if at least the *sign* of the ASC cannot be known, then all the rest counts for nothing.

His best known work in the English-speaking world is his characterization of the individual degrees of the zodiac. In the preface to his book he reviews the writings of previous authors on this subject.[104] Carelli's book characterizes each degree and gives one or more examples of its occupancy by a planet, the ASC, or the MC, in the chart of some well-known personage.

> The 360 Degrees of the Zodiac.
> Washington: A.F.A., Inc., 1951. 1st ed.
> Tempe, Az.: A.F.A., Inc., 1977. repr.

Capone

Federico Capone (1923-2001) was one of the founders of the CIDA, a director of its quarterly *Linguaggio Astrale*, and the author of a number of books on astrology, one of which is an ephemeris for the years 1700-1800.

Ghivarelli

Sergio Ghivarelli (b. 1926) is an authority on the philosophy of astrology and the author of works on esotericism and on the structure of astrological thought both ancient and modern.

Sementowsky-Kurilo

Nicola Sementowsky-Kurilo (1901-1979) was the author of *Astrologia/ Trattato Completo Teorico-Pratico* 'Astrology: A Complete Theoretical and Practical Treatise' (Milan: Ulrico Hoepli, 1972. 3rd ed. revised), a large comprehensive work covering the history and philosophy of astrology, the fundamentals of astrology, interpretation of natal horoscopes, a set of house tables for Rome-Naples and for Milan, and abbreviated ephemerides for 1890-1972 (daily for the Sun, at 8-day intervals for the Moon, and 5-day intervals for the planets and the Moon's node). This was an important book during the author's lifetime, but its popularity has slowly decreased in recent years.

One interesting feature of the book is what he calls Secondary Types—132 of the 144 possible combinations of the ASC sign and the Sun sign (he omits the cases where the signs are the same, since these are "pure" types of the signs). In some cases he gives references to other numbered interpretations in his book. Unlike some recent publications in the English language, these interpretations vary considerably in length. Here is one combination chosen at random:

> ASC Virgo/Sun Aquarius. The nature of the Virgo type

---

[104] See above under the heading "Degree Symbolism."

appears here again greatly accentuated. Since the position of the Sun in the sixth house in the sign Aquarius indicates the sense of a wearying and usually fruitless research for sympathetic persons, these individuals have to prepare themselves to confront the greatest difficulty and equally great obstacles; often, they do not quite succeed in creating a solid base of existence, either from the sentimental point of view or from the professional. At times—especially if it is a case of men—they have to suffer the fate of subdued victims from persons deprived of affection, preoccupied solely with safeguarding their own interests. As far as the health is concerned, ailments of lengthy duration are probable, for the most part incurable, that are primarily related to the circulation of the blood and to the metabolism. Lesions to the brain and to the spine are also noticed, especially if such planets as Mars, Saturn, or Neptune are in the twelfth house in the sign Leo.

Brunini

Angelo Brunini was a well-known esotericist and author of the best-seller *L'avvenire non è un Mistero* 'The Future is No Mystery' (Cassino, 1964).

Morpurgo

Lisa Morpurgo is the author of numerous astrological works. An innovative astrologer, she has a large following in Italy. Her fundamental work is her *Introduzione all'Astrologia e decifrazione dello Zodiaco* (Milan, 1972), which has run through many editions. Among her other books are treatises on the houses, the planets, and on transits.

Bordoni

Grazia Bordoni (b. 1945) is a prominent data-collector who has published a number of extensive collections of birth data from authentic sources. She offers her data on-line by subscription.

Dati di nascita interesanti.
[Interesting Birthdates]
Turin: C.I.D.A., 5 vols.

Mirti

Grazia Mirti is the former editor of the prestigious astrological quarterly *Linguaggio Astrale* published by the Centro Italiano di Astrologia (C.I.D.A.). She teaches astrology, writes a regular astrological column for the newspaper *Il Giornale*, is the author of a number of books, and has also published important historical material relating to the astrological activities of Galileo Galilei (1564-1642), including facsimiles from a private book kept by Galileo in which he had drawn the horoscopes of his children.

Bezza

Giuseppe Bezza (b.c. 1955) is a student of ancient and medieval astrology. He has translated some of the classic works into Italian and published a fine commentary on Ptolemy's *Tetrabiblos*. Bezza is the author of an extensive and excellent anthology of ancient and medieval astrological works, *Arcana Mundi* (Milan, 1995). 2 vols. boxed 1148 pp.

Astrology in Greece

Most of Greece was under foreign rule from the 12th century on, culminating with the Turkish domination from 1452 until 1821. Apparently astrology was not particularly studied or practiced then. And even after 1821 there was little stimulus to revive it. Consider that in the early 1930s some Greek newspapers were reporting astrology as "a magic art practiced by natives in Africa"! In 1936, the German-raised Greek engineer Peter Gravinger wrote a book entitled *Praktikon Enchiridion Astrologias* 'Practical Handbook of Scientific Astrology', much advanced for those days and largely unnoticed. It would be in the late 1950s before we began to see Sun-sign forecasts appearing in some popular magazines and newspapers.

But the true revival of astrology in Greece came about through the efforts of a lady named **Maria Metallinou** (1928-1974). In her youth she had become interested in astrology, and she maintained that interest through her polytechnic studies in northern Europe. She and her collaborator **Theodora Dakou** (b. 1942) took lessons at the Faculty of Astrological Studies, having as their tutor the legendary Charles E.O. Carter. Back in Greece, Metallinou and Dakou, possessing no ephemeris, contacted in the middle 1960s the director of the Athens Astronomical Observatory, **Konstantinos S. Chasapes** (1914-1972), who had a secret flair for astrology. He assisted them much with their calculations and interpretations! In 1969, Metallinou founded *Oroscopio*, the first astrological magazine in Greece. However, her untimely death caused the magazine's demise. Subsequently, Theodora Dakou founded the Ouranos Astrological Society, and in 1975 she published a quality astrological magazine named *Ouranos* that lasted until 1982. In 1980, she organized a pan-Mediterranean (F.I.M.A.) astrology conference in Athens.

In later years, astrologers **Thomas Gazis** and **Maro Ioannidou** organized two international conferences in Greece (Astromykonos 2000, featuring Robert Hand, and Astromykonos 2001, featuring Noel Tyl and Elizabeth Tessier). They also originated the idea (together with the Spanish astrologer Ernesto Cordero) for the formation of the F.A.E.S. (South European Astrology Confederation), which they promoted with other South-European colleagues. Thomas Gazis has lectured extensively in

Europe and has published a book in English. Today there are five astrology magazines being published in Greece, but commercial astrologers still dominate the scene, leaving little room for quality astrologers. The fact that no formal Federation of Greek astrologers has yet been established says it all!

Astrology in Some Other Countries

In this section I have placed some notes on astrological history, on individual astrologers, and astrological trends in a few other countries around the world. These are not intended to give a complete picture of the activity in those countries, but merely to mention some items of particular interest. Each country has its own astrological history, and we must depend on the national astrological historians to give a full account at some future date.

Argentina

In Argentina two immigrants, **A(nthony) P. Nelson Page** (1919-1970) and **Vendel Polich** (1892-1980), developed a new system of house division and primary directions, the Topocentric System. Unlike any previous system, Page and Polich derived their system from very precisely timed events. The mathematical basis of the house division is similar to that of Placidus and yields intermediate cusps that differ little from Placidus cusps in low and moderate latitudes, but differ increasingly as the latitude increases. Their aim, which they claim to have achieved, was to create a system that permitted precise prediction of events to the day or even to the hour. The system is set forth in English in Polich's book *The Topocentric System with Tables of Houses. . . .* (Buenos Aires: Editorial Regulus, 1975). Many examples are included.

The principal teacher and promoter of Argentine astrology in the 1970s and 1980s was the late **Eloy Ricardo Dumon** (1925-1991). He served as president of the Fundacion Centro Astrológico in Buenos Aires from 1965 until his death and was also editor of its journal *Astrologia*.

Australia
Zariel

In the early 1900s, **David Cope (Zariel)** proposed what amounts to a modification of the Morinus system of house division. It did not catch on but was later revived by the American astrologers Bruce Lloyd and Garth Allen under the name "Axial Rotation System." It again failed to find favor. The system is described by Ralph William Holden in his *The Elements of House Division*.

Kozminsky

Isidore Kozminsky wrote several books on numbers, precious stones, and the history of astrology, but he is best known today for his book:

Zodiacal Symbology and its Planetary Power.
[contains individual degree interpretations]
London: William Rider & Son, 1917.

De Dion

Arthur De Dion was a prominent Australian astrologer and teacher of astrology.

Furze-Morrish

L. Furze-Morrish in his younger days was an officer in the British field artillery (cf. Paul Choisnard). He practiced astrology professionally for more than forty years, and, like Choisnard, applied statistical analysis to astrology. Some of his research papers were published in American journals. He has written these books:

Outline of Astro-Psychology.
London: Rider & Co., 1952.

The Parallel in Astrology.
Seattle: Vulcan Books, 1974.

Furze-Morrish, L. & Kent, R.
Preliminary Investigation of Correlation between Celestial Patterns and Human Intelligence.
?: The Authors, 1973.

Greaves

Doris Greaves (b. 1919). Prominent Australian astrologer. Founder of the Federation of Australian Astrologers (FAA). She became interested in astrology in her teens and turned to it as a full-time occupation in her later years. Having become dissatisfied with standard horoscopes and the uncertainty about house systems, she tried Cosmobiology and found it more satisfactory. She has since become a leading exponent of that system of astrology. She also uses heliocentric positions and tertiary progressions. In an interview published some years ago she emphasized that "astrology was meant to predict the future and 90% of today's astrologers do not do this." She also cautioned against depending too much upon computers, especially without a basic understanding of chart calculation.[105]

Brazil

There is much interest in astrology in Brazil, and an outstanding series of publications is coming from that country. The late **James Martin Harvey** (1904-1993) was an astute and careful researcher into the birthdata of prominent people of the past. In addition to his articles written

---

[105]See the article "Doris Greaves, In Celebration" in the FAA *Journal* 17:2 (June 1987) for further details.

for the astrological magazines and the assistance he gave to other researchers, he kept a detailed notebook of his findings. Following his death, a memorial institution was established in São Paulo to propagate his work—TRIOM Centro de Estudos Marina e Martin Harvey. It has since begun to publish his notebooks in facsimile. These contain the results of his penetrating research into early books, archives, and original documents, as well as the horoscopes he drew and his own acute astrological observations on the charts. Three splendidly printed volumes have appeared so far:

James Martin Harvey
Nativitas. Astrological Studies
[with a prefatory essay by the author, entitled "Memories"]
São Paulo: TRIOM, 1992. vol. 1 4to. 190 pp. portrs.

James Martin Harvey
Nativitas. Astrological Studies.
[with a lecture "Astrology Pro and Con" delivered
to the Brazilian Society of English Culture in the 1960s]
São Paulo: TRIOM, 1993. vol 2 4to. 286 pp. portrs.

James Martin Harvey
Nativitas, Astrological Studies.
[with a preface by the author, entitled
"historical Nativities"]
São Paulo: TRIOM, 1997, vol. 3 4to 302 pp. diagrs.

Japan

Japanese astrology was in the Buddhist tradition until Western astrology as set forth by the English astrologer Sepharial was introduced into Japan by **Yushou Kumamoto** in 1914. Since that time, the trend has been to Western astrology. **H.M. "Gen" Ishikawa** (1921-2006), a retired electronics engineer and astrologer, worked in the Western tradition. He was a leader in modern Japanese astrology and a frequent visitor to the U.S. Mr. Ishikawa was a member of the Astrological Association in England. He was also a director of the American Federation of Astrologers and was the first member to join its Research Section when it was organized in 1981. Mr. Ishikawa was a frequent attendee and a lecturer at the AFA's biennial conventions. In Japan he published an astrological periodical, published a general textbook on astrology, and presided over a school of astrology. Living in an earthquake-prone country, he studied the incidence of earthquakes and their relationship to astrological factors, including the asteroid Juno.[106] He also wrote a book on a further development of Addey's Har-

---

[106]See his paper "Juno and Earthquakes" in the AFA *Journal of Research* 5, No. 1 (1989): 11-22.

monics:
Divisional Harmonics.
Tempe, Az.: A.F.A., Inc., 1984.

Ishikawa Genkou
Ensyuu Senseigaku Nyumon.
[in Japanese]
Tokyo: Hirakawa Publ. Co., 1992. paper. 246 pp.

Portugal

The Portugese astrologers Helena Avelar (b. 1964) and Luís Ribeiro (b. 1974) are interested in the history of astrology in their country. After diligent research into old books and documentary records, they have published a most excellent book containing the horoscopes of all the kings and queens of Portugal from Alphonso Henriques, the Conqueror (1109-1185) down to the last king, the unfortunate Manuel II (1889-1932).

The book is beautifully designed with horoscope diagrams and portraists of the monarchs. At the end the authors have added astrological notes, a bibliography, a list of sources, and a glossary of astrological terms.

Astrologia Real
A História de Portugal
à Luz da Astrologia
Cascais: Pergaminho, 2004. 279 pp.

Spain

There is much astrological activity in Spain with several magazines, among them Mercurio, and frequent conferences drawing attendes from all countries. The dean of the Spanish astrologers is Demetrio Santos (b.c. 1930). He has translated a number of medieval Latin astrological texts into Spanish, and he has also written a valuable historical work, Introduccion a la historia de la astrologia (Barcelona: Edicomunicación, 1986.

Some Remarks on Astrology

First, horoscopic astrology itself has little or nothing to do with religion.[1] It was not "revealed" in remote antiquity to priests of a particular religion or to leaders of mystical societies by divinities or "transcendental masters." It is not "occult" in the usual sense of the word. It is a clear-cut empirical science that was invented by human beings and that operates on the basis of definite rules that have been established by experience.

There is no essential conflict between astrology and religion unless the particular religion considers it impossible or blasphemous for anyone except a divinity (or an authorized prophet) to predict the future. Astrology does predict the future, but so do meteorology and economics and medicine and other sciences. Therefore, if it is irreligious for an astrologer to give a forecast, it is also irreligious for a weatherman to say it is going to rain, for an economist to predict a recession, or for a physician to issue a prognosis for a particular patient.

Throughout the ages some people who were devotees of a particular philosophy or religion, and some who practiced magic have also been interested in astrology. But this does not mean that astrology itself has anything to do with religion or magic, or, for that matter, with "New Age thought."[2]

---

[1] I mean by this that astrology itself is merely a set of rules by means of which astrologers interpret the astronomical configurations that are seen from a point on the earth's surface. As such, it is independent of religion and independent of philosophy. There has been and will continue to be much squabbling over "world views" and the philosophical framework and justification for the existence of a divinatory art, but the art itself is simply a set of rules, no more religious or mystical than those of algebra.

[2] In India, of course, the situation is different, since there is no conflict between

The earliest Greek and Roman astrological treatises that have been preserved occasionally mention that certain configurations in a horoscope indicate that the native (the person whose horoscope it is) will be a criminal or will be immoral or will be opposed to the gods. But that is as far as they go. There are no praises for a particular religion (or for any religion). The early astrologers were evidently moral people by the standards of their own culture, and they decried immorality and criminality, but that's it!

Second, astrology is based on observed correlations between horoscopes and human behavior. Anyone who studies the subject soon learns that a horoscope can give a fairly accurate description of the native's personality and behavior. An example: If you find in a man's horoscope that he has the Sun conjunct, square, or opposition Mars, then don't annoy that man and make him mad. He may hit you! In other words, his natural reaction to annoyance is forceful reprisal. However, this may have been modified by his rearing and cultural circumstances: if he was trained from birth to avoid violence, then he will want to hit you, but he may restrain himself (and get very frustrated); if he had an ordinary bringing-up, he may very well hit you; if he was reared or lives in a violent social environment, he may kill you if he has a deadly weapon handy. A woman may display the same tendency but with less violence. Why is this true? Astrologers don't know, but they see it happen over and over again in verification of the rule. Theoretically it makes sense, since Mars was the god of war.

Astrology cannot predict that a particular man will be rich or poor or great or humble except in relative terms. In a large city such as New York the child of a wealthy banker and the child of a poor welfare mother might be born at about the same time, so that their horoscopes are nearly identical. If the chart shows financial success, then the banker's child will in time become richer than his father, while the welfare mother's child may get a steady job and get off of welfare—in both cases the chart shows an *improvement* of financial status, not simply "he will be rich" in an absolute sense.

In the case of people like Napoleon, or Mussolini, or Hitler (or, to mention a more reputable character, George Washington), we cannot look at their charts and say that they will advance to become leaders of their nation (or of another nation). We can see in the chart that they will be successful in public life, but not that they will achieve the maximum possible success. There may be a way to predict such a big jump in social position, but astrologers haven't figured out yet how to do it. Still, there is no question that all four of those horoscopes showed success in public life and therefore necessarily an advancement from the social condition into

_____

astrology and religion. And in the Western world there are some astrologers who speak of "karma," which implies a vague belief in reincarnation, but this comes from an Eastern philosophical belief that they have adopted, not from Western astrology itself.

which the natives were born.

Similar considerations apply to the charts of men and women. In time of war, men are much more likely to be killed than women because they make up the warrior class. And in peacetime men and women live somewhat different lives (less so today than formerly, but still different). We cannot read sex in a horoscope, but we can say that a particular chart is more "masculine" or "feminine" in nature. Some geneticists have recently asserted that male homosexuals appear to have a distinctive genetic pattern. If this is true, then they may constitute a sort of third sex (and female homosexuals a fourth sex?), in which case we could no more expect to find a horoscopic indicator of homosexuality than we could expect to find an indicator of ordinary masculinity or femininity.

The famous American astrologer Evangeline Adams (1868-1932) tells an interesting story in her autobiography. The gist of it is this: a woman brought her a horoscope, which Miss Adams assumed was that of a child, and asked for a life reading (a character analysis and general prospects for the future). Miss Adams looked at the chart and said that the individual would be born in a slum but would advance to living in luxury. He would profit greatly from some woman. He would be intelligent but wouldn't read many books. He might be an actor and he might travel a lot. And he would live to a ripe, old age.

After having delivered these opinions, she was told that the birthdata was that of the pet dog of a well-known stage actress of the day. Well, it turned out that the actress had bought the dog from a man in a poor section of New York City. She had taught it tricks. It appeared on stage with her in one of her successful plays on Broadway. It accompanied her when the play went on tour. It certainly didn't read many books. And when Miss Adams wrote this account a decade and a half later, she said the dog was by then 18-years-old, which is of course old for a dog. Thus, the horoscopic indications fit the native (in this case a dog) as well as they could considering the circumstances.

Claudius Ptolemy put it all very well 1,800 years ago[3]:

> But in an inquiry concerning nativities and individual temperaments in general, one can see that there are circumstances of no small importance and of no trifling character, which join to cause the special qualities of those who are born. For differences of seed exert a very great influence on the special traits of the genus, since, if the ambient and the horizon[4] are the same, each seed prevails to express in general its own form, for example, man, horse, and so forth; and the places of birth bring about no small variation in what is produced. For if the seed is generically the same,

---

[3]*Tetrabiblos*, i. 2 (Robbins's translation).
[4]That is the planetary positions and their arrangement in the celestial houses.

279

human for example, and the condition of the ambient the same, those who are born differ much, both in body and soul, with the difference of countries. In addition to this, all the aforesaid conditions being equal, rearing and customs contribute to influence the particular way in which a life is lived. Unless each one of these things is examined together with the causes that are derived from the ambient, although this latter be conceded to exercise the greatest influence (for the ambient is one of the causes for these things being what they are, while they in turn have no influence upon it), they can cause much difficulty for those who believe that in such cases everything can be understood, even things not wholly within its jurisdiction, from the motion of the heavenly bodies alone.

Since this is the case, it would not be fitting to dismiss all prognostication of this character because it can sometimes be mistaken, for we do not discredit the art of the pilot for its many errors; but as when the claims are great, so also when they are divine, we should welcome what is possible and think it enough. Nor further, should we gropingly and in human fashion demand everything of the art, but rather join in the appreciation of its beauty, even in instances wherein it could not provide the full answer; and as we do not find fault with the physicians, when they examine a person, for speaking both about the sickness itself and about the patient's idiosyncrasy, so too in this case, we should not object to astrologers using as a basis for calculation nationality, country, and rearing, or any other already existing accidental qualities.

Newspaper Astrology—The Daily Guides

These are obviously general in nature. They are constructed in this manner: For each day, the astrologer in effect draws 12 charts, one with each of the signs of the zodiac on the first house. Then he notes the positions of the transiting planets (their current positions on that day). The same sign positions and aspects will appear in all twelve charts, but in different houses! This affects the way in which the positions will work out. For example if there is a bad influence in Gemini and it falls in the first house, it will affect the Gemini native personally; in the second house it will cause some financial problems for the Taurus native; in the third house, for the Aries native, it will cause some difficulty with siblings, with neighbors, or with communications ("You may get an unpleasant phone call" or "A letter may bring unsettling news"); in the fourth house, for Pisces natives, disturbance in the home or in relations with parents, etc.

Obviously these are very general indications based on nothing more than the house positions of the transiting planets. And they are usually given and read as solar house positions (measured from the native's Sun sign), although they work better if the native reads the paragraph for his rising sign. (But most people do not know their rising sign.) This is a far cry from a forecast based on your actual horoscope, just as those little psychological quizzes that appear in popular magazines from time to time that purport to give you a psychological profile based on your answers to a series of questions are a far cry from a personal analysis by a psychologist. In both cases, however, they are not wrong, but merely incomplete and more general.

Different Kinds of Astrology

Just as there are different kinds of physicians, different kinds of psychologists, and different kinds of economists, so there are different kinds of astrologers. Hindu astrology and Chinese astrology are both quite different from Western astrology. And among Western astrologers there are some who employ techniques that differ from those used by traditional or mainstream astrologers. Probably eighty percent or more of Western astrologers could be described as "traditional," which is to say that their main techniques are ultimately derived from those developed by the Alexandrian inventors of horoscopic astrology and refined by subsequent generations of Western astrologers.

The next most numerous group are the astrologers of the Hamburg (Germany) School and the Cosmobiologists. These astrologers use *midpoints* as their principal tool in analyzing charts. A midpoint is a point in the zodiac that is half way between two planets (or between a planet and the ascending or Midheaven degree). Suppose, for example that the Sun is in 20 Aries and Mars is in 28 Gemini. The distance between these bodies is 68 degrees. Take half of that and add it to the first body: 20 Aries + 34° = 54° Aries, which is of course 24 Taurus. The midpoint of Sun and Mars (usually written Sun/Mars) is 24 Taurus. This is assumed to be a point to which both of its components contribute their individual influences, and it is also a point that is sensitive to the presence of another planet.

The astrologer who uses midpoints makes an elaborate table of them and then notes the aspects that other planets make to them. This gives three-planet combinations (called "planetary pictures" by the Hamburg school practicioners) which are then looked up in the *Rule Book for Planetary Pictures* or (in the case of Cosmobiologists) *The Combination of Stellar Influences* that explains the signification attached to each combination. Astrologers who use these techniques typically ignore some other traditional techniques. This was a German invention of the 1920s that hasn't really caught on, although it has some enthusiastic devotees in Germany and in other countries around the world.

The astrologers of the Hamburg school use eight hypothetical "trans-Neptunian planets" that were postulated to exist by the founder and one of his associates. The Cosmobiologists reject these "trans-Neptunians," and they also claim to have refined the midpoint interpretations of the Hamburg School. At the present time Cosmobiology is somewhat more popular than the methods of the Hamburg School, perhaps merely because it is simpler.

A possible theoretical flaw in midpoint theory is that midpoints are calculated without regard to the "force" of the individual planets. Just as the *energy* midpoint between a roaring fire and a candle is certainly not half way between the two, it would seem that the midpoint between Jupiter, the largest of the planets, and Pluto, the smallest, could not reasonably be considered to be the actual midpoint of astrological "force." However, partisans of midpoints offer what they believe to be evidence that their theory does work.

Astrological Associations

There are many astrological associations in the world. Some are strictly professional, but most are open to both professionals and amateurs. The largest in the U.S. (and probably in the Western world) is the American Federation of Astrologers, which was founded in 1938 in Washington, D.C. In the 1970s it moved to Tempe, Arizona, a suburb of Phoenix. The next largest is the National Council for Geocosmic Research (NCGR), which is devoted primarily to astrological research. It was founded on the East Coast in the 1970s and is a parent organization for local research chapters. The other major research organization is ISAR (International Association for Astrological Research). A general organization is the Association for Astrological Networking (AFAN). Other national associations are smaller than those just mentioned. There are also local associations in many cities and states.

The various astrological associations hold conventions and lectures in many of the major cities in the U.S. Most of these are open to the general public as well as to members of the sponsoring associations. They offer an opportunity for the general public to learn something about astrology as well as an opportunity for professional astrologers and serious amateurs to learn about special techniques and advancements.

In Europe there are many astrological associations catering to the needs of the different language groups,[5] e.g. The Astrological Lodge of London and The Astrological Association in England, C.E.D.R.A. in France, the Ö.A.G. in Austria, and the Italian association C.I.D.A., to mention only a few. Likewise, in most other parts of the world, except in the former Communist countries, where astrology was generally frowned upon. Astrology, like religion, is coming back to life in Russia[6] and East-

---

[5]A comprehensive list is published annually in the *Astrological Journal*. It also covers periodicals and bookstores worldwide.

[6]There are said to be as many as 15,000 persons in Moscow who are attending classes in astrology or who belong to the new astrological organizations that have sprung up since 1990.

ern Europe. Its present status in mainland China is unknown to the present writer, although it was very popular there prior to the Communist take-over. However, astrology is popular in both Taiwan and Hong Kong. India is the great home of astrologers. There are many professional astrologers in India, probably more than in all the rest of the world put together. There astrology is considered to be an important and respectable profession. It is taught in the universities, and most Indians of all social classes consult astrologers for advice on personal matters and for life readings for new-born children.

Astrology is not very prevalent in the Islamic countries, especially since the recent upsurge of fundamentalist religion in some of those countries.

Professional Astrologers

In the U.S. the practice of astrology is generally unregulated. That is, anyone can offer his services as an astrologer to the public. He does not need to be certified by anyone to practice. However, in a few cities there are local ordinances that require some sort of certification. The AFA and NCGR both offer written examinations that a prospective professional astrologer can take to demonstrate proficiency in the subject. Some of the cities that require registration of professional astrologers accept these certificates as proof of professional competence (like an M.D. degree). There are a few cities that have local boards that give their own examinations to prospective astrologers (like the bar examination for lawyers). But in general the best recommendation for a professional astrologer comes from satisfied clients.

Astronomy and Astrology

Astronomers generally profess a disbelief in astrology. However, since few if any of them have ever studied astrology, their opinions are obviously worthless.[7] They would be the first to scream foul if astrologers were to offer opinions on the Big Bang theory, or on quasars, black holes, or some other pet astrophysical topic. They would immediately point out that since astrologers have not studied these matters, their opinions are therefore worthless. So, "turn about is fair play." Astronomers suffer from the disadvantage that at the present time their science is of little practical value (its main use is to regulate clocks and establish orbits for space vehicles), while astrology offers personal guidance and counsel to the individual citizen. Psychologically this may tend to engender an unconscious feeling of inferiority in astronomers which they try to assuage by asserting that astrological counsel is invalid.

---

[7]For examples of the arguments from ignorance and prejudice and the other devious twistings and turnings employed by some astronomers who have publicly opposed astrology, see the first fifteen chapters of Sydney Omarr's book, *My World of Astrology* (New York, 1965).

Science and Astrology

Scientists generally disbelieve in astrology because it is not in accordance with their current mindset, which assumes that there is no God, there is no elder race of superior beings, that today's universe is the result of a Big Bang that occurred 8 to 15 billion years ago (the age is disputed), and that all life is the meaningless result of the thoughtless process of evolution. They are careful, however, not to proclaim this world view too loudly, lest they come into conflict with organized religion. In fact, they neatly sidestep the religious question by asserting that "Science is not in conflict with Religion," which is another way of saying "We think it is nonsense, but we don't want to quarrel about it."

Along with this goes their belief that the major forces of nature have already been discovered and that faster than light travel is impossible. If pressed to give specific reasons why they disbelive in astrology, they usually mention these: (1) it is a touchstone of scientific orthodoxy to disbelieve astrology; (2) they think astrology has been scientifically disproved; and (3) astrologers offer no physical mechanism by means of which the planets could influence living creatures on earth.

The first reason is the main one. If an individual scientist should study astrology and decide that there is something to it and then be so incautious as to mention that to his fellows, he would be promptly and vehemently denounced as being something of an idiot, and his future career would be placed in jeopardy. The second reason is a mistake because there have been only a few "tests" that could even remotely be called scientific, and some of them have gone for astrology and some of them against, so there is no scientific disproof. The third reason is also a mistake because scientists really have no mechanism for gravity or the other natural forces. They claim to have mechanisms because they can write equations that describe motion under the forces. But writing an equation does not provide a mechanism. Astrologers can write planetary combinations that produce observable effects in human beings (like the Sun-Mars aspects I mentioned above).

Not understanding how something works is no reason why you shouldn't use it. Most people have no understanding of integrated circuits, but this does not prevent them from making use of watches, television and radio sets, computers, and other electronic devices. All that is required is the knowledge of how to use something, not how it works.

Actually, disbelieving astrology is in most cases merely the observation of an intellectual dogma accepted without thought. Since scientists don't make horoscopes and study them, they obviously can have no scientific basis for their disbelief in astrology.

The American astrologer Grant Lewi (1902-1951) makes the following statement in his book *Astrology for the Millions* (Garden City, 1940): "[Astrology] is 'believed in' by a lot of people who know practically nothing about it; and it is 'disbelieved in' by even more who know *absolutely* nothing about it." Astronomers in particular and other critics in general belong to the latter group. And, as Lewi observes, "Of no other art or science can this be said."

It is also worthy of note that scientists themselves make mistakes and maintain false beliefs. For example, in the 1930s they confidently stated that no rocket could ever be built with sufficient power to escape the earth's gravity. Therefore a trip to the Moon or Mars (not to mention the stars) was impossible. And they also taught that there could not possibly be more than 92 elements. It would be easy to make a longer list. Most scientists subscribe to the current scientific dogma that all life on earth originated entirely by accident from what an 18th century writer described as "a fortuitous concourse of atoms," and that all present-day lifeforms are merely the result of evolution through natural selection, with perhaps a bit of mutation thrown in. There is no proof of this, but it is also something that you must believe to be considered a true scientist.

Astrology and Medicine

The relationship between astrology and medicine goes back to Alexandrian times. Ptolemy, for example, says in *Tetrabiblos*, i. 3, ". . . . those who have most advanced this faculty of the art, the Egyptians, have entirely united medicine with astronomical prediction." There seems to have been a standard system of diagnosis and healing that was covered in books ascribed to Hermes Trismegistus. Some short treatises that were either part of this corpus or derived from it have survived, among them lists of herbs said to be useful in medicine.

During the 15th and 16th centuries many universities in Europe offered curricula in medicine that included the study of astrology, which was used for diagnosis, prognosis, and as an aid in choosing medicines to treat the patient's condition. The usual practice was to erect a chart for the moment when the patient took to his sick bed.[8] Inspection of the chart according to definite rules enabled the physician to determine the source of the illness, its probable course, and which medicines might be appropriate to prescribe.

With the decline of astrology in the late 16th and into the 17th centuries, the study of astrology was gradually dropped at one university after another. This was partly because the intellectual climate had turned against astrology and partly because physicians had accumulated and systematized more and more empirical medical knowledge, so that they were becoming able to diagnose, prognose, and treat at least the more common ailments without resorting to astrological assistance.

This trend continued as medical knowledge increased. The two most important discoveries came in 1616 when Harvey announced his discovery of the circulation of the blood and in the 1860s when Lord Lister and

---

[8]The technical term for this is "the decumbiture of the sick." It is of course a horary chart that is interpreted according to special rules.

others became aware that bacteria were the source of infections—the "germ theory of disease." It is not usually recognized that by today's standards every physician practicing prior to the latter discovery was to some degree a quack. Since that time, the application of advances in technology and specialized studies in medicine have equipped physicians with a good set of diagnostic tools. This has relegated medical astrology to a study mainly of interest to a few astrologers. Nevertheless, the few who are interested in it devote much time to their studies, and books on medical astrology continue to appear from time to time.

In the U.S. at least, the practice of medicine has been for most of the 20th century almost entirely in the hands of "doctors of medicine" (M.D.s), and in many states it has been illegal for anyone to "practice medicine without a license," for which the principal requirement was an M.D. degree from an accredited medical school. During the last few decades, however, other forms of medical treatment have slowly become recognized to the extent that the laws have been changed to permit the practice of "alternative forms of medicine" in some states. Still, anyone who announced openly that he was using astrology the way that the physicians of the 16th century used it would make himself liable to prosecution in many places.

One result of this is that those astrological software houses that offer medical astrology software have felt obliged to place restrictions on the purchase of their products. And professional astrologers generally shy away from offering medical advice to their clients.

Fate vs. Free Will

If an astrologer can determine future circumstances from a natal horoscope, doesn't that imply that future events are predetermined? Or, in other words, that there is such a thing as fate, and that an individual is fated to experience certain circumstances in his life? And if so, what good does it do you to find out what your future will be if you can't change it?

This brings up the question of fate vs. free will, which is a vexed question. There does not seem to be any definitive answer. However, some thoughts on the subject may be helpful. First, the terms should be defined. Fate is generally taken to mean an immutable future, while free will is taken to mean that the individual has full freedom of choice at every moment, and, by extension that there is no such thing as fate. Actually, the two terms are not necessarily mutually exclusive.

For example, at any point in time a man may be faced with two or more choices of action. He may choose whichever he wishes; but his choice is obviously conditioned by his personality, his past history, his assessment of the ramifications of any choice that he may make, and his feeling about the suitability of each of his possible choices judged by his own ethical concepts. In other words, he will make his choice based upon his own character and his assessment of the desirability of each of the choices.

Now if we have some means of knowing the circumstances, the available choices, and the man's character, we should be able to predict what choice he will make.

Hence, we can see that a man may have free will at every point and may in fact exercise it, but it might still be possible to predict what he will do in any given set of circumstances. Then, if we had some means of assaying a man's character and of predicting what his circumstances would be at any given moment, we would be justified in assuming that fate is what the man will choose to do—that is, it is the result of the man's free will choices. Thus, in effect, fate and free will are but two sides of the same coin.

Next comes the question of prophecy. Is it possible to know the future, either in outline or in detail? There are different answers to this question. Most religions assume the existence of an omnipotent deity who knows the future as well as the past. Hence, the future must be immutable, and fate is the answer. (This instantly brings up a serious problem, but religions prefer to gloss over it.)

Scientists on the other hand generally assume that the future is more or less random. Hence it is impossible (even for a hypothetical deity) to predict the future. If they are correct, then obviously free will is the answer.

How can we tell which of these answers is right? The touchstone is prophecy. If in the past there have been verified instances of specific, detailed prophecies of future events involving one or more humans, then we are forced to the conclusion that there is such a thing as fate, however we define it.

History is replete with instances of fulfilled prophecies, and many individuals have had the experience of receiving a forecast of future circumstances from someone—a forecast that later proved to be accurate. Scientists ignore these instances as long as they can, and, if challenged will deny that they ever occurred, or they will assert that the prophecies were so general that they had a good chance of being fulfilled, and therefore their fulfillment proves nothing. But this is simply refusing to face up to the facts.

It is, of course, true that some predictions or prophecies, even some famous ones, were sufficiently general to be easily fulfilled—a familiar example is the famous Biblical prophecy that ``there will be wars and rumors of wars.'' That was really a statement of fact and not a prophecy (although it was intended to be taken as one). Nevertheless, there have been many other prophecies that were narrowly specific and were later fulfilled. The scientific argument to the contrary is thus self-serving and unfounded. It is merely another instance of, "My mind is made up, don't try to confuse me with the facts"—especially with facts that cannot be explained by current scientific beliefs.

But, for the sake of argument, let us suppose that there is such a thing as fate and predestination. One might then ask, "What good is an astrological life reading or astrological counsel when a decision must be made if the outcome is preordained?'' In the 2nd century, Claudius Ptolemy answered the question like this[9]:

> To a general examination it would appear that those who find fault with the uselessness of prognostication have no regard for the most important matters, but only for this—that foreknowledge of events that will happen in any case is superfluous; this, too, quite unreservedly and without due discrimination. For, in the first place, we should consider that even with events that will necessarily take place their unexpectedness is very apt to cause excessive panic and delirious joy, while foreknowledge accustoms and calms the soul by experience of distant events as though they were present, and prepares it to greet with calm and steadiness whatever comes. A second reason is that we should not believe that separate events attend mankind as the result of the heavenly cause as if they had been originally ordained for each person by some irrevocable divine command and destined to take place by necessity without the possibility of any other cause whatever interfering. Rather is it true that the movement of the heavenly bodies, to be sure, is eternally performed in accordance with divine, unchangeable destiny, while the change of earthly things is subject to a natural and mutable fate, and in drawing its first causes from above it is governed by chance and natural sequence. Moreover, some things happen to mankind through more general circumstances and not as the result of an individual's own natural propensities—for example, when men perish in multitudes by conflagrations or pestilence or cataclysms, through monstrous and inescapable changes in the ambient, for the lesser cause always yields to the greater and stronger; other occurrences, however, accord with the individual's own natural temperament through minor and fortuitous antipathies of the ambient. For if these distinctions are thus made, it is clear that both in general and in particular whatever events depend upon a first cause, which is irresistible and more powerful than anything that opposes it, must by all means take place; on the contrary, of events that are not of this character, those which are provided with resistant forces are easily averted, while those that are not follow the primary natural causes, to be sure, but this is due to ignorance and not

---

[9]*Tetrabiblos*, i. 3 (Robbins's translation).

to the necessity of almighty power. One might observe this same thing happening in all events whatsoever that have natural causes. For even of stones, plants, and animals, and also of wounds, mishaps, and sicknesses, some are of such a nature as to act of necessity, others only if no opposing thing interferes. One should therefore believe that physical philosophers predict what is to befall men with foreknowledge of this character and do not approach their task under false impressions; for certain things, because their effective causes are numerous and powerful, are inevitable, but others for the opposite reason may be averted. Similarly those physicians who can recognize ailments know beforehand those which are always fatal and those which admit of aid. In the case of events that may be modified we must give heed to the astrologer, when, for example, he says that to such and such a temperament, with such and such a character of the ambient, if the fundamental proportions increase or decrease, such and such an affection will result. Similarly we must believe the physician, when he says that this sore will spread or cause putrefaction, and the miner, for instance, that the lodestone attracts iron: just as each of these, if left to itself through ignorance of the opposing forces, will inevitably develop as its original nature compels, but neither will the sore cause spreading or putrefaction if it receives preventive treatment, nor will the lodestone attract the iron if it is rubbed with garlic;[10] and these very deterrent measures also have their resisting power naturally and by fate; so also in the other cases, if future happenings to men are not known, or if they are known and the remedies are not applied, they will by all means follow the course of primary nature; but if they are recognized ahead of time and remedies are provided, again quite in accord with nature and fate, they either do not occur at all or are rendered less severe. And in general, since such power is the same whether applied to things regarded universally or particularly, one would wonder why all believe in the efficacy of prediction in universal matters, and in its usefulness for guarding one's interest . . . but, on the other hand, as regards particular matters . . . some people believe neither that foreknowledge is still possible nor that precautions can be taken in most instances. . . . For the cause of this

---

[10]A common (but erroneous) belief of the ancients.

error is the difficulty and unfamiliarity of particular prognostication, a reason which in most other situations as well brings about disbelief. And since for the most part the resisting faculty is not coupled with the prognostic, because so perfect a disposition is rare, and since the force of nature takes its course without hindrance when the primary natures are concerned, an opinion has been produced that absolutely all future events are inevitable and unescapable.

In short, Ptolemy says fate may be divided into two parts: general fate that affects large numbers of people and is generally immutable; and individual Fate, that without foreknowledge and deliberate effort is also immutable, but with foreknowledge and conscious effort can be, at least in part, altered. And, as he says earlier, foreknowledge has the added advantage that it enables one to face the future with philosophic calm.

Astrologers have generally adhered to the latter point of view. Namely, that fate will likely take its course if the individual has no foreknowledge. But, with foreknowledge of the future and the timely use of astrological counseling to make appropriate decisions at critical times, an individual's fate can be altered somewhat to his benefit.

Psychology and Astrology

Psychology is the study of human personality. There are several schools of psychology which disagree with each other. They have each developed their own terminology, tests, and interpretations of observed behavior. Astrologers also have theories of personality based upon the significations of the various parts of the horoscope. There is not much common ground, since each discipline approaches the subject from different vantage points. It is therefore difficult to try to compare the results obtained by the two sciences. Since there are many more psychologists than astrologers, and since psychologists are academics who can obtain grants to fund their experiments, many more tests and published investigations of human personality are produced by psychologists than by astrologers. A few astrologers have also studied psychology, and a few psychologists (mostly Jungians) have studied astrology. But by and large psychology and astrology are like two religious sects that have different dogmas that they apply to questions of human behavior. Each can best be investigated within its own context, not by trying to correlate one with the other.

Computerized Astrology

The advent of powerful and affordable desktop computers has already had a considerable impact upon astrology, and the strength of the impact grows year by year. Prior to computers, an astrologer had to learn something about astronomy, geography, time systems, and the calendar in addition to studying astrology itself in detail. Today that is no longer necessary. A good computer and 300 or 400 dollars worth of software will do all the work. If you can start the computer and type in the client's name, place of birth, birthdate and birthtime, the machine will look up the geographical coordinates of the place, determine from that plus the birthdate what time zone the place was in, whether daylight saving time was in effect, calculate the sidereal time of birth, the house cusps, and the planetary positions at that moment, and print out the chart in any one of 100 or more "designer formats."

Some computer software will also calculate the positions of innumerable asteroids. In recent years some astrologers have become fascinated with asteroids and have ascribed all sorts of special influences to them. Since there are now 50,000 or so that the astronomers have discovered, it has even been suggested by some enthusiasts that an asteroid that has "your name" or a name similar to yours is "your personal planet" and is very important in your horoscope.

The availability of computer assistance has also enabled astrologers to compute reliable, or at least consistent, ephemerides for a number of hypothetical celestial bodies, including the eight "trans-Neptunians" of the Hamburg School and the "Dark Moon" Lilith (a supposed satellite of the Earth).

In addition to chart-calculation and ephemeris programs, there are programs available today that will type out a character analysis and a time-table and analysis of future prospects. Other programs will determine if 9:00 AM tomorrow is a good time to open the doors of your new business or a good time to ask your boss for a raise. Another will apply the rules of horary astrology to answer any sort of question you care to enter into it. Still others will type out daily guides like the ones in the newspaper but made especially for the person whose birthdata you have entered. In short, if you can afford a computer, a printer, and several hundred dollars worth of software, you can become an instant astrologer. You don't have to know anything other than how to operate the machine.

Similar software is now available for physicians and lawyers and probably for several other professions. If it weren't for old-fashioned licensing requirements, you could become an instant doctor or lawyer just as easily as you can become an instant astrologer. There is no question about it. Computers will eventually take over the world.

Just as you do not need to know how the tiny wheels fit together in a mechanical watch (or how the integrated circuit on a chip works in an electronic one), in order to tell the time, neither will you in the future need to know anything about astrology, law, or medicine in order to get useful guidance in those fields. This brings up an important question: should a "professional" be required to know something about his field, or will it be sufficient for him to have an adequate computer and software combination? Competent professionals of today will insist that the professionals of the future should have an adequate understanding of their fields before they are allowed to practice. But history suggests that such restrictions may eventually be lifted in all fields.

Is computer astrology today as good as a well-trained and experienced astrologer? The answer is, "No." But ten or twenty years from now the answer may be "generally speaking, yes." And the same thing will probably be true of doctors, lawyers, and other professionals. Is this good? In some ways, yes; and in other ways, no. Is it inevitable? Probably.

An even more fundamental question might be asked, "Can computers think?" The answer is: not yet! But with the rapid advance of technology, they may become able to think sooner than we might suppose.

Can Astrologers Predict the Future?

Yes, but certainly not with one hundred percent accuracy. This is mainly because human beings are complex creatures and live in complex societies. Astrologers can generally tell what type of event will befall a given individual, but not its exact details. And they may not be able to determine exactly when the event will occur. This is due to the large number of variables that have to be considered, some of which cannot be known in advance. But the same thing is true of meteorologists, economists, physicians, political experts, etc. How many times have the weathermen predicted meteorological conditions that didn't occur or failed to predict those that did? How many economists have confidently predicted economic trends that never materialized or even went the other way? How many doctors have given a patient a clean bill of health only to have him fall over dead with a heart attack or stroke a week later? Or how many have misdiagnosed a patient's disease until it was too late, or given him pills that made him sicker? And how many political experts have misjudged the mood of the electorate?

But do we fire all the meteorologists, economists, physicians, and political experts and close their departments in the universities when they make false predictions? No! Unfairly, astrologers are held to a higher standard than these other professionals. If an astrologer makes a prediction that doesn't work out, the scientists and some of the public will immediately say, "See, that proves that astrology is false." But if one of those others makes a false prediction, everybody accepts it as just being bad luck in a particular instance, and the predictor goes right on making more predictions as if nothing had happened (except maybe in the case of the political expert).

The Three Wise Men— Were They Astrologers?

The Gospel according to Matthew, Chapt. 2, relates a birth story of Jesus in which "in the days of Herod the King" *mágoi apò anatolon* 'Magi from the East' came to Jerusalem saying that they had seen His star in the

East.[11] The author of Matthew has probably taken the name Magi from the Book of Daniel, where its exact significance is uncertain. (It does not seem likely that any Zoroastrian priests were at the court of the Assyrian king Nebuchadrezzar.) Nevertheless, recent translations of the New Testament have translated *mágoi* as 'astrologers', since the translators have presumed that only astrologers would have any interest in a miraculous star.

However, the Gospel according to Luke tells an entirely different story of Jesus's birth with no mention whatsoever of Magi or a Star. Nor do the other two gospels say anything about them.

But, elaborating on the story in Matthew and adding elements of Christian tradition, the usual modern picture of the event is of Jesus being born in a manger in Bethlehem on 25 December 1 A.D. and being visited by three Kings or Wise Men bearing gifts.[12]

Originally, most Eastern Christians believed that Jesus was born on January 6th, while Western Christians generally opted for December 25th. However, both of these dates were simply derived by adding nine months to the traditional date of the Crucifixion (6 April in the East and 25 March in the West)—the idea being that Jesus, being a perfect man, must have lived a definite number of complete years; consequently, He must have died on the date of His conception. December 25th eventually won out in the West, aided by the fact that it was already the date of an established Roman festival.

The gospel writers give neither the day nor the month of Jesus's birth, so the traditional dates just mentioned are obviously speculative dates that originated after the composition of the gospels. The year of His birth is also speculative. Herod the Great (c.73- 4 or 2 B.C.) was King of Judaea from 37 B.C. until his death, so, if the account in Matthew is correct, Jesus must have been born prior to 4 (or 2) B.C.

Astrologers and astronomers alike have relentlessly canvassed the possibility of finding some astronomical phenomenon that would agree with the story of the Star. Some have suggested planetary conjunctions, comets, or novas, but none have made a convincing case for their theories. In the early 17th century John Kepler (q.v.) proposed a conjunction of

---

[11]See the interesting discussion by Lynn Thorndike, HMES 1, pp. 473-479. The muddled Biblical accounts of Jesus's birth are reviewed in detail by Charles Guignebert, *Jesus* (New Hyde Park: University Books, 1956), Chapter 3 "The Place and Date of the Birth of Jesus."

[12]The Gospel does not say how many Magi there were, and the Venerable Bede (c.673-735) is the first writer to give their names in their present-day forms. But see Lynn Thorndike, *ibid.*, p. 476, who cites a still earlier version of the names from a 6th century Greek chronicle: "Bithisarea, Melichior, Gathaspa."

[13]In his tract *De Iesv Christi servatoris nostri vero anno natalitio . . .* 'The True Birth Year of Our Savior Jesus Christi . . .' printed with his book on the supernova of 1604, *De stella nova in pede Serpentarii . . .* (Prague, The Author, 1606).

293

Jupiter and Saturn as "the Star."[13] There were three such conjunctions in the same year, the last of which occurred in 16 Pisces (tropical) on the evening of 5 December 7 B.C., but the two planets were 1°03' distant in latitude, so they would not have appeared as a single star. However, King Herod is known to have been alive at that time, so that at least is consistent with the Biblical account.

Recently, the astronomer John Mosley at the Griffith observatory noticed that there was a very close conjunction of Venus and Jupiter on the night of 17/18 June 2 B.C. in 9 Leo. This conjunction would have appeared on that one night as a single very bright star. Some astronomical enthusiasts have even gone so far as to assert that this has solved the problem of Jesus's birthdate. But whether King Herod was still alive at that time is doubtful. And at any rate, the conjunction was a very transient phenomenon, which does not fit the Bible story.

None of the solutions that have been proposed is convincing. And the question becomes moot in the opinion of the so-called higher critics of the Bible, who are united in dismissing the whole story of the Magi and the Star as a pious fabrication. They point out that the earliest gospel, that of Mark, was composed after 70 A.D. and that those of Matthew and Luke were written perhaps ten years or more later. By the time the latter gospels were written, Jesus had been dead for more than fifty years.

In the opinion of the higher critics there was no longer any information available about Jesus's birth (Mark says nothing about it), so the writers of Matthew and Luke were free to invent whatever stories seemed appropriate to them—rather like the story M.L. Weems invented in 1806 about George Washington chopping down the cherry tree.

There is of course no mention of Jesus in the classical Greek astrological literature, so astrologers have no special information on the subject, although there have been many astrological speculations from the Middle Ages down to the present.[14]

---

[14]See my two papers, "Early Horoscopes of Jesus" and "Horoscopic Configurations Indicative of Crucifixion," the first of which is based on the Italian book, *Gli oroscopi di Cristo* by Ornella Pompeo Faracovi (Venice: Marsilio Edition, 1989), in teh AFA *Journal of Research*, vol. 12, no. 2 (Fall 2001).

SELECTED BIBLIOGRAPHY

There are numerous works that treat of the history of astrology, but there is no reliable technical history of astrology from its beginnings down to the present day. Most of the books listed below only cover specific periods and (with a few exceptions) are not technical, but they do give an insight into the place of astrology and astrologers in the times in which they lived.

The list that follows is mainly a selection of the books that are cited in the main text or in the footnotes. The majority of them are in English, since the present work is intended for an English readership. However, *L'Astrologie Grecque*, *L'Égypte des astrologues*, *Geschichte der Astrologie,* and *Arcana Mundi* have no equivalents in English, so they must be included.

I would also like to call the reader's attention again to the translations being published by Robert Schmidt and Robert Hand, which have the goal of translating all significant Greek and Latin astrological books into English. They are presently operating on a subscription basis; hence I have not mentioned any of the translations that have been issued so far. But the translated works will eventually be revised and published as separate volumes. When this is done, it will greatly facilitate the study of classical and medieval astrology.

Bouché-Leclercq, A.
L'Astrologie grecque.
[Greek Astrology]
Paris, 1899. 1st ed.
Paris: Culture et Civilisation, 1963. repr. in facs.
[the only extensive survey of Greek astrology; it is an academic study, and it has some errors]

Carmody, Francis J.
Arabic Astronomical and Astrological Sciences
in Latin Translation/A Critical Bibliography.
Berkeley and Los Angeles: Univ. Of California Press, 1956.
[the best English language bibliographical survey of Arabic astrological books that were translated into Latin]

Cramer, Frederick H.
Astrology in Roman Law and Politics.
Philadelphia: The American Philosophical Society, 1954.
[an excellent cultural history of astrologers and astrology under the Roman Empire down to about 200 A.D.]

Cumont, Franz
L'Égypte des astrologues.
[The Egypt of the Astrologers]
Brussels: Fondation Égyptologique Reine Élisabeth, 1937.
[a detailed study of Egyptian society in Ptolemaic times and
under the early Roman Empire, with references to astrological
literature and indexes of Greek and Latin words]

Gardner, F. Leigh
A Catalogue Raisonné of Works
on the Occult Sciences.
vol. II, Astrological Books.
with a sketch of astrological history by William Wynn Westcott
London: The Author, 1911. 1st ed.
Leipzig: The Author, 1923. 2nd ed.
reprinted as:
Bibliotheca Astrologica.
North Hollywood: Symbols & Signs, 1977. 2nd ed. [sic!]
[a facsimile repr. of the 1st ed.]

Howe, Ellic
Astrology/A recent history including the untold story of its role
in World War II.
New York: Walker and Company, [1968].
[originally published in 1967 in Great Britain as *Urania's Children* and since republished under still a third title]
[The author was an English publisher who served in British
military intelligence during World War II. An interesting and
informative book—probably the best cultural history of astrology in the modern period.]

Hübner, Wolfgang
Grade und Gradbezirke der Tierkreiszeichen.
[Degrees and Degree Areas of the Zodiac]
Stuttgart and Leipzig: B.G. Teubner, 1985. 2 vols.

Knappich, Wilhelm
Geschichte der Astrologie.
[History of Astrology]
Frankfurt am Main: Vittorio Klostermann, 1967. 1st ed
Frankfurt am Main: Vittorio Klostermann, 1988. 2nd ed.
[the best general history of astrology; the author was a learned Vi-
ennese librarian and astrologer; the 1988 edition is an unaltered reprint of the 1st edition with a new preface and a supplementary
bibliography of more recent books in the German language]

McCaffery, Ellen
Astrology/ Its History and Influence in the Western World.
New York: Charles Scribner's Sons, 1942.
[an excellent "cultural" history of astrology by a professional astrologer. Pages 383-396 contain lists of the books in the libraries of the famous John Dee and William Lilly. The author completed her MS in December 1941. On pp. 366-367 she predicts how long the war with Japan will last—four years! (Most Americans at the time believed it would be over in 6 months!) An interesting example of mundane astrological prediction.]

al-Nadîm (c.930-991)
The Fihrist of al-Nadîm.
ed. & trans. by Bayard Dodge
New York & London: Columbia Univ. Press, 1970. 2 vols.
[an annotated catalogue of Arabic books made by a Baghdad bookseller at the end of the 10th century; astrological books and their authors are covered in vol. 2]

Neugebauer, O. and Van Hoesen, H.B.
Greek Horoscopes.
Philadelphia: The American Philosophical Society, 1959.
[an edition and partial translation with elaborate notes, glossaries, etc. of all the horoscopes of the classical period that had been found on papyri or in literary sources at the time of writing]

Pingree, David
The Yavanajataka of Sphujidhvaja.
Cambridge, Mass.: Harvard Univ. Press, 1978. 2 vols.
[an edition and translation of the earliest preserved Sanskrit treatise of horoscopic astrology, with a very detailed commentary, and biographical notices of the leading Indian, Arabian & Persian, and Greek astrologers; a most excellent work, but one of reduced utility for those who cannot read Sanskrit, Arabic, Greek, and Latin, since parallel passages are cited in their original languages, usually without translation]

Thorndike, Lynn
A History of Magic and Experimental Science.
New York: Columbia Univ. Press, 1923-1958. 8 vols.
[the best available survey of astrology during the Middle Ages, Renaissance, and Early Modern periods]

Abu 'Ali al-Khayyat
The Judgments of Nativities.
trans. from the Latin version of
John of Seville by James H. Holden
Tempe, AZ: A.F.A., Inc., 1988.
[contains on pp. 11-16 of the Introduction a concise summary
of the history of horoscopic astrology with special reference to
Arabian and horary astrology]

Adams, Evangeline
The Bowl of Heaven.
New York: Dodd, Mead and Company, 1926. often reprinted
[an autobiography of the most famous of all American astrologers, containing many interesting anecdotes of her career as a
professional astrologer]

Avelar, Helena & Ribeiro, Luis
Astrologia Real.
A História de Portugal à Luz da Astrologia.
[Royal Astrology/The History of Porgugal in the Light of As-
trology]
Cascais: Editora Pergaminho, 2004, paper 279 pp. diagrs.
portrs.

Bezza, Giuseppe
Arcana Mundi.
Milan: Biblioteca Universale Rizzoli, 1995.
2 vols. 1148 pp. illus.
[a most excellent anthology of classical and medieval astrol-
ogy]

al-Bîrūnî
The Chronology of Ancient Nations.
trans. & ed. by C. Edward Sachau
London, 1879. 1st ed.
Frankfurt a/M: Minerva Verlag, 1984. facs. repr. of translation
[mainly on the calendars known to the author, but there is some
information on astrology]

al-Bîrūnî
Alberuni's India. [sic!]
trans. by Edward C. Sachau
London, 1888.
London: Routledge & Kegan Paul, 1910. 2 vols.
New Delhi: Ss. Chand & Co., 1964. facs. repr. 2 vols in one.

[a fascinating account of life in India in the early 11th century, with special reference to Hindu astronomy and astrology]

al-Bîrûnî
The Book of Instruction in the Elements
of the Art of Astrology.
Arabic text with a facing translation by
R. Ramsay Wright
[actually a textbook of mathematics, astronomy, and Arabian astrology written for a Muslim princess]
London: Luzac & Co., 1934.

Dean, Geoffrey, ed.
Recent Advances in Natal Astrology.
Subiaco, Australia: Analogic, 1977. paper.
[a very detailed survey by ten prominent astrologers of Western natal astrology in the period 1900-1976]

Holden, James H. & Hughes, Robert A.
Astrological Pioneers of America.
Tempe, AZ: A.F.A., Inc., 1988.
[biographical sketches of 1,300 American and 148 foreign astrologers of the modern period]

Kennedy, E.S. & Pingree, David
The Astrological History of Masha'allah.
Cambridge: Harvard Univ. Press, 1971.

Koch-Westenholz, Ulla
Mesopotamian Astrology.
Copenhage: Museum Tusculanum Press, 1995.
[an excellent and up-to-date survey of Babylonian astrology, with an extensive bibliography]

Leo, Bessie
The Life and Work of Alan Leo.
London: Modern Astrology Publ. Co., 1919.
[a biography by his widow]

Lilly, William
Mr. William Lilly's History of his Life and Times.
London, 1715. 1st and 2nd eds.
[a fascinating account of Lilly's career with many interesting anecdotes about his contemporaries]
Lilly, William

The Last of the Astrologers.
ed. by Katharine M. Briggs
London: The Folklore Society, 1974.
[a reprint of the 2nd. 1715 ed. of Lilly's autobiography under a
silly title, but with useful notes]

Oestmann, Günther
Heinrich Rantzau und die Astrologie.
[a beautiful and informative book]
Brunswick: Braunschweigisches
Landesmuseum, 2004. 4 to. 318 pp. illus.

Pingree, David
The Thousands of Abu Ma`shar.
London: The Warburg Institute, 1968.
[Albumasar's astrological history]

Stuckrad, Kocku von
Geschichte der Astrologie.
[History of Astrology]
[an excellent new history in the German language]
Munich: C.H. Beck, 2003. 412 pp. illus. 23 cm.

Wemyss, Maurice
The Wheel of Life *or* Scientific Astrology.
Vol. 5, pp. 67-130, Appendix 9 "The History of Astrology"
Edinburgh: International Publishing Co., n.d.
[some of the author's statements have been invalidated by later
studies]

Index Notes

The Index of Persons and Publishers contains the names of all persons mentioned individually as well as some collective categories of persons, e.g. "Arabs." It also contains the names of the publishers of books mentioned in the text. If a name occurs in both an English and a Latin (or another foreign language) form, I have usually indexed it under the English form. But some persons' names are commonly known in their Latin form, e.g. Regiomontanus, Junctinus, and Placidus. If the name has two forms, and it is not found under one form, then try the other.

The names of Arabian astrologers are generally given in both their Latinized and Arabic forms, e.g. Albumasar and Abū Ma'shar and Zahel and Sahl ibn Bishr.

Book titles in the Index of Subjects and Book Titles are handled differently. Titles in foreign languages are usually listed in their original language, but there is some redundancy—a few titles are listed in both their English translation and in their original language. (Most of the foreign language titles are translated at their first appearance in the text.)

The subject entries of the Subjects and Book Titles Index are a compromise between a "general category" type of index and a "concordance type." I have tried to index the topics and sub-topics most likely to be sought for. But rather than create a concordance, I have retained some general categories. For example, the entry "ASC" contains references to the origin of the term, to its primacy in Classical Greek astrology, and to incidental mention of it in connection with charts.

There is of course the usual confusion between topic and sub-topic. Should the reader look for "Subsidiary houses" or "Houses, subsidiary"? Or for "Domiciles of the planets" or "Planets, domiciles of"? Again, the advice is to try both ways. Some astrological terms have common synonyms. An example is "directions" and "progressions." Here, "Directions" is the main entry, but there is a cross-reference to it under "Progressions." I hope that the reader will be able to locate most of the topics and sub-topics he is interested in without undue effort.

Some book titles have been shortened in the index. This is usually indicated by an ellipsis. The indicated page may contain a fuller form of the title. But a few of the older books have "titles" that amount to wordy descriptions of the contents of the book. These are not given in full even in the text, but I have given enough to enable the reader to identify the book in library catalogues.

Additional references can sometimes be found by consulting both indices—one for a personal name reference and the other for a topical reference.

Most technical terms that are in common use (and a number that are antique or obsolescent) appear in the Index of Book Titles and Subjects. However, not all of them are defined in the references. The present work is a history and not an astrological dictionary. The reader who fails to find the definition of a technical term in the references can consult one of the numerous astrological dictionaries. However, some of the medieval and classical technical terms may not appear in the dictionaries or may even be incorrectly defined. To find the true meaning of the older terms, it is best to see how those terms are used in the referenced books mentioned in the present history.

Finally, I ask the reader's indulgence for the deficiencies of the indices. there are undoubtedly some omissions and errors of citation. I regret these, but circumstances prevented their complete elimination.

And I want to thank the editor, Kris Brandt Riske, for taking on the tedious task of revising the indices for the second edition.

Index of Persons and Publishers

Allen, Garth, *see* Bradley, Donald, A.
Almansor, *astrologer*, 114 n.25
Alphonso X the Wise, King of Spain, 130,135,146
Alphonso XIII, King of Spain, 223
American Federation of Astrologers, *publisher*, 4 n.15,6 n.20,14 n.15,15
n.17,50 n.117,109 n.12,112,159 n.6,197 n.8,199 n.13,204 n.25,200,222
n.52, 229,230,235,274,282,298,299
American Philosophical Society, *publisher*, 5 n.19,14 n.15,53 n.127,193
n.2,295,297
American University of Beirut, *publisher*, 132
AMS Press, *publisher*, 2 n.9
Analogic, *publisher*, 198 n.10,299
Andronicus IV, Emperor, 143
Angelus, Johannes *see* Engel, Johann.
Antarès, 253-254
Antigonus of Nicaea, 60-64,77,166
Antiochus III of Commagene, 29
Antiochus VIII, Seleucid king, 77
Antiochus IX, Seleucid king, 77
Antiochus of Athens, 64,65,66,85,89 n.207
Antipater, 8
Antîqūs, *see* Antiochus of Athens.
Anubio, 16
Anubis, *divinity*, 16 n.22
Aphrodite (Venus), *divinity*, 54 n.132
Apollonius, 149
Aposaites, *see* Abū Sa'îd Shādhān.
Appleby, Derek, 221
Arabs, 43,46,51,60,65,74,101,107,112 n.23,125,126,128,129, 132,134,138,
140,145,146,147,148,150,154
Arafat, Yasser, Palestinian president, xi
Arcandam, 151 n.99
Archbishop of Canterbury, see Sheldon, Gilbert.
Archilochus, *poet*, 77
Archimedes, *mathematician*, 67,77
Arco, *publisher*, 227 n.59
Ardashir I, King of Persia, 100
Ares (Mars), *divinity*, 54 n.132
Argapholon, 138
Argol, 171-172
Argoli, Andrea, *see* Argol.
Aries Press, *publisher*, 218 n.47,260
Aristokrates, *client*, 5
Aristotle, *philosopher*, 128
Arkana (Penguin Group), *publisher*, 212 n.37
Armenia Editore, *publisher*, 249

Arnold Birckmann's Heirs, *publisher*, 168
Arzachel, *see* al-Zarqālî.
Ashmand, J.M., 85,152,203
Ashmole, Sir Elias, 184,186 n.55
Ashurbanipal, King of Assyria, 1
ASI Publications, *publisher*, 240,250
Asimov, Isaace, *writer*, 126
Asklepios, 16 n.22
Assagioli, Roberto, *psychologist*, 269
Astro-Book Co., *publisher*, 240
ASTRO*CARTO*GRAPHY, *publisher*, 238
Astro Computing Services, *publisher*, 233,237,238,253
Astrolabe, *software publisher*, 238
Astrologer of the Year 82
Athenians, 7 n.22
Athenodorus, 8
Augustine, St., *Church father*, 160 n.9
Augustus, Emperor, 21,23,24,64,68
Aurum Verlag, *publisher*, 268
Avelar, Helena, *astrologer*, 298
Avelar, Ribeiro, *astrologer*, 298
Avon Books, *publisher*, 252
Azarchel, *see* al-Zarqālî.
Babylonians, xii,1,2,3,4,6,7,8,9,11,12,13,16 n.25,48,68,99,100
Bach, Eleanor, 232
Backmund, A., *see* Bethor, Alexander.
Bacon, Roger, *scholar*, 135,136-137
Baigent, Michael, 211 n.36
Bailey, Alice, 227
Bailey, E.H., 152,256
Baktay, Erwin, 263
Balbillus, Tiberius Claudius, 29-32,35
Baldwin, Richard S., *translator*, 174,176
Ballantrae Reprint, *publisher*, 200
Barbarians, 161
Barbault, André, *astrologer*, 249-250
Barbillus, *see* Balbillus, Tiberius Claudius.
Barclay, Olivia, 212
Bar-Hebraeus, *scholar*, 104
Barth, O.W., *publisher*, 260
al-Battānî, *astronomer*, 129,138
Bauer, Hermann, Verlag, *publisher*, 262,264
Baum, Julie, 260
Baumgartner Verlag, *publisher*, 264
Bayer, George, 240
Beck, C.H., *publisher*, 300

Beckerath, Erich, 262
Bede, The Venerable, *ecclesiastical historian*, 293 n.12
Behrend, *publisher*, 163 n.16
Belcher, Sir Edward, *critic of astrology*, 204
Belcsák, Sándor, xv,266
Belemith, 149
Belgian Royal Academy, *publisher*, 45 n.102
Bender, H., *psychologist*, 268,252
Benjamine, Elbert, *see* Zain, C.C.
Bennett, Sidney K., *see* Wynn.
Bentley, Richard, *publisher*, 202 n.17
Beraud, Symphorien, *publisher*, 167
Bernard Silvester, 151
Berosus, 7,8,9,47
Berti, Fabio Francesco, *astrologer*, 197
Besongne, Cardin, *printer*, 152,177 n.31
Bessière, Jany, xv,255
Best, Simon, 214
Bethem, 114 n.24-25,152,190
Bethor, Alexander, 257
Bezza, Giuseppe, 271,221,298
Biblioteca Universale Rizzoli, *publisher*, 298
Bickerstaff, Isaac, pseudonym of Jonathan Swift, 191
Bills, Rex E., 221
Birckmann's Heirs, Arnold, *publisher*, 168
al-Bîrûnî, 41 n.93,75 n.174,104 n.2,112 n.21,131-132,134,148,150,151,298,
   299
Bithisarea (Balthasar), "King," 293 n.12
Blake, William, 202
Boer, Emilie, *editor*, 28 n.55,45 n.102,65 n.157,79 n.180-181,152
Bollstädt, Count of, 135
Bonatti, Guido, 109 n.13,112 n.21,114,130,137-142,149,150,161,190
Bonattiis, Antonio Francesco de, 179-180,181 n.44
Bonatus, *see* Bonatti, Guido.
Bonatus, *nephew of* Guido Bonatti, 137
Bonelli, Antonio, 218
Bordoni, Grazia, 270
Borelli, Antonio, 218
Bouché-Leclercq, A., *scholar*, 25 n.48,295
Boulainvilliers, Henry de, Count of Saint-Saire, 181
Bourdin, Nicolas, Marquess of Villennes, 152,177
Boyko, Jolanda, *translator*, 177
Brackenridge, J. Bruce, *professor*, 214
Bradley, Donald A., 100,231,235-236,240,251 n.87
Brahe, Tycho, 170,172,173
Brahy, Gustav Lambert, 240,254

Bram, Jean Rhys, *translator*, 66 n.159
Brandler-Pracht, Karl, 256,257
Bressendorf, O. von, 261
Briggs, Katharine M., 300
Brignone, Jerry, xv
Brill, *publisher*, 44 n.100
Brookes, Nathan, *publisher*, 189
Broughton, Dr. L.D., 205,221,222-224
Brown University Press, *publisher*, 1 n.3,98 n.223
Browne, J., 200
Brunhübner, Fritz, 259-260
Brunini, Angelo, 271
Budai, Dr. E., 267
Buddha, *sage*, 9
Bulwer-Lytton, *see* Lytton.
Bylica, Martin, *mathematician*, 157 n.2
Byzantines, 31,89,107,120,149,153
Caesar, Caius Julius, Dictator, 7
Cambridge University Press, *publisher*, 25 n.48,29 n.60,299
Camden Society, The, *publisher*, 182 n.46
Camiade, Charles de, 167
Campanus of Novara, 144-145,158,214-215,231,261 n.100
Campion, Nicholas, 221
Cantera, Francisco, *editor*, 133
Canterbury, Archbishop of, *prelate*, 185 n.51
Cape, Jonathan, *publisher*, 184 n.49
Capone, Federico, 269
Capp, Bernard, *scholar*, 187 n.57
Cardan, Jerome, 19,60,165-166,169,171,190,266
Carelli, Adriano, 219 n.49,218,220,269-270
Carmody, Francis J., *scholar*, 90,126,128,129,130,131,132 n.61,143 n.85,
    149,295
Carter, Charles E.O., 208-209,212
Caslant, Eugène, 244
Castle Books, *publisher*, 212
Catherine de' Medici, Queen of France, 164
Celestes, mythical King of Greece, 161
Celestial Communications, *publisher*, 233
Chacornac, *publisher*, 244
Chaldeans, 8,20 n.32,47,92
Champion, Honoré, *publisher*, 159 n.7
Chand, Ss., *publisher*, 299
Chaney, W.H., 221
Charles V, Emperor, 167
Charles VIII, King of France, 161
Charubel, *occultist*, 218,220

Chasapes, Konstantinos, *astronomer*, 272
Chaucer, Geoffrey, 144,145,146,182
Chaucer, Lewis, *son? of* Geoffrey Chaucer, 144 n.89
Chennevière, Daniel, *see* Rudhyar, Dane.
Chinese, 101 n.230,151
Chiron, *centaur*, 161
Chnubis, 16
Choisnard, Paul, 274,245,251,268
Christian, Paul, *occultist*, 220
Christians, 136,137,155,292-294
Cicero, Marcus Tullius, *statesman*, 21,25 n.45
C.I.D.A., *publisher*, 270
Clancy Publications, *publisher*, 172 n.28,231
Clarendon Press, *publisher*, 13 n.6,90 n.209,184 n.50
Claudius, Emperor, 29
Clement IV, Pope, 136
Clement of Alexandria, *Church father*, 89
Cleopatra VI, Queen of Egypt, 43 n.96
Clerk, *character in* Chaucer's *Canterbury Tales*, 145
Climlas, George, *astronomer*, 233
Colbert, Jean Baptiste, *statesman*, 174
Coley, Henry, 152,153,142,187,190
Collección Mirach, *publisher*, 114 n.25
Colorado Astrological Society, *publisher*, 231 n.65
Columbia University Press, *publisher*, 100 n.228,297
Columbus, Christopher, *navigator*, 162
Constans II, Emperor, 68 n.163
Constantine I the Great, Emperor, 66,68 n.163
Constantine II, Emperor, 68 n.163
Cooper, John, 178 n.36
Cooper, Robert W., 235
Cope, David, *see* Zariel.
Cope, Lloyd, 240
Corfield, John, 202
Cornell, Dr. H.L., 225
Cornell University Press, *publisher*, 187 n.57
Corre, Robert, 236
Cory, I.P., *scholar*, 7 n.22
Cottrel, James, *publisher*, 189
Cramer, Frederick H., *scholar*, 5 n.19,20 n.31,20 n.32,29 n.60-61,60 n.145, 295
Critodemus, 32,47 n.109,52,53,59,74
Cronammon, son of Paul of Alexandria, 82 n.188,79
Crusaders, 101,103,135
CSA Press, *publisher*, 230
Culpeper, Nicholas, 188-189

Gauquelin, Michel, *statistician*, 214,236 n.68,238,241,242,245,250-253,268
Gaurico, Luca, 60,132,164-165,169
Gavorse, Joseph, *translator*, 21 n.34
Gazis, Thomas, xv
George, Demetra, 233
George, Llewellyn, 224 n.56
Gerbert, *see* Sylvester II.
Germans, 49,162
Gettings, Fred, *writer*, 212 n.37
Ghivarelli, Sergio, 270
Gingrich, Owen, *astronomer*, 193 n.2
Ginzel, F.K., *chronographer*, 193 n.3,194 n.4
Giuntini, Francesco, *see* Junctinus, Franciscus.
Glahn, A. Frank, 255,263
Gleadow, Rupert S., 212,231
Gods, 4,12,13,54 n.132,56,69,70,71,72,73,89,99,278
Goldstein, Jacobson, Ivy M., *see* Jacobson, Ivy M. Goldstein-.
Golik, Susan, xv
Goodman, Linda, 242
Goold, G.P., *scholar*, 23 n.40,25 n.48,26
Gordon, Henry J., 220
Gouchon, Henri, 249
Gould, Jay, *financier*, 223
Graham, G.W., *balloonist*, 203
Granger, Frank, *scholar*, 8 n.23
Grant, Catharine T., 229-230
Grant, Ernest A., 229-230
Grashof, Max, *see* Heindel, Max.
Greaves, Doris, 274
Greeks, 6,7,11,12,13,15,17,38,49,53,56,58,59,63,73,85 n.197,107,108,112
    n.23,122 n.42,143,145,161,175,179
Green, H.S, 207
Greene, Liz, 213
Gregory XIII, Pope, 183
Guignebert, Charles, *scholar*, 292 n.11
Guinard, Patrice, 253-254
Gundel, Hans Georg, *scholar*, 29 n.60,44 n.97,60 n.144,65 n.156
Gundel, Wilhelm, *scholar*, 29 n.60,44 n.97,60 n.144,65 n.156,216 n.42
Gustavus II Adolphus, King of Sweden, 170
Gutttman, Ariel, 238
Hadrian, Emperor, 60 n.146,61 n.147,64
Hagin le Juif, *translator*, 133
Halbronn, Jacques, 177,221
Hall, Manly Palmer, 21 n.36,221
Halliwell, J.O., *editor*, 182 n.46
Halma, Nicolas, *scholar*, 44 n.99

Haly Abenragel, 130-131
Haly Abenrudian, 130,132,152
Haly Embrani, 128-129
Hamaker-Zondag, Karen, 265
Hand, Robert, 238-239,272
Hamilton, John, Archbishop, 166
Hanubis, 16 n.22
Hanubius, 16,74
Harper & Brothers, *publisher*, 3 n.11
Harrassowitz, O., *publisher*, 2 n.4,44 n.100
Harris, B., *publisher*, 190
Hartmann, Franz, *occultist*, 256
Hārūn al-Rashîd, Caliph, 104
Harvard University Press, *publisher*, 7 n.22,32 n.71,109 n.10,297
Harvey, Charles, 200,211 n.35,214
Harvey, James Martin, 274
Harvey, Marina, 275
Harvey, William, *physician*, 285
Hawkins, John, 197 n.9
Heart Center, *publisher*, 200
Heiberg, J.L., *editor*, 44 n.98
Heindel, Augusta Foss, *Rosicrucian*, 225
Heindel, Max, *Rosicrucian*, 225
Heliodorus, 79,82,112 n.21
Heller, Joachim, *editor*, 112,135 n.65
Hellman, G., *meteorologist*, 163
Hemminga, Sixtus ab, 169-170
Henry VII, King of England, 142
Hephaestio of Thebes, 13,26,32,33,35,45,60,65,83-84,98,107,112 n.21
Hephaestus (Vulcan), *divinity*, 54 n.132
Herbais de Thun, Charles de, Viscount, 244,254
Hermann of Carinthia, *translator*, 115
Hermann Bauer Verlag, *publisher*, 262,264
Hermes (Trismegistus), 13 n.6,16,28,43,54,65,73 n.168,74,79,89-90,114 n.24-25,120 n.39,149,150,152,190,239,285-286
Hermogenes, 29
Herod the Great, King of Judea, 292-294
Hierocles, 29
Hieroz, Jean, 177,249
Hilty, Gerold, *editor*, 130
Hindus, 8,9 n.27,13 n.7,98 n.221,100,151,154
Hinrichs, J.C., *publisher*, 193 n.3
Hipparchus, *astronomer*, 9 n.27,17,23,45,46
Hippocrates, *physician*, 90
Hirakawa Publishing Co., *publisher*, 276
Hitler, Adolf, Chancellor of Germany, 278

H.M. Stationery Office, *publisher*, 47 n.108
Hoepli, Ulrico, *publisher*, 270
Holden, James Herschel, 4 n.15,6 n.20,12 n.2,14 n.12,15 n.17,32 n.38,50
  n.117,54 n.130,55 n.135,63 n.152,66 n.158,79 n.180,82 n.188,94
  n.215,109 n.12,111,112,119,134 n.64,159 n.6,174,176,222 n.52,223
  n.53,224 n.55,57,227 n.61,236,240 n.70
Holden, Ralph William, 215,273
Homer, *epic poet*, 77
Hone, Marguerite, 210,214
Honorius of Autun, 78
Housman, A.E., *scholar*, 25 n.48,29 n.60
Houwing, Gerhard, *astrologer*, xv
Howe, Ellic, *historian*, 201 n.15,202 n.18-19,204 n.23,24,205 n.29,207
  n.32,209 n.33,220 n.50,254 n.91,256,258 n.98-99,259,267 n.103,296
Huber, *publisher*, 259
Huber, Bruno, 255 n.94,269
Huber, Louise, 255 n.94,269
Hübner, Wolfgang, *scholar*, 27 n.51,296
Hughes, Robert A., 206,222 n.52,223 n.53,224 n.55,57,227 n.61,299
Hughes, W., *publisher*, 203
Huguetan & Ravaud, *publishers*, 166
Hulagu Khan, King of the Mongols, 132
Hypsicles, *mathematician*, 79,99
Ibn Ezra, Abraham, 109 n.13,112 n.21,109,112,114,132-134,153
Ibn Hibintā, 118
Ibn Khallikān, *historian*, 118
Ifram, Adnan, *translator*, 132
Indians, xii,3,8,76 n.175,105,107,108,111,123,131,145,146
Inner Traditions International, *publisher*, 239
Insititut Astrologique de Belgique, *publisher*, 254
Institute for the Study of Cycles in World Affairs, *publisher*, 178 n.36
Institute of Theoretical Astronomy, *publisher*, 203 n.21
Instituto Arias Montano, *publisher*, 134 n.64
Instituto Hispano-Árabe de Cultura, *publisher*, 104 n.3
International Publishing Co., *publisher*, 300
Inventors of horoscopic astrology, 52,215
Ishikawa, H.M., xv,213,275-276
Italians, 49,55,102,103,134,137,162,269
Jacob, Eugène, *see* Star, Ély.
Jacobson, Ivy M. Goldstein-, 199,208,229
Ja'far ibn Muhammad Abū Ma'shar al-Balkhî, *see* Albumasar
James, Colin, III, 231 n.65
Jay, Delphine, 199 n.13
Jayne, Charles A., 228 n.63
Jesus Christ, 136,161 n.12,292,293,294
Jethro, 109

314

Jews, 1,11,16 n.24,99,104,109,114,132
Jirjis, 128
John II, Duke of Bourbon, 159
John of Ashendon, 143,181
John of Seville, *translator*, 112,115,118,129,135,157,298
John of Vicenza, *friar*, 138
Johndro, L. Edward, 19 n.30,221,227-228,240
Johns Hopkins University Press, *publisher*, 45 n.103, 133 n.62
Johnson Reprint, *publisher*, 166
Jones, Mark Edmund, 219,220,228,230
Jordan, Clark L., *attorney*, 226
Josten, C.H., *biographer*, 184 n.50
Judar, 108
Julevno, 244
Julian of Laodicea, 107
Junctinus, Franciscus, 166-167,169,266
Jung, Carl, *psychologist*, 266-267,243
Juvenal, *poet*, 29
Kankah, 107
Kennedy, E.S., *scholar*, 109 n.10,111,118 n.35,132,299
Kent, R., 274
Kepler, John, 170,172-173,178,193,195,266,293
Kepler, Mrs., *mother of* John Kepler, 172
Khusrau Anushirwan, Shah, 111
al-Kindî, 115,126,128,138
King, Bruce, *see* Zolar.
Kitson, Annabella, 221
Kloeckler, Herbert von, Baron, 251 n.87,262
Klostermann, Vittorio, *publisher*, x,265,296
Knappich, Wilhelm, x,179 n.40,217 n.44,254 n.91-92,265-266,296
Kniepf, Albert, 255-256
Knupfer, Curt, 257
Koch, Walther, 214,261-262
Koch-Westenholz, Ulla, *scholar*, 1 n.1,2,3 n.10,4 n.16,5 n.18,12 n.3,299
Koechly, Arminius, *editor and translator*, 44 n.97
Kohlhammer, W., *publisher*, 165 n.22
Kollerstrom, Nicholas, 214,221
Koppenstätter, Ed., 260
Korsch, Dr. Hubert, 167 n.24,169 n.25,263,257,259
Kotulla, Alfred, 260
Kozminsky, Isidore, 218,220,273-274
Krafft, Karl E., 213,251,267-268
Krause, M., *scholar*, 99 n.224
Kritza, Theodore, xv,263 n.101
Kroll, Wilhelm, *editor*, 66 n.159
Kühr, E.K., 261-262

Kumamoto, Yushou, 275
Kündig, Heinrich, 268
Kunitzsch, Paul, *scholar*, 49 n.115
Labarta, Ana, *scholar*, 104 n.3
Laboratoire d'Étude des Relations entre Rhythmes Cosmiques et
   Psychophysiologiques, *publisher*, 252
Landscheidt, Theodor, 197 n.9
Langham, James Mars, 240
Le Brun, J., *publisher*, 174
L'Eclair, André, *see* Carelli, Adriano.
Lefeldt, Hermann, 258
Legrand, Amédée, *publisher*, 267
Lehman, J. Lee, 221,233
Leinbach, Esther, 232,233
Leland, Warren, *hotel proprietor*, 225
Leo I, Emperor, 89
Leo, Alan, 60,98 n.221,179,206-207,208,211,218,299
Leo, Bessie Phillips, 206-207,208,299
Leopold of Austria, 112 n.21,142
Leopold William of Austria, Archduke, 178
Leroux, *publisher*, 25 n.48
Lescaut, Jacques de, 254
LeVerrier, U.J.J., *astronomer*, 196,225
Levy, Raphael, *translator*, 133 n.62
Lewi, Grant, 227,231-232,284
Lewis, Jim, 238
Leymarie, *publisher*, 245
Libra, C.A., 265
Librairie Vega, publisher, 244
Liechtenstein, Peter, *publisher*, 126,128
Lilly, Ruth Needham, *wife of* William Lilly, 184 n.49
Lilly, William, 47 n.110,69,114,128,131,142,165,182,183,184-188,192
   n.63,189,204 n.22,299,300
Lincoln, Abraham, U.S. President, 222,223
Linser Verlag, *publisher*, 260
Lippincott, J.B., *publisher*, 149,152 n.102,210
Lister, Joseph Lister, Baron, *physician*, 285
Llewellyn Foundation, The, *publisher*, 236
Llewellyn Publications, *publisher*, 224 n.56,225,231,232,234,235,238
Llewellyn Worldwide, *publisher*, 221
Lloyd, Bruce, 273
Locatellus, Bonatus, *publisher*, 114 n.24
Loeb Classical Library, *collection*, 7 n.22,8 n.23,17 n.28,21 n.35,23 n.39-
   40,29 n.57,29 n.60,46 n.105
London astrologers, 189
London, Jack, *novelist*, 224

Long, Jeanne, 241
Lorenz, Dona Marie, 215
Louis XI, King of France, 159
Louis XIII, King of France, 173
Louis XIV, King of France, 173
Lowell, Laurel, 225
Luccans, 140
Lucis Publishing Co., *publisher*, 227,230
Luke, *Gospel writer*, 293,294
Lund Humphries, *publisher*, 4 n.14
Luther, Martin, *religious reformer*, 165
Luzac & Co., *publisher*, 2 n.9,132,299
Lydus, Joannes Laurentius, *scholar*, 22
Lyndoe, Edward, 178,209,264
Lyons, *Archbishop of*, 159
Lytton, Edward Bulwer-, Baron, *author*, 254
al-Ma'mūn, *Caliph*, 104,107
McCaffery, Ellen, 191,201 n.16,297
McGraw-Hill, *publisher*, 249 n.85
McKay, David, *publisher*, 21 n.36,228,265
McMinn, David, 240 n.70
Macnaughton, Duncan, *see* Wemyss, Maurice.
Macoy Publ. & Masonic Supply Co., *publisher*, 221
McWhirter, Louise, 240
Maghnal, *publisher*, 240
Magi, The, *Biblical figures*, 292-294
Magic Circle Publishing Co., *publisher*, 224
Magini, Giovanni Antonio, 171,266
al-Mahdî, *Caliph*, 104,105
Manasseh, 109
Manetho, *astrologer*, 43-44
Manetho, *historian*, 43 n.96
Manilius, Marcus, 23-26,44,95,98,157
Mansūr, *astrologer*, *see* Almansor.
al-Mansūr, *Caliph*, 103,104 n.2,106 n.7
Manuel II, Emperor, 143
Marcus, *friend of* Vettius Valens, 51
Margaret Rose, Princess, 209
Marie Louise, Queen of Poland, 174
Marinus, *biographer*, 84
Mark, *Gospel writer*, 294
Marr, Alexander, 264
Mary, *mother of* Jesus, 137
Mary I, Queen of England, 189
Māshā'allāh, xii,103 n.1,104,108-111,114 n.24,118,126,128,129,178 n.37,
   299

Master, The (Māshā'allāh), 138
Mather, Arthur C.M., 214
Matrix, *publisher*, 238
Matthew, *Gospel writer*, 292,294
Matthews, E.C., 219,220
Matthias, Emperor, 172
Mavortius, Quintus Flavius Maesius Egnatius Lollianus, Consul, 66,67,68, 69,76,77,78
Medici Family, 102,103
MEB, *publisher*, 177,185
Meier-Parm, H.C., 256,263
Melanchthon, Philip, *scholar*, 165
Melichior (Melchior), "King," 293 n.12
Menard, Pierre, *publisher*, 152,177
Meridian, Bill, 241
Messahalla, *see* Māshā'allāh.
Metallinou, Maria, 272
Michael de Petrasancta, *metaphysician*, 164
Michels, Agnes Kirsopp, *scholar*, 21 n.34,24 n.44
Michelsen, Neil F., 237-238
Minerva Verlag, *publisher*, 298
Mirach, *publisher*, 114 n.25
Mirti, Grazia, xv,185 n.52,217 n.44,271-272
Modern Astrology Publishing Co., *publisher*, 206,299
Modern Library, *collection*, 21 n.34
Mommsen, Theodor, *scholar*, 66,68 n.164,69,79 n.179
Mongols, 132
Montani & Neuber, *publishers*, 134 n.64
Moreau, J., *publisher*, 173 n.30
Morin, Jean Baptiste, 50 n.117,56 n.139,87 n.200,126,152,159 n.6,170,173-177,178,190,209,215,244,249,262,273
Morpurgo, Lisa, 271
Morrison, Al H., 232
Morrison, R.J., *see* Zadkiel I.
Moṣes, *Biblical figure*, 6 n.21
Mosley, John, *astronomer*, 294
Mostade, Georges, *see* Antarès.
Muhammad, *Prophet of Islam*, 115
Muhammad ibn Ahmad al-Bîrûnî, *see* al-Bîrûnî.
Mu'izz ibn Bādis, Prince, 130
Mull, Carol S., 241
Müller, Johann, *see* Regiomontanus.
Munkasey, Michael P., 221,240
Muratori, L.A., *historian*, 149 n.96
Mūsā ibn Nawbakht, 104,111 n.16, 118
Muse, 44

Museum Tusculanum Press, *publisher*, 1 n.1,299
Muslims, 101 n.230,145,155
Mussolini, Benito, *Italian dictator*, 278
al-Mutawakil, *Caliph*, 104
al-Nadîm, *bibliographer*, 100 n.228,107,112 n.19,126 n.48,128 n.52,132 n.61,297
Naibod, Valentine, 168-169
Nallino, C.A., *scholar*, 129,130
Napoleon I, Emperor of France, 278
Naq (Nahaq), 108
National Astrological Library, The, *publisher* 142 n.84,190,262,266
Navarro, Gilbert, 229
Navò, C.T., *publisher*, 165
Nawbakht the Persian, 103,104
Naylor, R.H., 209
Nebuchadrezzar II, King of Babylon, 293
Nechepso, 16,27,35 n.82,47,51 n.119,59,65,74
Neely, James, *programmer*, 233
Nergal-etir, 2
Nero, Emperor, 29,53,56,57,189
Neugebauer, O., *scholar*, 3 n.11,4 n.14,31 n.69,43 n.95,46 n.104,52 n.122, 53 n.127,60 n.145,84 n.192,98 n.223,99 n.224,109 n.13,129 n.55,297
Newcastle Publishing Co., *publisher*, 205 n.30
Newton, Robert R., *scholar*, 45,46
Nicholas II, Tsar of Russia, 268
Nicoullaud, Charles, Abbé, *see* Fomalhaut.
Niger, Pescennius Franciscus, *editor*, 76 n.176
Niggemann, Hans, 259
Nigidius Figulus, Publius, 20
Nine Judges, The, 128
Nobbe, C.F.A., *editor*, 44 n.100
Nolle, Richard, 233
Nordenskiöld, A.E., *geographer*, 44 n.100
Novello, Guido, Count of Poppi, 140
Noyes Press, *publisher*, 66 n.159
Occidental D.A.T.A., *publisher*, 145
Octavius, *see* Augustus.
Oedipus, King of Thebes, 77
Oestmann, Günther, 300
Old, W. Gorn, *see* Sepharial.
Olympiodorus, 79 n.181,82
Omar Tiberiades, 111-112,128,138
Omarr, Sydney, 227
Orion, 52,65
Orpheus, *astrologer*, 74,91
Osiander, Andreas, *religious reformer*, 165

Owen, Henry, Jr., xv
Oxford University Press, *publisher*, 104 n.4
Page, A.P. Nelson, 215,264,273
Palchus, 31,60,107,143
Palmer, Cecil, *publisher*, 210
Palmer, John, *see* Raphael II.
Pamprepius of Thebes, *poet*, 89
Para Research, *publisher*, 239
Paris Alexander, *Trojan prince*, 77
Parker, Else, 265
Parker, Derek, *writer*, 184 n.49,186 n.55,188 n.58
Parker, Richard A., *scholar*, 1 n.3,8 n.24,13 n.5,98 n.223
Parm, *see* Meier-Parm, H.C.
Partridge, John, 189,190-191
Partridge & Blunden, *publishers*, 69 n.166
P.A.S. Publications, Inc., *publisher*, 241
Paul I, King of Greece, 223 n.54
Paul of Alexandria, 28 n.55,79-82,89,93,99,216 n.42
Pauvert, J-J, *publisher*, 250
Payot, *publisher*, 249
Pearce, A.J., 15 n.19,248 n.81
Persians, 1,3,8,35 n.83,38,41,45,49,53,98,107,108,123,146,154
Pestalozzi-Fellenberg-Haus, *publisher*, 267
Petosiris, 15,27,35 n.82,43,44,47,51 n.119,59,65,74,78
Petreius, Johannes, *publisher*, 166
Petrus, H., *publisher*, 169
Peuckert, Will-Erich, *writer*, 165
Pfaff, J.W.A., 181
Pflaum, Jakob, *mathematician*, 158
Phenomena Publications, *publisher*, 233
Philip I, Emperor, 51
Philip II, King of Spain, 169
Philosophical Library, *publisher*, 221
Philosophical Research Society, *publisher*, 221
Picard, Eudes, 245-249
Pickering, W., *publisher*, 7 n.22
Pietro d'Abano, 217,220
Pindar, *poet*, 77
Pingree, David, *scholar*, 1 n.2,2 n.4,3 n.12,16 n.22,16 n.25,32,33,34,35 n.
83,85,36,Fig.4,Fig.5,39 n.88,41,53 n.126-127,54 n.130,64 n.153,83
n.190,85 n.195-196,85,86,100 n.226-227,229, 104 n.4,107,109 n.10-11,
111,115 n.29,118,120 n.38,143 n.86,151 n.101,297,299,300
Piobb, Pierre, 183
Pitois, J-B, *see* Christian, Paul.
Placidus, 48 n.114,50 n.117,92,97,158,159,171,173,178-179,187,190,195,
201, 206,210,215,231,245,258 n.96,261,266

Regulus Verlag, *publisher*, 261
Reiner, Erica, *scholar*, 1 n.2
Retz, *publisher*, 133
Rhetorius the Egyptian, 32,60,64 n.153,65,66,85-89,98,107,112,127 n.50, 129,216 n.42
Richelieu, Armand Duplessis, Duke of & Cardinal, 189
Rider, William & Son, *publisher*, 274
Rider & Co., *publisher*, 274
Righter, Carroll, 227
Rimbault, Olivier, 221
Ring, Thomas, 268
Riske, Kris Brandt, xiii,xiv,302
Riske, Philip, xiii
Robbins, F.E., *editor & translator*, 28 n.57,46 n.105,107;60 n.143,279 n.3,288 n.9
Robson, Vivian E., 47 n.110,149,151,152 n.102,210,245,248
Rochberg-Halton, F., *scholar*, 5 n.19
Rodden, Lois M., 237
Roffe, A.H. & Co., *publisher*, 203
Romans, 101
Romulus, *eponymous founder of Rome*, 21,22
Roosevelt, Franklin D., U.S. President, 229
Rosenberg, A., 268
Rosicrucian Fellowship, The, *publisher*, 225
Roussat, Richard, *editor*, 151 n.99
Routledge & Kegan Paul, *publisher*, 298
Rowse, A.L., *writer*, 182 n.47
Rozières, Jean, *see* Hieroz, Jean.
Rudhyar, Dane, 144,230
Rudolph II, Emperor, 172
Rudolph, Ludwig, 258
Rudolph, Udo, 258
Sabian Publishing Society, *publisher*, 219 n.48,228
Sachau, Edward, *scholar*, 132 n.97,298
Sachs, A., *scholar*, 5 n.19,50
Saffouri, Mohammad, *translator*, 132
Sahl ibn Bishr, *see* Zahel.
Saʿîd Shādhān, *see* Abū Saʿîd Shadhan.
Saint-Saire, Count of, *see* Boulainvilliers, Henry.
Salio (*or* Solomon), *translator*, 127
Sangreal Foundation, *publisher*, 176,264
Sanjahil, 108
Santos, Demetrio, 109 n.13,110 n.14,111 n.15,114,221,276
Sasportas, Howard, 213
Saurius, J., *publisher*, 172
Savoy, Duke of, *see* Emanuel Philbert.

Vibia Sabina, Empress, 61 n.147
Victoria, Queen of United Kingdom, 204,223
Vigoni, Francesco, *publisher*, 178 n.32
Vigot Frères, *publishers*, 243 n.76
Villennes, Marquess of, *see* Bourdin, Nicolas.
Vitruvius, *architect*, 8
Volguine, Alexandre, 249-250
Vollrath, Hugo, 257
Vuellius, *see* Valens, Vettius.
Vulcan Books, *publisher*, 233,274
Walker and Co., *publisher*, 201 n.15,296
Wallace, Athene Gale, 231
Wallenstein, Albrecht von, Count, 172
Warburg Institute, *publisher*, 118,151 n.101,300
Washington, George, President of the United States of America, 278,294
Wassilko-Serecki, Zoë, Countess, 266
al-Wāthiq, Caliph, 104
Weems, M.L., *biographer*, 294
Weingarten, Henry, 240
Weinstock, Stephen, *editor*, 45 n.102,65 n.157
Weiser, Samuel, *publisher*, 152,203,210,213,214,225,228,269
Weiss, Dr. Adolf, 176,177,265
Weller, Barbara L., *astronomer*, 193 n.2
Wemyss, Maurice, 144,173 n.29,210-211,214,300
Weschke, Karl, *publisher*, 227
Westerners, 46,102
Weston, L.H., 196 n.7,224-225
Whalley, John, 85 n.193,200
Wharton, Sir George, 190
White, Thomas, 201
Whitford Press, *publisher*, 212,233
Wickersheimer, Ernest, *scholar*, 159 n.7,160,161 n.11
Wife of Bath, The, character in *The Canterbury Tales*, 144
William II, Emperor of Germany, 223
William of Malmesbury, historian, 78
Williams, Elbert Benjamin, *see* Zain, C.C.
Wilshire Book Co., *publisher*, 212,227 n.60
Wilson, James, 85 n.193, 202, 203
Winkel, M.E., 259
Wise Men, Biblical figures, 292-294
Witte Verlag, *publisher*, 258
Witte, Alfred, 211 n.36,235 n.67,257-259
Wizard's Bookshelf, *publisher*, 7 n.22
Woden, divinity, 13 n.11
Wolf, H., *publisher*, 120 n.39
Worsdale, John, 201

Index of Subjects and Book Titles

Anaeretic place, *technical term*, 30,94
Analogy, *technical term*, 174
Analysis of the Horoscope by Ernest and Catharine Grant, 230
Anaphorikos by Hypsicles, 99
Ancient Astrology Theory and Practice trans. by Jean Rhys Bram, 66 n.159
Ancient Fragments, The trans. by I.P. Cory, 7 n.22
Ancient House Division, paper by James H. Holden, 15 n.17,94 n.215
Ancient sages, 68
Angles, *technical term*, 27,28,36,37,38,62,76,82,83,96,119,124,139,140
Angular, *technical term*, 20,61,62,63,65,83,175
Anima Astrologiae, or a guide for Astrologers by Henry Coley, 190
Animals, lists of, 90
Animodar, technical term, 49
Antarctic circle, 130
Anthology by Vettius Valens, 17 n.29,32,41 n.92,51-59,62,75 n.174,95, 99
Antiochus and Rhetorius, paper by David Pingree, 64 n.153,64 n.155,89 n.207
Antiscions, *technical term*, 45 n.101,69,92,175
Apheta, *technical term*, 31,38,52
Aphetic place, *technical term*, 30,38,49
Aphorisms, 8,32,87 n.200,127 n.50,152,153,157 n.1,165,167,182,190
Apollon, hypothetical planet, 257
Apotelesmatics of Hephaestio of Thebes, 31,32,35,43,45,60,65,79 n.180, 83-84
Apotelesmatics of Manetho, 43-44
Apotelesmatic Book, The of Palchus, 31,143
Appearances, *technical term*, 34,37,61,63,179
Application, *technical term*, 50,63,112,113,114
Applied Astrology by M.E. Hone, 210
Approximate Positions of Asteroids 1851-2050 by Emma Belle Donath, 233
Arabian astrologers, 43,46,75,103-131,132 n.61,147,153,154
Arabian astrology, 103-131,146,147,148,151,154,157,167
Arabic Astronomical and Astrological Sciences in Latin Translation by F.J. Carmody, *see* AAASLT.
Arabic literature, loss of, *see* Literature, Arabic, destruction of.
Arabic numerals, 108
Arabic Parts (see also Lots), 91,147,154,239
Arabic Parts in Astrology... , The by Robert Zoller, 239
Arabic translations of Greek books, 28 n.57,33,34,53,100,101
Arc of direction, *technical term*, 49,178 n.33,189 n.59
Arcana Dictionary of Astrology by Fred Gettings, 212 n.37
Arcana Mundi by Giuseppe Bezza, 272
Arcana of Astrology, The by W.J. Simmonite, 205 n.30
Arcandam doctor peritissimus... , by Alhandreus, 151 n.99
Archaeologists, 7
Architecture by Vitruvius, 8
Archives, 7

Arctic circle, 130
Aries, constellation, 76,77,78,147 n.92
Aries, First Point of, 47,151
Aries Ingresses, 15 n.20,119 n.36,111,118,146,147,163,209
Arms makers, indications of, 127
Art of Synthesis by Alan Leo, 207
ASC, abbreviation for ascendant, 8,17,18,23,24,27,28,29,30,31,34,35,37,38,39,40,41,42,48,51,52,55,56, 57,60,61,62,63,64,65,76,77,78,81,82,83,86,87,89,93,94,95,96,97,98,100, 112,113,116,117,119,120,123,124,127,130,141,211,246,247,258,270
ASC degree, 18,35 n.82,48,76,78-82,91,93,95,122 n.42,140,146,166,189 n.59,206,216,217,219,256,269
ASC degree, its signification from the Barbaric Sphere, 78,215
ASC degree, its signification in the terms of the planets, 76
ASC, Lord of the, 112,113,119
ASC/Sun combinations, 269
Ascendant, 12 n.4
Ascendant, errors in calculating the, 18
Ascendant, rectification of the, 19,48,51 n.121,82,93
Ascending sign, 15,47 n.111,94
Ascension tables, 145
Aspects, *technical term*, 14,26,33,34,35,37,38,39,42,43,52,53,61 n.148,62,63,73,76,82,88,91,93,94,95 n.216,97,109,110,111,112,113,114,115,116,117,124,125,127,128,133, 140,147,163,173,175,176,201,206,207,220,221,222,232,246,251,252 n.90,284
Aspects, hard, *technical term*, 258
Aspects, left and right, *technical term*, 27
Aspects, new, 173
Aspects to an empty sign, 112 n.23
Aspekt-Analyse by E.K. Kühr, 263
Assignment, *technical term*, 32 n.72
Association for Astrological Networking, organization, 282
Asterisms, 8 n.25,75 n.173,150
Asteroid Ephemeris 1883-1999, The by Rique Pottenger, 233
Asteroid Goddesses by Demetra George, 233
Asteroid Name Encyclopedia by Jacob Schwartz, 234
Asteroids, 196-198,202-203,211,232-235,263,275
Asteroids, colors of the, 234 n.66
Asteroids in Midpoints by Emma Belle Donath, 233
Asteroids in Synastry by Emma Belle Donath, 233
Asteroids in the Birthchart by Emma Belle Donath, 233
Astraea, 5th asteroid, 196
Astrobiology, 267
Astres royaux by André Barbault, 250
Astro*Carto*Graphy, 238

Astrology, traditional, 154,175,181,199,210,211,213,215,225,242,247,251, 252 n.90,262,281
Astrology, university chairs of, 137,157,158,178
Astrology, used for propaganda, 267
Astrology, viewed as an outdated superstition, 174,181
Astrology by Ellen McCaffery, 191 n.60,201 n.16
Astrology, article by David Pingree, 2 n.4
Astrology: A Recent History by Ellic Howe, 201 n.15,204 n.23-24,205 n.29, 207 n.32,208 n.33,220 n.50,255 n.91,259 n.98-99,257,268 n.103
Astrology and its Value for Living by Else Parker, 265
Astrology and Sex by V. E. Robson, 210,245 n.78,248
Astrology and Vocational Aptitude by Baron von Kloeckler, 251 n.87,262
Astrology for All by Alan Leo, 206,218
Astrology for Everyone by Edward Lyndoe, 209
Astrology For the Millions by Grant Lewi, 231,284
Astrology in Roman Law and Politics by Frederick Cramer, 5 n.19,20 n.31-32,29 n.61,60 n.145,295
Astrology of Accidents, The by C.E.O. Carter, 208
Astrology of America's Destiny, The by Dane Rudhyar, 230
Astrology of Personality by Dane Rudhyar, 230
Astrology Reborn by John Addey, 213
Astrology, The Astrologers' Quarterly, periodical, 208,212
Astrology: Your Place in the Stars by Evangeline Adams, 226 n.58
Astrology: Your Place in the Sun by Evangeline Adams, 226 n.58
Astro-Medical Diagnosis... by W.J. Tucker, 211
Astro-meteorology, 126,150,151,208,224
Astronomers, 13 n.9,15 n.19,17,44,45,46 n.106,47,49,51,95 n.216,103,117, 131,145,147,148,154
Astronomers, generally opposed to astrology, 283 n.7
Astronomica of Marcus Manilius, 23,25 n.48,157
Astronomical Cuneiform Texts by O. Neugebauer, 4 n.14
Astronomical midheaven, 19,95,96
Astronomy and Astrology in India and Iran, paper by David Pingree, 2 n.4,3 n.12,16 n.25
Astronomy and Elementary Philosophy trans. by Manoah Sibly, 178 n.36
Astronomy, not supported by Emperors Matthias and Ferdinand II, 172
Astrophysical Directions by Michael and Margaret Erlewine, 238
Astro-Psychology by Karen Hamaker-Zondag, 265
Astro-seismology, 208,275
Athena Astrological Society, organization, 232
Athla, *technical term*, 25
Atlantic Ocean, 67
A to Z Horoscope Maker and Delineator by Llewellyn George, 224 n.56, 227
Augustus, his Moon sign and ascendant, 24
Aus der Blütezeit der Astrometeorologie, paper by G. Hellman, 163 n.16

Ausdruck und Richtung der Kräfte by Thomas Ring, 268
Austrian Astrological Association, organization, 266
Autobiography of an Astrologer by W.J. Tucker, 211
Axial Rotation system, 273
Ayanamsa, *technical term*, 235
Babblings, 136
Babylonian astrologers, 4-7,9,32,68
Babylonian astrology, xii,1-9,40,299
Babylonian Horoscopes, paper by A. Sachs, 5 n.19
Babylonian Planetary Omens by Reiner, E. & Pingree, D., 1 n.2
Bad Daemon, name of the 12th house, 27,28,58
Bad Fortune, name of the 6th house, 27
Bad place, 6th, 8th, or 12th house, 37,38,42
Baghdad, foundation chart of, 104
Baghdad, sacked by Hulagu Khan, 132
Baktay Erwin Astrologiai Egyesület, organization, 264
Baldness, indications of, 127
Banquets, questions about, 139
Barbaric Sphere, The, 78,215
Basis, epithet of the ASC, 81
Battle, question about a, 134,139-142
Bausteine der Astrologie by F. Schwickert & A. Weiss, 177,265
Beagle, 656th asteroid, 235
Beauties of Occult Science Investigated ... , The by Thomas White, 201
Beginning of Wisdom, The by Ibn Ezra, 114,133
Beiträge zur Geschichte der Meteorologie, 163 n.16
Belgian Astrological Federation, *organization*, 255
Belgian Institute of Astro-Dynamics, *organization*, 255
Bell-shaped curve, *statistical term*, 125
Benefic planets, 30,37,39,40,41,42,50,58,78,106,133,174,216
Bergensen Tables of Johann Stadius, 169
Berechnung der Ereigniszeiten by E.K. Kühr, 263
Berufsbegabung und Schicksal by Baron von Kloeckler, 262
Besieged, *technical term*, 153
Bible, 132
Bibliographic works, 161 n.24
Bibliotheca Astrologica by F. Leigh Garnder, 167 n.24
Bicorporeal signs, *see* Signs, mutable
Big Bang, astrophysical theory, 284
Big Bear (Ursa Major), constellation, 67
Birth and Planetary Data Gathered Since 1949 by M. and F. Gauquelin,
   250-253
Birth of Jesus, date of, 292-294
Birthdata from public records, 241 n.72,250-253,255
Birthdata of occupational groups, 210,241,250-253
Birthplace system of houses, *see* Koch system.

Birth records, 148,242 n.72
Black holes, astrophysical theory, 283
Blockading, *technical term*, 62
Boat builders, indications of, 128
Boards for geomancy, 151
Bonding, *technical term*, 88 n.204
Book collectors, 101,102,128
Book of Daniel, 293
Book of Elections by Haly Embrani, 128
Book of Flowers, The by Albumasar, 118
Book of Fruit see *Centiloquy* of pseudo-Ptolemy.
Book of Hermes, 89,90,216
Book of Introduction to the Judgments of the Stars by Guido Bonatti, *see*
   Liber Introductorius... by Guido Bonatti.
Book of Instruction in the Elements of the Art of Astrology, The by
   al-Bîrûnî, 41 n.93,75 n.174,132
Book of Nativities by Māshā'allāh, 109,111,112
Book of Reasons by Ibn Ezra, 133
Book of Rulerships, The by J. Lee Lehman, 221
Book of the Fundamentals of the Tables, The by Ibn Ezra, 133
Book of the Interpretation of the Stars ... by Dr. Erwin Baktay, 264-265
Book of the Nine Judges, The, 128,131
Book of Times, The by Zahel, 114
Book of Twelve Genitures, The by Jerome Cardan, 166
Book on Nativities by Omar Tiberiades, 111
Books of Hermes, forty-two, 89
Books, licit and illicit, 136
Booksellers, 11,101
Botanic Practice of Medicine by W.J. Simmonite, 205
Bowl of Heaven, The by Evangeline Adams, 226
Brambilla, 640th asteroid, 235
Bridge builders, indications of, 128
Brotherhood of Light, *occult organization*, 228
Brotherhood of Light Lessons, 228
Burnt Path, The, *technical term*, 41
Business cycles, 239
Business Cycles and the Number 56, paper by David McMinn, 240
Byzantine astrology, 143-149
Cabala, xiii,207
Cabala of the Astrological Houses... , The by J.B. Morin, 173 n.30
Cabalistic astrology, 242
Cadent, *technical term*, 27,36,37,41,65,86,100,140,141,175
Cahiers astrologiques, periodical, 249
Calcul des probabilités appliqué à l'astrologie by Paul Flambart, 245
Calculations for Nativities by Kankah the Indian, 108
Calculators, electronic, 185

Calculators, mechanical, 197
Calendar of the Roman Republic, The by Agnes Kirsopp Michels, 21 n.34,24 n.44
Calendars, 3 n.11,6,7,8,17,18,20 n.34,22 n.37,24 n.44,25 n.46,52,145,150 n.98,162,183,189,193, 217, 290
Cambridge University, 182,188
Campanus system, 144-145,158,179 n.38,214,215,231,261 n.100
Campanus System Tables of Houses, 144
Candles as time keepers, 148
Canterbury Tales of Geoffrey Chaucer, 144,145
Cardinal houses, *technical term*, 14
Cardinal signs, *technical term*, 91 n.212
Carnegie Hall, 226
Carpenters, indications of, 127
Case Book of Medical Astrology by A. Charles Emerson, 235
Casting of rays, 30,114
Catalogue of Emperors, Kings, and Illustrious Men ... by Heinrich von Rantzau, 167
Catalogus Codicum Astrologorum Graecorum (CCAG), 26 n.49,29 n.61,31 n.68-69,64 n.154,65 n.157,82 n.189,85 n.196,104 n.5,105,107 n.8,143 n.68, 138
Catholic Church, 160 n.9
C.E.D.R.A., organization, 282
Celestial phenomena, viii,1,2,4,5,8
Celestial Philosophy or Genethliacal Astronomy by John Worsdale, 201
Celestial state, *technical term*, 175
Centiloquies, 90,152-153,190
Centiloquy of Bethem, 153,190
Centiloquy of Hermes, 90,152,190
Centiloquy of pseudo-Ptolemy, 54 n.131,132,152,165,177,190
Centro Italiano di Astrologia (C.I.D.A.), *organization*, 271,282
Ceres, *1st asteroid*, 196,202
Chaldeans, 8,20 n.32
Chaney's Ephemeris from 1800 to Date by W.H. Chaney, 224
Chaney's Primer of Astrology by W.H. Chaney, 224
Character reading, 145,207
Character traits, 251,252 n.90
Charts, *technical term*, 6,14,15,18,20,28,35,38,53,56,60,63,125,143,147, 148,186,215,285
Chess, 149
Chinese astrology, 281
Chiromancy, *see* Palmistry.
Chiron, asteroid or comet, 197,233
Chiron by Maritha Pottenger, 233
Chiron: The New Planet in Your Horoscope by Richard Nolle, 233
Choiac, 4th month of the Egyptian calendar, 21

Complete Arcana of Astral Philosophy by W.J. Simmonite, 205
Complete Book on the Judgments of the Stars, The by Haly Abenragel, 130
Complete Dictionary of Astrology, A by James Wilson, 202 n.20,203
Complete Illustration of the Celestial Art of Astrology, The by Ebenezer Sibly, 200
Computer databases, 237,241,243
Computer programs, *see* Software, astrological.
Computers, 195-196,197,200,203,207,213,221,228,233,234,237,238,240, 241,274,290-292
Conception charts, *see* Horoscopes, Conception.
Concerning the More Certain Fundamentals of Astrology by John Kepler, 172 n.28
Conditions of the Moon, *technical term*, 114
Confidences d'un astrologue by G.L. Brahy, 255
Conjunction, *technical term*, 5,9,48,58,61 n.148,74 n.171,75,93,97,108,114, 118,133,137,138,146,165 n.22,172,176,185,201,206,258,293
Conjunction figure, horoscope type, 263
Conjunction of 1524, The, 163-164
Conjunction of 7 B.C., 294
Conjunction of 2 B.C., 294
Conjunctions, of the superior planets, 110,115,116,137,146,154,161,163, 165,172,294
Conjunctions by Kankah the Indian, 108
Conjunctions by Māshā'allāh, 109
Conjurer's Magazine, The, 200
Constantinople, sacked by the Crusaders, 101
Constantinople, sacked by the Turks, 101
Constellational zodiac, *see* Fixed zodiac.
Constellations, 1,3,8,47,78,150
Constellations, zodiacal, 3,231
Consumption, disease, 166
Contrantiscions, *technical term*, 92
Contraparallels in declination, *technical term*, 92
Construction and Use of the Astrolabe, The by Māshā'allāh, 109
Contribution à l'étude de l'Astro-Dynamique by G.L. Brahy, 254
Copernican theory, xi
Copyists, 11
Cornerstones of Astrology by F. Schwickert & A. Weiss, 176,265
Corpus Hermeticum, 73 n.168,90
Correlation, periodical, 214,252
Corrupted, *technical term*, 37,41
Cosmic Clocks, The by Michel Gauquelin, 251 n.88,253
Cosmic state, *technical term*, 174-175
Cosmobiologie, periodical, 263
Cosmobiology, 261,263,274,281
Cosmocrator, epithet of the Sun, 61

Declination, *technical term*, 92,195
De cometis, libelli tres by John Kepler, 172
Decumbiture, *technical term*, 53,171,285 n.8
De diebus criticis et de aegrotorum decubitu by Argol, 171
De divinatione by Cicero, 21,25 n.45
De errore profanarum religionum of Julius Firmicus Maternus, 79
De exemplis centum geniturarum by Jerome Cardan, 166
Defectio Geniturarum by John Partridge, 190
De fundamentis astrologiae certioribus by John Kepler, 172
Degree areas, *technical term*, 210,215 n.40
Degree symbolism, *see* Degrees, interpretation of individual.
Degrees, bright and dark, 75
Degrees, full and empty, 75,147
Degrees, injurious, 25
Degrees, interpretation of individual, 76,78,215-220,228,269,274,270
Degrees, masculine and feminine, 52,75
Degrees, 360, invention of, *see* Circle, 360 degree, invention of.
Degrees of the Zodiac Symbolized, The by Sepharial, 218 n.47
De judiciis nativatatum libri tres by Johann Schoner, 165
De Iesv Christi servatoris nostri vero anno natalitio ... by John Kepler, 293 n.13
De la psychanalyse de l'Astrologie by André Barbault, 249
Delineation of nativities, 5,33,52,53,78,82,86,91,206,207,211,220,222,223, 275
De magnis conjunctionibus by Albumasar, 114
Demain, periodical, 254
Demons, 3,160 n.9
De nativitatibus secundum Omar by Omar Tiberiades,112
De nativitatibus by Albubater, 127
De revolutionibus nativitatum by Albumasar, 33 n.74,120 n.38
De revolutionibus nativatatum by Haly Abenrudian, 132
Der Kosmos in uns by Thomas Ring, 268
Der neue Planet Pluto by Fritz Brunhübner, 259
Der Planetoid Vesta by H.C. Meier-Parm, 263
Derived houses, *see* Houses, derived.
Desert Stars, The, a Hermetic tract, 90
Desktop computers, 195,203
De stella nova in pede Serpentarii by John Kepler, 172
Destiny, 20,286-290
Deterioration, *technical term*, 114
Determination, *technical term*, 174-175
Determination of longitude at sea, 173
Detriment, *technical term*, 175
Deutsche Kulturgemeinschaft zur Pflege der Astrologie, organization, 260
Development of the Personality, The by Green and Sasportas, 214
Diagrams, *see* Charts.

Diaries, astrological, 172
Dictionaries of astrology, 65,202 n.20,203,212 n.37,221,228,249,256,259
Dictionary of the History of Ideas, 2 n.4
Dictionary of Scientific Biography, 8 n.24,109 n.11,112 n.19,115 n.29,133
    n.62,158 n.3
Dictionnaire astrologique by Henri Gouchon, 249
Dido, hypothetical planet, 211
Die astrologische Synthese by F. Schwickert and A. Weiss, 177
Die Eigenschaften der Tierkreiszeichen in der Antike by Wolfgang Hübner,
    27 n.51
Die Mathematiker und Astronomen der Araber und ihre Werke by H. Suter,
    132 n.61
Die psychischen Wirkungen der Gestirne by Albert Kniepf, 255 n.93
Die psychologische Horoskopedeutung by E.K. Kühr, 263
Die Seele der Edelsteine by Walter Koch, 261
Dignities, *technical term*, 113,119
Dimming, epithet of the 8th house, 86
Direct, *technical term*, 34 n.80,37,39,153
Directions, not used by Grant Lewi, 231
Directions, primary, *technical term*, 35,48,49,50 n.117,82 n.187,95 n.216,
    97,159,168,169,170,174,158 n.4,175,178,179,189,201,205,206,207,262,
    264,273
Directions, secondary, *technical term*, 173,175,178,179,206,246,270
Directions, symbolic, *see* Profections.
Directions, tertiary, *technical term*, 209,210,264,274
Disasters, astrological studies of, 235
Discourses of Hermes to Tat, Hermetic tract, 13 n.6,73 n.168,90 n.210
Diseases, astrological indications of, 205,211,292
Diseases, lists of, 90
Dispositor, technical term, 119
Diurnal, technical term, 14,33,36,48,51 n.118,80,91 n.211,96,97
Diurnal signs, *technical term*, 34 n.79,40
Divination, 3,118,151,155
Divination, by extispicy, 3
Divination of thoughts, *technical term*, 83
Divine men, 68
Divisional Harmonics by H.M. Ishikawa, 276
Dizionario di astrologia by Henri Gouchon, 249
Dodecatemories, *technical term*, 4,12,30,75 n.174,83,84,93,245
Dogmas, scientific, 284
Domiciles of the planets, *technical term*, 27,33,38,47,59,61,62,86,87,93,
    109,110,111,113,115,119,141
Dominican Order, 135
Dorothei Sidonii Carmen astrologicum ed. by David Pingree, 34 n.77,111
    n.18
Doryphory, *technical term*, 61,62

Double-ought Seven (007), pseudonym of Dr. John Dee, 182
Dragon's Head, *see* Nodes of the Moon.
Dragon's Tail, *see* Nodes of the Moon.
Droughts, 208
DSC, abbreviation for descendant, 27,28,30,76,100,127,130
Dumbarton Oaks Papers, 143 n.86
Dwads, *technical term*, 4 n.17
Dyers, indications of, 128
Dynamics of the Unconscious by Green and Sasportas, 214
Earth in the Heavens, The by L. Edward Johndro, 228
Earth, the center of the universe, xi
Earth movers, indications of, 128
Earthquakes, 208,274
Easter, calculation of, 162,183
Eastern Orthodox Church, 101,183
Ecclesiastical frauds, 136
Eclipses, 1,2,4,7,12,15,17,21,22,41,66,67,163
Ecliptical Circle, *technical term*, 18 n.30,144
Economics, 277,281,292
Effective angles, *technical term*, 62
Effective houses, *technical term*, 62
Effective times, *technical term*, 52
Effects of the Position of the Fixed Stars by The Astrologer of the Year 379, 82
Egyptian astrology, 8,40,68
Egyptian Astronomical Texts by O. Neugebauer and Richard A. Parker, 98 n.223
Egyptian astronomy, 8
Egyptian Astronomy, Astrology..., article by Richard A. Parker, 8 n.24
Egyptian dates, *see* Dates, Egyptian.
Elder race, 284
Electional Astrology, 2,8,15,40,43,105,106,107,114,131,138,145,149, 151,152,153
Electional Astrology by V.E. Robson, 47 n.110,152 n.102,210
Elections by Zahel, 114
Electrical ascendant, *technical term*, 228
Electromagnetism, 228
Electronic calculators, 195
Electronic computers *see* Computers.
Elementary Astrology by Ernest and Catharine Grant, 230
Elements, the four, 13
Elements and Crosses as the Basis of the Horoscope by Karen Hamaker-Zondag, 265
Elements of Astrology, The by Dr. L.D. Broughton, 205 n.26,222 n.52,223
Elements of Esoteric Astrology by Dr. A.E. Thierens, 265
Elements of House Division, The by Ralph William Holden, 215,273

Giving Disposition, *technical term*, 114
Giving Virtue, *technical term*, 114
Glahn Life Circle, symbolic direction, 256,264
Glahn Method, interpretive and predictive procedure, 256
Glyphs, *see* Symbols.
God, 61,73,284
God, epithet of the 9th house, 55
Goddess, epithet of the 3rd house, 55 n.136,58
Good Daemon, name of the 11th house, 28 n.57,57,58
Good Fortune, name of the 11th house, 28,58,95
Gospel According to Luke, 293
Gospel According to Mark, 294
Gospel According to Matthew, 292,293,294
Grammar of Astrology, The by Zadkiel, 204
Grammatica astrologica, by Zadkiel, trans. by Franca Cargnello Ventura, 185 n.52
Grand Conjunction, *technical term*, 108
Grant Textbook Series by Ernest and Catharine Grant, 230
Great Conjunctions, The by Albumasar, 115,137
Great Introduction, The by Albumasar, 115
Great Year, *technical term*, 67
Greek astrologers, 4,12,143,152,179
Greek astrology, xii,11-102,143,145,146,147,148,153,154,175
Greek astrology, its preservation by the Medici, 102
Greek books translated into Middle Persian (Pahlavi), 34,53,100
Greek Horoscopes by Neugebauer & Van Hoesen, 14 n.15,31 n.69,43 n.95, 46 n.104,53 n.127,60 n.145,84 n.192,109 n.13,129 n.55
Greek language, loss of knowledge of the, 101
Greek literature, loss of, *see* Literature, Greek, destruction of.
Greek translations of Arabic books, 101,143
Greeks, 49,99
Greenwich Observatory, foundation chart of, 15 n.19
Gregorian calendar, institution of, 183,193
Griffith Observatory, 294
Grundlagen für die astrologischen Deutung by Baron von Kloeckler, 262
Grundriss der Geschichte der Astrologie by Dr. Hubert Korsch, 167 n.24,258
Guide to Horoscope Interpretation by Marc Edmund Jones, 228
Gulliver's Travels by Jonathan Swift, 191
Guides, daily, monthly, and yearly, 227
Gynecology, 88
Hades, hypothetical planet, 257
Hadîth, traditions of the Prophet Muhammad, 115
Hair cloth, 116
Hamburg School, 235,257-259,263,281
Hamburger Hefte, periodical, 258

Inferno of Dante Alighieri, 142
Influence astrale by Paul Flambart, 245
Influence of the Planet Pluto, The by Elbert Benjamine, 260
Institut Astrologique de Belgique, organization, 254
Institute of Theoretical Astronomy, 203 n.21
Integration factors, essential consideration in horoscopes, 242,278-279
Integration Factors, paper by James H. Holden, 242 n.74
Interception, of signs, *technical term*, 130
Interest on money to be shunned, 71
Internationale horoskopisches Lexikon by H-H Taeger, 264
International Society for Astrological Research, organization, 282
Interpreting Geo-Helio Planets by T. Patrick Davis, 237
Interrogations, *see* Horary Astrology.
Intihā' (pl. Initihā'āt), *Arabic technical term*, 118 n.34
Introductio in Tetrabiblum Ptolemaei by Porphyry, 65 n.157
Introduction by Antiochus of Athens, 62
Introduction to Astrology by Paul of Alexandria, trans. by J.H. Holden, 28 n.55,79-82,99
Introduction to Astrology, An by Zadkiel I, 185 n.52,204
Introduction to Astrology by Zahel, 114
Introduction to Political Astrology, An by C.E.O. Carter, 208
Introduction to the Art of Judgments of the Stars by Alchabitius, 129
Introduction to the Handy Tables of Ptolemy, trans. by N. Halma, 44 n.99
Introduction to the Sidereal Zodiac, An by R.C. Firebrace, 209
Introduction to Ptolemy's Tetrabiblos by Porphyry, 45,64,65,85,94
Introductorius maior by Albumasar, 115
Introduzione all'Astrologia ... by Lisa Morpurgo, 270
Introverts, *psychological term*, 242
Inventors of horoscopic astrology, 4,12,14,34,45,90,95,96,99,154,281
Iron workers, indications of, 127-128
Isis, periodical, 2 n.4
Iulii firmici Materni Matheseos libri viii ed. by Kroll, Skutsch, and Ziegler, 66 n.159
Japanese astrology, 274
Jason, hypothetical planet, 211
Jean Baptiste Morin's Comments on House Division, *paper* by J.H. Holden, 159 n.6,177
Jean-Jacques, 1461st asteroid, 235
Jesus by Charles Guignebert, 293 n.11
Jewish astrologers, 104,109,114,132-134
Journal of the Cuneiform Society, 5 n.19
Journal of Research of the A.F.A., 4 n.15,7 n.20,15 n.17,63 n.152,82 n.188, 94 n.215,134 n.64,159 n.6,177,240 n.70,243, n.74
J. Stoeffler's Forecast for the Year 1524, *paper* by G. Hellman, 163 n.16
Judgment on the Fiery Triplicity by John Kepler, 172
Judgments of Questions by Zahel, 114

La Volasfera, 218
L'avvenire non è un Mistero by Angelo Brunini, 270
Law of Sex, *technical term*, 152
Lawyers, 283,291,292
Learning during the Middle Ages, 152
Leather workers, indications of, 128
Lebensuhr im Horoskop by Bruno and Louise Huber, 268
Le centilogve de Ptolomee by Nicolas Bourdin, 152
L'École Polytechnique, 243
L'Égypte des astrologues by Franz Cumont, 11,296
Lehrbuch der astrologischen Technik ... by Baron von Kloeckler, 261
Leitourgoi, thirds of the decans, 13,41 n.93,73
*Le livre des fondements astrologiques...*by Ibn Ezra, 133
L'Encyclopédie du mouvement astrologique . . . by Viscount de Herbais de Thun, 253
Length of life, determination of the, 20 n.64,31-32,38,48,49,51 n.121,52,53, 79,93
Le premier traité d'astrobiologie by Krafft, Budai & Ferrière, 267
Les astres et l'histoire by André Barbault, 250
Les Cahiers Astrologiques, periodical, 249,250
Les hommes et les astres by Michel Gauquelin, 252
Les Mystères de l'Horoscope by Ély Star, 217,243
Les remarques astrologiques by J.B. Morin, 152,159 n.6,177
Letter on Eclipses by Māshā'allāh, 109
Li, asteroid, 235
Libellus in defensionem astrologorum ... by Michael de Petrasancta, 164 n.18
Liber astronomicus by Guido Bonatti, *see Liber introductorius...*by Guido Bonatti.
Liber Hermetis, see Book of Hermes, The.
Liber introductorius ad iudicia stellarum by Guido Bonatti, 109 n.13,112 n.21,114 n.26,129,137
Libraries, 1,6,11,101,104,132,143,155,159 n.7,184,185,199-200,230,231, 261
Lick Observatory, 259
Li compilacions de la science des estoilles by Leopold of Austria, 143 n.85
Life Clock by Bruno and Louise Huber, 267
Life, name of the 1st house, 27
Life forecasts, 145
Life of John Varley by A.T. Story, 202 n.17
Life of Romulus by Plutarch, 21
Life of Sulla by Plutarch, 20 n.32
Light of the Time, *technical term*, 34 n.79,91,96,97
Lights, (the Sun and Moon), *technical term*, 32,61,62,106
Lilith, hypothetical moon, 199,208,229,291
Lilith Ephemeris 1900-2000 by Delphine Jay, 199 n.13

Limburgia, 1383rd asteroid, 235
L'Influence des astres by Michel Gauquelin, 252
Linguaggio Astrale, periodical, 55 n.135,270,271
Literature, Arabic, destruction of, 155
Literature, Greek, destruction of, 100,103,155
Literature, Greek, its partial preservation by the Medici, 102
Literature, Persian, destruction of, 100
Livelihood, name of the 2nd house, 27,58
Lives of the Twelve Caesars, The by Suetonius, 21 n.34,23 n.43
LMT, abbreviation for Local Mean Time, 186,193-195
Locality chart, *technical term*, 228
Logarithms, 158 n.4,171,195,197,205 n.27
London, the Great Fire of, 187
London, the Great Plague of, 187
Lord of the action, *see* Signifiicator.
Lord of the lot, *technical term*, 38
Lord of the Year, *technical term*, 39
Lords of the triplicity, *see* Triplicity, rulers.
Lost Key to Prediction by Robert Zoller, 239
Lot of Basis, *technical term*, 81
Lot of Boldness, *technical term*, 80,81
Lot of the Daemon, *technical term*, 51 n.118,74-75,80,81,86
Lot of Faith, *technical term,* 127
Lot of Fortune, *technical term*14 n.13,25,46 n.105,47,50,51,52,58-59,59
    n.141-142,74,75,79,80,81,86,89,95,96,127,140,154
Lot of Friends, *technical term,* 112,113
Lot of Love, *technical term*, 80-81
Lot of Marriage, *technical term*, 38
Lot of Necessity, *technical term*, 80,81
Lot of Retribution, *technical term*, 80,81
Lot of Victory, *technical term*, 80,81
Lot of the Wedding, *technical term,* 37,38
Lots (Parts), 13,33,46 n.105,47 n.111,48,52,53,65,77,79-82,89,91,96 n.219,
    107,124,132 n.60,147,154,147,239,245
Lotteries, 240
Love Signs by Linda Goodman, 243
Lowell Observatory, 197
Luck, 126,188
Lumps in the Pudding, paper by James H. Holden, 234-235
Lunar apogee, *astronomical term*, 199
Lunar diameter, 27
Lunar returns, *technical term*, 175
Lunar tables, 16,17,23,51,173 n.30,193
Lunar theories, 3,170,173,193
McWhirter Theory of Stock Market Forecasting by Louise McWhirter, 240
Magi, The, 292-294

Magic, 149,150,151,154,182,277
Mainframe computers, 195
Male & female, alternation of, 13
Malefic planets, *technical term*, 37,38,39,40,50,62,78,86,93,97,106,115, 133,174
Man and his World by Bruno & Louise Huber, 269
Mansions of the Moon, *technical term*, 147,150-152
Manual of Computer Programming for Astrologers by Michael Erlewine, 238
Manuel d'astrologie sphérique et judiciaire by Fomalhaut, 243 n.76
Manuel pratique d'astrologie by Antarès, 255
Manzil, *Arabic technical term*, 150
Maps, orientation of, 14
Mariners, indications of, 128
Marriage, predictions about, 36-38,50,175-176,218
Mars, contrasted to Jupiter, 152
Mars effect, noted by Michel Gauquelin, 241
Masculine and feminine nativities, 53,279
Mathematical zodiac, 9
Mathematicians, 99,128,144,157,165,169,172,182,190,205
Mathematicus by Alhandreus, 151
Mathesis of Julius Firmicus Maternus, 4 n.16,13 n.5,16 n.22,26,33 n.76,35, 35 n.84, 45 n.101,49 n.116,53 n.128,66-79,79 n.179,86,97,127 n.50,157, 158,215
Mathesis, interpolations in the Aldine edition, 76 n.176
Mathesis, earliest notices of the, 78
Matutine, *technical term*, 88
MC, abbreviation for midheaven, 27,28,30,52,59,60,62,63,75,76,81,82,83, 89,91,100,119,124,130,140,146,166,206,211,258,270
MC degree, astronomical, 19,48,80 n.183,91,93,95,96,140,146,189 n.59
Mean time *see* Time, reckoning of.
Medical astrology, 90,91,132,157,171,182,188,211,225,235,262,285-286
Medical Botany ... by W.J. Simmonite, 205 n.28
Medical conditions, 210
Medicine, 161,169,180,185 n.51,190-191,205,222,285-286
Memoirs of Cornelius Sulla, 20
Mensch im All, periodical, 263
Mercury, contrasted to Venus, 152
Mercury, errors in its position, 141 n.80,146
Mercury, perihelion of, 46,225
Merlinus Anglicus, Junr., almanac issued by William Lilly, 187,190
Merlinus Liberatus, almanac issued by John Partridge, 191
Message of the Stars by Max & Augusta Foss Heindel, 225
Mesopotamian Astrology by Ulla Koch-Westenholz, xii,1 n.1,2 n.8-9,3 n.10,4 n.16,18;5 n.19,12 n.3
Meteorological astrology, 126,150,208,224

Naibod's Measure, *technical term*, 168
Nakshatras, Indian asterisms, 132,151
Natal astrology, 2,5,9,15,32,48,90,112,125,127,147,154,164,169,181,251,
  286-288
National Council for Geocosmic Research, organization, 235,282
Nativitas/Astrological Studies by James Martin Harvey, 273
Nativities by Judar the Indian, 108
Nativities by Naq (Nahaq) the Indian, 108
Nativities, diurnal and nocturnal, 33,34 n.79,36,48,51 n.118,96
Nativities, *see also* Natal astrology and Horoscopes.
Natural History by Pliny, 7 n.22,17 n.28,23 n.39,32
Navamsa chart, Indian auxiliary horoscope, 13 n.7
Navāmśas, *Indian technical term*, 13,41
Nebulo Anglicanus . . . by John Partridge, 189
Necromancy, 136
Neptune, 8th planet, 163,196-197,205,211,257,271
Neue astrologische Texte des Hermes Trismegistos by Wilhelm Gundel, 216
  n.42
New Age thought, 277
New Almanac Serving for Many Years to Come, A, by Johann Stoeffler, 163
New and Complete Set of Astrological Tables, A by James Wilson, 203
New Directions in Astrology by R.C. Firebrace, 209
New Manual of Astrology, The by Sepharial, 207
New Moon, 31,50,63
New Style (calendar), 183,193
New Year's Day, different dates of, 183,193
New York Daily News, newspaper, 229
Newspaper astrology, 209,272,280-281
Newtonian gravitational theory, 196,225
New World, discovery of the, 162
Ninetieth Degree, significance of, 78
Nocturnal, *technical term*, 33,34 n.79,36,40,41,96
Nocturnal sacrifices, *to be shunned*, 71
Nocturnal signs, *technical term*, 41
Nodes of the Moon, 32,52,86,87,119,240 n.70,258,270
Non-Reception, *technical term*, 114
Normal Stars, *scholarly technical term*, 3,5,9
Notable Nativities by Alan Leo, 167,207,211
Novae caelestium motuum ephemerides (1620-1640) by Argol, 171
Nove lettere astrologiche ad un antroposofo by André L'Eclair, 269
Novas, 293
Numerical theories of celestial motions, 3,9,16 n.25
Numerology, xiii,29,155,207,240,243 n.75
Observations of Ptolemy, mostly fraudulent, 44-45
Occidental, *technical term*, 34 n.80,39,62
Occidental quadrants, *technical term*, 50

Papyrus, as a writing material, 14,19,98
Papyrus horoscopes, 14,45
Parallax of the Moon, 207,235
Parallax Problem in Astrology, The by Donald A. Bradley, 235
Parallel in Astrology, The by L. Furze-Morrish, 274
Parallels in declination, *technical term*, 92
Paraphrase of Ptolemy's Tetrabiblos by Proclus, 84,191,203
Parisian Epitome of astrological works, 29 n.62,31 n.68,32,64
Part of Faith, *see* Lot of Faith.
Part of Fortune, *see* Lot of Fortune.
Part of Plastic, 132 n.60
Partile, *technical term*, 61
Parts, *see* Lots.
Parts of the body in each sign, 78
Pauli Alexandrini elementa apotelesmatica ed. by Emilie Boer, 28 n.55,79 n.180
Pentateuch of Dorotheus of Sidon, 33-43,45,83,95 n.217,100,111,112
People, The, London newspaper, 209
Peregrine, *technical term*, 186
Perfection, *technical term*, 114
Perihelion of Mercury, 16 n.25
Persian astrology, 100,107,108,111,145,146,154
Persian astrologers, 103,104,111
Persian astronomy, 3,100,103
Persian books, translated into Arabic, 103,111
Personal Name Asteroids by Nona Press, 233
Personality traits, 251, n.90,278
Pharmacopoeias, 188
Pharmouthi, 8th month of the Egyptian calendar, 21
Philosophical considerations, 51,78,277
Philosophy, xi,23,25,136,213,269
Physical Directory, A by Nicholas Culpeper, 188
Physicians, 143,144,161,165,166,169,173,179,182,185 n.51,188,222,225, 257,285-286
Physikalische Begründung der Horoskopie und Astrologie by Albert Kniepf, 254 n.93
Physiomathematica or Celestial Philosophy by Placidus, 187,178
Picatrix, 151 n.101
Piezoelectric, *technical term*, 228
Pinax of Critodemus, 32
Pinax of Thrasyllus, 26
Pirate, ambition to be a, 224 n.56
Place of Fortune, *see* Lot of Fortune.
Place of the Daemon, *see* Lot of the Daemon.
Places, *see* Houses, celestial.
Placidus measure of time in directions, 178 n.33-34,258 n.96

Planets, symbols of the, 15
Planets, their significations in the houses, 14,34,35,38,37,46
   n.105,52,53,74,86-88,134,270-271
Planets, their significations in the signs, 14,37,46 n.105,69,75
Planets, their significations in the terms, 14,35,41,76,77,92,93
Planets and Asteroids by Esther Leinbach, 233
Planets in Composite by Robert Hand, 239
Planets in Transit by Robert Hand, 239
Planets in Youth by Robert Hand, 239
Plants, lists of, 91
Pleiades, an asterism, 150
Pluto, hypothetical planet, 211
Pluto, 9th planet, 197,231,243 n.70,244,257,258,259-260
Pluto by Fritz Brunhübner, trans. by Julie Baum, 260
Poetae bucolici et didactici, 44 n.97
Poles, *technical term*, 179,245,261 n.100
Political astrology, 208,264
Political Astrology by Alexander Marr, 264
Political experts, 292
Popes, 73,78,160,162,164,180
Porphyry system, 52,65-66,89,96,215
Poseidon, hypothetical planet, 257
Potentiators, *technical term*, 174
Praeclarissimus liber completus in judiciis astrorum by Haly Abenragel,
   131
Prana, occult magazine, 257
Precession, 17
Precious stones, 261,273
Predestination, *see* Fate
Predictions, 56,73,96,107,126,143,145,150,159,160,161,163-164,169,170,
   175,180,187,188,191,203,204,209,213,222,223, 226,227,229,273,277,
   287,292
Prediction I, II, III by Alexander Marr, 264
Predictive Astrology by Ernest and Catharine Grant, 230
Predominance, *technical term*, 28,38
Preliminary Investigation of Correlation... by L. Furze-Morrish and R.
   Kent, 274
Prenatal Epoch, 54,152,256
Prenatal Epoch, The by E.H. Bailey, 152
Presidents dying in office, 20-year cycle of, 224
Priests, 2,70
Primary progressions, *see* Directions, primary.
Prime Vertical circle, 19 n.30,144
Primer of the Sidereal Zodiac by Cyril Fagan & R.C. Firebrace, 209 n.34,
   231
Primum mobile... by Giovanni Antonio Magini, 171

Reports of the Magicians and Astrologers... by R.C. Thompson, 2 n.9
Reports, astrological, 2
Rerum Italicarum Scriptores by L.A. Muratori, 149 n.96
Retrograde, *technical term*, 34 n.80,39,134,153,185
Return, *technical term*, 114
Revolutionizing Astrology with Heliocentric by T. Patrick Davis, 237
Revolutions of the years of nativities, *see* Solar returns.
Revolutions of the years of the world, *see* Aries ingresses.
Revolutions of Nativities by Albumasar, 114 n.32,120
Revolutions of Nativities by Haly Abenrudian, 132
Revolutions of Nativities by Hermes, 120 n.39
Revolutions of the Years of Nativities, The by Albumasar, 120-125
Revolutions of the Years of the World, The by Māshā'allāh, 109,118
Revolutions of the Years of Nativities, The by Māshā'allāh, 109,126
Rings, with planetary images, 149
Rising crooked, *technical term*, 40
Rising decan, 12
Rising degree, 39,268
Rising sign, 12,14,18,19,40,64,94,98,163,269
Rising sign, interpretation of, 269
Rising signs, illustrations of their physical appearance, 202
Rising straight, *technical term*, 40
Rising times of the signs, 17,40,52,65,79,99
Rituals, 3,70
Roman astrologers, 21-26
Roman emperor, his fate not discernible, 70
Roman emperor, ranked with the gods, 70
Roman Empire of the East, 101
Roman Empire of the West, its collapse, 101
Roman Republican Calendar, 21 n.34,24
Romans, fondness for astrology, 20
Rome, its Moon sign, 25 n.45
Romulus, horoscope of, 21-23
Rosicrucianism, 183,225
Royal stars, 76
Rudolphine Tables of John Kepler, 172,183
Rudolphine Tables of J.B. Morin, 173 n.30
Rulebook for Planetary Pictures by Alfred Witte, 257-259
Ruler of the nativity, *technical term*, 33,38 n.87,75,87,93,250
Ruler of the Nativity, The by Alexandre Volguine, 250
Ruler of the Sect, *see* Light of the Time.
Rulership Book, The by Rex E. Bills, 221
Rulerships, 4,13,25,29 n.59,39,47 n.109,57,90,98 n.221,174-175,185,198,
    211,221,228,243 n. 76,257
Rules for Planetary Pictures, by Witte-Lefeldt, 258
Rusthawelia, 1171st asteroid, 235

n.22,130,146,154,215 n.39
Sign positions, 5,8,9,12,15
Significator, *technical term*, 38,48,116,120,121,140,153,154,175
Significator, universal (the Moon), 114
Significators, accidental, 48,154,174,175
Significators, false, 153
Significators, general, 48,154,174,175
Signs, 3,9,12,23,27,67,107,123,251,252 n.90
Signs, bicorporeal, *see* Signs, mutable.
Signs, cardinal, *technical term*, 40,113,153
Signs, common, *see* Signs, mutable.
Signs, crooked, *technical term*, 27,40
Signs, indications of direction from, 185-186
Signs, equivalent to houses, 94
Signs, fixed, *technical term*, 113,153
Signs, moveable, *see* Signs, cardinal.
Signs, mobile, *see* Signs, cardinal.
Signs, mutable, *technical term*, 40,113,153
Signs, natures of the, 27,32,46,47,52,87
Signs rising rapidly, *technical term*, 40
Signs rising slowly, *technical term*, 40
Signs, rulers of the, 13,39,205-206,211,221,257
Signs, straight, *technical term*, 40
Signs, symbols of the, 15
Signs, their significations on the angles, 76
Signs, tropical, *see* Signs, cardinal.
Signs, twin, *see* Signs, mutable
Signs of the Zodiac, origin of the, 3
Silk, 116
Simplified Horary Astrology by Ivy M. Goldstein-Jacobson, 229
Sixteen Modes, The, *technical term*, 114
Sobre las natividades by Demetrio Santos, 127
Society reflected in astrological writings, 11
Software, astrological, 196,203 n.21,213,221,230,234,238,240,241,286,291
Solar arc, *technical term*, 178 n.33,257
Solar diameter, 27
Solarhoroskop, Transite, usw. by Baron von Kloeckler, 262
Solar-Lunar polarities, *technical term*, 206,232
Solar returns, *technical term*, 98,109 n.11,120-125,126,147,154,167,173,
    175,178,229
Solar Revolutions, The by Alexandre Volguine, 250
Solar tables, 16,17,23,147,163,169,173 n.30,189,190
Solar theories, 3,167,170,193
Solstices, 15 n.20,46,91,92,150 n.98
Solunars, series of articles by Cyril Fagan, 231
Solunars Handbook, The by Cyril Fagan, 231

Space vehicles, 283
Spectacles, to be shunned, 72
Speculum astronomiae by Albertus Magnus, 136
Speculum astronomiae by Junctinus, 167
Sphere, The of Archimedes, a celestial sphere, 67
Spica, fiducial star, 235
Spica, periodical, 209
Square, the 90° aspect, 34 n.78,75,93,111,112-113,127,140,153,175,220, 258
Standard & Poor's 500 by Carol S. Mull, 241
Star, The, 292-294
Star Signs by Linda Goodman, 243
Stars, catalogues of, 17,45,75 n.173,82,190,216 n.43,217 n.44,238
Stars, nature of the, 47,82
Stars and constellations in medieval magic, 149
Stars, How and Where They Influence, The by L. Edward Johndro, 228
State of a planet, *see* Celestial state and Cosmic state.
Static Direct, *technical term*, 34 n.80,134,153
Static Retrograde, *technical term*, 34 n.80,134,153
Stationary, *technical term*, 134,153
Stationers, 11
Stations of the Planets, *technical term*, 34 n.80
Statistical analysis, *see* Astrological statistics.
Stoic philosophy, xi,23,25
Stones, lists of, 90
Story of Astrology by Manley Palmer Hall, 21 n.36
Straggling Astrologer, The, astrological magazine, 203
Strength, of a planet, *technical term*, 113
Student's Textbook of Astrology, A by V.E. Robson, 210
Succedent, *technical term*, 27-28,37,59,61,63,65,100
Summary of Judicial Astrology Related to Mundane Occurences by John of Ashendon, 143 n.88,182
Sun, altitude of the, 140
Sun and Moon Polarity in Your Horoscope, The by Robert A. Hughes, 206
Sun conjunct Mars, indicative of a short temper, 278
Sunday Express, London newspaper, 209
Sundials, 19,146,195
Sundial time, 146,195
Sun is Shining: Helio, The by Michael Erlewine, 238
Sun Sign astrology, 243,280-281
Sun Signs by Linda Goodman, 243
Supernovas, 170,172
Swedenborgians, 200
Swift, *technical term*, 86 n.199
Swift's joke on Partridge, 191
Symbolic directions, 35,98,208,256

Appendix 1
Terms According to the Egyptians

	Aries			Taurus			Gemini			Cancer	
Ju	6	1-6	Ve	8	1-8	Me	6	1-6	Ma	7	1-7
Ve	6	7-12	Me	6	9-14	Ju	6	7-12	Ve	6	8-13
Me	8	13-20	Ju	8	15-22	Ve	5	13-17	Me	6	14-19
Ma	5	21-25	Sa	5	23-27	Ma	7	18-24	Ju	7	20-26
Sa	5	26-30	Ma	3	28-30	Sa	6	25-30	Sa	4	27-30

	Leo			Virgo			Libra			Scorpio	
Ju	6	1-6	Me	7	1-7	Sa	6	1-6	Ma	7	1-7
Ve	5	7-11	Ve	10	8-17	Me	8	7-14	Ve	4	8-11
Sa	7	12-18	Ju	4	18-21	Ju	7	15-21	Me	8	12-19
Me	6	19-24	Ma	7	22-28	Ve	7	22-28	Ju	5	20-24
Ma	6	25-30	Sa	2	29-30	Ma	2	29-30	Sa	6	25-30

	Sagittarius			Capricorn			Aquarius			Pisces	
Ju	12	1-12	Me	7	1-7	Me	7	1-7	Ve	12	1-12
Ve	5	13-17	Ju	7	8-14	Ve	6	8-13	Ju	4	13-16
Me	4	18-21	Ve	8	15-22	Ju	7	14-20	Me	3	17-19
Sa	5	22-26	Sa	4	23-26	Ma	5	21-25	Ma	9	20-28
Ma	4	27-30	Ma	4	27-30	Sa	5	26-30	Sa	2	29-30

The sum of the degrees allotted to each of the planets is this: Saturn 57, Jupiter 79, Mars 66, Venus 82, and Mercury 76; their total is 360.

Lightning Source UK Ltd.
Milton Keynes UK
UKOW03f1614240217
295276UK00001B/35/P